Poverty and Power

The Problem of Structural Inequality

Third Edition

Edward Royce
Rollins College

ROWMAN & LITTLEFIELD
Lanham • Boulder • New York • London

Executive Editor: Sarah Stanton
Assistant Editor: Carli Hansen
Senior Marketing Manager: Kim Lyons

Published by Rowman & Littlefield
An imprint of The Rowman & Littlefield Publishing Group, Inc.
4501 Forbes Boulevard, Suite 200, Lanham, Maryland 20706
https://rowman.com

Unit A, Whitacre Mews, 26-34 Stannary Street, London SE11 4AB,
United Kingdom

British Library Cataloguing in Publication Information Available

Library of Congress Cataloging-in-Publication Data
Names: Royce, Edward Cary, author.
Title: Poverty and power : the problem of structural inequality / Edward Royce, Rollins College.
Description: Third Edition. | Lanham : Rowman & Littlefield Publishing, [2018] | Revised edition of the author's Poverty and power, [2015] | Includes bibliographical references and index.
Identifiers: LCCN 2018002948 (print) | LCCN 2018005546 (ebook) | ISBN 9781538110461 (electronic) | ISBN 9781538110447 (cloth : alk. paper) | ISBN 9781538110454 (pbk. : alk. paper)
Subjects: LCSH: Poverty—United States. | Equality—United States.
Classification: LCC HC110.P6 (ebook) | LCC HC110.P6 R696 2018 (print) | DDC 339.4/60973—dc23
LC record available at https://lccn.loc.gov/2018002948

Printed in the United States of America

To my parents, Dick Royce and Phyllis Royce

Brief Contents

Detailed Contents

Preface to the Third Edition

Despite the many changes in this new edition, some of which are listed below, my essential argument remains the same. (1) Poverty is a serious problem in the United States, more so than commonly imagined, more so than in other industrialized nations, and increasingly so since the 1970s. (2) Poverty is a structural problem. Individualistic theories maintain that poverty derives from the moral weaknesses, inferior abilities, and deviant behaviors of the poor. Taking a structural perspective, I argue instead that poverty is due primarily to a shortage of decent-paying jobs, an inadequate safety net, a cultural discourse that disparages the poor, and a multitude of social forces (residential segregation, to cite one example) that deliver cumulative advantages to the affluent and cumulative disadvantages to the impoverished. (3) Poverty is rooted in and perpetuated by large and growing disparities in economic, political, and ideological power, with business groups and their allies occupying a dominant position over the working class and the poor. (4) A war on poverty can be won, but only by confronting the deep-rooted inequalities in income, wealth, power, and opportunity so visibly on display in today's American society.

NEW TO THE THIRD EDITION

The basic organizational structure of the book remains the same, but this third edition is more extensively revised than the second edition. I have done considerable rewriting throughout the book in an effort to enhance clarity and sharpen arguments. I have updated the statistical data where possible. And I have integrated new findings and ideas from dozens and dozens of recently published books, journal articles, research reports, government documents, and newspaper clippings.

The most significant change is a thorough reworking of chapter 5, "The Economic System and Poverty." Segments on deindustrialization and globalization have been carried over in revised form from the previous edition. But I have added two entirely new segments, one on automation and the threat of technological unemployment and the other on financialization and the shift in corporate management practices since the 1980s. Against the backdrop of these four large-scale economic developments—deindustrialization, globalization, automation, and financialization—I examine, in another entirely new segment, the current "jobs crisis" in the United States. Among other topics I discuss here are restrictions on workers' freedom to move from one job to another, changes in the distribution of employment by sector and industry, corporations' increasing reliance on subcontracted workers, and the growth of "alternative" or "nonstandard" work arrangements. This restructuring of employment, I argue, has significantly diminished the quality of job opportunities in the United States, making millions of Americans chronically vulnerable to poverty.

Among the many other changes in the third edition are the following:

- A more extensive discussion of the weakening of the safety net, with reference to both policy changes over the past couple of decades and new proposals put forward by the Trump administration.
- A stronger emphasis on the theme of poverty as a social justice issue.
- A brief critique of J. D. Vance's *Hillbilly Elegy*, a popular new contribution to the cultural theory of poverty.
- A discussion of partisan gerrymandering, the "small-state" bias of the US Senate, and how these issues affect the balance of political power.
- A revised and lengthened treatment of the political marginalization of the working class and the poor, including a new segment on voter suppression.
- An analysis, drawing on recent survey research data, of the growing partisan divide between people leaning Democrat and people leaning Republican and a look at how this played out in the 2016 presidential election.
- An updated overview of findings on residential segregation, concentrated poverty, and geographical or place-based disparities.
- A revised listing of policy recommendations, presented in the final chapter.
- Throughout the new edition, where appropriate I have also taken note of relevant policy changes proposed, and in a few cases already enacted, by the Trump administration and congressional Republicans.

A new edition of this book has been prompted, in fact made necessary, by the quality of poverty as a moving target. On this topic no last word is possible; no final account can ever be written. Indeed, the ink is barely dry on this completed third edition, and I have already accumulated a large stack of new material for what I hope will be a fourth edition sometime down the road.

Acknowledgments

I could not have completed the first edition of this book without the help I received from Doug Amy, Fran Deutsch, Eric Schutz, and Larry Van Sickle. These four friends kept me going, reading chapters as I wrote them and providing essential feedback and encouragement along the way. And now, with the third edition, showing remarkable patience, they continue to serve as invaluable readers, advisers, and critics. I am extremely grateful for all the time and effort they have devoted to this project. Several other people offered useful comments on parts of the manuscript in one or more of its three editions. For their generosity, support, and criticism, I would like to thank Wendy Berg, Wendy Brandon, Dan Czitrom, Denise Cummings, Rick Eckstein, Jerry Epstein, Michele Ethier, Meryl Fingrudt, Susan Libby, Shannon Mariotti, Julia Maskivker, Matt Nichter, Ellen Pader, Susan Rosen, Lisa Tillmann, Dave Walsh, and Tom Wartenberg.

Eight anonymous reviewers, adopters of *Poverty and Power* in one or more of their courses, provided impressively thoughtful suggestions for the third edition. I have tried to incorporate their ideas as far as possible, and the book is improved as a result. To avoid excessive length, however, I was unable to follow through on some of their most worthwhile and interesting recommendations. I want to thank these reviewers sincerely, and I hope they will be pleased by the new edition.

I would also like to thank everyone at Rowman & Littlefield. Special thanks to Executive Acquisitions Editor Sarah Stanton, who has been a pleasure to work with over the past several years, and Assistant Editor Carli Hansen, who so ably responded to all of my questions concerning the preparation of the third edition. I also, once again, wish to express my gratitude to the late Alan McClare for all of his help and encouragement with the first edition.

Chapter One

Poverty as a Social Problem

The most telling fact about poverty in the United States is how thoroughly it is ignored. Poverty is rarely depicted on television shows or in the movies, receives only passing coverage from the news media, and is largely absent from the political agenda. Not even once did a moderator in the televised 2016 presidential debates ask the candidates about poverty.[1] Nor did either Donald Trump or Hillary Clinton feel compelled to raise the topic during the run-up to the November election.[2] The nation's political leaders don't talk much about the poor when they are in office, either. Looking at the past fifty State of the Union addresses, Jeff Shesol finds that "presidents of both parties have shown a rare, bipartisan resolve to avoid the subject."[3] With neither elected officials nor the media treating poverty as an urgent social issue and the public response amounting to "a great big national shrug," there is little chance that any new government initiative will soon be launched.[4]

Poverty has not always been so invisible. In the early 1960s, in the wake of the civil rights movement, politicians and the press discovered the poor, and in 1964 President Lyndon Johnson declared an "unconditional war on poverty." Martin Luther King Jr., along with other political and civil rights activists, kept the issue alive throughout most of the 1960s. Frustrated by the timidity and inadequate funding of Johnson's antipoverty program, King put forward a more radical vision. He called upon the country to live up to its democratic ideals and moral principles: "The time has come for us to civilize ourselves by the total, direct and immediate abolition of poverty."[5]

More than five decades later, not only have we failed to eradicate poverty, but the very idea of such an undertaking is barely contemplated in the mainstream public discourse. At best poverty is considered a low-priority concern, or even worse, it is perceived as a problem that does not merit the expenditure of public resources. After all, so it is imagined, poor people in the United

States, especially compared to their counterparts in the Third World, do not really have it so bad. Many even own their own refrigerators and microwave ovens, as the conservative Heritage Foundation likes to remind us.[6] This inclination to downplay the problem—"poverty denialism"—is not uncommon.[7] Politicians and pundits are often heard complaining that the poor, thanks to a multitude of overly generous government programs, are so comfortable in their poverty they have little incentive to take responsibility for their own lives. Among the larger public also, this is a common opinion. More than one-third of Americans, and two-thirds of those leaning Republican, say that "poor people have it easy."[8]

The silence and denialism surrounding poverty contribute to its absence from the political agenda. Public figures also give us license to wash our hands of the problem by portraying poverty as a hopelessly baffling phenomenon, "mysterious" and "unknowable," to cite *New York Times* columnist David Brooks.[9] As mere mortals, we are told, there is just nothing we can do to fix something so utterly perplexing. We've made every effort too, this line of thinking implies, more often than not managing only to make a bad situation worse. It is not for lack of trying that we have been so unsuccessful. Maybe poverty is just one of those unsolvable problems. Maybe what they say is true: "The poor shall always be with us." This "poverty befuddlement," as we might call it, encourages a do-nothing approach. At the same time it reinforces low expectations about government's ability to combat poverty and raises the suspicion that money spent helping the poor is wasted.[10] Poverty is a complicated problem, to be sure, but it is neither incomprehensible nor intractable. After all, many industrialized nations have made remarkable progress in reducing poverty. What *is* truly baffling though is why US policy makers refuse to learn from the successful antipoverty efforts undertaken by other countries.[11]

Why is the plight of the poor not a matter of more sustained public discussion and more decisive government policy? Why have we not heeded Martin Luther King's appeal to rid our society of poverty once and for all? Poverty invisibility, poverty denialism, and poverty befuddlement provide partial answers. But another explanation is this: for many Americans, the real problem is not *poverty* at all; the real problem is the *poor*. They have only themselves to blame. They have bad genes, poor work habits, and inadequate skills. Poverty is a symptom, a regrettable by-product of individual failings. The hardships experienced by the poor stem from their own shortcomings, not from any dysfunctions of the system; thus grand schemes to alleviate poverty are inherently misguided. It might be appropriate, according to this view, for government to lend a modest helping hand, aiding the poor to overcome their deficiencies, but in the end, self-improvement, not social reform, is the only credible remedy.

Against this perspective, I argue that we need to abandon the simplistic idea that poverty results from the moral weaknesses, bad behaviors, and inferior abilities of the poor. This conception of poverty misrepresents the nature of the problem, obscuring its root causes and tragic consequences, and it constitutes a powerful barrier to a workable solution. What we need instead is an alternative *structural* perspective, what Mark Rank calls a "new paradigm" and what Alice O'Connor calls a "new poverty knowledge."[12] We need to recognize that problems of poverty and inequality are inextricably bound to power-laden economic and political institutions. These determine the allocation of resources and opportunities, who gets what and how much. Theories attributing poverty to the deficiencies of the poor neglect the big picture: the severity of the poverty problem ultimately depends on the availability of decent-paying jobs and the responsiveness of government to the needs of less-advantaged citizens.

THE PROBLEM OF POVERTY

Despite living in one of the world's richest countries, millions of Americans experience genuine economic hardship and are denied equitable access to opportunities for a quality education, a healthy living environment, a decent-paying job, and a meaningful life. Poverty is hard on the poor. It is also inconsistent with the principles of equality and fairness to which most Americans subscribe. Can we be the kind of society we want to be with so many of our fellow citizens suffering from an inadequate standard of living? Indeed, one important reason for investigating poverty is precisely to determine what kind of society we really are. To study American poverty is simultaneously to study American society.

In this first section of this chapter I set the stage by briefly introducing several key aspects of the poverty problem in the United States. My objective here is to provide readers with an overview of certain disturbing facts and, in opposition to the denialist standpoint, to demonstrate that poverty in the United States is a serious issue, deserving far more public awareness and political attention than it currently receives. I then, in a preliminary manner, lay out the contrast between a structural perspective on poverty and the more conventional individualistic perspective. I follow this with a brief description of how this book is organized.

The Official Rate of Poverty in the United States Is Very High

The level of poverty in the United States is substantial by any yardstick. In 2016, according to the official poverty measure, 40.6 million Americans were poor, 12.7 percent of the population. The rate of poverty is higher for selected subgroups: 18.0 percent for children, 22.0 percent for African

Americans, 30.8 percent for black children, 19.4 percent for Hispanics, and
26.6 percent for Hispanic children.[13] Millions of other Americans live on the
edge of poverty, barely scraping by. Approximately 14 million people—the
nearly poor—reside in households with incomes between 100 and 125 percent of the poverty line.[14]

The Real Rate of Poverty in the United States Is Even Higher

The Census Bureau in 2016 counted a four-person family with two children
as poor if its yearly pretax income totaled less than $24,755.[15] Opinion polls
show that the majority of Americans believe this is not nearly enough money
to make ends meet. When asked what the poverty line should be for a family
of four, the average response in a 2013 survey was approximately $30,000,
far more than the official figure.[16] The current poverty threshold, in the
judgment of the US public, is too low. For most Americans, the *real* poverty
population is substantially larger than the *official* poverty population.

Many experts agree. As one alternative to the official measure, Elise
Gould and her colleagues estimate "basic family budgets." Adjusted for family size, family type, and geographical location and factoring in the costs of
child care, transportation, housing, health care, and other essentials, these
budgets are designed to "measure the income families need in order to attain
a secure yet modest living standard." By this calculation, even in the least
expensive parts of the country, the income required to meet a basic family
budget is more than twice the official poverty threshold.[17] According to the
Census Bureau estimate, there are a lot of poor people in the United States,
but in the assessment of the American public and many policy specialists as
well, the level of real poverty is much greater than the official numbers
indicate.

Poverty in the United States Is Worse Than in Other Developed Countries

The rate of poverty in the United States is high, and it looks even higher,
extraordinarily so in fact, when compared to the rate of poverty in other
industrialized nations. The United States may be falling behind on some
counts, but when it comes to producing poor people, we outperform our chief
competitors by a wide margin. In a study of eight developed countries from
circa 2000, using a "relative poverty line" set at 50 percent of median income, the United States comes out on top, with a poverty rate of 17 percent,
easily beating out our closest rivals, the United Kingdom with 12.3 percent
and Canada with 11.9 percent.[18] Data on twenty-three developed nations
from the late 2000s show the United States still leading the pack with a
relative poverty rate nearly twice the average of our peer countries.[19] Other

recent studies reveal the same pattern, with the United States standing out among rich countries as a high-poverty outlier.[20] The real purchasing power of poor families in the United States is also lower than in other advanced economies, and the income gap between the rich and the poor is larger.[21] The poor in the United States are worse off in absolute terms than are the poor in many other developed countries, and they are worse off relative to their fellow citizens as well.[22] Based on a comprehensive examination of the cross-national data, Alberto Alesina and Edward Glaeser conclude that, compared to the poor in European countries, the "American poor are really poor."[23]

The rate of poverty among children in the United States is particularly high by international standards. In 2009 the United States ranked number one in child poverty among twenty-six developed nations, with a rate more than twice that of other wealthy countries. Not only are there more poor children in the United States than elsewhere in the industrialized world, but American children are more deeply poor as well, living further below the poverty line.[24] A 2017 report from the United Nations Children's Fund (UNICEF) paints a similarly negative picture. Out of thirty-seven "high-income" countries, the United States ranked well below the average: thirty-third on child poverty, better only than Israel, Romania, Mexico, and Bulgaria, and thirty-sixth on children's general health and well-being.[25] The sorry fact is this: children in the United States are more likely to be poor than in just about any other developed nation, far more likely than in most. They are also more likely to be deeply poor. And beyond simply lacking money, they are also more likely to suffer from a variety of material hardships, including food insecurity and substandard housing. Poverty is a common occurrence for American children, and child poverty in the United States is an uncommonly harsh experience, with lasting consequences for children's health and educational outcomes. "If nations are judged by the way they treat their children," Tim Smeeding observes, "the United States is currently failing the test."[26]

Poverty in the United States Is a Persistent Problem

Not only is there a lot of poverty in the United States, but the rate of poverty has remained persistently high over the past half century. The official poverty rate declined substantially during the 1960s, reaching a historic low of 11.1 percent in 1973. It remained relatively stable during the 1970s, increased during the 1980s, and exceeded 13 percent throughout most of the next decade. As the employment picture improved in the late 1990s, the rate of poverty also declined, falling to a near-record low of 11.3 percent in 2000. Since then it has trended upward, hitting new highs in the aftermath of the Great Recession. Though down from the 2010 peak of 15.1 percent, the rate of poverty in 2016 was still higher than during the years immediately preceding the 2007–2009 financial collapse.[27]

While the size of the poverty population fluctuates from year to year, the longer-term trend line is sobering: even during periods of economic growth there has been no large or lasting reduction in the rate of poverty since the 1960s.[28] Since the beginning of the new century, in fact, almost 10 million people have been added to the poverty population. It is remarkable to consider, moreover, that at no point since the government began collecting data on poverty have fewer than one in ten Americans been poor.

More of Today's Poor Are Severely Poor

The poor today are also poorer than in the past, with many suffering "severe deprivation." The severely poor, Matthew Desmond explains, endure "acute hardship," a lack of essential resources. They encounter "compounded hardship," confronting on a daily basis a multitude of difficulties simultaneously. And they experience "persistent hardship," rooted in early-life traumas, long stretches of social and economic disadvantage, and a life of poverty extending from one generation to the next.[29]

One way to calculate the severity of poverty is to measure the "poverty gap" or "income deficit": how far the average poor person or poor family falls below their respective poverty threshold. Between 1959 and 1973 the average income deficit for families declined from $7,126 to $6,373. Since then, however, the poverty gap has increased, growing even during the boom years of the late 1990s. It has continued to climb, rising to $10,505 in 2016. Today's poor are worse off because they have a longer climb to get out of poverty.[30]

Another way to assess the severity of poverty is to calculate the percentage of the poverty population—the deeply poor—whose income puts them below 50 percent of the poverty line. Poverty by this measure has become more prevalent over time as well, rising to record highs in the wake of the Great Recession. The size of the deeply poor population, as a percentage of the total poverty population, increased from less than 30 percent in the mid-1970s to 45.6 percent in 2016. In that year, 18.5 million people lived in households with incomes of less than half the poverty line.[31]

A third measure, developed by Kathryn Edin and H. Luke Shaefer, calculates the number of households in the United States that suffer from "extreme poverty." These are the "poorest of the poor." Households are considered extremely poor if they report two dollars or less per person per day in total cash income in a given month. The number of such households, Shaefer and Edin find, more than doubled between 1996 and 2011, increasing from 636,000 to 1.65 million, including 3.55 million children.[32] This striking growth in extreme poverty, they claim, is due largely to the combination of a persistent shortage of decent-paying jobs and the 1996 reform of the welfare system, which resulted in a sharp decline in the availability of cash assistance for needy families.[33]

The Relative Deprivation and Social Exclusion of the Poor

The official poverty measure in the United States, devised in the early 1960s, is based on an "absolute" standard. The poverty line is set at a fixed level of income, just enough to meet basic subsistence needs, and it is adjusted only for family size and the rate of inflation. It is not revised to take into account changes in patterns of consumption, customary notions about what people need to live a minimally decent life, or the prevailing standard of living. The definition of poverty stays constant over time; the criterion for counting someone as poor in 2016 is the same as it was in the 1960s.[34] But what it means to be poor today differs from what it meant in the past. Consider for example that in 1963, the income of a family of four right at the poverty line was about 50 percent of the median. In 2016 the income of that same family, once again right at the poverty line, is about 42 percent of the median. Compared to a family counted as poor in the past, a family counted as poor today is worse off relative to the typical family.

Though the poverty threshold remains unchanged, the standard of living for average Americans has improved modestly over the past several decades, while at the same time the poor have become more deeply poor. As illustrated above, the gap between the income of those officially regarded as poor and the income of households at the median has widened, and so too has the distance between the social worlds they inhabit. Today's poor, compared to the poor in the 1960s, can less afford the life of the average American, in which, for example, cable television, cell phones, computers, and internet access are the norm. Even less can they afford those commodities whose prices have risen faster than the rate of inflation, including middle-class essentials such as child care, health care, housing, and college tuition. The poor today, either as consumers or citizens, are less financially able than in the past to participate as equal and full-fledged members of society. The bar has been raised for entry into the social and economic mainstream, leaving poorer Americans vulnerable to "social exclusion."[35] The deprivation endured by poor families is greater nowadays because they are worse off relative to middle-class American households than the poor of earlier decades and because they are much worse off relative to the rich.

More of Today's Poor Are Stuck in Poverty

The United States is not the unique land of opportunity we like to think it is. Over the past several decades the dream of economic mobility has faded, and poverty has become more of a trap. Compared to the 1960s and 1970s, people today are less likely to experience upward mobility in occupational status and earnings over the course of their lifetimes (*intragenerational mobility*). And they are also less likely as adults to reach or exceed the socioeconomic level achieved by their parents (*intergenerational mobility*).

In the current era of increasing inequality and wage stagnation, it is more difficult for low-income families to rise into the middle class or even work their way above the poverty line.[36] According to Annette Bernhardt and her collaborators, the decline of earnings mobility is due especially to the proliferation of low-wage jobs and the conversion of low-wage work into a lifetime career. They compare two cohorts of male workers, the first tracked from 1966 to 1981 and the second from 1979 to 1994. Over these two periods, they find, "wage growth has both stagnated and grown more unequal," "there has been a marked deterioration in upward mobility," the percentage of workers who are stuck in low-wage jobs has more than doubled, and workers at the bottom of the wage distribution are especially liable to fall into the "bad-job trap."[37] More recent research, also focusing on men's earnings mobility, confirms this pattern well into the 2000s. On average, every cohort of men entering the workforce since the late 1960s has started out at a lower income level than the previous cohort and ends up making less money during their working lives. The lifetime earnings of men, in short, has declined steadily for several decades, with younger workers faring progressively worse than older workers. This trend, the research suggests, is likely to persist into the future.[38] Economic mobility, in sum, is harder to attain in today's economic environment. A job is not enough, hard work does not necessarily pay, and fewer individuals than in the past are able to pull themselves up by their own bootstraps.[39]

Family background, whether one is born into poverty or wealth, is a particularly powerful determinant of adult economic outcomes in the United States. Among twenty-four industrialized nations, the United States ranks only sixteenth in its level of intergenerational mobility. The American Dream is less a reality in the United States than it is in Denmark, Norway, Finland, Canada, Germany, France, and many other countries.[40] Because economic inequality in the United States is so extreme, the class structure, particularly at the top and the bottom, is unusually sticky. American children born into poor families, with all their accumulated disadvantages, have nowhere near the same life prospects as American children born into rich families, with all their accumulated advantages. The rich and the poor do have one thing in common, though: they both tend to pass along their economic standing to their children, and this is more true in the United States than just about anywhere else in the industrialized world. We do indeed stand out from other countries, not because we have *more* opportunity and economic mobility, but because we have *less*.[41]

Not only is the level of intergenerational mobility lower in the United States than in most other developed countries, the trend, due largely to increasing inequality, is one of declining mobility over time. According to a recent study by Raj Chetty and his colleagues, the share of children achieving a higher standard of living than their parents fell from 90 percent for children born in the 1940s to 50 percent for children born in the 1980s.[42] The social mobility prospects for children born into low-income households in particular have worsened over the past four decades and, barring any major policy initiatives, the life chances of poor children are likely to deteriorate even further going into the future.[43]

The intergeneration mobility among African Americans over the past 150 years has persistently lagged behind that of white Americans. The chance of black sons faring better than their parents, for example, is far less than for comparable white sons. This racial mobility gap is not shrinking over time, either, suggesting the enduring presence of racial discrimination and race-based inequalities of opportunity.[44] Edward Rodrigue and Richard V. Reeves also document racial disparities in intergenerational mobility. Compared to their white counterparts, African Americans born into poverty, they report, are much more likely to end up in poverty as adults, and African Americans born into middle-class households are much more likely to experience downward mobility.[45] Most Americans still believe in the American Dream. They think it is possible to start out poor, work hard, and become rich. It is possible, just not likely, increasingly unlikely in fact, and even less likely for racial and ethnic minorities.

The Shredding of the Safety Net

A country's safety net provides assistance to low-income households, helping them satisfy their basic needs for food, housing, health care, child care, and other essentials.[46] The safety net in the United States is the least generous in the industrialized world, and if the Trump administration and congressional Republicans get their way, it will become even less generous in the near future. Consider first some examples of how the safety net has been weakened over the past couple of decades and how public policies currently in place fail to address adequately the needs of the poor. (1) The 1996 reform of the welfare system—with the Temporary Assistance for Needy Families program replacing Aid to Families with Dependent Children—has resulted in a steady decline in the number of poor families receiving cash assistance and a corresponding increase in the ranks of those experiencing deep or extreme poverty. (2) Due to inadequate funding, the "Section 8" housing voucher program, which helps low-income renters cover housing costs, serves only one-quarter of eligible families. (3) Government officials in eighteen states have refused to extend Medicaid coverage to low-income workers as permitted by the Affordable Care Act. (4) The Unemployment Insurance program, which once distributed benefits to 75 percent of unemployed workers, now provides assistance to less than 25 percent. (5) The federal minimum wage, which peaked at $9.68 an hour in 1968 (in 2016 dollars) has been stuck at $7.25 for almost a decade.[47]

With the 2016 election, the safety net, in tatters but still providing essential benefits, has become further endangered. To offset anticipated tax cuts and increases in military spending, the budget proposed by the Trump administration for fiscal year 2018, crafted by budget director Mick Mulvaney, calls for the elimination or reduction of numerous programs that currently aid poor and low-income families.[48] Among the most important of these is the Supplemental Nutrition Assistance Program (SNAP). Previously known as food stamps, this program is already under assault by conservative state legislators around the country pushing for work requirements, time limits, and tougher eligibility restrictions.[49] The federal government now appears ready to follow the example set by the states. By limiting nutrition assistance to the "neediest" people only, tightening eligibility rules, and asking states to assume more of the cost while giving them "flexibility" in setting benefit levels, the Trump administration projects spending reductions in the SNAP program of $190 billion over ten years.[50] The 2018 budget also calls for the elimination of at least two dozen programs from which poor people benefit, including the Low Income Home Energy Assistance Program, the Neighborhood Reinvestment Corporation, the Community Services Block Grant, and the Legal Services Corporation. Other programs, including Medicaid, are scheduled for reductions in funding or are being overhauled to make it more difficult for people to receive benefits.[51] The Trump budget, economist Pavlina R. Tcherneva argues, represents a continuation of the Republican Party's traditional "devolve, defund, and destroy" attack on the public sector: "devolve essential federal functions to the states, provide increasingly small or strictly capped grants-in-aid, and eventually shrink, privatize or eliminate programs altogether."[52] If passed in anything like its present form, this budget will bring increasing economic adversity to people already struggling to make ends meet.

Low-income Americans are due to be hammered on the front end by budget cuts and are also in danger of suffering furthers costs on the back end by the Republican tax bill currently making its way through Congress. On the one hand, the Trump administration proposes spending reductions for safety net programs to pay for tax breaks for corporations and the wealthy. On the other hand, these tax breaks, by increasing the deficit and the national debt, will create pressure down the road for additional reductions in funding for social programs, not only those serving low-income households, but also popular middle-class programs like Medicare and Social Security. This combination of budget cuts and tax cuts, as it plays out over the next several years, most economists agree, will do little to boost economic growth, job creation, or wage rates, but it will make the rich richer, with low- and middle-income households paying a steep price.[53]

Most Americans Are Vulnerable to Poverty

In any particular year since 1970, somewhere between 11 and 15 percent of the population was counted as poor. This is a lot of poverty, especially for a country with such great wealth. But on the brighter side, these numbers might leave the impression that for the vast majority of Americans a lifetime of economic security is the norm. The reality is quite different. The composition of the poverty population, keep in mind, is constantly changing, as each year millions of Americans climb out of poverty and millions more fall into poverty. The people we sometimes refer to as "the poor" are not the same people from one year to the next.[54] The majority of Americans, in fact, experience at least a year of poverty during their adult lives, and about a third experience four years or more.[55] Looking at adults between the ages of twenty-five and sixty, Mark Rank and Thomas Hirschl find that 61.8 percent fall into the bottom 20 percent of the income distribution for at least a year ("poverty"), and 42.1 percent fall into the bottom 10 percent for at least a year ("extreme poverty").[56]

The likelihood of Americans experiencing an episode of poverty has increased over the past few decades, a product of what Jonathan Morduch and Rachel Schneider call the "Great Job Shift." Since the 1970s, they argue, "steady work that pays a predictable and living wage has become increasingly difficult to find." Americans today are thus vulnerable to economic instability. They lose a job, their hours are cut, or their earnings fluctuate over time. Between 2009 and 2011, as a result of this "income volatility," 90 million people, almost a third of the country, had a spell of poverty lasting at least two months, with even the shortest episode long enough for families to deplete their savings, accumulate debt, and find themselves even less prepared to weather future economic downturns.[57]

In the American society of today, poverty is a "common life course event,"[58] even more common for racial and ethnic minorities. Relatively few African Americans manage to stay above the poverty line over the entire course of their lives. Over 90 percent endure at least one year of adult poverty. But even for non-Hispanic whites, poverty is an ordinary occurrence. It is not a paradox or an anomaly, and it is not something that happens only to inner-city minorities, teenage mothers, or other "marginalized groups." Poverty, Mark Rank emphasizes, is "endemic to our economic structure." It is "as American as apple pie."[59]

Living without an Economic Cushion

Income consists of a periodic stream or flow of revenue, including wage earnings, private pension benefits, and government transfers—welfare, unemployment, and Social Security payments, for example. We count on income to pay for our daily expenses. Wealth consists of an accumulated stock or reserve of resources, including savings, home equity, business assets, stocks, bonds, and real estate. We count on wealth to supply us with an economic cushion. The distribution of wealth (or assets) is far more unequal than the distribution of income, and like income inequality, wealth inequality is greater in the United States than in other developed countries.[60] In 2016 the top 1 percent of American families received a 23.8 percent share of the nation's total income, and the top 10 percent received a near-record high 50.3 percent share, with the bottom 90 percent splitting up the rest.[61] This level of income inequality is extreme, but nowhere near as extreme as the level of wealth inequality. In 2016 the top 1 percent of households owned 38.6 percent of the nation's wealth, and the top 10 percent owned approximately 77 percent, with the bottom 50 percent of households possessing only about 1 percent of the country's wealth.[62]

Families possessing an asset cushion have something to fall back on during hard times. They also benefit from access to capital and credit that can be invested in housing, education, and retirement. Assets help families achieve upward mobility and avoid downward mobility. Millions of Americans, however, are "asset poor." Households are considered asset poor if their wealth holdings are insufficient to cover the cost of basic needs for a period of three months. Asset-poor households are vulnerable to economic shocks. They do not have a reserve of funds they can use to pay the bills and put food on the table should they experience a job loss or some other interruption in their flow of income.[63]

The level of asset poverty in the United States, which has increased dramatically since the early 1980s, is substantially greater than the level of income poverty. In 2014 nearly half of American households were "liquid asset poor," meaning they did not have enough cash or savings to cover expenses for three months without a paycheck, and about a third of American households did not even have a savings account.[64] One recent study of low-income and middle-class families reported that more than half had no personal safety net at all, no "rainy-day" funds they could draw on to cope with a medical crisis or a spell of unemployment.[65] A Federal Reserve survey of five thousand people likewise found that an astonishing 44 percent did not even have enough cash on hand to pay for a $400 emergency expense.[66]

For African American and Hispanic families, possessing only 10 percent and 12 percent respectively of the median wealth of white families, asset poverty is the norm.[67] More than two-thirds of households of color are asset poor, with the incidence of financial insecurity extending well up the income ladder.[68] For African Americans, a large percentage of whom have no economic cushion at all, "any setback, from a medical emergency to the unexpected loss of hours at work, can be devastating"; the electricity may be cut off, cars repossessed, renters evicted, and wages garnished.[69] In the absence of assets, "small crises" can turn into "major disasters."[70]

Millions of American families do not make enough money to enjoy a minimally decent standard of living. An even greater number are asset poor, a worsening problem over the past two decades, with younger cohorts experiencing heightened financial insecurity. More families today live on the edge, from paycheck to paycheck, often deep in debt, and persistently vulnerable to economic adversities. Even if their income puts them above the poverty line, they have little or nothing in reserve to smooth out the ups and downs that have become commonplace for working families in today's economy.

Economic Growth Is Not the Cure for Today's Poverty

The level of economic inequality remained stable for the first quarter century after World War II but has increased dramatically since the 1970s. Nowadays the rich are taking a much bigger slice of the economic pie, at the expense of everyone else, including those at the low end of the income distribution. In 2016 the hourly wages of workers in the bottom two deciles were only slightly higher than they were in 1979—an eight cent raise for those in the tenth decile, up to $9.35 per hour, and a thirty-five cent raise for those in the ninth decile, up to $10.91 per hour. Workers at these hourly wages, even if employed full-time, year-round, would be unable to support a family of four above the official poverty threshold.[71]

The past four decades teach a clear lesson: a growing economy by itself is no solution to the problem of poverty. Economic growth won't cure poverty if the benefits of increasing output are not widely shared, a sufficient number of new jobs are not created, those jobs don't pay a living wage, or the safety net fails to provide adequately for those who can't work. Nor will economic growth cure poverty if the gains achieved during periods of expansion are wiped out during periods of contraction, with each new downturn pushing low-income households back to square one. Economic growth may be necessary for the alleviation of poverty, but as the historical record reveals, it is not sufficient.

A war on poverty cannot be won by unleashing the forces of the free market or by stimulating growth through corporate tax cuts and deregulation. In an era of rising inequality, weak job creation, and stagnant wages, an expanding economy will do little to improve the long-term well-being of low-income households. Absent targeted policies specifically designed to increase the earnings of low-wage workers, millions of Americans will continue to be poor. An antipoverty program can be effective only if it addresses the problem directly, through a strategy combining economic growth with better jobs, a living wage, a stronger safety net, and a more equitable distribution of the national income. This will require a fundamental change in political policy. Poverty demands serious attention because it is a problem that cannot be cured by economic growth alone.

The Conditions That Cause Poverty Harm Most Americans

Middle-class Americans ignore the poor at their peril, for the conditions that give rise to poverty cause hardships that touch the lives of nearly everyone other than the privileged few at the top. The share of Americans living in middle-class households—defined as those with an income between 67 and 200 percent of median household income—has been shrinking for several decades, declining from 61 percent in 1971 to 50 percent in 2015.[72] As a proportion of the total population, there are both more poor people and fewer middle-income people living in the United States than in most other developed countries.[73] With a small slice of high earners capturing most of the gains from economic growth, average Americans are not as well off as they used to be either. The share of the nation's income going to the middle class has been trending downward since the late 1960s. In 2016 the middle 60 percent of households took home less of the national income than the top quintile, 45.4 percent compared to 51.5 percent, and in recent years the American middle class has also lost its status as the most affluent in the world.[74]

Since the 1970s an increasing number of middle-income Americans have become financially squeezed, trapped on a treadmill, running harder and harder just to stay in place. Households around the median are holding their own, maybe gaining a little ground, but only because family members are working more hours, and even then the distance between the middle class and the rich continues to grow. With the cost of essentials rising faster than the rate of inflation, moreover, millions of Americans, approximately 30 percent according to a recent Federal Reserve report, have difficulty making ends meet.[75] Middle-income families today occupy the same leaky boat as the poor, buffeted by the same economic and political forces responsible for the persistence of poverty: job instability, stagnant or volatile earnings, rising personal debt, burdensome rental costs and mortgage payments, inadequate health coverage, retirement insecurity, expensive child care, soaring tuition costs, and stressful family lives.

Poverty Is a Social Justice Issue

The rich are advantaged way beyond anything one can reasonably say they deserve, and the working class and the poor are disadvantaged way beyond anything one can reasonably say they deserve. Poverty and inequality, for this reason alone, are social justice issues. Consider as evidence the profoundly skewed performance of the US economy. Because wage rates have become largely unresponsive to economic growth, less affluent Americans have not gained any ground at all for decades. The average pretax income for the bottom 50 percent of adult earners has been stagnant since 1980. Their share of the increase in economic output over the past quarter century or so has been *zero*. "For the 117 million US adults in the bottom half of the income distribution," the authors of a new study declare, income "growth has been non-existent for a generation." For affluent Americans, things are quite different. Since 1980 those at the top of the income distribution have seen huge gains: 121 percent for the top 10 percent, 205 percent for the top 1 percent, and 636 percent for the top 0.001 percent.[76] The number of billionaires in the United States is on the rise too, reaching a record high of 565 in 2017. Topping the list were Bill Gates ($86.0 billion), Warren Buffet ($75.6 billion), and Jeff Bezos ($77.8 billion), with brothers Charles and David Koch worth a combined $96.6 billion. Gates, Buffet, and Bezos combined have "more wealth than the entire bottom half of the American population."[77]

More than 40 million Americans are poor, and millions more are near poor. Many of these people live desperate lives. They suffer from substandard housing, poor health and inadequate medical attention, unreliable transportation, and low-quality child care. In 2016, according to the latest report from the US Department of Agriculture, 41.2 million people, including 12.9 million children, experienced "food insecurity" at some point during the year: they worried about running out of food, ate less than they should, skipped meals, went hungry, and in some cases did not eat for an entire day because they didn't have enough money.[78] If they are lucky enough to find regular employment, jobs for low-income workers not only fail to pay a living wage and offer reasonable benefits, they are also often alienating and exploitative, demeaning, and dangerous. In the current economic environment opportunities for average working-class Americans to improve their lives or ensure their children will have a better future are scarce. For low-income racial and ethnic minorities, matters are even worse. Several million impoverished African Americans and Hispanics live in segregated, high-poverty neighborhoods and send their kids to segregated, high-poverty schools, all but guaranteeing that the disadvantages of the current generation are passed along to the next.

In this "tale of two countries," to borrow a phrase from Thomas Piketty and his collaborators, it is difficult to say which is more mind-boggling: the level of hardship experienced by Americans in the bottom half of the income distribution or the enormous riches enjoyed by the handful of those at the top of the economic pyramid. In any case, the presence of a large poverty population in such a wealthy country and the massive and growing gap between the rich and the poor, inhabitants of two vastly different worlds, is not only a societal health hazard, it also runs contrary to any sensible notion of fairness. Granted, it would be no easy matter to specify precisely what an equitable distribution of society's resources might be. But it is difficult to imagine how anyone reflecting on the data presented above, along with the information already provided in this chapter (with more to come), could arrive at the conclusion that the United States is the embodiment of a just society.

The widening economic divide represents a deep contradiction between American ideals and American realities. It undermines the principle of equality of opportunity, erodes feelings of social solidarity, reinforces huge and dangerous disparities in power, and subverts the democratic ideal of political equality. Widespread poverty amid great wealth: What does this say about the kind of society we are and aspire to be? The seriousness of this problem is not just found in the facts conveyed by economic indicators, but also in the troubling moral questions it compels us to consider. At the end of his award-winning book, *Evicted*, Matthew Desmond raises just this point. By "no American value," he says, are current levels of inequality and deprivation justified. "No moral code or ethical principle, no piece of scripture or holy teaching, can be summoned to defend what we have allowed our country to become."[79] This is a thought readers might ponder as they make their way through the following pages.

THE INDIVIDUALISTIC PERSPECTIVE AND THE STRUCTURAL PERSPECTIVE

To acknowledge that American poverty is a serious problem would be a step forward. But a contentious question remains: What causes people to be poor? The debate on this issue is framed by the opposition between two perspectives: the individualistic and the structural. Is poverty caused by lack of effort on the part of the poor or by circumstances beyond their control? Are people poor because of their own failings or because of the failings of the American political economy? Do poor people themselves bear the burden of responsibility for overcoming their deprivation, or should government do more to alleviate problems of poverty and inequality? Is poverty best combated by reforming the poor or by reforming society?

My approach in this book is to sharpen and underscore the contrast between these two perspectives. This strategy is intended to draw detailed attention to the divergence in the assumptions, arguments, and implications of these opposing views. And, as I hope to show, the added benefit of placing these two ways of thinking about poverty alongside one another and closely examining their differences is that it brings to the surface the inherent deficiencies of the individualistic perspective and the comparative strengths of the structural perspective.

These two viewpoints propose radically dissimilar theories of poverty. For the individualistic perspective, poverty results from personal weaknesses, failings, and inadequacies. People are poor for some combination of the following reasons: they are deficient in intelligence, competence, and ability; they are insufficiently experienced, skilled, and educated; they lack ambition, determination, and perseverance; they have poor attitudes, motivations, and values; they make bad choices and engage in self-destructive behaviors; and they are unable or unwilling to exert the necessary effort or take advantage of the opportunities available to them. Poverty is an individual problem, according to this perspective; it is a by-product of the characteristics and behaviors of the poor.

The structural perspective attributes poverty to an assortment of economic, political, cultural, and social forces outside the immediate control of the individual: a shortage of jobs that pay a living wage; a corporate profit-making strategy predicated on the reduction of labor costs; government policy that caters to the concerns of the wealthy while ignoring the interests of working-class families; a political and media rhetoric that variously disparages the poor, treats them as objects of charity, and renders them invisible; and the persistence of discrimination, residential segregation, and social isolation. Poverty is a social problem, according to this perspective; it is a by-product of the distribution of power and the institutional features of society.

The individualistic perspective explains poverty mainly by reference to the choices and behaviors of the poor. They drop out of high school; they reject marriage and sexual monogamy; they have children out of wedlock; they join gangs, do drugs, and commit crimes; and they refuse to stick with a job. For the individualistic perspective, poor people are victims of their own bad decisions and lifestyle preferences. The structural perspective, conversely, explains poverty mainly by reference to the choices and behaviors of the people who occupy positions of political and economic power. They downsize the workforce, relocate factories overseas, and impose wage and benefit reductions. They legislate cutbacks in social welfare programs, enact tax cuts for the rich, craft trade agreements that profit multinational corporations at the expense of workers, and pass laws hindering the ability of employees to form labor unions. They also spend millions of dollars to disseminate the message that the "free market" is fair and efficient, government programs are wasteful and counterproductive, and poverty is the fault of the poor. For the structural perspective, poor people are victims of the decisions and actions of political and economic elites.

Theories of poverty imply theories of society. And these two perspectives convey sharply conflicting images of the United States. For the individualistic perspective, American society is a meritocracy in which hard work and determination pay off. Through the magic of the market, the rewards people receive correspond to their economic contribution. For the structural perspective, the distribution of earnings, income, and wealth is less a reflection of differences in individual ability and effort than it is an outcome of economic and political struggles, past and present, and enduring disparities in power. The individualistic perspective and the structural perspective disagree about a variety of related issues as well: Are current inequalities fair or unfair, are opportunities for getting ahead plentiful or scarce, do individuals compete on a level or tilted playing field, does discrimination continue to play a significant role in explaining race and gender inequalities, and is the American Dream a reality or a myth? The appendix at the end of this book provides a summary overview of the key differences between the individualistic perspective and the structural perspective.

ORGANIZATION OF THE BOOK

Grounded in a synthesis of current research findings and recent studies of American poverty, this book develops a sustained critique of individualistic theories and makes a case for an alternative structural perspective. It is intended for classroom use, written in an accessible manner, and targeted specifically to undergraduate students. The book is organized into three parts, plus this introductory chapter and a concluding chapter. In part I, consisting of chapters 2 through 4, I summarize and critique in turn each of the three main individualistic theories of poverty: the biogenetic theory, the cultural theory, and human capital theory. These theories, often found in some combination, attribute poverty to the failings of the poor, though they each underline a somewhat different set of failings. For the biogenetic theory, the poor are deficient in cognitive ability; for the cultural theory, they are deficient in achievement motivations; and for human capital theory, they are deficient in education and skills.

My plan in each of these chapters is to highlight the central claims of the theory in question, describe as clearly as possible the logic of its argument, flesh out the underlying assumptions and implications, and identify its conceptual and empirical weaknesses. Along the way, I begin making the case that we need to abandon individualistic theories in favor of a structural alternative. These three chapters constitute only an opening salvo in my critique of the individualistic perspective, as many of the criticisms presented here are expanded and new ones introduced in later chapters.

In parts II and III I rely on two different organizational devices, each designed to spotlight specific structural causes. First, in what I refer to as the "systems" chapters (chapters 5 through 8), I examine the economic, political, cultural, and social forces affecting the rate and severity of poverty. This familiar four-systems format expressly shifts the focus from individual-level variables to larger societal forces. Second, in what I refer to as the "obstacles" chapters (chapters 9 and 10), I devote about five pages each to ten structural obstacles or institutional problems that contribute to the adversity of the poor and hinder their ability to survive and overcome their poverty. This framework of four systems and ten obstacles is intended to portray poverty as both a social condition and a lived experience. In the systems chapters I conceptualize the determinants of poverty more from the top down, while in the obstacles chapters I take a more bottom-up approach, examining the day-to-day problems regularly encountered by low-income households as they struggle to make ends meet.

The "systems" and "obstacles" format is intended to highlight features of the larger societal context that shape people's access to resources and opportunities. This is what makes it useful for presenting a structural perspective and for drawing attention to the blind spots and flaws of the individualistic perspective. But it is an organizational device only, a useful means to communicate information. The four systems format is not meant to suggest that economic, political, cultural, and social forces are separate from one other, operate independently of one another, or exist only within their own system domains. Nor is it meant to imply that all pertinent phenomena can be fitted into one and only one system. The same is true of the obstacles. They are intertwined with each other in numerous and complex ways. There are also continuous and multiple points of contact between the four systems and the ten obstacles. The framework of systems and obstacles is an organizing device intended only to help readers make their way through a large amount of material by bringing some order to the disorderly phenomenon of American poverty.

The four chapters in part II focus in turn on the economic, political, cultural, and social systems. Each of these systems consists of a *structure of power*: a hierarchical distribution of access, influence, and decision-making authority. The unequal distribution of power within these systems enables some individuals and groups more than others to shape the course of the economy (the economic system); to dictate the direction of government policy (the political system); to influence the opinions, preferences, and beliefs of the public (the cultural system); and to control avenues of social and economic mobility (the social system). Power is always contested, however, so each of these four systems also constitutes a *site of conflict*: an arena within which contending groups struggle to achieve favorable outcomes and vie for access to scarce opportunities and resources. My objective in these chapters, challenging the logic of the individualistic perspective, is to demonstrate the significance of a wide range of system variables: economic, political, cultural, and social forces beyond the immediate control of the individual. These variables exert a decisive influence on the rate and severity of poverty, and they help explain why some people are more vulnerable to economic hardship than others.

I examine five structural obstacles in each of the two chapters in part III. In chapter 9 I address problems of racial discrimination, residential segregation, housing, education, and transportation. In chapter 10 I address problems of sex discrimination, child care, health care, retirement insecurity, and legal deprivation. I refer to these obstacles as *structural* because they originate from the combined workings of the economic, political, cultural, and social systems; because they are caused by social forces, arrangements, and practices outside the control of any particular individual; because they are experienced by the poor and the near poor as elements of the external social landscape, circumscribing their lives and limiting their options; and because they reflect the allocation of political and economic power and the distribution of resources and opportunities. Poverty is a *structural* problem insofar as the hardships of the poor and the persistence of their poverty can be traced back to these obstacles rather than to the failings and deficiencies of poor people themselves.

The main argument of this book is that the key to the persistence of poverty in the United States is not the intractable deviance of the poor, but the increasingly unequal distribution of power. The current problem of American poverty is the consequence of an economic, political, and cultural transformation ongoing since the 1970s, accompanied by a growing imbalance of power between business and labor, the haves and the have-nots, the Right and the Left. Employers have gained the upper hand in the labor market and workplace, putting a downward pressure on wages. Corporate interests have achieved a dominant position in the political arena, reinforcing the conservative tilt of government policy. And the ideology of the Right has come to prevail in the public discourse, thanks especially to a compliant news media and the ascendancy of conservative think tanks, talk radio, and social media. On the other side of the class divide, working Americans and the poor have been shunted to the margins. They are trapped at the low end of the economy, competing for dead-end jobs that pay less than a living wage. They are deprived of political influence, disenfranchised in some cases, and otherwise denied equitable access to a system in which money and connections count more than ever. And their voices are largely excluded from the mainstream political debate. Only from the standpoint of a structural perspective, I argue—only by bringing power, politics, conflict, and inequality into the story—can we begin to understand and address effectively the problem of poverty in the United States.

Part I

Individualistic Theories of Poverty and Inequality

Chapter Two

The Biogenetic Theory of Poverty and Inequality

OUR FATE IS IN OUR GENES

People differ. Some are high school dropouts; others have PhDs. Some have jobs pushing paper; others flip hamburgers. Some give orders; others take orders. Some are law abiding; others spend years in prison. Some have a lot of money, power, and prestige; others have little. The future is bright for some, bleak for others. When sociologists are called upon to explain such differences, they usually commence by invoking the triumvirate of gender, race, and class: the kind of life we live depends on whether we are born male or female, white or black, blueblood or redneck.

In sharp contrast to the sociological tradition, for the biogenetic theory the characteristic with the most profound influence on people's life prospects is not their social status, but their native intelligence.[1] Nature, not society, dictates our place in the world. Inequalities in educational achievement, occupational attainment, and other social outcomes are due to inherited differences in cognitive ability. People endowed with a high level of intelligence are destined to be rich, the moderately intelligent are slated for the middle class, and those born with low intelligence are doomed to poverty. Regardless of the circumstances of their birth, smart people rise to the top and dumb people fall to the bottom.

In this chapter I focus on Richard J. Herrnstein and Charles Murray's controversial book *The Bell Curve: Intelligence and Class Structure in American Life.*[2] This is the most widely cited statement of the biogenetic theory of poverty and inequality. It received extraordinary attention in the popular media when it was published in 1994, and it has since generated a small library of reviews, commentaries, replications, and critiques.[3]

25

According to the authors of *The Bell Curve*, modern American society is becoming increasingly segregated into unequal social classes. The "decisive dividing force" in this new class system is not family background, but inherited "cognitive ability."[4] The distinction between the upper class and the lower class is more and more a distinction between bright people and dull people. Intelligence is also unevenly distributed by race and ethnicity, they argue, with black people being generally less intelligent than white people. This intelligence gap, they propose, not discrimination, is what explains the persistence of racial inequality.

Two developments, according to Herrnstein and Murray, have transformed the system of social stratification in the United States such that cognitive ability is now the key to economic success. First, equality of opportunity has come to prevail, diminishing the influence of race, gender, and class background on individual achievement and social mobility. People now compete for access to schools and jobs on a level playing field. Who wins and who loses in this competition is due primarily to merit, merit is primarily a matter of intelligence, and intelligence is primarily a matter of genes. Second, the technological upgrading of the economy has engendered a growing demand for workers with sophisticated cognitive skills. Today's high-tech economy places a premium on intellect. The result is increasing inequality between the high-IQ people who possess the requisite brainpower and the low-IQ people who do not. Modern "technological society" has thereby given rise to a new upper class, a "cognitive elite" occupying the top echelons by virtue of its superior intelligence.[5]

For Herrnstein and Murray, the class divide in the United States has become a cognitive divide, with rich bright people on one far end of the class spectrum and poor dull people on the other. Nowadays, IQ rather than family status, inherited wealth, or social connections is what gets people into the good schools and the good jobs. With the "democratization of higher education," admittance into college is open to anyone with the necessary intellectual qualifications. The same "cognitive partitioning" occurs within the occupational system, as workers are sorted into jobs on the basis of their IQs.[6] In the modern meritocracy, how far individuals advance within the educational and occupational arenas is dictated by their inborn mental ability. High intelligence yields success and low intelligence yields failure. Not much can be done to alter this equation, either, at least not without undermining economic efficiency and social justice. In sum, innate cognitive ability, because it governs access to educational institutions and occupational positions, is the principal determinant of who gets ahead. "Putting it all together," Herrnstein and Murray conclude, "success and failure in the American economy, and all that goes with it, are increasingly a matter of the genes that people inherit."[7]

Just as rich people are rich because they are smart, so too poor people are poor because they are not so smart. For the biogenetic theory, poverty results from individual deficiencies in cognitive ability. People with low IQs are vulnerable to poverty because their intellectual inferiority makes them less able to learn, attain a quality education, acquire advanced skills, and perform competently in mentally demanding jobs. The intellectually dull are also prone to bad decisions and self-destructive behaviors that lead them into poverty and keep them there. They are likely to have irregular job histories, indulge in excessive drug and alcohol consumption, have unplanned pregnancies and out-of-wedlock births, drop out of high school, and participate in criminal activities and other forms of deviance. Since low cognitive ability is generally associated with "socially undesirable" behaviors, according to Herrnstein and Murray, the less intelligent are not only impeded in their economic mobility, they also tend to create problems for everyone else. People with low IQs, *The Bell Curve* alleges, are the source of most of society's troubles: a "large proportion of the people who exhibit the behaviors and problems that dominate the nation's social policy agenda have limited cognitive ability."[8]

My critique of *The Bell Curve* is divided into three sections. In the first I discuss Herrnstein and Murray's view of intelligence, in the second I examine their analysis of the relationship between IQ and life outcomes, and in the third section I focus specifically on their analysis of poverty.

GENES, IQ, AND INTELLIGENCE

The argument of *The Bell Curve* rests on a conception of human intelligence consisting of four disputable propositions: (1) Intelligence is a single, unitary phenomenon consisting of a "core human mental ability." This "general intelligence" underlies all forms of "complex mental work." (2) Standardized intelligence tests provide a precise measure of general intelligence, making it possible to rank individuals on a linear scale according to their capacity for cognitive functioning. (3) Intelligence is "substantially inherited," with genes accounting for at least 40 percent and as much as 80 percent of the variation among individuals in cognitive ability. (4) People are at birth either blessed or doomed with a level of intelligence that is largely unalterable. Social and educational interventions cannot appreciably raise the cognitive ability of people born with low IQs.[9] I briefly discuss each of these issues in turn.

First, many critics of *The Bell Curve* argue that intelligence is a multidimensional rather than a unidimensional phenomenon. It is not one thing but many different things, and these are not all strongly correlated with one another or equally derivative of "general intelligence."[10] People may be smart in some respects, in some contexts, and at some tasks, but not in others. Some may have a facility for numbers, others for words; some may have good business sense, others artistic talent; some may have classroom smarts, others street smarts. The kind of intelligence facilitating high performance in one arena does not necessarily have the same payoff in another. Individuals cannot be classified as uniformly bright or dull, therefore, and their ranking on a single intelligence continuum cannot explain much about their social and economic outcomes. The multidimensional view implies that success and failure, to the extent these have anything to do with intelligence, are not predicated on the one single property, "general intelligence," that conventional IQ tests presume to measure. There are many kinds of cognitive abilities and many kinds of social endeavors as well, each favoring a somewhat different set of skills and talents. IQ scores, therefore, tell us little about people's overall practical competence, nor do they dictate social and economic destinies.

Second, standardized intelligence tests are direct measures of *performance* only, not ability, and how well test takers perform may be affected by anything from mood to comfort level to test-taking experience.[11] Such tests measure ability only indirectly, and even then they measure a "developed" ability, a quality formed over time and within a specific social context, not an "innate" ability.[12] As measures of intelligence, standardized tests are also limited because they assess only a specific set of test-taking competencies, skills associated with achievement on time-restricted, paper-and-pencil examinations. They do less well at measuring diverse forms of practical intelligence; cognitive abilities exhibited in everyday problem solving; or the broader, more context-dependent kinds of "intellectual functioning" individuals employ in navigating classrooms and workplaces.[13] Indeed, recent research by psychologist Keith Stanovich has found only a small to moderate correlation between intelligence (as measured by IQ tests) and "rationality"—referring to such mental qualities as reflexivity, adaptive decision making, cognitive flexibility, sensitivity to inconsistencies, and responsiveness to evidence. A high IQ is not a requisite for good thinking, nor are intelligent people immune from dumb behavior. Furthermore, thinking rationally is something we can learn, as Richard Nisbett argues, and while such learning may not give us a higher IQ, it will make us smarter, and in ways that matter, too. The "intelligence" measured by IQ tests, in sum, does not capture the full range of valued cognitive traits, nor is it a reliable predictor of people's ability to function effectively in the day-to-day worlds of school, work, and family life.[14]

Third, *The Bell Curve*, according to many critics, overestimates the genetic basis and heritability of IQ and underestimates the influence of the social environment. Herrnstein and Murray's method for calculating heritability and the implications they draw from this exaggerate the extent to which cognitive ability is an inborn and unchanging trait genetically transmitted from one generation to the next.[15] While they claim the heritability of IQ may be as much as 80 percent, other research, drawing on a wider range of studies, suggests a much lower figure, somewhere between 30 and 50 percent.[16] The reality is even more complex, however, because how much genes matter depends on the social context. For children raised in poverty, for example, where material deprivation suppresses the full realization of intellectual potential, the heritability of IQ approaches zero.[17] To many experts, indeed, genetic and environmental factors are so closely intertwined that it is impossible to parcel out to each a fixed percentage of influence.[18]

Fourth, according to Herrnstein and Murray, intelligence, because it is substantially genetic, cannot be easily raised, and efforts to do so have yielded "disappointing results." "For the foreseeable future," they state, "the problems of low cognitive ability are not going to be solved by outside interventions to make children smarter." Though it is not impossible to boost IQ, they admit, it is impractical because of insufficient knowledge and limitations in "the available repertoire of social interventions." The problem is not that nothing can be done, but that an *"inexpensive*, reliable method of raising IQ is not available."[19] This is a political, not a scientific, judgment, however, and as James Heckman observes, Herrnstein and Murray fail to carry out the appropriate cost-benefit analysis required to justify their do-nothing standpoint.[20]

The deeper problem with their argument is that Herrnstein and Murray misleadingly equate heritability with immutability. They falsely assume that if there is a large genetic component to IQ, then social reforms cannot significantly raise intelligence. But as the title of one critique puts it, "The malleability of intelligence is not constrained by heritability."[21] The empirical evidence, moreover, does not support *The Bell Curve*'s pessimism about the prospects for improving cognitive ability. Herrnstein and Murray tend to overlook or dismiss studies documenting how social and educational interventions, especially in early life, can increase children's intelligence, enhance their ability to benefit from school, and aid them in the acquisition of marketable skills.[22] One review of the literature concludes that "intelligence can be increased substantially without the need for heroic [or prohibitively expensive] intervention."[23] Simply improving children's prenatal or maternal environment, for example, can produce significant gains in IQ.[24] Intensive early childhood education, the earlier the better, and schools with high-quality teachers can also improve the cognitive skills of poor children.[25] Other research shows that schooling improves people's economic outcomes regardless of IQ, and that educational policies "have the potential to decrease existing, and growing, inequalities in income."[26] Contrary to the biogenetic theory, neither people's level of cognitive ability nor their socioeconomic fate is sealed at conception.

IS IT BETTER TO BE BORN SMART OR BORN RICH?

In part II of *The Bell Curve*, the core of their book, Herrnstein and Murray purport to demonstrate that inherited cognitive ability exerts a powerful influence on people's life outcomes. They make their case not by showing that IQ matters greatly, but by showing that IQ matters more than family background, as measured by parental socioeconomic status (SES). They proceed by comparing how much IQ and SES affect various "social behaviors." Included among these "behaviors" are poverty, unemployment, welfare usage, and crime. Are people with low IQ scores more or less likely, for example, to drop out of high school than people with low SES? The authors' purpose in weighing IQ and SES in this manner is to determine which is more important, nature or nurture, genes or environment. The data they report generally reveal IQ to have a larger influence than SES on social behaviors. The problems people experience in their lives, poverty and unemployment, for example, appear to be due more to lack of cognitive ability than to adverse upbringing. The implication is that genes count more than the social environment in shaping economic outcomes. People fare poorly in their lives, Herrnstein and Murray insist, not because they are socially disadvantaged, but because they are intellectually inferior.[27]

Among the many problems with Herrnstein and Murray's analysis of the relative importance of IQ and SES, three stand out: they employ a questionable measure of intelligence, they treat IQ as though it were entirely the product of genes, and their index of SES fails to capture the full range of relevant social variables. *The Bell Curve*, as a result, overestimates the influence of innate cognitive ability on life outcomes, including poverty, and underestimates the influence of the social environment.

Herrnstein and Murray measure IQ using the Armed Forces Qualification Test (AFQT). This test, administered to respondents between the ages of fifteen and twenty-three, with years of accumulated experiences and schooling, measures achievement more than aptitude; it measures what people have learned more than their inborn capacity for learning.[28] In their reanalysis of the data, Janet Currie and Duncan Thomas find that AFQT scores reflect the influence of socioeconomic status rather than genetics, and that such scores are less indicators of innate intelligence than of family background.[29] Perhaps it is possible to construct and administer an IQ test that actually measures native intelligence, but the AFQT is not such a test, and it cannot justifiably serve to estimate the influence of genes on social outcomes.

Herrnstein and Murray recognize, in principle, that intelligence is not *entirely* a product of genetic inheritance. As much as 60 percent and at least 20 percent of the variation in IQ, they acknowledge, is due to nurture rather than nature, or at least to nurture-nature interaction. They typically neglect this qualification in their interpretation of the data, however, and implicitly treat IQ (as measured by the AFQT) as though it were a purely genetic product.[30] By their own account, however, far from simply attesting to the potency of genes, any correlation between IQ and life outcomes reflects in part—and probably in large part—the influence of social conditions on cognitive ability. Weighing the effects of SES and IQ on life outcomes is not an appropriate test of the power of social background versus the power of genes, because IQ, by their own admission, is itself partly an expression of the social environment.

In addition, Herrnstein and Murray's conception of SES, to cite the strong words of one critic, is "unspeakably crude."[31] They measure respondents' social environment by constructing an index of parental SES consisting of four variables: mother's education, father's education, family income, and parents' occupational status. This index is limited even as a measure of family background; as an instrument for estimating the cumulative effects of "social and economic disadvantage," it is exceedingly narrow.[32] It excludes an assortment of important social variables pertaining both to respondents' parental background and to their own current social and economic circumstances, including family size and composition, quality of education, local employment opportunities, community and neighborhood characteristics, and quality of social contacts.[33] Several replications of Herrnstein and Murray's analysis using more refined measures of socioeconomic background find that *The Bell Curve* consistently underestimates the influence of the social environment relative to IQ on life outcomes.[34]

Perhaps the most serious problem with Herrnstein and Murray's argument is that their own data, buried in one of the appendixes to their book, reveal only very weak correlations between IQ scores and social outcomes.[35] According to the statistics they report, IQ has at best a modest effect on how individuals live their lives; contrary to their central argument, it is not "a major predictor of income."[36] One team of economists, reanalyzing the data used in *The Bell Curve*, found that cognitive ability, *even in combination with education and experience*, explains "at most one third of the total variance in wages." Herrnstein and Murray, they report, "dramatically overstate the degree to which differences in wages among individuals can be attributed to differences in cognitive ability."[37] This conclusion would not be so damaging if the objective of *The Bell Curve* were only to prove that IQ, along with many other variables, has *some* influence on life outcomes. But Herrnstein and Murray maintain that intelligence is the *predominant* force in people's lives, and this claim is refuted by the "small to middling" correlations they report.[38] Though not entirely irrelevant to economic achievement, IQ, inherited or not, does not play anything like the powerful role Herrnstein and Murray attribute to it.

GENES, IQ, AND POVERTY

The Bell Curve proposes a simple theory of poverty: people are poor because they are deficient in inherited cognitive ability. The poor are victims of their own bad genes, and social and educational interventions can do little to remedy the problem. In what follows, I identify five key weaknesses of Herrnstein and Murray's theory: their individualistic premise blinds them to the structural causes of poverty, their argument rests on the erroneous assumption of equality of opportunity, they misrepresent the relationship between IQ and poverty, they present an unrealistic analysis of how people are matched to jobs, and they fail to address the problem of poverty in the aggregate.

Individualistic Bias

The very language of *The Bell Curve* reveals an "individualistic bias."[39] Herrnstein and Murray describe poverty, unemployment, and the like not as social conditions, but as "social behaviors," implying that these are purely personal problems arising from individual misconduct and unrelated to the structure and functioning of society. Poverty, they suggest, is a predicament low-IQ people get themselves into because they are unable to perform adequately in school and on the job and because they are prone to bad choices and self-destructive behaviors. The authors' terminology conveys the message that poverty is not so much a condition of society as it is an instance of individual inferiority and deviant behavior.

More important, Herrnstein and Murray's individualistic bias is reflected in their assumption that poverty can be explained solely in terms of personal attributes. Indeed, they propose a *single-factor* individualistic theory, pinpointing just one variable as the key to explaining the complex phenomenon of poverty. And while they emphasize the limits set by genes from the inside, Herrnstein and Murray acknowledge no outside obstacles to achievement. They consider parental SES, only to dismiss it, and they otherwise disregard the numerous external social forces affecting life outcomes. They not only deny the influence of family circumstances on people's economic outcomes, but they also ask us to believe that the incidence of poverty is unrelated to the state of the economy or to government social welfare and labor market policies.

Inequality of Opportunity

In modern American society, Herrnstein and Murray insist, individuals compete for access to schools and jobs under conditions of equality of opportunity.[40] Cognitive ability, not family background or social status, is the key to success or failure. In reality, however, neither the educational nor the occupational systems come close to being meritocracies. Children encounter vast and cumulative educational inequalities from the very first moment they begin learning all the way through their college years and beyond. Poor children are less likely to receive high-quality child care, attend high-quality preschool programs, or benefit from a cognitively stimulating home environment. By the time they are old enough for kindergarten, they are already well behind their more affluent peers. Once they enter the highly segregated school system, packed into the country's worst classrooms, they encounter a new round of disadvantages. And while Herrnstein and Murray proclaim the "democratization of higher education," an outpouring of recent research demonstrates increasing class disparities in access to college. The combination of budgetary constraints, rising tuition costs, declining financial aid, and stagnant family incomes has made higher education unaffordable for many qualified students. Money, indeed, has increased in importance relative to brains as a determinant of who gets a college degree. As Peter Sacks finds, "a wealthy low-achiever in America has a significantly greater chance of attending a four-year university than a highly accomplished student from a lower-income family."[41]

Herrnstein and Murray fail to acknowledge inequalities of opportunity in the labor market as well. In particular, they downplay racial and gender discrimination and the persistent disadvantages associated with social class. A study conducted by a team of economists, drawing on the same data used in *The Bell Curve*, shows wage levels for women and racial minorities are lower compared to white males at the same level of cognitive ability. A white man might earn a decent living even with a relatively low IQ, while a woman or an African American might struggle even with a relatively high IQ.[42] The data on earnings, the authors conclude, are "inconsistent with Herrnstein and Murray's claim that the labor market is meritocratic."[43] The rates of poverty for African Americans and women are also significantly higher than what would be expected if equal opportunity prevailed and if cognitive ability were the primary determinant of economic outcomes. The evidence reveals, contrary to the meritocracy ideal, that women and racial minorities are unable to cash in on their cognitive ability to the same extent as their white male counterparts.[44]

More generally, Herrnstein and Murray refuse to recognize how life chances are structured by "durable inequalities" and how such inequalities are transmitted through the family, along with genes.[45] As one critique of *The Bell Curve* concludes: "Parents' advantages—property, learning, personal contacts, practical crafts, social skills, cultural tools, and so on—are passed on to their children and are also passed from older members of a community to younger ones. Disadvantages are passed on, too."[46] Contrary to Herrnstein and Murray's assumption, neither the educational system nor the occupational system deserves the meritocracy label. Significant and enduring disparities in access to education and employment persist. Poor people are poor not because they have limited intelligence, but because they have limited opportunities for gaining a quality education and securing a decent job.

The Correlation between IQ and Poverty

People with low IQs are more likely to be poor than people with high IQs. Herrnstein and Murray infer from this correlation that inherited cognitive ability exerts a causal influence on economic status—low intelligence leads to poverty.[47] They jump to this conclusion for two reasons. First, they treat intelligence as a cause, never as an effect; they refuse to see intelligence as "responsive to social conditions."[48] Second, they treat poverty as an effect, never as a cause; they refuse to see poverty as something that shapes behavior and life outcomes. Poor children are raised in poor families, and they often live in poor housing, reside in poor neighborhoods, and attend poor schools; they suffer disproportionately from nutritionally inadequate diets and from poor mental and physical health; and if they are African American or Latino, they experience prejudice and discrimination, residential segregation, and social isolation. Children born into poverty face multiple and cumulative disadvantages, and they live stressful lives. If their IQ scores were not lower than average, it would be nothing short of miraculous.

By downplaying the influence of the social environment on cognitive ability, Herrnstein and Murray overlook a highly plausible alternative to their interpretation of the modest correlation between IQ and poverty: "*It is not that low intelligence leads to inferior status; it is that inferior status leads to low intelligence test scores.*"[49] Poverty hinders the full development of cognitive functioning. Low-income families often lack the financial means, social supports, and institutional resources necessary to nurture fully the abilities and aptitudes of their children.[50] Perhaps the issue is as simple as this: rich kids score higher on intelligence tests mainly because they are raised in rich environments with an abundance of resources and opportunities, and poor kids score lower on such tests mainly because they are raised in poor environments with a paucity of resources and opportunities. The fundamental problem for the poor is their poverty, not their IQs.

Getting a Job

Herrnstein and Murray claim that individuals, through the operation of an "invisible hand," are sorted into the occupational system according to their cognitive ability.[51] Differences in intelligence are thereby translated into differences in earnings. High-IQ workers are slotted into the good jobs and low-IQ workers, if they are not entirely superfluous, are slotted into the bad jobs. This occupational sorting process, for Herrnstein and Murray, is uniform, objective, rational, inevitable, and meritocratic: *uniform*, because all employers rely on essentially the same criteria for evaluating workers; *objective*, because the screening process is relatively free of subjective judgment, prejudice, and false impressions; *rational*, because it maximizes efficiency; *inevitable*, because it is bound to the imperatives of a technological society; and *meritocratic*, because it guarantees that ability is the primary determinant of who gets ahead.

Herrnstein and Murray's theory of occupational sorting rests on an implausible assumption: the only handicap people suffer in the labor market is a low IQ. Independent of cognitive ability, however, as a vast social science literature shows, individuals may be disadvantaged by, among other things, their race, ethnicity, gender, age, and sexual preference. They may be bumped from the inside track because they lack the requisite references. They may be perfect for a job, but unaware that an opening exists. Employers might overlook cognitively qualified candidates because they have the wrong social or cultural background, have the wrong credentials, come from the wrong neighborhoods, know the wrong people, have the wrong physical appearance, or speak with the wrong accent. Applicants might be rejected because they are perceived to be lacking in proper work attitudes, loyalty, discipline, compatibility, people skills, or willingness to obey authority. The occupational sorting process is way too messy to imagine that workers are matched to jobs primarily on the basis of their "general intelligence." A good theory of poverty needs to be able to explain, among other things, why particular individuals lose out in the labor market. But it is implausible to think this is simply a matter of some people having low IQs.

Poverty in the Aggregate

The individualistic bias of *The Bell Curve* is evident also in how Herrnstein and Murray frame the poverty problem. They implicitly conceive the central empirical issue as one of identifying the characteristics of individuals that make them more or less vulnerable to poverty. This is an important topic, but because of this narrow focus, they fail to address adequately the problem of poverty in the aggregate.[52] Their theory purports to explain why some people are poor, but it cannot explain why *anyone* is poor, or why there is as much (or as little) poverty as there is.[53] And it cannot explain why the gap between the rich and the poor is so large, why those at the low end of the occupational system are rewarded so much less for their labor than those on the high end, or why day-care workers, say, earn eight dollars an hour rather than sixteen dollars an hour. It is not a requirement of genetics that millions of workers in the US economy are paid less than a living wage.

The flaw in Herrnstein and Murray's theory derives from the fact that individual deficiencies, in themselves, do not cause people to be poor. During an economic boom, for example, a person with few skills may have no trouble earning a decent living. But during an economic bust, as jobs become scarce, that same person might end up unemployed and in the ranks of the poor. Whether or not a low IQ, or any other individual-level characteristic, leads to poverty depends on the availability of decent-paying jobs. The biogenetic theory can predict (though, as it turns out, not with a great deal of accuracy) who is likely to fall into poverty when the economy goes sour. But it cannot explain the fluctuations in the rate of poverty over time or the causes of the economic booms and busts underlying those fluctuations. Was the decline in the rate of poverty in the United States from 12.8 percent in 1989 to 11.3 percent in 2000 due to an upsurge in the average IQ of Americans during that period, and why has the rate of poverty increased since 2000? Does the United States have the highest rate of poverty in the industrialized world because Americans on average are so much less intelligent than people in other countries? Some individuals are bound to be less able and less skilled than others, of course, but whether this leaves them above or below the poverty line depends largely on government policy and the state of the economy.

The statistical relationship Herrnstein and Murray find between IQ and poverty in the United States is not a fact of nature. It is a contingent product of the existing economic and political rules of the game. Change the rules, and the relationship between IQ and poverty likewise changes. Under a different regime, with different economic and political structures, different cultural norms and ideals, different conceptions of fairness, different regulations governing the operation of the labor market, and different social policies, cognitive ability might play less (or more) of a role in the allocation of income and wealth. Herrnstein and Murray argue that intelligence cannot be raised; but even accepting this dubious assertion, it does not follow that people with low cognitive ability are destined to be poor. As the authors of *Inequality by Design* emphasize, the fate of low-IQ people is not set by their genes, but by social structure and public policy. And these can be altered.

CONCLUSION

Herrnstein and Murray propose that people are poor for the simple reason that they are born with a deficiency in cognitive ability. This view of poverty, and the more general biogenetic theory of inequality that underlies it, is flawed in many respects. I do not attempt to summarize here the numerous weaknesses of *The Bell Curve*, but I do restate four key problems. First, Herrnstein and Murray's own statistical findings, confirmed by subsequent studies, show that differences in IQ account for only a very small portion of the variation among individuals in wages and income, approximately 10 percent.[54] Individuals differ in their economic standing and their vulnerability to poverty for many reasons. Cognitive ability, whether inherited or not, far from being a predominant factor, plays a relatively small role in determining people's life outcomes. Second, the modest relationship between cognitive ability and poverty testifies more than anything to the influence of social and economic deprivation on children's test performance. The biogenetic theory overstates the influence of IQ on poverty and understates the influence of poverty on IQ. Third, contrary to the supposition of *The Bell Curve*, research shows that social, political, and educational policies can raise children's cognitive ability and can improve their later-life economic outcomes. People's life chances are not fixed at birth. Fourth, the biogenetic theory completely ignores the myriad economic, political, cultural, and social forces that influence the distribution of resources and opportunities, the rate of poverty, and the severity of the hardships experienced by the poor.

Herrnstein and Murray's analysis serves less to illuminate the problem than to divert attention away from the real causes of poverty and inequality in the United States. Their theory, with its potent mixture of individualism and racism, plays naturally into the prevailing blame-the-victim mentality. While Herrnstein and Murray do not quite hold poor people themselves responsible for their own poverty (after all, the problem is in their genes), at the same time their theory does not attribute poverty to any sort of inequity or injustice. The conclusion that people are poor because they are deficient in inherited cognitive ability, at the very least, adds fuel to an already fashionable cynicism, one that dovetails with a prevailing skepticism about the ability of government to remedy social problems. Herrnstein and Murray, indeed, go out of their way to cast doubt on the practicality of policies intended to achieve greater equality or improve the economic prospects of the poor. Their book contributes to an atmosphere in which poverty is perceived as a quasi-natural phenomenon, problems of poverty and inequality are absent from the political agenda, and the larger structural forces that underlie increasing inequality and persistent poverty are ignored.

Chapter Three

The Cultural Theory of Poverty and Inequality

POVERTY AS DEVIANCE

The underlying logic of the cultural theory resembles that of the biogenetic theory. Both attribute poverty to the failings of the poor: low IQs for the one and bad values for the other. In the biogenetic theory, the poor lack the requisite cognitive ability; in the cultural theory, they lack the motivation to achieve. In either case, poverty is blamed not on the deficiencies of the American political economy, but on the deficiencies of poor people themselves.

In calculating the size of the poverty population, the Bureau of the Census employs a monetary definition: individuals and families are counted as poor if their income falls below a certain threshold. From the standpoint of the cultural theory, however, poverty—insofar as it is deemed a social problem—is not primarily a matter of economic resources. The poor become visible from a policy standpoint not because of the hardships they endure, but because of the troubles they cause. They come into public view only when they are jobless, are unmarried with children, abuse alcohol and drugs, commit crimes, or receive food stamps. Public assistance, job training, and other conventional antipoverty policies, according to this theory, are bound to be ineffective. Such remedies, based on the assumption that poverty is essentially an economic condition, fail to address the root problem: the deviant way of life of the poor. A war on poverty can be won, the cultural theory submits, only by changing poor people themselves, only by compelling them to embrace the values of family, work, and personal responsibility.

THE ORIGINS AND DEVELOPMENT OF THE
CULTURAL THEORY

The modern cultural theory of poverty came on the scene in the United States in the early 1960s and has been the subject of controversy ever since.[1] While it subsequently became the centerpiece of conservative analysis, the culture of poverty concept, ironically, was introduced to American audiences through the work of two men on the left, Michael Harrington and Oscar Lewis.[2] Unlike many later advocates of the cultural theory, neither Harrington nor Lewis held poor people solely responsible for their condition, and both regarded the culture of the poor as a symptom of poverty, not its cause. They employed the culture of poverty concept to underline the multifaceted, persistent, deep-rooted, and tenacious nature of the problem. By drawing attention to its cultural dimension, moreover, neither Harrington nor Lewis intended to downplay the economic and political causes of poverty. Indeed, they both understood poverty to be an outgrowth of capitalism, and they both regarded the culture of the poor as a by-product of economic deprivation, social segregation, and political exclusion.

By the end of the 1960s the culture of poverty theory had become a staple of conservative social criticism in the United States. In their adaptation of this theory, conservatives shifted the onus of responsibility for poverty from society to the individual, prompting liberals to charge them with "blaming the victim."[3] Unlike Harrington and Lewis, conservatives regarded the culture of the poor as the cause of their poverty, not its consequence. This version of the cultural theory has gained intellectual and political prominence since the 1970s, contributing to a shift in the public discourse on poverty away from concerns about inequality, discrimination, and job scarcity and toward issues of welfare dependency, the underclass, and the decline of family values.[4]

THE CULTURE OF THE POOR

The cultural theory maintains that poor people have a distinct set of values, aspirations, beliefs, attitudes, dispositions, and psychological characteristics. These putative cultural traits and the style of life corresponding to them constitute a unique culture of poverty, one often conceived as the antithesis of mainstream culture. In an influential early statement of this theory, Edward Banfield posits a "class-cultural scale," with "lower-class" culture at one end of the continuum and its opposite, "upper-class" culture, at the other. The culture of the lower class, he states, is characterized by "the existence of an outlook and style of life which is radically present-oriented and which therefore attaches no value to work, sacrifice, self-improvement, or service to family, friends or community."[5] People from the lower class, Banfield asserts, have little awareness of the future, they are incapable of self-discipline, and their behavior is governed by impulse and "bodily needs (especially for sex)." The poor, he declares, are also inclined toward "violent crime and civil disorder," they are "not troubled by dirt and dilapidation," and they prefer "the 'action' of the street to any steady job." Their presence turns neighborhoods into "slums" and schools into "blackboard jungles."[6] The poverty of this lower class, furthermore, Banfield alleges, is "'inwardly' caused," the outcome of a psychological inability to plan for the future. The habitual "ways of thinking and behaving" that characterize the poor are deeply rooted as well, such that "improvements in external circumstances" are likely to have little effect. For Banfield, lower-class "attitudes, habits, and modes of behavior," as with cognitive ability for Herrnstein and Murray, cannot be easily changed. His call for action, accordingly, consists mostly of measures that would subject the lower-class poor to more stringent mechanisms of social control—intensified policing and swift imprisonment, for example.[7]

For other proponents of the cultural theory, the problem is not so much the deep attachment of the poor to a deviant subculture as it is their superficial allegiance to mainstream norms. The poor give "lip service" to middle-class values, William Kelso contends, but they rarely abide by these and "feel no sense of obligation to harmonize their beliefs with their actions."[8] They might talk the talk, but they don't walk the walk. For Lawrence Mead, similarly, the poor affirm cultural ideals "in principle but not in practice."[9] They profess adherence to values of work and marriage, but they do not have regular jobs or stable family lives. The inability of the poor to live up to conventional norms, he insists, is not due to any external obstacles, but to their own negative outlook on life. They are imbued with a "defeatist culture," and this mentality is the "chief cause" of their poverty. The poor remain poor because they are resigned to failure, easily discouraged, and do not try very hard to get or keep a job. They are deficient in the "self-discipline" necessary "to get through school, obey the law, work steadily, and avoid trouble." The persistence of poverty, according to Mead, is due primarily to poor people's misguided defeatism and their lack of "personal organization."[10] Ben Carson, appointed by Donald Trump to head the Department of Housing and Urban Development, offers a similar conclusion. People remain stuck in poverty, he states, because they have "the wrong mind-set"; instead of striving to get ahead, they passively embrace "the status of victim."[11]

Employment opportunities are plentiful, the cultural theory implies, and anyone can work their way out of poverty if they are willing to put in the necessary effort. Joblessness among the poor, Mead argues, is not caused by discrimination, disability, or low wages, nor is it due to unaffordable child care or unreliable transportation.[12] The real problem is psychological: the

long-term poor are simply incapable of mobilizing the inner resources necessary to secure a job. Charles Murray offers an even harsher judgment. The
"underclass" is chronically unemployed, he asserts, not because they lack
opportunities or skills, but because they are unwilling and unable "to get up
every morning and go to work."[13] For Myron Magnet, likewise, the poor are
held back not because they are unfairly denied the chance to succeed, but
because of their own inferior psyches; they are "equipped with different, and
sparser, mental and emotional furniture, unhelpful for taking advantage of
the economic opportunities that American life offers." The poor, he concludes, are victims of their own bad behavior and "the worldview from which
that behavior springs."[14]

Whether the poor have succumbed to a deviant subculture or a defeatist
psychology, the implication is the same: poverty is the result of poor people's
own impaired values. They have only themselves and their families to blame.
They lack ambition and initiative, perseverance and diligence; they have
weak moral convictions and are easily lured into delinquency and crime; they
are lazy and unmotivated, preferring government handouts or criminal activity to hard work; they lack strength of character and are too quick to give up
in the face of adversity; and they reject the values of personal responsibility,
sexual restraint, and monogamous marriage. As a result of their inner defects,
the poor are likely to drop out of high school, become unmarried mothers and
fathers, experience chronic joblessness, and surrender to welfare dependency. The negative psychological and behavioral traits of the poor persist from
generation to generation as well. Through the process of socialization and the
bad example set by their parents, poor children learn to emulate the errant
behaviors of their elders. Poverty and its culture endure, this theory proposes,
because the poor "pass on to their children a self-defeating set of values and
attitudes, along with an impoverished intellectual and emotional development, that generally imprisons them in failure as well."[15]

To conclude this section, I have a few words to say about J. D. Vance's
Hillbilly Elegy (published in 2016), worth singling out because it is a new
and highly popular addition to the cultural theory library. This book is a
memoir, a family history. It is not an investigative report or a social science
study. Nor does it present a deeply researched and methodical analysis of the
lives and circumstances of poor white Americans. Nevertheless, Vance has
come to be seen as a fresh conservative voice on the topic of poverty. He
even appeared alongside distinguished sociologist William Julius Wilson in a
September 2017 forum, "Race, Class, and Culture," sponsored by the Brookings Institution.[16]

Vance grew up poor in an "Ohio steel town" that had long been "hemor-
rhaging jobs."[17] His book, however, where relevant to the issue of poverty, is
not an account of how those jobs came to disappear or how their disappear-
ance undercut the employment and mobility prospects of his friends and

neighbors. Nor does it contain much information about current economic conditions.[18] Many "distressed" areas throughout the rust belt and the Appalachian South have experienced negative business creation and negative job growth since 2000 and, not surprisingly, persistently high rates of unemployment and poverty.[19] The grim economic realities, however, are not what capture Vance's attention. What interests him instead is the culture he perceived during his youth and as a young man, a culture, he says, that encouraged "social decay instead of counteracting it." The white working class of his community, he maintains, or some portion of it anyway, responded to a changing economic landscape in a thoroughly self-destructive manner. They reacted to their "bad circumstances in the worst way possible," giving rise to a social world—Vance's world—marred by "truly irrational behavior." "Our homes are a chaotic mess." "We choose not to work when we should be looking for jobs." "We don't study as children, and we don't make our kids study when we're parents." "We spend our way into the poorhouse," buying "giant TVs and iPads," fancy clothes, and homes we "don't need" and can't afford. Thrift, he states, "is inimical to our being." These are not problems government can remedy, he insists. "We created them and only we can fix them."[20]

Betsy Rader, another product of Appalachian poverty and now a lawyer, disputes what she refers to as Vance's "sweeping stereotypes" and "inaccurate and dangerous generalizations." "Who is this 'we' of whom he speaks?" she asks. In her memory of growing up in a poor "hillbilly" family, thrift "was the very essence of our being."[21] People's recollections, inevitably selective and sometimes tendentious, even if unknowingly so, give rise to divergent pictures of the same world. And here we see the problem, and the limitations of a memoir, a genre that by definition relies on hearsay, remembrances, and personal observations. These might point to fruitful areas of investigation, but they don't yield the kind of evidence required to carry the weight of an argument. The allegations Vance makes—as in his lament about "the many food stamp recipients who show little interest in honest work" or the broad-brushed passages cited above—are too anecdotal and impressionistic to be counted as reliable indicators of a pathological culture and even less to serve as an explanation for the enduring poverty of his hometown region.[22] *Hillbilly Elegy* is an interesting memoir. But it lacks the systematic empirical grounding to be considered a credible statement about American poverty.

THE SOURCES OF THE CULTURAL DEVIANCE OF THE POOR

If, as the cultural theory contends, people are poor because they are deficient in the values and motivations that lead to economic achievement, then what is the source of this deficiency? The challenge for this theory is to come up with an explanation for what are presumed to be the distinct psychological and cultural traits of the poor without conceiving these as consequences of their poverty. For some proponents of this theory, the cultural characteristics imputed to the poor are simply taken as given. For others, the culture of poverty is a product of some combination of (1) the legacy of slavery, (2) the political and cultural revolutions of the 1960s, and (3) the liberal welfare state.

Addressing specifically the case of black poverty, one version of the cultural theory attributes the psychological and behavioral deviance of the poor to the legacy of slavery. Daniel Patrick Moynihan, in a controversial government report made public in 1965, proposed that slavery and Jim Crow, along with urbanization and unemployment, undermined the ability of black males to assume the breadwinner role. To fill the vacuum, a matriarchal family structure, a maladaptive arrangement "out of line with the rest of American society," came into being. The resulting weakness of the black family, according to Moynihan, engendered "aberrant, inadequate, or anti-social behavior" among the younger generation, thus causing an ongoing "cycle of poverty and deprivation." This "tangle of pathology," he argues, highlighting the point that racial discrimination is no longer the fundamental problem, "is capable of perpetuating itself without assistance from the white world." The legacy of slavery, in Moynihan's view, gave rise to a now autonomous matriarchal subculture, and this is the central causal factor in the continuation of black poverty. [23]

According to another formulation of this thesis, the slave experience had lasting effects not just through its influence on black family formation, but also through its broader impact on black culture. Mead surmises, for example, that the worldview of African Americans, formed by "group memories of slavery and Jim Crow," promotes a powerful hopelessness that inhibits effort. [24] Dinesh D'Souza proposes a more elaborate theory. Black people, he claims, devised various strategies of resistance under slavery. They refused to work hard, stole from their masters, and acted in a defiant manner. Over time, D'Souza imagines, these traits congealed into a "distinctive ethnic identity" that lives on today in the form of "destructive and pathological patterns of behavior." Included among these, he asserts, are "excessive reliance on government, conspiratorial paranoia about racism, a resistance to academic achievement as 'acting white,' a celebration of the criminal and outlaw as authentically black, and the normalization of illegitimacy and dependency." Originating as a "response to past oppression," these behaviors are now "dysfunctional and must be modified." [25] By underscoring the cultural and distant historical roots of African American poverty, D'Souza and others want to suggest that the impoverished circumstances of today's black poor have nothing to do with current economic conditions or with the persistence of racial segregation and discrimination. Poverty, they conclude, is the fault of black people themselves; they have been too slow to shed the values and attitudes that grew out of the slave experience and that have since turned pathological.

A second version of the cultural theory ascribes the presumably aberrant values and behavior of the poor to the social, political, and cultural changes of the 1960s. According to Magnet, Kelso, and others, the ascendancy of liberalism, the sexual revolution, and the hippie counterculture combined to create a new and pernicious set of values, norms, and beliefs.[26] Liberal social programs, from the war on poverty to affirmative action, fostered ideologies of victimization and entitlement, undermining traditional ideals of individual initiative, hard work, and merit. The sexual revolution, along with feminism, sparked a transformation of values that "reshaped family life, increasing divorce, illegitimacy, and female-headed families." And the sixties counterculture inspired a do-your-own-thing hedonism that demeaned precisely those moral principles—the work ethic, sexual responsibility, and deferred gratification—most conducive to individual achievement.[27] The cultural upheaval of the 1960s, Magnet and Kelso believe, had an especially adverse effect on the poor. As the "Victorian principles" of self-control and hard work gave way to a "more laissez-faire morality," poor people, only weakly committed to conventional norms to begin with, "abandoned the values of self-restraint even more quickly than the rest of society." This cultural devolution left "many indigents without a moral compass" and caused the "economically poor" to mutate into a destructive "underclass."[28] While in the past the poor just lacked money, today they lack values.

A third version of the cultural theory holds the welfare state responsible for the deviant values and behaviors of the poor.[29] According to this thesis, the welfare system rewards poor people for not working, for not marrying, and for having babies out of wedlock. By offering money for nothing, welfare encourages the laziness of the poor, sunders "the psychological link between effort and reward," and destroys the motivational foundation of "long-run upward mobility."[30] It undermines personal responsibility, saps individual initiative, and fosters an ethos of dependency. The welfare system, according to its conservative critics, perpetuates a dysfunctional culture of poverty, inhibiting the poor from achieving economic independence.

These hypotheses assume the existence of what they set out to explain: a deviant black identity, the decline of moral standards, and a destructive welfare culture. They posit a connection between today's poverty and past developments, but establish this more through supposition than careful investigation. And they rest on the dubious assumption of a bifurcated poverty population, one divided into the "bad" and the "good": the black poor versus the white poor, the post-1960s poor versus the pre-1960s poor, the welfare poor versus the working poor. Though lacking empirical credibility, these arguments enable conservative critics to ignore issues of economics, inequality, and discrimination, while at the same time giving them a platform to extol traditional values, vent their hostility toward the decade of the 1960s, and denounce the welfare state.

THE CULTURAL SOLUTION TO THE PROBLEM OF POVERTY

To conquer the problem of poverty, according to the cultural theory, the poor must be induced or compelled to renounce their self-destructive lifestyles and adopt the values of hard work, self-restraint, and individual responsibility. "The opportunity is there," Lawrence Harrison avows. What the poor need is a new message: "Go for it!"[31] According to Republican congressman Paul Ryan, the poor can replace their "vicious cycle of despair" with a "virtuous cycle of hope" only by "embracing the attributes of friendship, accountability, and love."[32] George Gilder also exhorts the poor to change their ways. The "only dependable route from poverty," he declares, "is always work, family, and faith."[33] Explicitly urging "moral reform," Joel Schwartz proposes that the poor can best escape their poverty by adhering faithfully to traditional virtues of diligence, thrift, sobriety, and family responsibility.[34] Kelso, likewise, calls for a "strenuous effort . . . to resocialize the poor into playing by the 'rules of the game.'"[35] Conventional solutions, which throw money at the problem or seek only to expand opportunities, are doomed to failure, conservative critics charge. Such remedies ignore the deep cultural roots of poverty. An intervention into the lives of the poor is required, something invasive enough to undo their counterproductive values, attitudes, and behaviors.[36]

For many adherents of the cultural theory, the necessary first step toward rehabilitating the poor is to dismantle a welfare state that creates incentives for people to behave badly. According to Dick Armey, former congressional representative and now Tea Party front man, the key to ending poverty is to "scrap today's failed welfare system and replace dependency with work, marriage, and personal responsibility." He favors the "'Tough Love' option": kick the poor off welfare and trust they can make it on their own. And for those who do fall through the cracks, the solution is not "Big Government," but "the natural safety net" of "family, friends, churches, and charities."[37]

Armey's solution builds on the thinking of Marvin Olasky, the architect of "compassionate conservatism."[38] Like other adherents of the cultural theory, Olasky believes poverty is less a problem of economics than attitudes. What the poor need is not a government handout, he contends, but a strong dose of spiritual reform and moral instruction. Poor people are "caught within a dysfunctional culture," Newt Gingrich explains, summarizing Olasky's theory, and the only way for them to change their behavior and escape poverty is to "transfer their loyalties, beliefs, and practices to another culture." Government bureaucrats and welfare agencies lack the competence to effect such a transformation. Faith-based organizations are the only institutions capable of mounting such a momentous undertaking. The poor can be moved out of "the culture of violence and poverty and into a better culture" only through the moral influence of religiously inspired "missionaries."[39]

Mead also believes the poor need to change their outlook on life and patterns of behavior. But unlike right-wing critics of the welfare state, he thinks government can play a positive role in helping poor people to "reorganize their lives." Calling for a "new paternalism," Mead proposes that public authorities, to address the "lifestyle causes of poverty," place recipients of government assistance under close supervision.[40] By monitoring the poor and enforcing mandatory compliance with conventional values and behavioral rules, such as work requirements, government agencies might be able to steer poor people into the cultural and economic mainstream.

The cultural theory, in sum, makes five key claims: (1) The psychology and worldview of the poor differ markedly from those of the middle class, with poor people being deficient in the attitudes, beliefs, and commitments that promote stable families and economic achievement. The poor have, at best, a weak commitment to the values of work, marriage, and personal responsibility. (2) Because of their deviant cultural and psychological traits, the poor are predisposed toward a self-destructive lifestyle, leaving them trapped in welfare dependency, single parenthood, and chronic joblessness. (3) The cultural and behavioral deviance of the poor—not economic conditions, lack of opportunities, or discrimination—is the primary cause of their poverty. (4) The psychological and motivational deficiencies of the poor are transmitted through the process of socialization from one generation to the next. Because of their deep cultural origins, these deficiencies have the status of relatively fixed personality traits and cannot be remedied simply by changing the socioeconomic environment of the poor. (5) Only by uprooting the culture of poverty itself, only by subjecting the poor to a regimen of resocialization and moral reform, can the problem of poverty be alleviated.[41]

IS THE CULTURAL THEORY PLAUSIBLE?

The appeal of the cultural theory is understandable. It affirms the American Dream ideology; it accords with popular narratives recounting tales of individual success and failure; it sends a positive message, telling us that opportunities are abundant and anyone can make it if they try; it conveys the comforting idea of a just world where everyone gets what they deserve; it fits our natural inclination to favor explanations for people's behaviors and life outcomes in terms of personal dispositions rather than larger social forces; it plays on popular stereotypes about the poor, the black poor in particular, while presenting a flattering picture of a virtuous middle class; and, by proposing that poverty can best be combated by cutting social welfare programs, it promises a solution that goes easy on the pocketbook of the taxpaying public. This theory is plausible also because poor people, consumed by the stressful experience of "resource scarcity," do sometimes make bad decisions or engage in seemingly imprudent behavior, splurging on an expensive meal, for example.[42] And nearly everyone, moreover, can point to a poor person or two who seemingly fit the theory's negative image. For these and other reasons, it is not surprising that Americans are attracted to the cultural theory. But even at first glance there are good reasons to doubt the validity of this view of poverty.

One reason to be suspicious is that the cultural theory purports to explain poverty by reference to one chief cause: the mental outlook of the poor. Any single-factor theory such as this lacks surface plausibility, especially when applied to an extraordinarily complex and multifaceted phenomenon such as poverty. This theory would have us believe that values and attitudes are the only things that matter, and that larger economic and political forces exert little influence on people's life trajectories. Even in the wake of the Great Recession, proponents of this theory dismiss or give short shrift to a host of potentially relevant structural forces: the accelerated pace of globalization, the loss of manufacturing jobs, the decline of trade unions, the erosion in the real value of the minimum wage, and the surge of inequality. The cultural theory's interpretation of recent American history and its analysis of poverty largely ignore these developments, offering up instead a simpleminded story of family breakdown, moral decline, and personal irresponsibility.

We should be skeptical about this theory for other reasons as well. The proposition that poor people share certain deviant norms and values that diverge from the mainstream and are passed on from generation to generation is inconsistent with certain basic facts about the poverty population. First, as Jens Ludwig and Susan Mayer show, most of today's poor grew up in precisely the sort of families celebrated by conservative critics: mainstream families in which parents were married, had regular jobs, and attended religious services. The majority of today's poor adults were not reared in some aberrant cultural environment, and they did not inherit bad values from their parents. Contrary to the thesis of the cultural theory, there is no massive family-values upbringing gap that explains why some children become poor adults and others do not.[43]

Second, while the poor are alike in that they do not have much money, they are otherwise a diverse group, contrary to popular impressions and common stereotypes. Some are old and some young, some male and some female. Some are disabled, some suffer from temporary health problems, and others are caregivers for incapacitated relatives. Many of the poor are African American and Latino, and a smaller number are Asian American and Native American, but most are non-Hispanic white. Some poor people live in single-parent households, some in two-parent households, and others alone. The poor vary also in their residential location: they reside in inner cities, in the rural countryside, and increasingly, in the suburbs. Some poor people are unemployed or out of the labor force, but many have jobs in the low-wage service sector. Some are poor for only short periods of time, others for many years. It is difficult to imagine that the poverty of this heterogeneous group is due to their all sharing a common set of achievement-inhibiting beliefs and values.

Third, the poor are not only a diverse population, they are a constantly changing population as well. The number of people below the official poverty line increases in some years and decreases in others. The poverty population undergoes regular turnover as well, with thousands of people moving into poverty and thousands of others moving out of poverty all the time. As Mark Rank shows, it is not just marginal groups that experience poverty; indeed, a majority of the American population is poor at least one year during their adult lives. Poverty is a "'mainstream event," Rank argues; it is not something unique to a deviant "other" or to those who are somehow culturally disfigured.[44]

Fourth, contrary to the cultural theory's "us" versus "them" imagery, the poor on the whole are not all that different from the nonpoor. In its determination to represent the poor as some deviant underclass, the cultural theory exaggerates the divide separating the poverty population and the working population.[45] It maintains credibility by suppressing the similarities between the poor and the nonpoor, by depicting the poor as falling outside the mainstream of American culture, and by assuming the values and behaviors attributed to the poor cannot also be found among the middle class. Only through this strategy can the cultural theory sustain the argument that the problems of the poor are of their own making and have little to do with the social and economic forces that cause great hardship also for the more respectable members of society.[46]

The poor, in sum, comprise a diverse population, and one that, as Bradley Schiller emphasizes, is "not markedly different from . . . the rest of society."[47] It is implausible to think this varied and changing group possesses a common mental outlook, much less one antithetical to conventional values, that exerts an autonomous and decisive effect on people's life outcomes. The very heterogeneity of the poverty population casts doubt on the cultural theory's simpleminded, single-factor psychological explanation.

HOW WELL DOES THE CULTURAL THEORY KNOW THE POOR?

Most of the poor do not fit the cultural theory's stereotypical portrait. Consider, for example, the millions of Americans, increasingly visible since the Great Recession, who adhered faithfully to mainstream values throughout most of their lives and yet now suffer from long-term unemployment. Or consider the millions of Americans who fall into poverty due to a family crisis, a medical emergency, a job loss, or a decline in earnings. These people, and the vast majority of the poor more generally, are not averse to hard work, they are not lazy and irresponsible, they are not living on government handouts, and they are not engaged in criminal or immoral activities.[48] Though proponents of the cultural theory say little about such people, they at least sometimes admit that many of the poor do not conform to the theory's psychological and demographic profile. They sidestep this inconvenient fact by specifying the theory so that it pertains not to the *entirety* of the poverty population, but to a restricted *segment*—an "underclass" (or "black underclass") that is typically said to include long-term welfare recipients, the chronically unemployed, teen mothers, and assorted troublemakers.[49] By targeting this ill-defined "underclass," and by conceding that most poverty falls outside its purview, the cultural theory strains for empirical credibility, but it also sacrifices any standing it might claim as a general theory of poverty. At the same time, it is forced to acknowledge, if only implicitly, that the larger problem of poverty is not foremost a cultural phenomenon. But even in this narrowed-down version, the cultural theory lacks plausibility. Its sweeping and highly stereotypical claims about the deviant values, negative attitudes, pernicious motivations, and self-destructive behaviors of the poor (or some segment of the poor) presume intimate knowledge of the daily lives and state of mind of millions of people spread all across the country. It is difficult enough to gain insight into the psychology of any single individual or even come to understand our own personal mental world. On what basis can one claim to comprehend the "inner life" of the poor as a whole—to know with such certainty the "values and aspirations" of this large population and "the particulars of their daily decisions"?[50]

The cultural theory's conclusions about the worldview and lifestyle of the poor would be more credible if they were derived from hours of in-depth interviews or years of close-up observation in low-income communities. In fact, however, they are mainly the results of armchair psychological speculation and dubious inference. Advocates of this theory sometimes generalize from their own personal experiences, extrapolate from small and unrepresentative samples, or summon a handful of cases tailored to fit their negative profile. Consider Myron Magnet's statement that the five million or so people who make up the "underclass" are poor because of their sparse "mental and emotional furniture" and because they suffer from an "inner defect." The evidence marshaled in support of this far-fetched contention is not impressive. Magnet cites a smattering of newspaper articles and a couple of sensationalistic anecdotes.[51]

In fact, proponents of the cultural theory rarely provide direct evidence about poor people's values, attitudes, and beliefs; they rely on indirect evidence instead. Rather than studying the world of the poor firsthand, an admittedly laborious task, their typical approach is to infer the psychological dispositions of the poor from more easily accessible data on the observable circumstances of their lives. If the employment and family status of the poor diverge from the mainstream, it follows that they must be in the grips of a deviant culture. If black people comprise a disproportionate share of the long-term poor, they must be "uniquely prone to the attitudes contrary to work." If poor people live in slums, they must prefer a life of "squalor and misery." If they fail to climb out of poverty, they must be lacking in perseverance.[52] If they are unemployed, they must be unwilling to work. If they receive government assistance, they must have surrendered to an ethic of dependency. The difficulty with such inferences, of course, is that individuals do not always have the means to conform to their cultural preferences, live up to their ideals, or realize their desires. People's circumstances inevitably impose constraints on their options, causing them to do one thing even while they believe in another: to be a single mother, even though they dream about marriage; to be unemployed, even though they desperately want a job; to be on welfare, even though they prefer self-sufficiency. What the cultural theory overlooks is that the lives people lead are shaped not just by their psychological and cultural dispositions, but by their access to resources and opportunities as well.

DO THE POOR DIFFER FROM THE NONPOOR, AND IF SO, HOW AND WHY?

Since the cultural theory appeared on the scene in the 1960s, social scientists—through a combination of survey research, in-depth interviews, and ethnographic studies—have sought a more empirically grounded understanding of the values, beliefs, and way of life of the poor. Many of these studies have focused on precisely those people presumed to be most susceptible to the culture of poverty, including single mothers, welfare recipients, and the residents of urban ghettos. This research reveals a complicated picture, but one that clearly contradicts the cultural theory's image of poverty and the poor. No brief summary can do justice to the numerous studies that have been conducted in recent decades. Nevertheless, two key conclusions deserve to be singled out from this body of research. (1) The fundamental values and aspirations of the poor do not differ significantly from those of the middle class. (2) Many of the poor lead lives that diverge from what is presumed to be the norm—they are unemployed, they live in single-parent households, and they sometimes receive government assistance—but these outcomes are due largely to inadequate opportunities, not deviant values.

The vast majority of the poor, for better or worse, adhere to traditional cultural ideals. They believe in the importance of individual effort, education, family, and personal responsibility.[53] Despite experiences that might be expected to teach a contrary lesson, most poor people remain wedded to the ideology of individualism. They think opportunities are available and education and hard work are the keys to success. Even residents of the poorest Chicago neighborhoods, according to William Julius Wilson, "agreed that America is the land of opportunity where anybody can get ahead, and that individuals get pretty much what they deserve."[54] Though they tell complicated stories, Jennifer Hochschild and Alford Young both cite a surprisingly strong belief in the American Dream among poor African Americans.[55] In a study of impoverished households in Chicago, Sandra Barnes reveals a widespread endorsement of a conventional "achievement ideology" emphasizing the importance of work, education, and merit.[56] Naomi Farber shows that poor teen mothers, just like their middle- and working-class counterparts, "hold aspirations that reflect mainstream values about educational and vocational achievement."[57] Poor people, it seems, are not so different, certainly not the alien "other" envisioned by the cultural theory. They want what most Americans want: a decent education, a good job, a stable family, a happy marriage, and a nice home. Based on data from a large national sample, Rachel Jones and Ye Luo conclude that on issues of work, family, and welfare, there is little empirical support for "traditional culture of poverty arguments."[58]

There is no vast cultural divide that separates the poor from the nonpoor. But in several respects rarely mentioned by proponents of the cultural theory, the poor are certainly different. They lack money, prestige, power, and all the advantages that go along with these, including safe neighborhoods, good schools, social connections, secure jobs, and political influence. The aspirations of the poor resemble those of the affluent, but the poor are limited in their access to the means required to realize those aspirations. I briefly illustrate this point for the two key areas of work and family. The essential message is this: while most poor people are mainstream in their ambitions, they often lack the opportunities and resources necessary to secure full-time jobs and establish stable marriages. The poor do in fact sometimes live unconventional lives, but this does not mean they adhere to unconventional values, much less that their values are the cause of their unconventional lives.

Work

"I just want to become able, stable, with a life, you know, a good life," one black man explained. "I just want to work man. I just want to work."[59] This man, and millions of others like him, contrary to the diagnosis proposed by the current Speaker of the House, Paul Ryan, does not suffer from a reluctance to work.[60] Indeed, most poor people, even the jobless, are work oriented, and few seem resigned to their fate or think they deserve a free ride.[61] Roberta Iversen and Naomi Farber show that young black women, many already employed, place a high value on work, are encouraged by their parents to become self-supporting, and hold largely negative attitudes about welfare.[62] In a study of labor force activity among poor parents in Chicago, Marta Tienda and Haya Stier find that only a small minority do not want to work. Most are either working or looking for work. According to their evidence, "willingness to work" is the prevailing norm, and joblessness is largely involuntary, not a sign of "shiftlessness."[63] Barrio residents, like those of the ghetto, Daniel Dohan reports, also demonstrate a strong commitment to the work ethic. Despite often being treated shabbily in the low-wage labor market, poor Mexican Americans share a common belief that work is "a worthwhile and important activity."[64] Interview data reveal that welfare recipients also have conventional attitudes toward work. They dislike being on welfare, they want jobs that will allow them to support their families, and they often struggle to survive in the low-wage labor market.[65] "I hate being on welfare," one young black woman explained. "I want to be independent; I want to be on my own. I want to have a good job."[66]

These expressions of support for the work ethic are not just a case of respondents paying lip service to socially sanctioned ideals. Attesting to their willingness to work, Stephen Petterson finds that African American men regularly settle for jobs that pay less than their "reservation wage"—that is, less than what they regard as a fair wage.[67] Rather than seeking to avoid work, the unemployed indeed seem desperate for a good job. When 250 positions opened up for carpenter apprentices in Manhattan recently, several hundred men and women lined up in the August heat—some as early as eight days in advance—hoping to fill out an application.[68] We should also keep in mind that millions of Americans, making up the ranks of the working poor, show up every day at grueling low-wage, dead-end jobs.[69] And if they are complaining about anything, it is not about working *too much*, but working *too little*. More than 5 million men and women in early 2017 were involuntarily stuck with part-time jobs; they preferred *more* hours of work per week, not *fewer*.[70] This is hardly evidence of an antiwork, freeloader mentality. Many low-income people are understandably worried and frustrated about their economic prospects, and some do withdraw from the labor market, as evidenced by the figures on the declining labor force participation of working-age males. The central problem, however, is not that we have too many people "who don't want to work," as claimed by Mick Mulvaney, the Trump administration's budget director, but too few jobs that offer a living wage.[71]

The work effort of the poor varies in tandem with the ups and downs of the economy, and this also suggests that joblessness is more a function of employment opportunities than bad values. Several studies show that when labor markets are tight, the unemployed poor, including less-educated minority youths, are drawn into the labor force. When jobs are available, the poor go to work.[72] For example, the rates of poverty for African Americans and Hispanics fell significantly between 1995 and 2000, as poor minorities took advantage of the unusual upsurge in the availability of jobs.[73] And when in 2015 the economy finally started to recover from the Great Recession and jobs became available, unemployed people rejoined the workforce, with several million Americans managing to "raise their chins above the poverty line."[74] The big problem poor people face is that periods of sustained job growth and low unemployment are rare and short-lived, and even when labor markets are at their tightest, there are still never enough job vacancies to absorb the pool of willing workers.[75]

Most able-bodied, working-age poor people participate in the paid labor market. Some have steady jobs, some cycle in and out of the labor force, and some work in the underground economy. But many of the poor, especially young, less-educated black males, do have extended bouts of unemployment, experience chronic joblessness, or are only marginally attached to the labor market.[76] This problem cannot be reduced to one of insufficient motivation and bad values. To be sure, some of the long-term unemployed are not adequately prepared for vocational success. They lack skills, work habits, employment experience, and knowledge of the ins and outs of the labor market and the workplace. They are not very confident, sometimes unrealistic in their expectations, and uncertain how to translate their occupational aspirations into a regular job.[77] They sometimes have physical and mental health issues and other personal difficulties that inhibit work effort. An increasing number of young black men are also burdened with the "mark of a criminal record," making it nearly impossible for them to find work no matter how hard they try.[78] They also encounter a variety of other structural problems limiting their ability to work their way out of poverty, including racial discrimination, residential segregation, and the low quality of available jobs. Single mothers, including welfare recipients, face additional hurdles, including assorted child-care, health-care, transportation, and housing problems.[79] Poor people who are disconnected from or only weakly attached to the labor market need help as individuals, certainly. But no amount of resocialization, moral reform, or faith-based inspiration will fix the multifaceted problems that keep the jobless poor out of work and trapped in poverty.

Family

Contrary to the assumption underlying marriage-promotion initiatives, poor women "do not have to be convinced about the value of marriage."[80] Most, single mothers included, affirm conventional family values and extol the virtues of two-parent child rearing. Kathryn Edin and Maria Kefalas, having spent five years doing research in inner-city communities, report "astonishingly little evidence of the much-touted rejection of the institution of marriage among the poor."[81] Regardless of class or race, low-income teen mothers, according to Naomi Farber, uphold "ideal visions" about marriage and childbearing that "are congruent with traditional values."[82] Robin Jarrett discovered nearly unanimous support for the concept of marriage among the eighty-two never-married African American women she interviewed. "I would like to be married," one woman declared, expressing the general sentiment. "I want to be married. I'm not gonna lie. I really do."[83]

Though professing adherence to the ideal of the two-parent family, many poor women have children as teens and experience years as single mothers. This outcome does not reflect a weak commitment to traditional values, however. The relationship between poverty and single motherhood is due primarily to the circumstances under which poor women make decisions about marriage and childbearing. As in the case of work, the behavior of the poor with respect to family formation is largely a product of the limited options available to them.[84] Many poor mothers are reluctant to marry because the fathers of their children are themselves poor, sometimes incarcerated, jobless, or otherwise "unmarriageable."[85] As one teen mother explained, "If I can't find [a man] that got a job or that can help me in some way, I don't want him."[86] According to another woman: "I don't want to marry nobody that don't have nothing going for themselves. . . . I could do bad by myself."[87] An environment of poverty contributes to single motherhood also because it heightens women's mistrust of the men in their lives; it makes them more cautious about marriage and more determined to preserve their independence. Poor single women have difficult lives, and they are wary of making a bad situation worse by entering into a potentially troublesome long-term relationship.[88] For some poor women, in addition, motherhood, even in the absence of marriage, is a desirable route to social standing, maturity, and respect, particularly when other paths to adulthood and a meaningful life are closed off.[89]

In a direct challenge to the cultural theory, Edin and Kefalas show that poor women are prone to single motherhood not because they repudiate family values, but, paradoxically, because they value marriage and children so highly, even more so perhaps than their middle-class counterparts. Poor women, they report, fully embrace the ideal of lifelong marriage, so much so in fact that they are reluctant to tie the knot even when they become mothers, for fear that they may face the disappointment and stigma of a divorce down the road. It is worse to be an ex-wife than an unwed mother, they believe, and pregnancy is no excuse for foolishly rushing into a marriage. Their first priority is to get financially established, get settled in their lives, and get to know their prospective husbands to make sure their relationships will last. They want to be married, to be sure, but they do not want to be trapped in a bad marriage or face the humiliating prospect of abandonment or divorce. Poor women are also eager to be mothers and cannot imagine a life without children. But because "good, decent, trustworthy men are in short supply," they cannot wait for a husband to appear on the scene before taking up motherhood.[90] Given the options available to them, poor women are led to elevate the institution of motherhood over marriage. Their choices may not be conventional, but they are an understandable response to difficult circumstances—an adaptation to poverty, not its cause—and they certainly do not constitute evidence of cultural pathology.[91]

The poor and the middle class are similar in their aspirations and ideals, but they differ in their life circumstances. Despite the value they place on work, education, individual responsibility, and the two-parent family, the poor are more likely to be chronically unemployed, drop out of high school, be on welfare, and raise their children in single-parent homes. These are not lifestyle choices, however, and they are not indications of character flaws or a deviant culture. The unconventional lives of the poor are predictable consequences of residential segregation, racial discrimination, social isolation, poor schools, lousy jobs, and an inadequate system of public support. Poor people do not lack mainstream values. They lack the means to get a quality education, secure a good job, and create a stable marriage. The problem for the poor is their poverty, not their culture.

CULTURE AND POVERTY

Despite the deficiencies of the cultural theory, it does not follow that culture is irrelevant to the study of poverty. It is plausible, for example, that cultural and psychological variables can help explain why some people who are born into poverty or reside in high-poverty neighborhoods do better in their lives than others. It is also plausible that cultural factors can account for differences in the coping strategies of the poor, how they respond to economic hardship, how they interpret their experiences, and how they navigate their social worlds. Where human behavior is at issue, culture is bound to play a role.[92]

Poverty, however, is not a *behavior*. It is *experienced* by individuals, but it is a *condition* of society. It varies in its severity from one country to another, with the United States having an unusually high rate of poverty; it varies by geographical location as well, with the poor having it harder in some regions, states, and cities than others; and it varies over time, worsening in the United States since 2000. As social circumstances change, so too does the incidence of poverty, sometimes increasing and sometimes decreasing. Poverty is not a state of mind; it is a state of society, and as such it is bound up with certain structural forces. Among the most consequential of these are racial discrimination and residential segregation; unaffordable housing; an egregiously inequitable educational system; lack of reasonable access to child care and health care; an extraordinarily high rate of imprisonment; a gilded-age level of inequality in the distribution of income and wealth; a political system in which elected officials are unresponsive to the preferences of the poor; and a massive shortfall of jobs that provide meaningful and dignified work, pay a living wage, offer health and retirement benefits, and hold out the possibility of some margin of economic security and upward mobility. A serious-minded cultural theory—one not intended simply to blame the poor for their poverty or divert attention from enduring structural inequalities—can conceivably shed light on the everyday lives of the poor. The essential point to keep in mind, however, is this: *there is only so much one can learn about poverty from studying poor people*. If we hope to understand the *condition* of poverty and the *causes* of this ever-changing condition, and if we are committed to winning a war on poverty, we need to turn our attention to the structure and workings of the American economic and political systems.[93]

CONCLUSION

Poor people are not saints, and in this respect they are like everyone else. In all fairness, though, we should acknowledge that the circumstances of the poor are less conducive to saintliness than are those of the affluent. As Michael Zweig observes, it is far more difficult to manage "mainstream" behavior when one lives under "non-mainstream conditions."[94] This is not to imply, of course, that poor people bear no responsibility for their actions or that economic deprivation excuses bad behavior. Nor is there anything wrong with wishing that some of the poor would conduct themselves in a more virtuous manner, though this end might be more effectively achieved by changing their "non-mainstream conditions" than by pious exhortation, public condemnation, or punitive reform. We should also keep in mind, however, that most of the poor already live respectable lives: working hard at thankless jobs, raising their children as best they can, and tending to their communities. They do not need resocialization, government supervision, or an education in the rules of the game.

Proponents of the cultural theory have brought issues of values and morality into the poverty debate. In one important example, Joel Schwartz proposes "fighting poverty with virtue." He maintains that "mundane moral virtues such as diligence, sobriety, and thrift . . . make it easier to escape from poverty."[95] This seems sensible enough as far as it goes, but he does leave some important empirical questions unanswered. How widespread is the lack of virtue among the poor? Is it a serious problem? More so than lack of jobs, inferior schools, and unaffordable child care? How much of a difference would adherence to traditional values make in the lives of the poor, particularly those subject to residential segregation and racial discrimination, and how much would it increase their probability of escaping poverty? Virtuous behavior might conceivably give this or that person an edge over more profligate rivals in the labor market, but given the relative scarcity of jobs that pay a living wage, how far can good behavior go toward reducing the level of poverty in the aggregate?

Schwartz rightly criticizes theorists who represent the poor as nothing other than passive victims. But his conception of moral agency is exceedingly narrow. He emphasizes diligence, sobriety, and thrift, but ignores other virtues, including compassion, empathy, and generosity. He insists that poor people take responsibility for their own lives, but focuses only on their conduct as individuals, overlooking how they might pursue worthy goals by rallying together as a group, a community, or a political movement. When Schwartz calls upon the poor to take moral action to overcome their poverty, he is not thinking of *collective* action; he is not suggesting that poor people organize among themselves to press for social reform. When he admonishes the poor to "act in ways that are self-advancing rather than self-defeating," he means they should exercise self-control, not that they should mobilize for political purposes.[96] Schwartz may be correct in his assumption that self-help is the only reliable means through which poor people can improve their circumstances. But what form of self-help is likely to be most helpful: diligence or militance, sobriety or solidarity, thrift or protest?

Schwartz believes that moral reform must have a prominent place in the antipoverty arsenal. But his conception of what this entails is astonishingly one-sided. He urges the poor to embrace virtue in the expectation that this will ease their path out of poverty. The persistence of poverty in the United States, however, is due far less to the misbehavior of the poor than to the irresponsible and sometimes just plain mean-spirited conduct of the men and women who occupy positions of political and economic power.[97] If we are really serious about fighting poverty with virtue, we need to take a look at the criminal justice system, the pharmaceutical industry, payday lenders, corporate lobbyists, and Wall Street. We need to talk about employers who cheat their employees out of overtime pay, illegally fire workers with prounion sentiments, and seek to reduce labor costs by replacing full-time workers with part-timers and temps. We need to talk about corporate executives who negotiate exorbitant salaries for themselves while imposing pay and benefit reductions on the workers they have not yet downsized; who travel around the globe in search of the most easily exploitable labor force; and who devise clever financial schemes to enrich themselves at the expense of employees, customers, and the larger taxpaying public. We also need to talk about politicians who refuse to raise the minimum wage or extend Medicaid benefits to the working poor, who cut back social programs while enacting massive tax cuts for the rich, and who provide generous subsidies to corporations while turning a blind eye to deteriorating inner cities and distressed rural areas.

Moral and cultural reform has a legitimate place on the poverty agenda. But why target only the culture of the poor? The corporate culture and the political culture seem every bit as dysfunctional—the media culture, too—and with a far greater impact on the larger society. Why not expand our moral vision beyond the values of diligence, sobriety, and thrift to incorporate also the principles of equity, fairness, and honesty? More virtuous behavior on the part of the poor might prove beneficial, but we are likely to achieve substantial progress in the war against poverty only if we are prepared to conduct a moral crusade on a much larger scale. As a strategy for fighting poverty, moral reform requires the creation of a "moral economy"—one in which self-interest and the bottom line are not the only standards of behavior.[98] In their call for a renewed emphasis on values, proponents of the cultural theory set their sights too low. The demand for moral reform cannot be separated from the larger movement for social justice.

Chapter Four

The Human Capital Theory of Poverty and Inequality

EDUCATION IS THE KEY TO SUCCESS

When asked the best way to alleviate poverty, Americans commonly reply that government should see to it that everyone is furnished with a good education.[1] Education is the key to success and lack of education is the primary cause of poverty. Human capital theory, an important strand of mainstream economics, offers a technically sophisticated version of this popular adage. The central claim of this theory, as it pertains to the issue of poverty, is that people are poor because they are deficient in education, skills, and work experience. For more than fifty years the idea that education is the solution to poverty has occupied a prominent place in the thinking of social scientists, the lay public, and policy makers on both sides of the aisle. Human capital theory, for this reason alone, demands critical scrutiny.

Differences in earnings, human capital theory maintains, correspond to differences in productivity. The most capable and proficient workers get the best jobs, while less competent workers, if they are able to find employment at all, are channeled into the low-wage sector. Workers are more or less productive, in turn, because they possess more or less *human capital*: education, training, and skills. Those rich in human capital contribute more to economic output, growth, and profitability, and they rightfully command a higher wage. For this theory, the American economic system, thanks to the magic of the free market, is a well-functioning meritocracy, with workers getting what they deserve and deserving what they get.

Individuals vary in their level of human capital, this theory states, because of differences in the choices they and their families have made about how much time, energy, and money to put into their education and training. These choices are thought of as investment decisions. They come into play as individuals consider how to live their lives and as they select between immediate and future rewards, leisure and work. How much people choose to invest in education and training depends on their personal preferences. From the standpoint of human capital theory, these are exogenous variables. This means the theory does not presume to explain people's desires (assigning this task to other disciplines, like psychology and sociology), but rather takes these as given. In mainstream economics, there is no accounting for taste. For whatever reasons, people vary in their aspirations and how they wish to spend their time and are thus led to differ in their decisions regarding education and work.

With respect to poverty specifically, human capital theory, like the biogenetic and cultural theories, maintains that people are poor because they are lacking in qualities associated with job performance. In the biogenetic theory the poor have low IQs, and in the cultural theory they have negative attitudes. In human capital theory, similarly, people are poor because a history of unwise investment decisions has left them deficient in education, skills, and training. Poverty can best be reduced, accordingly, by exhorting the poor to invest more in themselves and their children or by implementing government policies to assist the poor in overcoming their human capital shortcomings. In either case, proponents of this theory recommend as an antidote to poverty that individuals stay in school, earn a degree, build a record of stable employment, and take advantage of training opportunities. From the human capital perspective, the most effective way to combat poverty is to build up the skills of the poor. Whether through individual initiative or government programs, efforts to enhance the education and training of the poor will improve their prospects in the labor market and enable them to avoid or escape poverty.

In the following sections I discuss two broad problems with human capital theory. First, with its emphasis on individual investment decisions, this theory fails to deal adequately with the structural constraints hindering disadvantaged individuals from acquiring productive skills. How much training and education people receive is not primarily a matter of personal choice. It is dependent on family resources, access to educational opportunities, and business strategies and government policies beyond the control of the individual. Second, this theory also presents a misleading picture of the labor market. The process through which individuals convert their education into employment and earnings is not nearly as uniform and equitable as human capital theory implies. Employers do not hire on the basis of human capital alone, people vary in how much they are compensated for their skills, a good job does not necessarily follow from a good education, and economic success is dependent on a host of factors other than human capital, not least the state of the economy and the availability of employment opportunities. At best, this theory offers a partial explanation for earnings differences, and the education and training proposals it recommends for fighting poverty are likewise bound to have only limited effectiveness.

ACQUIRING HUMAN CAPITAL

People are poor, according to human capital theory, because they are deficient in education and skills, and this deficiency is primarily the consequence of their own personal investment decisions. This supposition places human capital theory in the same camp as the cultural theory: for both poverty results ultimately from the ill-considered preferences and misguided choices of the poor.[2] Their earnings are low because they have elected to live their lives in a manner that has left them inadequately prepared for the world of work. This excessively individualistic view of economic behavior fails to acknowledge how the goals people pursue and the choices they make are shaped by the means at their disposal. As Jon Elster observes, preferences are "adaptive"; they reflect our social and economic circumstances. We adjust our desires according to the possibilities allowed by our place in society.[3] Children from affluent families aspire to attend elite colleges and secure high-paying professional jobs in part because they are made aware from an early age that the resources to make this dream come true are readily available. Children from poor and working-class families, on the other hand, may scale down their ambitions to conform to their less-favorable circumstances. And if they do not envision themselves going off to an Ivy League college in preparation for some lucrative career, the fundamental cause may not be an aversion to education or a lack of ambition, but a lifetime of inadequate resources.

Human capital theory's conception of investment behavior gives priority to preferences over constraints, choice over opportunity. It emphasizes the decisions people make concerning their education and training, but says little about the opportunities available to them and even less about the social, economic, and political forces shaping those opportunities. People succeed or fail not only because they make good or bad decisions, but also because of the circumstances under which they decide and the menu of alternatives placed before them. Individuals make choices, but they always do so within a given social context.[4] The residents of poor communities, for example, confront a severely restricted range of educational alternatives. "What if all your [educational] choices are bad ones?" This is the dilemma faced by many parents in impoverished and segregated neighborhoods.[5] However determined they might be to ensure their kids get the best possible education, the schooling their children receive is still likely to be inferior. The extent and quality of the human capital people acquire, and their economic outcomes more generally, are not simply products of their investment *decisions*; they are products of their investment *options* as well.

People's decisions about education and training are conditioned not only by the opportunities at hand but also by their financial resources. Though free to choose, people can only make the choices they can afford to make. Money matters. And because it does the reality as far as education is concerned—more so in the United States than in other developed countries—does not even remotely approach the ideal of equality of opportunity.[6] Poor parents do not have sufficient income to enroll their children in high-quality preschool programs, send them to private schools, hire tutors, purchase homes in neighborhoods with superior public schools, or ensure their children are afforded an abundant variety of educationally enriching experiences. And with tuition costs skyrocketing and government aid in short supply, an increasing number of high school graduates from poor and working-class families have been priced out of a college education. Even many solidly middle-class parents struggle to pay for their children's schooling. Resource constraints may also limit access to forms of human capital other than formal education. Unemployed workers, for example, may not have the funds needed to go back to school, enroll in a job-retraining program, or finance a move across the country in search of better employment opportunities.

Individuals and families make human capital investments, but so do businesses and governments. Business firms invest in their employees by introducing new technologies and implementing training programs to upgrade workers' skills. Federal, state, and local governments invest in citizens, spending billions of tax dollars on education. How much human capital an individual accumulates is not simply a function of personal choice; it is contingent also on business practices and government policies. Employers decide whether or not to offer job-training opportunities in the workplace and which employees are eligible to benefit. This is not something that is normally at the discretion of the individual worker. Parents, likewise, do not in any simple manner choose how much public money is apportioned to the education of their children. This is determined in the political arena, with politicians making spending decisions, voters contending over tax issues, and communities and neighborhoods competing to maximize their share of scarce educational resources. The allocation of public funds for education is a matter of political power, not individual choice.

Poor people are disadvantaged because they lack the opportunities and resources to invest sufficiently in human capital. In addition, they often work in jobs with limited prospects for training and advancement, and they often reside in neighborhoods lacking the political clout to ensure their children's schools receive adequate funding. Bringing opportunities and resources more fully into the picture and acknowledging the role played by business and government investors make it clear that the amount of education and training people acquire cannot be attributed primarily to personal preferences and individual choices. Human capital differences, indeed, are as much the *consequence* of inequality as its *cause*.

An antipoverty strategy predicated on enhancing the human capital of the poor would seem to place the cart before the horse. It is precisely their poverty—their economic deprivation, residential segregation, and political marginalization—that limits poor people's access to education and training. In the absence of reforms addressing these more fundamental inequities, it is difficult to envision how the deep class and race disparities in access to education might be eradicated. In any case, recognizing the influence of economic and political resources on the accumulation of human capital turns the basic thesis of this theory on its head. *People are not poor because they are deficient in human capital; they are deficient in human capital because they are poor.* Of course not all poor people *are* deficient in human capital. Many have a high school degree and some even have a college degree. Some also have considerable job experience and work skills. Human capital matters, but it does not guarantee success or prevent people from falling into poverty. This takes us to the second problem with human capital theory.

CONVERTING HUMAN CAPITAL

It is one thing to acquire human capital, but it is quite another to cash in on the human capital one acquires. And just as people may encounter barriers in their efforts to accumulate productive skills, they may also face difficulties converting their education and training into earnings, employment, and social mobility. A diploma, after all, cannot be turned in at the bank for a weekly paycheck. Education is the key to success only if it unlocks the door to a good job, and there is nothing automatic about this, as many of today's college graduates are discovering.[7] Despite human capital theory's belief in the abundance of opportunities and the efficacy of market forces, there is no assurance that investments in human capital will be rewarded or rewarded equitably. The meritocratic idea that we are all paid what we are worth, however "worth" might be measured, is difficult to square with the empirical evidence.[8]

From 1948 to 1973, just as human capital theory might predict, workers' compensation rose in tandem with productivity growth. Since 1973, however, while labor productivity has continued to rise, though more slowly, there has been little or no improvement in the pay of the typical worker. The bulk of the gains from increasing productivity, rather than being widely shared, has gone instead to a small minority consisting mostly of top earners and owners of capital. Corresponding to this productivity-pay disconnect, there has been, on the one hand, an increase in the concentration of income and wealth at the upper tier of the class structure and, on the other hand, wage stagnation for the majority of American workers. Relative to their human capital, the few at the top are being paid way more than they deserve, and the many at the bottom are being paid way less than they deserve.[9]

Whether overall productivity growth leads to overall wage increases—and whether the productivity of any particular individual worker is duly compensated—depends on the larger political and economic context and, more specifically, on the balance of power between capital and labor. Since the 1970s, more so in the United States than in other developed countries, the distribution of economic and political power has shifted to the advantage of business, giving employers an upper hand in their dealings with workers. The result of this power shift, due especially to the decline of unionization, is that wage levels are no longer responsive to increases in productivity. Lacking sufficient bargaining power, American workers are unable to convert their human capital into a decent wage and claim their rightful share of the economic pie.[10]

Human capital theory tells only a small part of a complicated story. People's employment and earnings outcomes are influenced by many variables besides education, training, and job experience. One of these variables, as we have seen, is the distribution of economic and political power. Wages are not simply a payoff to human capital; they are an expression of power relations between employers and employees. In addition, as I explain in the following four sections, the degree of success we experience in the labor market and the workplace is not simply a product of what we know, as human capital theory implies. It is also dependent on (1) who we are, (2) who we know, (3) where we work, and (4) the availability of jobs.

WHAT YOU KNOW OR WHO YOU ARE?

What counts most in the labor market according to human capital theory is what you know. But who you are makes a big difference, too, and one aspect of who you are is your appearance. Some retail and service firms, for example, only hire individuals with the right look and the right sound—workers who can represent and embody the company's "brand."[11] Looks count for women especially. As Dalton Conley shows, physical attractiveness, weight in particular, has a significant effect on women's life chances. Women who are overweight suffer a wage penalty, while women who are conventionally good looking "can get a boost in their economic status." The "bottom line," Conley concludes, is that success for women "is less related to talent and hard work, since beauty muscles into the equation too."[12] In the following pages I briefly discuss three other aspects of who you are that also matter in the labor market: gender and race/ethnicity, cultural capital, and psychological capital.

Gender and Race/Ethnicity

Women and racial/ethnic minorities encounter numerous disadvantages in the labor market and are more vulnerable to poverty than white males. Even when comparing workers with equivalent levels of human capital, significant employment and wage inequalities by gender and race remain. As Elise Gould reports, at all levels of education, men have higher earnings than women, and white workers have higher earnings than African Americans.[13] A college education is worth less on average for a woman than for a man, and less for a Latino or black man than for a non-Hispanic white man. Merit is not the only factor at play in the labor market. Race and gender influence which candidates get what jobs, who is promoted and who is not, who is fired and who is retained, and how much money workers make. Individuals are not equal in their capacity to convert their human capital into employment, nor are they equal in the rate of return they receive on their investments in education, training, and experience. The monetary value people derive from their human capital depends on a variety of ascribed traits, including whether they are male or female, black or white, Asian or Latino.[14]

Cultural Capital

The French sociologist Pierre Bourdieu is usually credited with bringing the concept of cultural capital into the study of inequality. Cultural capital refers to certain dispositions, preferences, and competencies acquired through the process of socialization that influence social and economic outcomes.[15] As a result of their upbringing, people differ not only in their education, but also in their "class-specific" tastes and values, interaction styles and conversational skills, and familiarity with mainstream social practices. They differ in their self-presentation; their "tastes in music, leisure, food, fashion"; and their ability to "fit in" comfortably in diverse settings.[16] The cultural signals people transmit in the course of job interviews and workplace interactions influence gatekeepers' appraisals of merit and decisions about hiring and promotion.[17]

Individuals have a competitive edge if their cultural capital puts them on the same page as employers, supervisors, managers, and coworkers, and if it furnishes them with an understanding of the "rules of the game," the ins and outs of workplace settings and affiliated social institutions.[18] Individuals who are attuned to the ways of the dominant culture are more at ease and perform better in the prejob interview, they feel comfortable seeking advice and mentoring from coworkers, they are less likely to fall victim to misunderstandings in the workplace or experience prejudice and discrimination, and they are more likely to be perceived in a positive light by gatekeepers. The problem faced by many poor and working-class individuals, and by women and racial and ethnic minorities in particular, is that they do not automatically project an acceptable or suitably comforting image. Their cultural repertoire may be dissimilar from, sometimes even at odds with, those of people in positions of authority. Because of differences in demeanor, dress, and linguistic style—to say nothing of the tensions typical of interactions across race, gender, and class boundaries—some workers might inadvertently prompt negative impressions or evoke antipathy and hostility on the part of employers, coworkers, or customers. The hiring process, as Lauren Rivera argues, is not simply a matter of finding the best match between the skills applicants possess and the requirements of the job; it is also a matter of finding a good "cultural and emotional" match. "Whether they are hiring restaurant servers, fashion models, or high-tech workers, US employers emphasize their personal feelings of fit, chemistry, and like-mindedness, often over applicants' prior work experience and job-specific skills."[19] While human capital theory gives primacy to what you know, the concept of cultural capital draws attention to how job seekers may also be advantaged or disadvantaged in the labor market by who they are.

Psychological Capital

Another body of research highlights the importance of a different aspect of who you are: "noncognitive traits" and behavioral and personality attributes.[20] Employers hire and promote not just on the basis of workers' training and skills, but also on the basis of their "attitudes" and "character."[21] They desire *good* workers, not just skilled workers. They seek workers who are diligent, responsible, and conscientious, of course. But from a management standpoint, a good worker is also someone who is psychologically predisposed to obey the rules, comply with authority, perform in a habitually dependable manner, and identify with the firm. In addition to "purely technical skills," employers value personality and behavioral traits that facilitate the accommodation of employees to the workplace "system of power."[22] In the blunt words of Roger Waldinger and Michael Lichter: "Bosses want *willing* subordinates."[23] Employers are likely to be wary of job applicants who display a strong independent streak, are prone to questioning orders, appear to have issues with authority, or exhibit prounion sentiments. The workplace, particularly in the low-wage sector of the economy, as Barbara Ehrenreich observes, is more a dictatorship than a democracy.[24] Employers want subjects, not citizens. The most desirable workers are those who fit in rather than stand out, follow rules rather than assert rights, are dutiful rather than demanding, exhibit loyalty to the employer rather than solidarity with coworkers, and are inclined to go along rather than speak out.[25]

Some of the characteristics employers might desire in their employees—subservience and docility, for example—are not qualities normally valued in individuals outside the workplace. A "cheerful robot" might make a good worker, but not so much a good family member, friend, or citizen.[26] In the short run, workers gain a paycheck by submitting to the workplace regimen. In the longer run, however, compliance with "workplace authoritarianism" may take a "psychological toll." "If you're made to feel unworthy enough," Ehrenreich suggests, "you may come to think that what you're paid is what you are actually worth."[27] In addition, by reinforcing the attributes often demanded of the working poor, low-status jobs, rather than serving as stepping stones to upward mobility, might leave workers unprepared and unqualified for higher status jobs, where different psychological and behavioral traits are deemed desirable. A worker in the fast-food industry who is taught to perform strictly according to the workplace manual may end up lacking in the qualities of self-determination and initiative that better jobs sometimes require.

The challenge posed by this research goes even deeper. The premise of human capital theory is that schooling influences earnings by imparting productivity-enhancing skills. Among the key pieces of evidence in support of this contention is the correlation, albeit modest, between education and income. But as Samuel Bowles and Herbert Gintis argue, education raises earnings not only because students acquire valuable skills in the classroom, but also because the school experience promotes attitudes and patterns of behavior that "assist in the exercise of the employer's authority."[28] Schools transmit knowledge, but they also function as agents of socialization, preparing students psychologically and behaviorally for the world of work.[29] Employers want educated workers not just because schooling makes students more skilled, but also because it habituates them to a regimented environment and renders them more easily subject to discipline and control. The statistical relationship between education and earnings does not unequivocally support the thesis of human capital theory. Schools increase what you know, making graduates more educated and skilled, but they also affect who you are, molding students into the kinds of people valued by employers.

The quality of employers' information about the competence and character of job candidates is highly imperfect, with the result that hiring decisions, especially in the low-wage service sector, are based on inherently subjective judgments. Women and racial/ethnic minorities are particularly disadvantaged in this environment because there is so much room for stereotypes, prejudices, and cultural misconceptions to influence employers' assessments of who is an acceptable employee. Employers' preference for *good* workers, not just skilled workers, in combination with racial and gender stereotypes, means that many poor people cannot necessarily expect to lift themselves out of poverty simply by increasing their education, training, and job experience.

WHAT YOU KNOW OR WHO YOU KNOW?

Two individuals with equivalent levels of human capital may experience very different labor market outcomes due to differences in the characteristics of their social networks. One person is not well connected. She has few acquaintances outside a close circle of family members and neighbors; she has limited personal contacts in the work world; and she has no friends in high places. She is aware of job vacancies only when they are advertised in the media; she lacks influential contacts who might advocate on her behalf when she does submit an application; and even when she lands a job, she cannot count on anyone to acquaint her with the ins and outs at her new place of employment. A second person knows people who know people. He regularly hears about job openings through the grapevine, he gets unsolicited calls from employers requesting he submit a résumé, he can depend on a small army of acquaintances to certify he is the right man for the job, and friends of friends at his new workplace are eager to show him the ropes. While the first person may have her nose to the grindstone, the second has his foot in the door.

Human capital theory maintains that what you know is the key to success. As we have seen, who you are also matters. People's fortunes in the labor market are also conditioned by their social capital: the extent and quality of their social networks, social connections, and social ties. *Who* you know is often as important in getting ahead as *what* you know. The earnings and employment differences among individuals do not simply reflect inequalities in human capital; they reflect inequalities in social capital as well.

Social networks are important because they are potential conduits of information and influence. They vary, however, in their value, in the extent to which individuals can exploit them to improve their life chances. Some social networks are "resource rich," while others are "resource poor."[30] Some individuals are embedded in networks yielding extensive and high-quality information and comprising people far enough up in the social hierarchy to sway the hiring decisions of prospective employers. Other people are embedded in networks conveying little useful information and made up of people—like themselves—who lack leverage in the labor market. Social capital is a valuable resource because it facilitates the conversion of human capital into employment and earnings; it lubricates the process through which workers are matched to jobs. High school graduates, for example, can more easily make the transition into the labor market, turning their degree into a job, if they have numerous friends who are already working, who keep them informed of employment vacancies, and who are willing to put in a good word for them. How well people are connected is one of the main determinants of who wins and who loses in the competition for jobs.

People differ in the extent and quality of their ties to others and in the resources available through such ties, and these differences influence their economic prospects. If someone is mired in poverty, the chief cause might not be so much a human capital, skills deficiency as a social capital, connections deficiency. The problem of resource-poor social networks is especially common among racial minorities isolated in segregated neighborhoods.[31] In a study of the working poor in the Harlem fast-food industry, Katherine Newman found that residents had strong connections, but mainly to other workers in the low-wage labor market. These "lateral" networks made it relatively easy for workers to move from one low-wage job to another, but they rarely had friends, acquaintances, or personal contacts who could help them move up into higher status jobs. While they were able to gain skills and experience on the job and to learn proper work attitudes, they nevertheless lacked the social network resources necessary to convert their accumulated human capital into a viable career.[32]

Racial minorities also encounter blocked opportunities because they are excluded from white social networks, which tend to be more resource rich. In a remarkable study, Deirdre Royster compared the employment experiences of black and white working-class males, all graduates from the same trade school. The black males in her sample were equal, if not superior, to their white counterparts in human capital and in the personal qualities typically valued by employers. But black students did not receive the invaluable "networking support" from teachers and older workers that enabled white students, though often less qualified, to succeed in the labor market. Particularly in an environment where most employers are white, black job seekers, despite having the requisite education and training, are significantly disadvantaged by their lack of well-placed connections.[33] In their study of the life trajectories of disadvantaged young adults in Baltimore, Karl Alexander and his collaborators report a similar pattern. They found that while less-educated white men were often able to exploit their connections to get jobs in construction or other skilled trades, their black counterparts, due to a combination of racial discrimination and network disadvantage, were largely barred from access to desirable blue-collar employment. These studies provide strong evidence that who you know may be more important than what you know, especially when race too enters into the picture.[34]

WHAT YOU KNOW OR WHERE YOU WORK?

People differ, and so do jobs. Some are located in the manufacturing sector, others in the service sector; some in the private sector, others in the public sector; some in large corporations, others in small businesses; and some in growing and highly profitable industries, others in declining industries. The relationship between employers and employees is cooperative in some work-places, antagonistic in others; some jobs are typically occupied by men, others by women; some are full-time and secure, others part-time and precar-ious; some offer opportunities for advancement, while others are dead end; and some are unionized, though most are not. Jobs differ in many, many other respects as well, but the bottom line is this: some are better than others.

Individuals succeed or fail not just because they are good or bad workers, but also because they have good or bad jobs. What you know certainly influences where you work, but the process through which people are matched to jobs is contingent on many other factors besides human capital, including who you are and who you know. It is not simply the case that good workers are inevitably slotted into good jobs and bad workers into bad jobs. Indeed, a good job might turn an otherwise bad worker into a good worker; and a bad job might turn an otherwise good worker into a bad worker. The recognition that some jobs are better than others underlines a key problem with human capital theory: by focusing exclusively on the qualities of work-ers, it downplays the independent influence of job characteristics on people's economic outcomes and on their ability to cash in on their skills and experi-ence. Success or failure, contrary to the premise of human capital theory, depends on where you work, not just what you know.[35]

Human capital theory posits a causal relationship between productivity and earnings, suggesting that low-income workers can increase their wages by investing in productivity-enhancing human capital. An alternative per-spective, drawn from "efficiency wage" theory, implies a reverse relation-ship.[36] According to this theory, higher wages—because they have a positive effect on motivation, effort, morale, loyalty, and a sense of fairness—can stimulate an increase in the productivity of the workforce. Well-paid employ-ees are less likely to quit, shirk, or complain; they have an incentive to work hard because they have more to lose if they are fired; and they are less likely to require costly supervision. If the working poor are not very productive, perhaps this is due to their being stuck in low-wage jobs in which effort reaps few rewards and prospects for advancement are limited. Low-income work-ers have low productivity (and low earnings) not just because they are defi-cient in human capital, but also because they are trapped in bad jobs. How productive workers are and how much money they make depends on where they work, not just what they know.

Most work skills are not learned in the classroom; they are learned in the workplace. Jobs differ, however, in the extent to which they enable otherwise equal workers to acquire valuable skills. Workers accumulate human capital not just from the choices they *make*, or even the education they receive, but also from the jobs they are *given*. Human capital, this suggests, may be less a ticket to a good job than something one obtains from having a good job. The key to getting ahead, accordingly, is not just what you know, but where you work; and where you work, furthermore, influences what you eventually come to know. Human capital theory assumes that poorly skilled workers end up in bad jobs. But the opposite is also true: bad jobs cause workers to be poorly skilled. People are poor not just because their choices have left them deficient in human capital, but also because they lack access to jobs that offer opportunities for training and skill enhancement.

SKILLS DEFICIT OR JOBS DEFICIT?

One popular offshoot of human capital theory attributes increasing inequality and persistent poverty to "skill-biased technological change" or skills mismatch. According to this theory, technological advances, including the introduction of computers into the workplace, have increased the skill requirements necessary for getting a good job. Changes in technology have induced a shift in the demand for labor—to the advantage of those with more education, increasing their employment prospects and earnings, and to the disadvantage of those with less education, decreasing their employment prospects and earnings. Because they are deficient in the skills needed in today's increasingly high-tech industry, less-educated workers are unable to benefit from a growing economy and are at greater risk of poverty. The solution to problems of unemployment and low earnings, this line of thinking suggests, is the old human capital standby: education and training.[37]

Though the theory of skill-biased technological change (SBTC) enjoys widespread support, it cannot easily be reconciled with the data on income inequality. The big earnings gains since the 1970s have not gone to the wide swath of college graduates or technically trained workers, but to the top 1 percent or even the top 0.1 percent.[38] Nor is it the case that workers in the STEM (science, technology, engineering, mathematics) fields or in the high-tech, computer-related fields have experienced notably rising wage levels in recent years.[39] Today's chief winners, making vast sums of money, consist of a small elite of corporate executives, investment bankers, and hedge fund managers.[40] The theory of SBTC, William Lazonick and his collaborators observe, simply cannot account for this extreme concentration of income at the top.[41] It is not just high-school dropouts who are struggling in the current economy, furthermore. Approximately 15 percent of workers in the bottom quintile of the wage distribution and over 20 percent in the lower-middle quintile have a college degree.[42] The problem with the SBTC thesis is this: way too few people are gaining ground in today's economy, and way too many are losing ground, to believe that skills are the key determinant of earnings.

The earnings gap between college-educated workers and those with a high school degree or less narrowed during the 1970s, but widened significantly in the two subsequent decades, particularly during the 1980s.[43] This finding is often cited as evidence in support of the theory of SBTC. Economists, observing this pattern, often speak of a growing "college premium" or a rising "return to skills." College graduates, this language implies, are outpacing their less-educated counterparts because, with information technology invading the workplace, they possess increasingly valuable knowledge and abilities. This is misleading, however. In fact, the growing wage gap between college- and non-college-educated workers is due more to the declining earnings of the latter (especially men) than to the rising earnings of the former. Between 1979 and 1994, according to Peter Gottschalk, the earnings of high school graduates decreased by 20 percent, while the earnings of college graduates increased by only 5 percent.[44] Since 2000, moreover, employment growth in low-wage service jobs has increased, while the demand for workers with a four-year college degree has diminished and the college wage premium has ceased growing. The result is stagnant earnings for many college graduates and higher levels of unemployment and underemployment.[45] Nor does it appear that the jobs of the future will be open only to those with high-tech skills. Nine of the fifteen occupations projected to add the most jobs to the US economy through 2024 require "no formal educational credential" or a "high school diploma or equivalent" only.[46] The major story—and the phenomenon most requiring explanation—is not that educated workers have gained so much ground in recent decades, but that most workers since 2000, college graduates included, have not fared well at all.

College graduates and high school graduates differ, of course, in their level of education, and college graduates, presumably (though with less certainty), are also more skilled than high school graduates. But because they differ in many other respects as well, the earnings gap between the more- and the less-educated may be due to factors other than skill differences. For example, non-college-educated workers are more likely to be found in industries and occupations affected by the minimum wage, international trade, and unionization. Earnings for high school graduates have declined or stagnated over the past three or four decades not necessarily because technology has rendered less-educated workers obsolete, but because they have been hit especially hard by the fall in the real value of the minimum wage, heightened competition with cheaper foreign workers, and a decline in the size and strength of labor unions.[47] These developments have increased the exposure of high school graduates to competitive market forces, driving their wages down. On the other hand, for the time being anyway, at least some college graduates occupy protected professions. Their income is "safeguarded by elaborate systems of immigration control, licensing, educational credentials, and legal mandates." The salaries of professionals, Gordon Lafer argues, have been "propped up not by the rarity of their skills but by their ability to erect institutional barriers to competition."[48] The disadvantage faced by less-educated workers is not so much a deficit of skills as it is a deficit of institutional support and bargaining power. Compared to college-educated workers, high school graduates are less able to shield themselves from the ravages of the market or to protect themselves from management cost-cutting strategies.

The major flaw in human capital theory's account of employment and earnings outcomes is the tacit assumption that suitable employment opportunities are sufficiently available for all qualified individuals. If workers are doing poorly in the labor market, according to this theory, the only possible explanation is that they are poorly skilled. Human capital theory implies that jobs are essentially unlimited, such that all workers, at least over the long run, will find employment that corresponds to their level of education and training. It is not necessary, therefore, to change the economic system to remedy the problem of poverty. In this "field of dreams" fantasy, as Ruy Teixeira and Lawrence Mishel describe it, all that is needed is for poor people to acquire more education: "If we build the workers, jobs will come."[49]

From the human capital perspective, the problem of poverty is one of deficient workers, and the solution is to make workers less deficient. For many critics, however, poverty results more from a shortage of good jobs than a shortage of skilled workers.[50] D. W. Livingstone, in a sustained analysis of the problem of "underemployment," documents a persistent and growing "education-jobs" gap.[51] More and more workers, he shows, are overqualified for their jobs, as in the case of the proverbial college graduate employed at Starbucks. Millions of people possess credentials, knowledge, skills, and talents that are underutilized in their work. Frederic Pryor and David Schaffer find that over the quarter century going into the 1990s, "jobs requiring relatively little education have increased faster than the number of less-educated prime-age workers," while "jobs requiring more education have increased more slowly than the number of more-educated prime-age workers."[52] Stephen Vaisey also documents widespread underemployment. He estimates that between 20 and 55 percent of full-time workers were overqualified for their jobs in 2002, almost double the rate for 1972.[53] This trend has become even more pronounced since 2000. According to Richard Vedder and his collaborators, more than 20 million college graduates were underemployed in 2010, with this number projected to rise to nearly 30 million by

2020. Over the next decade millions of college graduates will likely be stuck working at jobs requiring only a high school degree.[54] Many already are. A 2016 survey found that 41 percent of workers with a bachelor's degree stated that their qualifications exceeded what was required for their jobs.[55] Education does not guarantee success, because the economic system cannot absorb the increasing number of men and women entering the labor market with a college degree. The problem is not a shortage of good workers; it is a shortage of good jobs.

What is bad news for college graduates is disastrous news for the less educated. When well-educated people are unable to find employment appropriate to their credentials, they search for jobs lower down in the labor market. The effect is to crowd out less-educated workers who would otherwise get those jobs. These workers are then bumped down to an even lower tier or driven out of the labor force altogether.[56] The less-educated are caught between a rock and a hard place. They are impeded from moving up into better jobs because of growing competition from more educated workers moving down. And if not forced into joblessness, they are confined to the low end of the labor market, where employment opportunities offer little prospect of a decent living or upward mobility.

With a surplus of educated workers, employers can afford to be choosy. They now hire college graduates for jobs that used to be filled by high school graduates. They may even insist that applicants have a college degree, even though less-educated job seekers are sufficiently skilled to do the work. Such credential inflation—raising the level of education required of workers to be considered for a job—creates the illusion that occupational skill demands are increasing. The larger reality, however, contrary to the skill-deficit thesis, is that the American economy is simply not generating enough solidly middle-class jobs to accommodate the supply of able workers. Because of this jobs deficit, an increasing number of people are unable to convert their human capital into a meaningful career. This problem hits the least-educated hardest of all, limiting them to a low-wage career or pushing them out of the labor market entirely. Less-educated workers are forced to choose between a bad job and no job at all.

CONCLUSION

Human capital theory maintains that people are poor because a history of bad investment decisions has left them deficient in education, training, and job skills. This theory misdiagnoses the causes of poverty and prescribes remedies that will not solve the problem.

First, in human capital theory people are poor because they lack education. The more valid conclusion, however, is that people lack education because they are poor. Low-income families do not have the resources and opportunities to make sufficient investments in schooling and training, either for themselves or their children. Nor, typically, are such families the chief beneficiaries when governments and businesses make collective human capital investments. Some poor people do indeed suffer from a deficiency in human capital, but this arises largely from the constraints of poverty and powerlessness, not the misguided choices of the poor.

Second, in human capital theory the more skilled workers are, the more productive they are, and the more productive they are, the more they are paid. In contrast to this theory's highly idealized image of the labor market, human capital in the real world is not so easily converted into employment and earnings, and it is not a surefire determinant of economic outcomes. How much labor is rewarded is not simply a function of workers' efforts, skills, and productivity; it depends also on the balance of power between capital and labor, employers and employees. Race and gender matter too, and so do other forms of capital, including cultural, psychological, and social capital. Success or failure is not just due to what you know; it is also contingent on who you are, who you know, where you work, and whether you have any bargaining power.

Third, in human capital theory poverty is best alleviated by increasing the education, training, and job experience of the poor. This remedy ignores many other barriers commonly encountered by poorer Americans, including discrimination. More fundamentally, however, the human capital solution to poverty addresses only the problem of skills deficit and ignores entirely the problem of jobs deficit. The human capital remedy, making poor people into more productive workers, will not solve the problem because there are not enough good jobs to accommodate the supply of good workers.

Fourth, as Harvey Kantor and Robert Lowe argue, by putting all our eggs in the education basket, we slight more direct and effective solutions to problems of poverty and inequality, including a higher minimum wage, redistributive tax and spending measures, and the strengthening of workers' rights. And by asking schools to shoulder the burden of fighting poverty, we are also setting ourselves up for disillusionment with the current system of public education while opening the door to privatization and other education reforms likely only to deepen existing inequalities.[57]

Part II

A Structural Perspective on Poverty — Four Systems

Chapter Five

The Economic System and Poverty

THE ECONOMICS OF POVERTY

José Gutiérrez, fifty-two, father of two daughters, works thirty hours a week as a busboy in Manhattan. He barely makes enough money to cover the rent. He hasn't gotten a raise in five years, has never received a holiday bonus, and despite repeated requests, his boss refuses to give him more hours. Dawn Nasewicz found steady employment in retail, eventually becoming manager of a store at a local mall. But with declining industry in her community and competition from e-commerce, she lost her job. "I need my income," she says. "I'm fifty-three. I have no idea what I'm going to do." Frank Walsh, a dues-paying member of the Brotherhood of Electrical Workers, has been out of work for four years. He and his family live on his wife's earnings from a part-time job and a small inheritance from his mother. But the money is running out. He needs a job. Local restaurants are hiring, but they pay only $10 an hour. "I'm 49 with two kids," he says, "$10 just isn't going to cut it." Working thirty hours a week at two jobs, Stephanie Douglas, fifty, stopped paying her health insurance premiums. "When you owe on your house, on your truck, when you're a single parent of a college student and you have other bills," she said, "it just doesn't work."[1]

The ongoing transformation of the American economy has turned many lives upside down, as the experiences of these people and millions of others attest. Though certainly making the rich richer, four decades of economic restructuring, topped off by the most severe recession since the Great Depression, have brought significant hardship to average Americans: long-term unemployment for some, reduced earnings for others, mounting indebtedness for many, and economic insecurity for most. Millions of families are falling behind, and millions more, in what some economists fear has become a permanently slow-growth economy, have little chance of getting ahead. Contrary to what the individualistic perspective would have us believe, the problem is not that Americans are deficient in cognitive ability, lacking in skills, or unwilling to work. The problem originates from a succession of troubling changes in the American political economy since the early 1970s.

Most of us need to find employment to earn a living and keep our heads above the poverty line. As individuals, however, we have little control over whether or not jobs are available and how much they pay. We are subject to the vicissitudes of the labor market. This market dependence is precisely what makes poverty a structural problem. Our life chances are contingent on external circumstances, on the dynamics of distant and seemingly mysterious economic powers. Far from being masters of our own fate, we are at the mercy of larger social forces: the vagaries of supply and demand, the questionable judgments of policy makers, the management strategies of business firms, and the hiring practices of employers.

Change in the structure of employment opportunities is a primary determinant of variations in the rate of poverty. As a result of economic fluctuations and the policy decisions of corporate and political elites, it is sometimes easier to find a decent job and sometimes downright impossible. When jobs are plentiful and wages high, the income of Americans goes up and the rate of poverty goes down, as happened, for example, during the short-lived boom of the late 1990s. When jobs are scarce and wages low, the income of Americans goes down and the rate of poverty goes up, as was the case during the Great Recession. The story is more complicated than this, of course. But still, if the objective is to understand the causes of poverty, the most sensible approach is to begin by investigating the economic and political forces determining the quantity and quality of available jobs.

The economic well-being of the American population depends on the state of the economy. Nothing could be more obvious. Most people, even if they do not always read the financial tea leaves correctly, know that economic indicators convey good news or bad news: interest rates rise or fall, the value of the dollar weakens or strengthens, the stock market turns bullish or bearish, productivity growth speeds up or slows down, the trade deficit expands or contracts. Most people are also familiar with the vocabulary of economic turmoil: plant closings, outsourcing, offshoring, downsizing, layoffs, bankruptcies. Americans realize, certainly, that external economic forces affect people's chances for a good life. They see abandoned factories, jobs moving overseas, and communities decimated by mass unemployment; they experience wage reductions, benefit cuts, bouts of unemployment, and downward mobility; and they recognize that some people enjoy tremendous advantages in life while others suffer great disadvantages. And yet, despite all evidence to the contrary, many Americans persist in believing that individual effort is sufficient for success and that people are poor because they are lazy. Even in the midst of hard times, the individualistic perspective exerts a powerful hold on Americans' understanding of poverty and inequality.

A SHIFT IN THE BALANCE OF ECONOMIC POWER

Looking back at American history since the end of World War II, we can discern two distinct eras: the period from 1945 to 1973 and the period from 1973 to the present. During the first period, sometimes referred to as the "golden age" of American capitalism, the standard of living in the United States, fueled by strong economic growth and rising productivity, more than doubled. Real wages for workers rose steadily, and the rate of poverty declined sharply, from over 20 percent in the early 1960s to a historic low of 11.1 percent in 1973. This was an era of unprecedented economic prosperity. The future looked bright. The American Dream had become a reality, even if considerably less so for racial and ethnic minorities. During this golden age the rising tide of economic growth did indeed lift most boats. As the economy grew, nearly everyone benefited: the rich got richer, the middle class thrived, and the poor became less poor and fewer in number.

Beginning in the early 1970s, however, the American economy came unglued. Increasing prosperity turned into persistent stagnation. The economic boom of the postwar period gave way to what Harold Meyerson calls a "forty-year slump."[2] The pace of productivity growth and economic expansion slowed, real earnings declined for much of the workforce, and unemployment and inflation increased simultaneously, yielding the new phenomenon of stagflation. The 1970s heralded the onset of a profound economic transformation, one that would change the relationship between business and labor, the nature of work, and the economic future of American households.

In the 1950s and 1960s a growing economy fostered job creation and wage increases, enabling many low-income families to work their way into the middle class. Since the 1970s, however, with the "great stagnation of American wages," the antipoverty effectiveness of economic growth has diminished; there has been "a reduced 'bang' for the economic growth 'buck.'"[3] An expanding economy in the current era, compared to the 1960s, generates fewer new jobs and has a less positive effect on wage levels. Even in the midst of an economic upturn, it is more difficult to get a job nowadays than it was in the past and much harder to earn enough with a job to enjoy a satisfactory standard of living.

This breakdown in the relationship between economic growth and poverty reduction resulted from a combination of forces, including the weakened state of organized labor; an upsurge in inequality; and the rise of a more ruthless form of capitalism, with big business abandoning "norms of fairness" in its treatment of workers.[4] In the 1970s and 1980s corporate managers went on the offensive. By altering investment strategies, transforming employment relations, and squeezing wages, they sought to boost profits, primarily on the backs of the working class. To remain competitive, business firms might have pursued a "high-road," "carrot" strategy. They might have tried to enhance productivity by enlisting the cooperation of the labor force, investing in the human capital of their workers, and winning the commitment of employees through an equitable sharing of the fruits from increased profitability. Despite the success of this "high-road" strategy in other countries, most American corporations, wedded to the short-term goal of maximizing shareholder value, adopted a "low-road," "stick" strategy instead. With a single-minded devotion to the bottom line, they disinvested in basic industry; relocated manufacturing plants to low-wage countries; initiated an aggressive campaign against labor unions; assumed an adversarial stance in labor negotiations, threatening layoffs and plant closings to force employees to accept wage concessions and benefit cuts; and downsized the labor force, eliminating many standard jobs and replacing permanent employees with a disposable workforce of temps, part-timers, and contract laborers. American corporations since the 1970s—placing their interests and the interests of shareholders above those of workers, customers, communities, and the country itself—have followed the "low road" to profitability. This management strategy, which both issued from and added to the growing imbalance of power between business and labor, has resulted in a decline in the rewards from work.[5] As evidence on this point, consider a small sample of striking disparities.

The labor share disparity. The labor share—"the fraction of economic output that accrues to workers as compensation in exchange for their labor"—reached a peak of 66 percent in the early 1960s and then began to decline slowly until the turn of the century. Since 2001 the labor share has fallen more rapidly, hitting a low of 56 percent in 2011 and then rising to its current level of 58 percent, still well below the historic norm.[6] Labor's share of corporate income, a somewhat different measure, has also shrunk since 2000, costing workers in the corporate sector, according to one estimate, a total of $535 billion.[7]

The bottom 50 percent–top 1 percent disparity. Since 1980 the average pretax income of adults in the bottom 50 percent of the income distribution has stagnated, while the average pretax income of adults in the top 1 percent has increased from $420,000 to about $1.3 million. Between 1980 and 2014 the share of total income received by the bottom 50 percent decreased from 20 to 12 percent, while the share received by the top 1 percent increased from 12 to 20 percent.[8]

The pay-productivity disparity. In the 1960s workers' earnings rose proportionate to productivity. Beginning in the 1970s, however, with business leaders determined to cut labor costs, a sizable pay-productivity gap emerged. Worker compensation fell behind productivity growth. Between 1973 and 2015 labor productivity increased by 73.4 percent, while hourly wages grew by only 11.1 percent.[9] Workers nowadays produce more, but their earnings, siphoned off by shareholders and corporate managers, no longer keep pace with their labor contributions.

The corporate executive-worker pay disparity. From 1978 to 2016 CEO compensation rose by over 800 percent, while the average worker during this period enjoyed an earnings increase of barely 11 percent. The typical CEO of a large firm in 2016 received in compensation 271 times that of the typical worker. This was down from a peak compensation ratio of 411 to 1 in 2000, but far greater than the quaint 1965 ratio of 20 to 1. And it is far greater too than what average Americans think it is, 30 to 1, or what they think it should be, 7 to 1.[10] The highest paid chief executive in 2016 was Thomas M. Rutledge of Charter Communications, whose pay package was $98 million, approximately 2,617 times the salary of the average American worker.[11]

During the golden age of the immediate postwar years, it was not implausible to imagine that what was good for business was also good for workers and that rising profits would rebound to the benefit of all. In the current era, however, the supposition that we are all in the same boat—that when business prospers everyone wins—is no longer credible. The gains from wealth creation and productivity growth have become increasingly monopolized by financial and corporate elites, and as a result, people in the bottom half of the income distribution are less able than in the 1960s to achieve a decent standard of living through work.

According to the individualistic perspective, wages are regulated by neutral market mechanisms, ensuring a fair distribution of earnings. People get what they deserve. According to the structural perspective, wages are set by antagonistic power relations, with *might* more than *merit* determining the distribution of economic output. In the structural perspective, there is a fundamental opposition of interests between business elites, impelled to reduce labor costs and maximize profits, and workers, seeking job security and good wages. The conflict between these two classes—played out in the labor market and the workplace, the political arena and the news media—is a primary determinant of wage levels and profit rates. Over the past thirty years employers have had the upper hand, with this shift in the balance of power between business and labor producing an increasingly skewed distribution of income and wealth. The poor and the near poor suffer from low earnings not because they are deficient in intelligence, work motivation, or human capital, but because they are deficient in the economic and political power needed to bargain effectively for improved working conditions and a more equitable slice of the economic pie.

In the following pages, in defense of a structural perspective, I show how large-scale economic changes since the 1970s—including deindustrialization, globalization, automation, and financialization—have caused a deterioration in the quality of employment opportunities, resulting in persistent poverty, rising inequality, and widespread economic insecurity.

DEINDUSTRIALIZATION

In June 2003 the Hoover vacuum cleaner factory located in Canton, Ohio, laid off much of its workforce, including fifty-five-year-old Jim Greathouse. He had worked for Hoover for nearly three decades, sometimes earning as much as $50,000 a year. Because of plant closings and downsizing throughout the Midwest, Greathouse was unable to find another blue-collar job. As of September 2003 he was contemplating personal bankruptcy and awaiting career advice from a vocational counselor. Many displaced workers like Greathouse will never again be employed in the manufacturing sector, and if they remain in the labor force at all, will be drawn instead into the burgeoning service sector. "A lot of people are going to work at Wal-Mart," explained one longtime veteran of Republic steel. "But how do you live on the $7.50 an hour Wal-Mart pays?"[12]

Jim Greathouse, along with thousands of other workers like him, is a victim of "one of the major transformations of the twentieth century."[13] In a landmark study from the early 1980s, Barry Bluestone and Bennett Harrison refer to this transformation as the "deindustrialization of America." Beginning in the 1970s, they argue, US corporations, in response to declining profits and increased international competition, undertook "a widespread, systematic disinvestment in the nation's basic productive capacity." Instead of using earnings to develop new technologies, upgrade equipment, and refurbish essential industries, corporate executives diverted the nation's financial resources into "unproductive speculation, mergers and acquisitions, and foreign investment."[14] Meanwhile, firms remaining in the business of manufacturing sought to reduce labor costs by offshoring, relocating operations to the nonunion South and Southwest, or demanding concessions from vulnerable workers. As a result of this shakeup of American industry, the quality of the current generation of blue-collar jobs is not what it used to be. Due especially to the decline of unions and employers' growing reliance on temporary hires, factory workers today have less bargaining power and lower wages. Compared to the 1970s, manufacturing jobs in the twenty-first century are both fewer in number—*much* fewer relative to the size of the workforce—and less likely to support a secure middle-class way of life.[15]

Between 1959 and 1969 the number of US workers in manufacturing increased from 15.3 to 18.6 million. Three decades later, in 1999, with an additional 60 million people in the civilian labor force, the number of factory jobs was down to 17.3 million. Partly due to increased trade competition from China, the decline of manufacturing employment escalated in the 2000s, hitting a historic low of 11.5 million in 2010 and then rising modestly thereafter, reaching 12.3 million in late 2016. The number of workers employed in retail trade alone, one of the lowest-paying job classifications, has exceeded the number of workers in manufacturing every year since 2004.[16]

The scale of this economic transformation is made even more apparent by looking at changes in the share of employment by industry. The broad trend shows a marked decline in the percentage of workers in the "goods-producing" sector, consisting mostly of manufacturing jobs, and a significant increase in the percentage of workers in the "service-providing" sector.[17] Between 1972 and November 2016 the share of private-sector nonagricultural employment in manufacturing declined from 29 percent to 10 percent, about 12 million workers, while the share of employment in the service sector increased from 63 percent to 84 percent. This pattern is anticipated to continue into the future, with the number of manufacturing jobs projected to decline throughout the next decade.[18]

The phenomenon of deindustrialization has occurred, with regional variations, throughout the country, upending the world of countless blue-collar families and leaving in its wake "shuttered factories, displaced workers, and a newly emerging group of ghost towns."[19] The wreckage is plainly visible in cities throughout what is now called the "rust belt," including Camden, New Jersey, Youngstown, Ohio, Gary, Indiana, and Detroit, Michigan.[20] Joblessness is at the heart of the problem, with working families suffering manifold consequences. Since plant closings are localized and the effects concentrated, the larger community too experiences repercussions. Households headed by laid-off workers cut back on expenditures, accumulate debt, and struggle to make ends meet. They may lose their homes, their health insurance, and their retirement savings. The financial strains they endure are associated with high levels of stress, anxiety, depression, and other health problems. With job openings in short supply, many people pack up and leave, resulting in a shrinking population and a shrinking tax base. Local businesses, with fewer paying customers, reduce their payrolls, further depressing consumer demand, or they shut down completely, leaving communities littered with boarded-up buildings. Unemployed workers and closed businesses translate into lower property values and lower tax revenues, while at the same time growing economic hardship increases the need for public funds and services. A declining tax base also means that local and state governments have less money for schools, libraries, parks, garbage collection, and police and fire protection. When factory workers are hit by plant closings, the ripple effects are felt by other workers as well, including public employees and workers in the service sector. Deindustrialization wreaks hav-

oc on affected communities, creating sites of concentrated economic hardship, undermining the social fabric, and jeopardizing people's hopes for the
future.[21]

The decline of the manufacturing sector and the rise of the service sector
have significantly altered the characteristics of the jobs available today, the
kinds of careers people might pursue, and the opportunities for Americans to
avoid or escape poverty. Service jobs, on average, pay less than manufacturing jobs, and wage levels in the service sector, compared to those in the
manufacturing sector, are also much more unequal. At one end are high-paid
lawyers, doctors, and investment bankers, while at the other end are low-paid
child-care workers, waitresses, and home health-care aides. A shift in the
composition of employment from manufacturing, where there is less inequality and fewer low-paying jobs, to services, where there is greater inequality
and more low-paying jobs, yields an overall rise in earnings inequality and an
increase in the ranks of the working poor.[22]

In the immediate postwar years young men just out of high school could
reasonably hope to get a union job in a factory and build a successful career
in manufacturing. By closing off the traditional blue-collar route to the
American Dream, deindustrialization and deunionization have hit non-college-educated workers especially hard. Relatively few entrants into the labor
force in the twenty-first century will work in what remains of the automobile
or steel industries, and those who do will discover that manufacturing jobs
today do not pay nearly as well as they did during the heyday of American
industry.[23] In any case, most new job seekers without a college degree will
end up working as waiters and waitresses, food preparation workers, nursing
aides, janitors, receptionists, and security guards. Compared to the manufacturing jobs of the past, the service jobs of the present are inferior in pay,
benefits, hours, advancement prospects, and job security. In general, the
contrast between the manufacturing sector and the service sector is not one of
good jobs versus bad jobs. But from the standpoint of the working class, this
is the essential reality. Deindustrialization, along with the proliferation of
low-paying service-sector jobs, has eroded opportunities for workers without
a college degree to earn a minimally decent living.

Well-designed policies, including perhaps a public works program to develop clean energy sources and repair the nation's infrastructure, can increase the number of blue-collar jobs. In any conceivable future, however,
the vast majority of Americans are destined to work in the service sector.
This is not such a bad thing. As Ruth Milkman reminds us, many of the
bygone factory jobs were brutal. The workers in the General Motors automobile plant she studied, despite receiving a decent paycheck, commonly used
the "metaphor of imprisonment" to describe their term of employment.[24] Nor
is it inevitable that the replacement of manufacturing jobs by service jobs
will be accompanied by a decline in the standard of living for the working

class. In some European countries, where the minimum wage is higher and institutional protections are in place, the quality of retail jobs, for example, is much better than in the United States.[25] Service workers in the United States fare poorly not because of any iron law of economics or some inherent characteristic of the service industry, but because they lack the leverage to bargain for better pay, are poorly protected by existing labor laws, and are rarely unionized, and because the minimum wage remains too low. The key point is this: without a general improvement in the quality of low-end service jobs—turning these bad jobs into good jobs—millions of Americans, however hard they might work, will continue to earn less than a living wage.

GLOBALIZATION

The term "globalization" is used to refer to the growing integration of national economies, an outcome of increased international trade. Compared to the 1950s and 1960s, countries today are more interdependent: more reliant on exports, imports, foreign investment, and immigrant labor. What most characterizes the current era of globalization is the increased permeability of national borders and the heightened velocity of capital mobility, evidenced by the incessant and worldwide movement of production facilities and investment funds. Technological advances, including the development of giant shipping containers, have facilitated globalization by lowering the costs of air and sea transportation. Because shipping is cheaper, business firms are less tied to a single location. They can readily manufacture goods in one country and sell them in another; they can fabricate a final product by assembling components produced in plants at multiple and distant sites. And with new information and telecommunication technologies, a corporation headquartered in one country can monitor and coordinate business activities in far-flung places around the world.

Globalization is not only an economic and technological phenomenon, however; it is a political phenomenon as well. The particular configuration of the present-day global regime—its characteristics and consequences—is not the product of impersonal economic laws. Nor, as the term "free trade" suggests, is it simply the expression of unfettered market forces. It is instead the contingent outcome of explicit policy decisions made by national governments, multinational corporations, and international organizations. "Where there is globalization," Dani Rodrik observes, "there are rules," and these rules determine how the game is played and who wins and who loses.[26] Operating largely behind closed doors, with little publicity or accountability, the power holders making these rules are drawn overwhelmingly from the ranks of the economic elite. The trade agreements crafted through their efforts, not surprisingly, serve less to promote the rights and interests of workers and the larger public than they do to promote the rights and interests of financial institutions and multinational corporations. The wealthy reap the benefits from globalization, while workers absorb the costs.[27]

During the quarter century following World War II, imports composed only a small portion of domestic purchases, and American corporations in the US market were relatively insulated from foreign competition. Consumers did not have to be urged to "buy American"; they had little alternative. By the 1970s, however, Japan and Western Europe, rebuilt from wartime destruction, emerged as powerful economic rivals to the United States. Foreign businesses came into competition with American corporations not only in markets abroad, but also for the dollars of American consumers. In the 1980s and 1990s international competition intensified, as developing countries in Asia and Latin America, vying to export their own goods, entered the fray. In more recent years China and India—benefiting from rapid technological development, the expansion of higher education, and a seemingly endless supply of low-wage labor—have become major players in the global market. With the world economy becoming increasingly intertwined, the value of imports to the United States as a percentage of gross domestic product (GDP) has increased steadily—rising from 4.2 percent to 14.3 percent between 1960 and 2000, reaching a peak of 17.4 percent in 2008, then slipping back down to 15.4 percent in 2015.[28] Since the 1980s, due in large part to the acceleration of manufacturing imports from developing countries, the ratio of imports to exports in the United States has also been trending upward, resulting in a growing trade deficit.[29]

In a global economy, in which trade and investment funds flow freely, workers in relatively high-wage countries like the United States, particularly those with no more than a high school degree, find themselves in competition with millions of low-wage workers in less-developed countries. This circumstance places US workers in a precarious position, especially those in the trade-sensitive manufacturing sector. By enlarging the "global labor pool," doubling its size according to Richard Freeman, the internationalization of the economy has made American workers more replaceable, diminishing their bargaining power and putting a downward pressure on wages.[30] China's emergence as a powerful exporter of manufactured goods, corresponding to its 2001 entry into the World Trade Organization (WTO), has had a particularly significant and sustained effect on the employment prospects of less-educated workers. For the period from 1999 to 2011, according to one estimate, job losses in the United States attributable to competition from China ranged from 2.0 to 2.4 million.[31] Globalization has its benefits, but the course of international trade over the past two or three decades, as both major political parties have apparently come to recognize, has caused lasting harm to the American working class.[32]

The phenomenon of globalization, like deindustrialization, attests to the profound influence of larger structural forces on people's life chances and economic outcomes. Globalization has reshaped the labor market, reducing the quality of jobs available to many Americans. It has shifted the balance between multinational corporations and national governments, limiting the scope for democratic decision making. And it has altered the relationship between business and labor, weakening the ability of workers to negotiate a fair share of the nation's growing wealth. In what follows, to underline its relevance to the problem of poverty, I identify several pathways, both direct and indirect, through which globalization adversely affects the employment opportunities and economic prospects of American workers.[33]

Offshoring. With the aim of lowering labor costs, many American businesses—though attracted also by favorable tax treatment, less regulation, and the absence of unions—have turned to outsourcing or offshoring. The goods sold by an increasing number of US-based firms are assembled from imported components that used to be manufactured by American workers.[34] In other cases, corporations have shifted their entire production facilities to low-wage countries. Levi Strauss, for example, along with other jeans manufacturers, ended all production in North America in the early 2000s, laying off thousands of workers and moving its operations to the Caribbean, Latin America, and Asia, where labor is cheaper. "What happens to our American dream?" asks one twenty-four-year veteran of the jeans industry now facing an uncertain future in the service sector.[35] Apple is another, somewhat different, example. Almost all the millions of iPhones and iPads sold each year, along with most other consumer electronics, are manufactured outside the United States. Many of the workers who assemble iPhones at the Foxconn facility in China make less than $17 a day, generating huge profits for American corporations.[36] Blue-collar workers have been hit hardest by globalization, but with employers seeking to benefit from the surplus of educated labor in China, India, and elsewhere, the movement of jobs overseas is now also a growing concern for skilled service-sector workers.[37]

Defensive innovation. Global competition also affects job quality in the United States by pressuring American firms to lower labor costs. International trade, Adrian Wood argues, prompts "defensive innovation." To "fight off" imports and remain competitive, domestic businesses introduce new "methods of production" that reduce the need for or price of unskilled labor.[38] This has occurred, for example, in the agricultural industry. Farmworkers in the United States barely average $6 an hour. But while agricultural labor in this country is cheap, as one California raisin grower states, it "isn't cheap enough." To remain competitive with foreign industry, whose labor costs are much lower, American agribusiness has turned to labor-saving technologies, replacing hand harvesting of crops with mechanical harvesting.[39] In a competitive international environment, American-based firms have become exceedingly cost conscious, determined to reduce labor costs, whether by replacing workers with machines or by forcing workers to accept lower wages.

Generalized wage suppression. Workers displaced by plant closings and layoffs due to globalization, if they remain in the labor force, typically have to settle for service-sector jobs with lower wages and fewer benefits. Former blue-collar workers, along with new entrants into the labor force, are thrown into the already crowded low-wage market. International trade not only threatens US manufacturing employment, it also keeps a lid on the wages of service workers, even though many service jobs are not directly exposed to foreign competition. The negative effects of globalization on workers' earnings and bargaining power are thus not confined to the rust belt or even to the manufacturing sector as a whole. By intensifying the competition for jobs, globalization suppresses wage growth throughout the economy, putting a downward pressure on earnings for the entire working class. [40]

Union avoidance. Globalization is also a threat to American workers because it provides employers with a powerful weapon in their battle to discourage the formation of labor unions. As plant closings and outsourcing have become everyday realities, business firms can credibly threaten to shut down or relocate operations if workers attempt to unionize. In a study of a large sample of union-organizing drives in 1998 and 1999, Kate Bronfenbrenner found that plant-closing threats, in combination with other tactics both legal and illegal, were a "pervasive and effective component of employer anti-union strategies." "In the current climate of corporate restructuring, burgeoning trade deficits, constantly shifting production, and the fear of job loss these have engendered," Bronfenbrenner argues, "most workers take even the most veiled employer plant closing threats very seriously." Globalization creates an economic environment in which employers are more effectively able to resist unionization. [41]

Employment insecurity. Global competition and plant closings have engendered an atmosphere of "heightened job insecurity," which partly explains why wage levels have failed to keep up with productivity growth. [42] Even when unionization is not an issue, employers—invoking the specter of international competition—exploit worries about job security to force workers into accepting wage cuts and benefit reductions. [43] In the new global context, employers have the upper hand, and they are not reluctant to use it. According to a *New York Times* report, "even many employers with solid profits are demanding concessions." [44] By fueling fears of job loss, globalization has augmented business's power over labor, enabling employers to insist that workers accept cutbacks in wages and benefits. [45]

Undermining democracy. The increased mobility of capital adds to the leverage corporations have over local, state, and national governments. Because firms nowadays are freer to relocate, governments are even more constrained to accommodate corporate demands. "When business can produce and invest abroad as easily as at home," James Crotty observes, "any government policy not perceived to be business friendly may induce the export of jobs and productive capital."[46] The threat of capital flight keeps the pressure on governments to resist policies that might increase workers' income: raising the minimum wage, easing requirements for unionization, or increasing taxes to strengthen the safety net. Globalization limits the leeway for political officeholders to introduce redistributive tax and spending policies, including programs that might compensate the losers from international trade.

The deterioration of the earnings and employment prospects of American workers is due to a variety of economic and political forces. Globalization is only one cause among many, and it does not inevitably generate job losses or wage reductions. The culprit, indeed, is not globalization as such, but its existing form, a product of the 1980s and 1990s, what might be called procorporate, "neoliberal," or "hyperglobalization."[47] Four characteristics of the procorporate regime stand out: (1) a philosophy preaching the dangers of interference by national governments (e.g., regulatory policies, tariff barriers, and protectionism) and heralding the superiority of free-market and free-trade practices; (2) a system of rules governing trade established by international agencies, such as the WTO, which limit the latitude for policy making on the part of national governments—regarding workers' rights and environmental standards, for example—and infringe on the scope of democratic decision making;[48] (3) the premise that good trade policies are those that best serve the goals of multinational corporations; and (4) the assumption, repeatedly asserted by mainstream economists, that since free trade produces gains in the aggregate, it is therefore good for the country as a whole, even though it may cause severe and lasting losses for a sizable minority of the population.[49] With little regard for the interests of labor, procorporate globalization promotes free-market capitalism on an international scale, and in this incarnation, globalization does indeed perpetuate poverty and inequality. Even so, however, national political institutions and policies mediate the effects of international trade on employment and earnings.[50] The impact of globalization is more or less severe, depending, for example, on the strength of a country's welfare state and on whether or not social programs exist to compensate the victims of economic dislocation. Many of the negative consequences of globalization in the United States arise not from international economic imperatives, but from domestic political choices. The problem in this country is that we have a "more cutthroat form of capitalism" in which individuals, more so than in other developed countries, are left to their own devices to manage the harsh consequences of an increasingly global economy.[51]

TECHNOLOGICAL UNEMPLOYMENT

New digital technologies, including smart machines, high-speed computers, and artificial intelligence, are invading work settings throughout the world, automating jobs previously performed by human workers. Self-driving vehicles, a potential threat to truckers and taxi drivers, are still in the future. But already technology has eliminated numerous blue-collar jobs in manufacturing and mining and is making inroads in the service sector as well, evidenced by the appearance of self-serve checkout counters, salad-making robots, online shopping sites, and restaurants that are almost fully automated. Retail salespeople, food and beverage servers, cashiers, and office clerks—the four most common occupations in the United States—are all also highly susceptible to automation. Many professional jobs are also at risk, with increasing reliance on computers in legal discovery, medical diagnosis, music composition, journalism, and stock trading.[52]

Oxford researchers Carl Frey and Michael Osborne estimate that nearly half of all jobs in the United States—more so jobs paying less than $20 an hour, but many solidly middle-class jobs as well—fall into the "high risk category," meaning they are vulnerable to automation "relatively soon, perhaps over the next decade or two."[53] Researchers from the McKinsey Global Institute offer a more sanguine prognosis. Though acknowledging that "the latest technological developments will touch every job in every sector and in every country," automation, they argue, will eliminate specific work activities *within* occupations but will displace relatively few occupations in their entirety.[54] Using a similar methodology, researchers for the Organisation for Economic Co-operation and Development estimate that on average 9 percent of occupations in OECD countries are vulnerable to automation. They admit, as do other commentators, that new technologies, even if they do not necessarily cause widespread joblessness, will likely increase inequality, with less-educated workers hit hardest.[55] Prompted by these "sharply contrasting" findings, Richard Berriman and John Hawksworth, applying a more refined methodology, reexamine the data in the Frey and Osborne study and the OECD study, along with additional data. They estimate that about 38 percent of jobs in the United States are at "high risk of automation" by 2030.[56]

In 2014 the Pew Research Center solicited the opinions of 1,896 experts, asking them how the development of advanced digital technologies might alter people's lives between the present and 2025. The central question concerned the economic and employment effects of robotics and artificial intelligence. The experts were divided, with 52 percent (the optimists) believing that new technological advancement will create as many jobs as it destroys, and 48 percent (the pessimists) anticipating significant job loss for both blue- and white-collar workers. The optimists base their case primarily on the historical record. They point out that despite warnings of mass unemployment, previous waves of technological innovation, beginning with the Industrial Revolution itself, have not resulted in long-term job loss and increasing poverty, but have instead stimulated job growth and a rising standard of living. If the past is any guide to the future, the optimists assert, technology will change the mix of jobs and perhaps cause some short-term disruption, but it will not lead to any substantial displacement of human labor.[57]

The pessimists too look to the past, but they cite the more immediate past—a three-decade-long period marked by weak job creation, wage stagnation, long-term unemployment, and declining labor force participation. These indicators suggest that technology might already be creating fewer jobs than it is destroying. Though admitting that automation and computerization are not solely, or even mainly, responsible for the current economic malaise, they are contributing factors, the pessimists argue.[58] One study, looking at the period from 1990 to 2007, estimates "large and robust negative effects of robots on employment and wages."[59] And according to a 2014 poll, 35 percent of nonemployed, job-seeking Americans between the ages of twenty-five and fifty-four attribute their unemployment to their "jobs being replaced by technology."[60] If the present is any guide to the future, the pessimists hold, the new technologies of the digital age may very well give rise to a full-blown jobs crisis. This assessment has added weight because the optimists have yet to explain where the millions of new jobs promised for the future might come from, especially in an environment in which labor-intensive industries are on the wane, or why those new jobs too won't eventually be automated out of existence.[61]

While acknowledging that fears of technological unemployment have turned out to be unwarranted in the past, this time, the pessimists argue—challenging the key plank of the optimists' case—there are several good reasons to think that things are different and that, in a departure from the historical pattern, the current wave of technology might indeed cause extensive joblessness.

First, *the rapid pace of technological development.* The capabilities of new technologies are growing more quickly than was the case for past technologies. The processing power of computers is increasing at a phenomenal rate, doubling approximately every eighteen months. Since this has been happening for many years now, each subsequent doubling means a phenomenal jump in computational power. This pattern of *exponential* growth is the distinguishing feature of today's computer-based technologies.[62]

Second, *the rapid decline in the price of new technologies.* In combination with the growth in their capabilities, the ever-cheapening cost of digital technologies creates a powerful—and, over time, increasing—incentive to substitute machines for human labor. In the short run workers might be able to fend off unemployment by accepting rock-bottom wages, thus reducing employers' incentive to invest in labor-saving devices. In the longer run, however, it is difficult to imagine how human workers can compete effectively against ever-smarter and ever-cheaper machines.

Third, *the general-purpose quality of new technologies*. Not only is digital technology getting more powerful and cheaper, it is also uniquely versatile, subject to continuous improvement over time, and capable of performing any number of tasks, thus conceivably replacing human labor up and down the entire occupational structure. In contrast to, say, the cotton gin, whose effects were confined to the textile sector, information technology is not industry specific; it has a "general-purpose" quality. Analogous to electricity, it is applicable in nearly every work setting and liable to spread across all industries, eliminating numerous jobs along the way.[63]

Fourth, *the displacement of both unskilled and skilled labor*. Automation thus far has mechanized forms of labor that are mostly manual and routine; its impact today has been felt mainly by blue-collar factory workers and low-wage service workers. With current technological developments, however, it is apparent that many complex cognitive tasks, "which, until now, have largely remained in the human domain," are also vulnerable.[64] The intellectual skills possessed by educated workers can be programmed into the machines themselves. Smart workers, such as translators and radiologists, can be replaced by smart machines.[65] Indeed, James Manyika argues that "knowledge workers at the middle and the top" are even more susceptible to technological displacement than those engaged in physical labor.[66] The new technologies are different in part because they are a threat not only to less-skilled jobs, but also to "high-wage, high-skill jobs as well."[67] It follows, furthermore, that conventional education, training, and skill-upgrading solutions to unemployment will not suffice to remedy the looming problem of twenty-first-century joblessness.

Fifth, *modern machinery is more dependable than human workers*. Business firms substitute machines for workers when it is cost-effective, either because of a decline in the price of technology or an increase in the price of labor. Besides being potentially cheaper, however, modern digital technologies have other qualities that, from the standpoint of employers, make them superior to workers. Machines are more predictable, more manageable, and more quickly fitted to a variety of tasks. They don't daydream, shirk, or spend time socializing on the job. They don't foul up, forget, or otherwise make avoidable mistakes. They are easier to program, control, and replace. They can work 24/7—all day and all night—and, depending on the task, they can operate at speeds impossible for human workers. They also don't need periodic breaks or lunch hours, nor do they require sick days or vacation time. They don't demand pay raises, better working conditions, or flexible hours. They don't complain, threaten lawsuits, organize unions, or go out on strike. They are the epitome of the ideal worker: no family responsibilities, no extraneous needs that have to be fulfilled, no life whatsoever outside the job. Though not suited to every task, of course, machines generally meet the needs of employers better than humans. The upshot is this: if a job can be automated, it will be automated.

The growing presence of labor-saving technologies in the workplace—machines that learn, robots that mimic human behavior, and computers capable of mining vast amounts of data—is likely to exacerbate the already troubling disparity between the number of people desperate for work and a regular paycheck and the number of jobs that offer steady employment and a decent wage. This time things might really be different, and if they are, as Farhad Manjoo warns, we may "end up with a society in which there's not enough work for everyone, and especially not a lot of good work."[68] This prospect—a more or less permanently weak market for labor—by intensifying the competition for employment, will diminish further the already limited bargaining power of workers and place additional downward pressure on wages. The painful predicament many workers face already—a choice between a bad job and no job at all—is likely to become an increasingly common reality.

Technology per se is not the cause of technological unemployment, nor is it inevitable that a decline in the demand for labor will bring about economic ruin for the working population. Everything depends on who controls the trajectory of technological development, who specifies the purposes served by automation, who determines the allocation of gains and losses, and who decides how we deal with the repercussions of a changing economy. In short, everything depends on the balance of economic and political power and the interplay of conflicting interests.[69] At present one certainty is this: machines are not being introduced into workplaces for the purpose of improving the economic well-being of the larger population; quite the contrary. The current course of technological change, as Robert McChesney and John Nichols observe, "is taking *all* the trends toward increased inequality and poverty already in existence and making them worse."[70] The problem, to reiterate, is not technology per se; it is the system within which technology is embedded and the interests it serves. In the existing regime of unregulated capitalism, the guiding interest is profit maximization, and the main function of technology is to lower the costs of production by replacing workers—not even to increase the productivity of workers, but to replace them altogether. As the founder of a start-up company in the business of automating the production of gourmet hamburgers puts it: "Our device isn't meant to make employees more efficient. It's meant to completely obviate them."[71]

Technology holds out the promise of bringing untold benefits to humanity. But in the current system, the lion's share of the gains from technological innovation is monopolized by economic elites while the losses are borne by working- and middle-class families. This is a *structural* problem, one rooted in the normal workings of the current political and economic order. The solution is not to renounce progress, but to effect changes in a system in which technology—rather than being used to enhance the general quality of human life—is deployed instead with the sole purpose of improving the corporate bottom line.[72] These changes might include, among others, a universal basic income so families are not exclusively dependent on earnings to maintain a decent standard of living; a true commitment to full employment, with government serving as an employer of last resort; the creation of a system of portable health-care and retirement benefits, not tied to employment; and the reining in of the power of corporations to set economic policy, with no accountability to the larger public, on a wide range of issues, including investment, jobs, and wages.[73] In the absence of such changes, the continued application of technology in the workplace, even if automation does not usher in a world without work, is certain only to worsen the already severe problems of inequality, unemployment, and poverty.

FINANCIALIZATION AND THE SHAREHOLDER REVOLUTION

From the 1940s into the 1970s—the bygone days of "boring banking"—the financial system, in addition to offering services to private households, played a modest role in support of industry, lending investment funds to business start-ups and firms seeking to renovate or expand.[74] Since the 1980s, however, financial institutions, financial markets, and financial activities have experienced substantial growth and have attained a commanding place in the overall functioning of the American economy. Financial assets as a percent of GDP more than doubled between 1980 and 2014; salaries in the financial sector, particularly for investment bankers and securities broker-dealers, have skyrocketed; and financial profits as a share of total corporate profits have increased enormously, rising from 10 percent to 15 percent in the early 1980s, reaching a high of over 40 percent in the early 2000s, and then, after taking a nose dive during the Great Recession, climbing back up again to a range of 25 percent to 30 percent.[75] The lure of financial profits has even enticed nonfinancial firms—including General Electric, General Motors, and Sears—to move into lending, insurance, consumer credit, and other financial ventures.[76] Not only are nonfinancial corporations behaving more like financial firms, but financial firms have also become major owners of nonfinancial corporations. Never before, according to Gerald Davis, has the United States "seen corporate ownership this concentrated in the hands of a small number of financial institutions." As of 2011, one investment firm alone, BlackRock, owned at least 5 percent of more than eighteen hundred companies, and the combination of three institutional investors—BlackRock, Vanguard, and State Street—has the largest ownership share of 88 percent of the companies in the S&P 500.[77] Commonly referred to as *financialization*, this ascendancy of the financial system—with Wall Street gaining supremacy over Main Street—has allowed corporate investors and top managers to amass immense wealth and power. But while investment bankers, private equity firms, hedge fund managers, and other rich financiers have made billions, the ongoing subordination of industry to finance has jeopardized the economic security of working families and the health of the American economy.

As we have seen already with deindustrialization, globalization, and automation, the decisions made by corporate elites play a decisive role in shaping people's opportunities for employment, the pay and benefits they receive, and their chances for a piece of the American Dream. The corporate regime in place during the immediate postwar years, roughly 1945 to 1975, operated reasonably well, partly due to the strength of organized labor, which enabled workers to receive a share in the gains from economic growth and rising productivity. Under this system of corporate governance—which came to be called *managerialism*—large corporations were run by professional managers, with shareholders playing a largely passive role as recipients of dividends. Though remaining attentive to the bottom line, managers had considerable discretionary authority while also acknowledging obligations to other stakeholders, including customers, employees, and the surrounding community.[78] "Retain and reinvest" was the guiding strategic principle of this managerial system. Rather than passing earnings along to shareholders, corporations reinvested profits to finance research and development, technological innovation, workforce training, and wage increases. In adopting this reinvestment strategy, managers sought to increase market share and promote the long-term health and stability of the firm.[79]

In the 1980s the managerial system and its corresponding business practices came under fire. Changes in the legal/regulatory environment tipped the balance of power between shareholders and managers and opened up new opportunities for shareholders to assert their ownership rights. Changes in the intellectual/ideological environment also empowered shareholders vis-à-vis managers. The idea that corporations, beyond profit making, had broader social responsibilities receded during this period, as "activist investors" and free-market enthusiasts articulated a different philosophy. The corporation, it was now proposed, had one purpose and one purpose only: the maximization of shareholder value. This conception of the corporation conveyed a clear message: the interests of investors come first and the public good, if it counts at all, is incidental.[80]

These changes set in motion what came to be called the *shareholder revolution*, with open conflict breaking out between shareholders—including corporate raiders, institutional investors, and public pension funds—and top managers. Intent on boosting share prices and establishing their claim on the flow of corporate cash, shareholders demanded that CEOs focus on the "core competencies" of their firms and eliminate wasteful expenditures, sell off less productive divisions, lower labor costs, and subcontract jobs that could be done more cheaply by subsidiary businesses. In an effort to sway recalcitrant managers, shareholders in the 1980s resorted to hostile takeovers and leveraged buyouts, resulting in changes in management, the bust-up of many companies, and the outright demise of numerous corporations.[81] In the 1990s, as legal obstacles made takeovers more difficult and less profitable, shareholders turned to other forms of pressure. They sponsored stockholder resolutions, demanded seats on the board, publicly criticized management, initiated shareholder lawsuits, and threatened stock dumping. Most managers eventually came to embrace the shareholder value mandate, partly because they were forced to, but also because the financial incentives for doing so were considerable. By the mid-1990s top executives were receiving the bulk of their earnings in the form of stock options and other types of stock-based remuneration. This system of compensation gave managers a major stake in the game, aligning their interests with those of shareholders: both profited when stock prices rose.[82]

By the mid-1990s the concept of shareholder value was enshrined as the governing principle of corporate America. To take one notable example, while the Business Roundtable, an elite group of top CEOs, had once emphasized the public responsibility of the corporation, its 1997 mission statement sang a different tune, no longer even paying lip service to larger social purposes: "The paramount duty of management and of boards of directors is to the corporation's stockholders; the interests of other stakeholders are relevant as a derivative of duty to stockholders."[83] The success of the shareholder revolution shifted corporate strategy from "retain and reinvest" to "downsize and distribute," from "value creation" to "value extraction."[84] Corporate earnings, rather than being reinvested, were used to award payouts to shareholders. Instead of supplying money *to* the real economy, financial elites began siphoning money *from* the real economy. Under this new regime, corporations focused on financial speculation rather than productive investment, downsizing rather than growth, and short-term earnings rather than long-term sustainability. The ideological shift initiated by the shareholder revolution—the proposition that the sole purpose of the corporation is the creation of shareholder value—has since become the reigning orthodoxy.[85]

One important outcome of the shareholder revolution is the phenomenon of stock buybacks, with corporations using their earnings to repurchase shares of their own stock, thus rewarding investors by bolstering share prices. This practice was once regarded as a form of stock market manipulation. Since the early 1980s, however, buybacks have not only become legal, they have become a commonplace corporate practice, and massive in scale. As "a mode of distribution of corporate cash to shareholders," stock repurchases have even surpassed dividends. Between 2005 and 2014, William Lazonick finds, the companies listed in the S&P 500 Index "expended $3.75 trillion on stock buybacks, representing 52.7 percent of net income, plus another 35.7 percent of net income on dividends"—a total of approximately $6 trillion turned over to shareholders, almost 90 percent of corporate net income. Many American corporations, Lazonick adds, "routinely distribute more than 100 percent of net income to shareholders, generating the extra money by reducing cash reserves, selling off assets, taking on debt, or laying off employees."[86] If the maximization of shareholder value is the fundamental purpose of the corporation, then corporate America is fulfilling its mission with a vengeance.

Corporations today are fixated on stock prices, but equally important, this fixation has a short-term horizon. Pressured by activist investors out for a quick buck, top executives can afford to look ahead no further than quarterly earnings. As William Galston and Elaine Kamarck argue, all the incentives line up in favor of short-term gains rather than long-term growth, payouts to shareholders rather than capital investment, and immediate returns rather than a sustainable future. Investors benefit from this "quarterly capitalism," as do managers who receive stock options. But the combination of "short-termism" and outsized shareholder payouts is unhealthy for the future of the American economy: it reduces the pool of funds available for reinvestment, creates a bias against projects with a long gestation period, slows growth in the real economy, causes unemployment and wage stagnation, and yields a system in which "corporate profitability is not translating into economic prosperity."[87]

The "business of America isn't business anymore," Rana Foroohar observes. "It's finance."[88] And what's good for finance is *not* good for America, certainly not good for the American working class. Financialization has given rise to a new group of wealthy elites possessing inordinate economic and political power. It has altered corporate managerial practices, prioritizing short-term profit making at the expense of productive investment. It has promoted rising inequality and a reduction in labor's share of the nation's income. It has contributed to reduced business investment, slowing productivity, and weak economic growth. And it is partly responsible for the uncertain employment picture in the United States and the decline in the lifetime economic mobility of workers.[89] Financialization, as should be apparent, is not just a story of how the rich have become richer. It is also a story of how changes in the structure of the US political economy have diminished the availability of good jobs and made the circumstances of millions of Americans increasingly perilous. More than this, it is also a story of how the economic trajectories of the rich and the poor are connected—how the suffering on Main Street is a by-product of the prosperity on Wall Street.

Deindustrialization, globalization, automation, and financialization—these large-scale structural developments have transformed the economic landscape in the United States and have contributed to rising levels of poverty and inequality. Since the onset of the Great Recession and into the current recovery, the economic bad times have remained unusually bad. Weak economic growth, slow productivity growth, insufficient aggregate demand, and a low level of investment spending are among the chief culprits.[90] This combination of structural change and a persistently sluggish economy have diminished opportunities for employment, exacerbating a problem endemic to American capitalism: a shortage of good jobs.

The basic thrust of the analysis presented here is that the rate of poverty remains extraordinarily high in the United States not because so many Americans are deficient in intelligence, determination, and skills, but because the number of people who would like to have a job far exceeds the number of job openings, and because a growing proportion of the jobs being created in today's economy, besides being demeaning and exploitative, cannot support a decent standard of living. In short, despite a current rate of unemployment not much higher than 4 percent, the American economy suffers from a jobs crisis.

A JOBS CRISIS

There are two aspects to the current jobs crisis: the job availability problem and the job quality problem. First, there are not enough employment opportunities to enable every aspiring worker to find a job. Second, and more important, there are even fewer opportunities for every job seeker to find employment that pays a living wage, offers health and retirement benefits, and promises some measure of economic security. Moreover, the job quality problem has worsened over the past few decades, raising troubling questions about the current trajectory of the American economy. In the first subsection below I discuss the problem of job availability. In the second subsection, delving into the heart of the crisis, I turn to the problem of job quality.

The Job Availability Problem

The Bureau of Labor Statistics (BLS) counts people as being in the "labor force" if they are either "employed"—having some paid work, however little, during the reference week—or "unemployed"—jobless but actively looking for work. If they are neither employed nor unemployed, a category including many retirees, students, and full-time parents, they are considered *not* in the labor force. According to the latest "employment situation" report from the BLS, the rate of unemployment (the "seasonally adjusted" share of the labor force fitting the definition of "unemployed") was 4.1 percent in November

2017, about 6.6 million people. Another 1.5 million were "marginally attached to the labor force." They would like to have a job, they say, and they have searched for a job at some point over the past year, but they are not actively looking for one at the moment. Among those defined as marginally attached, 469,000 ceased looking for work because they believed no suitable jobs were available. These people are officially classified as "discouraged workers." Including workers who are discouraged or otherwise marginally attached increases the unemployment rate from 4.1 to 5.0 percent. An additional 4.8 million people would like to have full-time jobs but are currently working less than thirty-five hours per week, often much less, because they can't get more hours at their current job—a persistent complaint among Walmart workers—or find a full-time job.[91] Including these "involuntary part-time workers" in the count raises the unemployment rate to 8.0 percent, about 13 million people, double the official estimate.[92]

But even this broad measure of unemployment understates the extent of the current jobs shortage. In November 2017, the BLS reports, there were an additional 5.2 million people not in the labor force—meaning not having looked for work for a year or more—but wanting a job nevertheless. This group, Edward Fullbrook suggests, might be called "very discouraged workers." Counting these people among the unemployed—along with the officially unemployed, the marginally attached, and involuntary part-time workers—we arrive at an "augmented unemployment rate" of approximately 10.6 percent, more than 17 million people, almost three times the official number.[93] Even this measure, however, does not fully capture the weakness of the labor market or the extent of the job availability problem, because it does not factor in the millions of people who are "underemployed," working at jobs below their level of qualifications.

A job availability problem is also suggested by the large number of potential workers missing from today's labor market. If employment opportunities were available in sufficient numbers, we would expect to see the reentry into the labor force of people who had lost their jobs and left the workforce during the recession. This has happened, but only to a limited extent, suggesting inadequate job growth in the postrecession period. The rate of labor force participation in the year prior to the financial crash was 66.4 percent. It fell to a low of 62.4 percent in September 2015. Remarkably, however, even with the economy in recovery, the labor force participation rate has regained little ground, rising only to 62.7 percent in November 2017. We see a similar pattern looking at the employment-to-population ratio for prime working-age men and women, those between the ages of twenty-five and fifty-four. Though this ratio has improved since the depths of the recession, increasing from a low of about 75 percent to 78.5 percent in 2017, it is still considerably less than what it was prior to 2007.[94]

The existence of so many unemployed, underemployed, discouraged, and very discouraged workers, along with the figures on the labor force participation rate and the employment-to-population ratio, are evidence of an unhealthy economy. The slow pace of wage growth and a rate of inflation below 2 percent also suggest continued weakness in the labor market.[95] Though one might quibble over the numbers, it cannot be denied that a sizable segment of the population, disproportionately African American, is unemployed.[96] These are people who want employment, but the jobs aren't there, don't pay enough to live on, don't offer a sufficient number of hours, or are located in places too expensive to live.[97] This is indicative of an economy in a slump. The recession is over, but the economy continues to suffer from inadequate demand, slow growth, a slack labor market, and a sizable jobs deficiency.[98]

The Job Quality Problem

There are currently not enough jobs to go around, but this may be the least important aspect of the problem. The more pressing issue, one with worrying implications for the future, is the shortfall of jobs that pay a satisfactory wage, have regular hours of work, offer health-care and retirement benefits, provide opportunities for upward mobility, and enable workers to achieve a middle-class standard of living. Over the past four decades, measured by these criteria, the proportion of "good" jobs in the American economy has declined sharply. Wages are so low, in fact—with approximately 40 percent of workers making less than $15 per hour—that millions of employed Americans are able to put food on the table only by drawing on public assistance programs, with taxpayers asked to fill the gap between what employers are willing to pay and what workers need to live.[99]

As we have seen, deindustrialization, globalization, automation, and financialization, along with the decline of unions, have contributed to the deterioration of job quality in the United States. Connected to these larger economic forces, I discuss in what follows four additional, closer-to-the-ground developments, which have also played a significant role: (1) barriers to workers' mobility, (2) changes in the distribution of employment by sector and industry, (3) the "fissuring" of the workplace, and (4) the growth of alternative work arrangements.

Barriers to workers' mobility. A high rate of unemployment enhances employers' leverage, enabling them to dictate terms to desperate job seekers. A low rate of unemployment enhances workers' leverage, enabling them demand higher wages or move from a worse job to a better job. In the current economic environment, however, despite a relatively low rate of unemployment, workers' mobility and wage growth remain weak. One explanation for this puzzle, as argued in the previous section, is that the real level of joblessness is greater than what the official unemployment numbers suggest. But there are other factors involved as well. I focus here on three barriers that limit the job mobility and bargaining power of workers.

First, it is not so easy to pack up and move from an area of high unemployment to an area of low unemployment. Besides having to cut long-standing ties to one's community, leaving neighbors, friends, and relatives behind, the upfront monetary costs of relocation and resettlement are considerable. Housing, for example, is expensive just about anywhere, and especially so in cities and states with good job prospects. How is a family living paycheck to paycheck expected not only to finance a move across the country but also to come up with a down payment for a home or a first and last plus security deposit for a rental unit? Because of high transaction costs, along with the lack of affordable housing, many workers tend to be stuck in place, not altogether free to quit a bad job in favor of a good one.[100]

Second, owners of franchises, including Jiffy Lube and H&R Block, but particularly fast-food franchises, such as Domino's and Pizza Hut, are often contractually prohibited from hiring workers already employed in the same franchise chain. These collusive "no-poaching" agreements, present in more than half of all major franchise operations, undermine workers' right to switch jobs, such as leaving one Burger King for a better job at another Burger King, thus limiting their bargaining power and putting a downward pressure on wages.[101]

Third, 18 percent of all workers, nearly 30 million people, are bound by noncompete agreements. Whether knowingly or not, these employees have signed labor contracts forbidding them—if they quit, are fired, or are laid off—from accepting employment in a competing firm or industry. They are locked into their current jobs, barred from exercising their exit option and thus prevented from pricing their worth in the market. And because quitting means they would have to take up a new trade or profession, they cannot effectively bargain with their existing employer for better wages or working conditions. As one economist observes: "People can't negotiate when their company knows they won't leave."[102] Non-compete agreements are typically justified as a means for employers to protect trade secrets. But only a small percentage of those subject to these agreements possess any such secrets. Many are employed in low-wage jobs as beauticians, warehouse laborers, and workers in the fast-food and restaurant industries. Like no-poaching agreements, noncompete clauses restrict workers' freedom to leave one job for another job, while enhancing the ability of employers to control labor costs and dictate the terms of employment.[103]

Changes in the distribution of employment by sector and industry. Shifts in the distribution and availability of jobs by sector and industry also bear some of the responsibility for the decline in job quality. First, as we have already seen, the proportion of jobs in manufacturing, which are typically better paying, has shrunk, while the proportion of jobs in the largely nonunion service sector, many of which are part-time and low-paying, has grown. Second, just as manufacturing jobs have become harder to get, so too have government jobs. The public sector, where in the past African Americans in particular have found a gateway into the middle class, has not added any jobs since the onset of the Great Recession, and astonishingly, the federal government today employs fewer people than it did way back in 1972.[104] Third, the prospects for getting lifetime employment in corporate America have also dried up. In the 1960s and 1970s top corporations, including AT&T, GM, and IBM, each employed several hundred thousand workers, most receiving good wages and benefits. Today, however, the largest corporations as measured by revenue, including Apple, Google, and Microsoft, employ relatively few people. The biggest corporate employers are in retail—Walmart, Kroger, Home Depot, and Target—"where the wages are low, turnover high, benefits modest, and upward mobility minimal."[105] Fourth, among the industries with the strongest employment growth in recent years are "food services and drinking places," including restaurants and fast-food establishments. In 2017 the number of people employed in eating and drinking places was just about the same as the number of people employed in manufacturing. The working class, previously located at Ford Motor Company and U.S. Steel, can now be found at Taco Bell and Kentucky Fried Chicken. These are not good jobs. Though the average pay for workers in eating and drinking places is about $14 per hour, many employees make less than $10 per hour, and the average number of hours is only twenty-six per week.[106] As Jerry Davis observes, there is little chance that firms in the retail and eating and drinking industries, where so many Americans work today and where even more are likely to work in the future, "will transform into providers of the stable career employment that characterized the postwar era in the U.S."[107] Or at least they won't do so without a big push.

The "fissuring" of the workplace. A third development contributing to the decline of job quality is what David Weil calls the "fissuring" of the workplace. Under pressure from shareholders and investors, corporations since the 1980s have been divesting assets and shedding employment peripheral to their "core competencies," such as product innovation or brand promotion. Many jobs—for example, janitorial labor, cafeteria work, security, maintenance, human resources, payroll, accounting, and even manufacturing—that once might have been carried out within the firm, relying on workers employed directly by the firm and paid according to the reigning compensation standards of the firm, are instead farmed out to subordinate businesses located beyond the firm's boundaries, where market conditions are more competitive and workers receive lower wages and fewer benefits.[108] Just as Apple does not make iPhones and Nike does not make tennis shoes (these jobs are outsourced), so too, Weil notes, hotel maids work at Marriott, but they are employed by a hotel management company; cable installers are employed by an intermediary, not by Time Warner itself; and Big Macs are not made by McDonald's Corporation, but by the employees of franchise owners. The same pattern, taking a variety of forms, is replicated throughout the economy. In their relationship with subordinate businesses, intermediaries, and franchises, major corporations, committed to protecting their brand name and fulfilling consumer expectations, still set standards for job performance and product quality. But by outsourcing employment they unburden themselves from any responsibility for the workers they profit from, with those workers now coming under the control of sometimes dubious and exploitative subcontractors and franchise owners who operate in a ruthlessly competitive market. At the same time, by ridding themselves of low-value assets and reducing labor costs, these downsized corporate firms are able to increase profits and shareholder value. "Shifting work outward," Weil says, "allows redistribution of gains upward."[109]

The growth of alternative work arrangements. A fourth development contributing to the worsening of job quality is the proliferation of new labor arrangements. As part of their restructuring efforts, US corporations and businesses, abetted by the weakness of organized labor and the absence of countervailing public policies, have replaced many of their regular, full-time employees with workers who occupy a "contingent" or "nonstandard" status.[110] This enables employers to fulfill their need for labor without making any costly long-term commitments to the human beings who supply that labor. Robert Kuttner describes this "move to insecure, irregular jobs" as the "most profound economic change of the past four decades."[111]

While the growth of nonstandard employment increased during the Great Recession, it has been ongoing for some time. Even as early as 1993, Lance Morrow, writing for *Time* magazine, announced the advent of a new epoch: "America has entered the age of the contingent or temporary worker, of the consultant and subcontractor, of the just-in-time work force—fluid, flexible, disposable. This is the future. Its message is this: You are on your own." In this new regime, he reports, companies have become "strangely conscienceless," jobs are "vanishing into thin air," full-time workers are reduced to part-timers, and employees are "throwaway." The "human costs" of this "merciless and profound" transformation, Morrow declares, are "enormous."[112]

There is no agreed upon definition of nonstandard or contingent work, and different definitions yield different estimates of its size. In one recent high-profile study, Lawrence Katz and Alan Krueger include in their definition of "alternative work arrangements" the following: "temporary help agency workers, on-call workers, contract workers, and independent contractors or freelancers."[113] What is common to all of these jobs is the lack of permanent employment and regularly scheduled hours. Temps are paid and assigned jobs by whatever agency they work for. On-call workers, typically hired part-time as needed, operate on a standby basis. Contract workers are employed by companies that sell their employees' services to other businesses. And independent contractors are freelancers, finding customers on their own. Based on this definition, Katz and Krueger find a remarkable growth in the percentage of workers employed in alternative work arrangements, rising from 10.1 percent in February 2005 to 15.8 percent in late 2015, an increase of 8.6 million workers. Over the same period, by contrast, the number of employees in regular jobs increased by just 0.5 million. What this adds up to is striking: *"94 percent of the net employment growth in the U.S. economy from 2005 to 2015 appears to have occurred in alternative work arrangements."*[114]

Though not all contingent workers have bad jobs, the displacement of standard employment by nonstandard employment generally translates into an overall decline in job quality. If they are day laborers, picking up work at informal street markets, curbside labor pools outside places like Home Depot, or through temporary employment agencies, they are especially vulnerable to violations of labor law, including wage theft.[115] If they are temps or part-timers, making do while waiting for a better job to come along, they are in danger of finding themselves among the ranks of the "perma-temps" or full-time "part-time" workers.[116] If they are independent contractors in the "gig economy," they might really be employees, as some Uber drivers assert, who have been purposefully misclassified so employers can avoid paying payroll taxes; providing health-care and retirement benefits; and abiding by labor laws, including rules governing overtime pay and minimum wages.[117] And if they are employed in any nonstandard position, they generally work fewer hours than they would like and make less money per hour than otherwise equivalent workers in standard jobs. They have more job instability and are less able to map out a long-term career for themselves. They are less likely to have retirement and health-care benefits, paid sick days, or parental leave options, and they are more likely to have irregular and unpredictable work schedules. They are also more likely to be poor and to receive public assistance.[118] As Katz and Kruger point out, with the exception of independent contractors, most nonstandard workers are forced into these precarious and unrewarding labor arrangements and, not surprisingly, would prefer to have regular jobs.[119] The increasing prevalence of alternative work arrangements is driven by the desires and interests of employers, not workers. Because it increases flexibility and reduces labor costs, nonstandard employment is a good deal for business, but it leaves many workers permanently trapped in the low-wage labor market.

Millions of Americans do not have jobs, millions more do not have good jobs, and millions of households as a result are chronically vulnerable to poverty. This is a structural problem. It derives from the workings of the political economy, not from the deficiencies of the workforce. Deindustrialization, globalization, automation, and financialization—these economic forces, along with cost-cutting corporate strategies and business-friendly government policies, have exacerbated an enduring problem of American capitalism: a shortage of good jobs.

In an article published in 2002, Bob Sheak and Melissa Morris calculate the level of "subemployment" in the American economy for every year in the period stretching from 1972 through 1999. People are counted as subemployed if they fall into one of four groups: (1) the officially unemployed; (2) discouraged workers; (3) involuntary part-time workers; and (4) full-time, year-round workers who earn less than a poverty-level wage. With the inclusion of this fourth criterion, Sheak and Morris are able to assess not only job *availability*, but at least one dimension of job *quality*: the adequacy of earnings. Though not quite reaching the highs attained in the early 1970s, the booming economy of the late 1990s resulted in a significant improvement in employment prospects. Nevertheless, the rate of subemployment in 1999 was remarkably high at 22.9 percent, meaning approximately 33 million workers in what was a very good year lacked an "adequate" job. Using a more realistic earnings threshold, set at 150 percent of the official poverty line, Sheak and Morris estimate that more than 50 million people were subemployed in 1999.[120]

Though pertaining to an earlier period, this finding conveys an important message. While the jobs crisis has been worsening over the past decade, the problems of job availability and job quality, as Sheak and Morris demonstrate, are long-standing. Even in the best of times—as in the case of the booming late 1990s—there exists a massive shortfall of adequately paying jobs. While the 2007–2009 financial meltdown and its aftermath have aggravated the difficulties people experience in securing stable employment, the Great Recession is not the ultimate cause of the present-day shortage of employment opportunities. The current jobs crisis, rather, is an outgrowth of the normal functioning of the American economic system, particularly in the configuration this system has taken since the 1970s. This is precisely what makes poverty a structural problem. It originates from political and economic forces limiting the availability of good jobs. Instead of asking what is wrong with poor people that they do not want to work, the structural perspective poses a better question: What is wrong with the American political economy that millions of people cannot find a job that pays a decent wage?

CONCLUSION

In September 2016 presidential candidate Donald Trump promised, if elected, to create 25 million new jobs over the next decade.[121] He offered no

details at the time, but he deserves some credit at least for implicitly acknowledging the existence of a serious jobs shortage. With his ill-conceived
infrastructure program in a state of limbo, President Trump, to the extent job
creation is still on the agenda, appears to think that corporate tax cuts, deregulation, and redrawn trade agreements will be sufficient. [122] But no matter
how far the Trump administration might go in lowering taxes for the rich and
freeing American business from government regulation, the private sector on
its own, as the record of the past half century attests, cannot generate anywhere near the number of good jobs needed to accommodate the supply of
potential workers. It is not an impossible task to create the millions of new
jobs we need now and into the future. But this would require a genuine
commitment to a full employment policy and a greatly enlarged public sector. Overcoming the current jobs crisis and ensuring meaningful employment
for every willing worker is achievable only through a guaranteed jobs program of some kind, with government serving as the employer of last resort,
something along the lines of the Works Progress Administration established
during the New Deal era. [123] In the current political context, of course, especially when the chief priority is to shrink government rather than expand it,
an audacious jobs policy along these lines is unlikely to receive serious
consideration. Things change, however, and the looming danger of an enduring and worsening jobs shortage, the effects of which are already being felt
all around the country, might yet give rise to a constituency willing to support, or even demand, a more far-reaching, full-employment program.

Chapter Six

The Political System and Poverty

THE POLITICS OF POVERTY

Government is a pervasive force in society. Public officials, elected and appointed, exercise authority on a wide range of matters from international trade to criminal justice, from health care to housing, from education to retirement, and from the environment to national security. Executive orders, court rulings, and legislative measures establish—to the detriment of some and the benefit of others—innumerable procedures, regulations, and laws that dictate, among other things, the distribution of the tax burden; the disbursement of government revenues; eligibility requirements for social programs and subsidies; the prerogatives and obligations of businesses and unions; the organization and operation of election systems and political parties; and the rights and responsibilities of employers and employees, producers and consumers, creditors and debtors.

Through these and countless other means, government sets forth the rules of the game. These inevitably favor some interests over others. The normal functioning of the political system unavoidably allocates costs and benefits, powers and privileges. Everything government does—whether at the federal, state, or local level—redistributes resources and opportunities. The share of the economic pie we each receive is not proportionate to some combination of cognitive ability, work effort, and human capital. It is instead a product of myriad social conflicts, political choices, legislative battles, and court cases, past and present. As we saw in the previous chapter, the state of the economy shapes our economic outcomes and, as this chapter shows, so too does government policy.[1]

Who wins and who loses in the political process reflects the balance of power between contending groups. Government is most responsive to those who speak loudest. If people have plenty of time and money, if they benefit from social status and insider connections, they can effectively turn up the volume for their side. They can publicize political causes, attract the attention of the news media, finance and manage advocacy groups, lobby legislators, and get candidates elected to office. Poorer Americans cannot so easily make themselves heard. On top of their many other disadvantages, they suffer from a shortage of political assets. This is an important cause of poverty. Poor people lack money, but they also lack political power, and one reason they lack money is precisely *because* they lack political power.

Whether we have more or less poverty in the United States depends on a multitude of political factors. Both through what it does and what it refrains from doing, government causes the rate of poverty to sometimes rise and sometimes fall, and it makes the lives of the poor sometimes better and sometimes worse. Fluctuations in the amount and severity of poverty mirror changes in government policy, and the composition of government policy, in turn, reflects the alignment of political forces. Poverty is an economic problem, as we saw in the previous chapter, and it is a political problem as well. To understand the dynamics of poverty, therefore, rather than dwelling on the characteristics and behavior of the poor, it is more productive to examine the structure and functioning of our political institutions, the mobilization and exercise of political power, and the causes and consequences of government policy.

WE'RE NUMBER ONE: THE UNITED STATES IN COMPARATIVE PERSPECTIVE

Compared to other developed nations, whether looking at income or at wealth, the United States has an exceptionally high level of inequality. The gap between America's rich and poor has also widened more over the past several decades than elsewhere in the industrialized world.[2] The United States has an inordinately large poverty population as well. In 2000 the poverty level dropped to a near record low, but even so, the United States at the turn of the century had a poverty rate higher than any other affluent nation.[3] Since then, with the recession of 2001, followed by a jobless recovery, and the Great Recession of 2007–2009, followed by yet another stubbornly anemic recovery, the rate of poverty has increased substantially and remains much higher than the cross-national norm. In 2014, 17 percent of Americans fell below the poverty line, compared to an average rate of 11 percent for thirty-six other developed countries. American children have it even worse, with a poverty rate of 20 percent, well more than twice the level found in Norway, Denmark, Finland, Iceland, Switzerland, South Korea, and Sweden, and greater also than in France, at 12 percent, and Germany, at 10 percent.[4] We are indeed number one. Measured against other advanced countries, the rich in the United States are richer and the poor are poorer and more numerous.[5]

As we saw in the previous chapter, economic forces play a major role in the perpetuation of American poverty. But politics matters, too. Relative to our peers, policy makers in the United States have been less than zealous in their response to problems of inequality and poverty. As a percentage of GDP, government spending on assistance to low-income households is lower than in other developed countries. The United States ranks at or near the bottom for public expenditures on (1) income support policies targeted to the working-age population; (2) unemployment compensation; (3) benefits for families with children, including child allowances; (4) child care and early education; (5) support for the sick and the disabled; and (6) labor market programs, including job training and public job creation.[6] In addition, many other countries have a higher minimum wage and labor market regulations that do more to protect the rights and safeguard the living standard of the working class.[7] Unlike Americans, most Europeans and Canadians also have universal health care, guaranteeing access to medical attention, and they are eligible for paid parental leave.[8] Poverty is worse in the United States than in other developed nations not only because of the prevalence of low-wage work, but also because the United States devotes far less money to social programs for low-income families and working-age adults.[9] As David Grusky and his collaborators observe, the United States not only has a "distinctly unequal" distribution of income and wealth, it also has a "distinctly anemic safety net."[10]

We can assess more precisely the efficacy of government social welfare programs by comparing the "posttransfer" rate of poverty and the "pretransfer" rate of poverty. Pretransfer poverty is calculated by counting the share of the population whose income falls below the poverty line *before* adding in the effects of government benefits and taxes. Posttransfer poverty is calculated by counting the share of the population whose income falls below the poverty line *after* adding in the effects of government benefits and taxes. The difference between the posttransfer rate and the pretransfer rate measures the antipoverty effectiveness of government policy. This before and after comparison tells us how much government contributes to the reduction of poverty.

By international standards, the antipoverty effectiveness of government policy in the United States is astonishingly low. Janet Gornick and Markus Jäntti report that the United States ranks close to the bottom among twenty-four "high-income" countries in the extent of poverty reduction achieved through tax and spending policies.[11] Similarly, Karen Jusko, based on an analysis of thirteen developed countries, finds that the United States ranks last in its "poverty relief ratio," a measure of the level of support provided to low-income households relative to their needs. The American safety net, her data reveal, is relatively ineffective, leaving "significant needs unmet."[12] Platitudes about "big government" notwithstanding, social expenditures for the poor in the United States, and for poor families with children in particular, are among the lowest in the western world.[13]

Conservative critics maintain that government programs intended to help the poor have the perverse effect of causing more poverty.[14] The reality is quite the opposite. Cross-national data demonstrate that social welfare policies reduce poverty, and generous policies reduce poverty a lot.[15] While government in the United States has not won as much ground in the war on poverty as other countries, this is more from lack of trying than anything else. The simple story is this: when government allocates more resources to fighting poverty, the result is fewer poor people and less economic hardship; when government allocates fewer resources to fighting poverty, the result is more poor people and greater economic hardship. Other industrialized nations have less poverty for the obvious reason that their governments do more to help the poor.

Poverty in the United States is not an intractable social problem; it is not a by-product of uncontrollable demographic forces; it is not the outcome of inviolable economic laws; and it is not the result of Americans being unusually deficient in intelligence, values, or skills. Poverty, fundamentally, is a political phenomenon, an outgrowth of government policy. Poverty remains high because the level of political commitment to assisting the poor remains low. Why is the United States so much less successful at combating poverty than other industrial nations? "It's simple," Timothy Smeeding says. "We choose to tolerate a lot more poverty than do other countries."[16] This of course begs the question of who precisely this "we" is and why "we" make the political choices we make. Nevertheless, cross-national studies of tax, spending, labor market, and social welfare policies demonstrate that explicit political decisions decisively affect the extent of poverty in society and the severity of the hardships experienced by the poor. The problem of poverty cannot be explained by reference to individual deficiencies. To understand the persistence of poverty in the United States, we need to shift our focus from the values and behaviors of the poor to the workings of American political institutions and the forces that shape government policy.

THE STRUCTURE OF THE AMERICAN POLITICAL SYSTEM

Though most countries in the industrialized world are nominally democratic, their governing systems differ. Some are more genuinely representative than others, more responsive to the needs of ordinary citizens, and more open to egalitarian social reforms. The American political system, contrary to the popular image, falls well short of conventional "democratic standards."[17] Compared to those in Western Europe, political institutions in the United States favor the rich over the poor, business over labor. They are unique also in the extent to which they limit the exercise of majority rule and create an "inequality-inducing" bias in government policy.[18] The institutional features of American politics help explain why the rate of poverty remains persistently high and why governing officials, even in a period of skyrocketing inequality, fail to enact compensatory tax and spending measures. The two-party, winner-take-all election system, the absence of Left political parties, a bicameral legislature, the presence of multiple veto points and elaborate checks and balances, partisan gerrymandering, a federal system that divides political power between the central government and the states, and the distorting effect of money in the political process—these and other characteristics of the American political system weaken democracy and constrain the capacity of government to fight poverty and promote equality.

The American Election System

Elections in most European democracies operate according to one or another system of proportional representation.[19] Though the procedures vary from one country to the next, the basic principle underlying this type of system is straightforwardly democratic: political parties are allocated legislative seats according to their share of the vote. A party that wins 20 percent of the votes receives approximately 20 percent of the seats in the legislature. This election method encourages the formation of multiple political parties, and it enables minority parties, including labor and socialist parties, to participate effectively in the exercise of political power. Proportional representation offers voters more choices, opens up political debate to a wider range of views, and allows the working class and the poor to gain a real voice in the legislative process. It also engenders government policies more favorable to the interests of less-advantaged citizens. Social welfare expenditures, for example, are significantly higher in countries where legislators are elected through proportional representation.[20]

The principal method for choosing legislators in the United States, by contrast, is the single-member-district, winner-take-all system.[21] In the House of Representatives, for example, candidates in 435 separate geographically defined districts compete for office every two years. The winning candidate in each district is the one receiving the most votes. This sounds very democratic, but it can produce perversely undemocratic outcomes. For example, if a single party receives 51 percent of the votes in every district election in a state, that party would get 100 percent of the legislative seats, leaving almost half of the electorate without anyone to speak for their interests. This procedure for selecting legislative members violates the principle of fair representation. It "tends to overrepresent majority constituencies and under-represent minority constituencies." The winner-take-all system yields governing bodies that do not truly reflect voter preferences.[22]

Political parties operating under the winner-take-all formula are viable only if they are consistently capable of attracting the support of a majority of the electorate. This voting system is usually coupled with a two-party political structure, such as in the United States, where the only real choice is between the Republicans and the Democrats. A vote for a third party is typically a wasted vote, and the supporters of such parties, even though they may constitute a sizable percentage of the populace, cannot normally expect to gain representation in the legislative arena. The winner-take-all election system thus inhibits the formation of parties on the left that can usually be counted on to support egalitarian causes, and it favors the appearance of more conservative political regimes. Cross-national studies show that multi-party proportional representation systems typically give rise to left-center governments that favor redistribution, while majoritarian two-party systems typically give rise to right-center governments that oppose redistribution.[23] American-style electoral institutions hinder social democratic and leftist political parties from gaining a presence in government, thus weakening the influence of constituencies likely to press for and benefit from more expansive and generous tax and spending policies. This explains, in part, why social welfare expenditures in the United States are relatively stingy and why levels of poverty and inequality are relatively high.[24] The essential reality is this: the American voting system, through its effects on the distribution of political power, causes poor people in the United States to be worse off than their counterparts in other modern democratic societies.

Small-State Bias and Partisan Gerrymandering

Each of the fifty states is represented by two senators, regardless of the size of its population. This system produces a small-state bias, with voters in less-populous states having more of a say than voters in more-populous states. Consider, for example, that the approximately 40 million people living in the twenty-two smallest states have a total of *forty-four* senators representing their interests, while the approximately 40 million people living in California have only *two* senators representing their interests.[25] This gross malapportionment corrupts the principle of equal representation and violates the democratic ideal of "one person, one vote."[26] And since less-populous states also tend to be disproportionately white, rural, and conservative, the small-state bias results in the overrepresentation of Republicans as well. The GOP's share of Senate seats exceeds by a wide margin its share of the national popular vote. Conservative lawmakers are thus awarded political power beyond what is consistent with voter preferences and democratic principles.[27]

The practice of gerrymandering adds to the undemocratic distortions built into the American election system. Every ten years, with the completion of the decennial census, electoral districts are redrawn to account for population shifts. Though this could be done by nonpartisan bodies, redistricting in the United States is typically the responsibility of state legislatures. The majority party in any particular state is thus periodically given the opportunity to stack the electoral deck—to strategically slice and dice congressional districts with the aim of maximizing its own voting power and minimizing the voting power of the opposition. For example, a "red" state legislature might seek to dilute the influence of likely Democratic voters (e.g., African Americans) by sprinkling them across several districts ("cracking"), thus limiting the number of districts in which Democratic candidates can win a sufficient number of votes (typically a majority) to claim a seat in the state legislature or the House of Representatives. Or they might concentrate likely Democratic voters in a handful of districts ("packing"), sacrificing these to give Republicans an edge throughout the rest of the state. These examples are illustrative, but appropriate too, because the GOP in recent years, outmaneuvering the Democratic Party, has attained political preeminence at the state and national levels by successfully exploiting the opportunities made available through gerrymandering.

Shaken by Obama's victory in 2008, Republican operatives, looking ahead to the midterm election, went on the offensive. With a $30 million war chest, they launched a precisely targeted campaign to win gubernatorial elections and secure majorities in state legislatures. A big victory in 2010, they recognized, with district lines due to be redrawn that year, would give the GOP control over redistricting. This is precisely what happened. And in subsequent electoral contests, the Republican Party has been able to achieve a commanding position in the House of Representatives and in statehouses around the country. In the 2012 election, for example, the first with the new redistricting in place, Republicans added thirty-three seats in the House, even though Democratic candidates overall received 1.4 million more votes than Republican candidates.[28] Gerrymandering—with one political party capturing seats in governing bodies out of proportion to its share of the popular vote—perverts the system of representative democracy and adds to the rightward tilt of American politics. The combination of small-state bias and partisan gerrymandering, in sum, undermines the principle of majority rule, magnifies the influence of conservatives in Congress, and solidifies the state and national legislative power of a Republican Party that has demonstrated little sympathy toward the working class and the poor.

Checks and Balances

The American political system consists of three independent branches of government—the executive, the legislative, and the judicial. It has two congressional chambers—the House and the Senate—and a legislative process that operates according to a byzantine set of rules and procedures. Legislative proposals are shuffled back and forth through numerous committees and subcommittees in both the House and the Senate, and they also require the approval of the president and sometimes the courts. This complex arrangement of separated powers, established less to promote than to restrain democracy, results in a law-making process that is prone to gridlock.[29] In the American political system—described by Francis Fukuyama as a "vetocracy"—there are a million ways for a bill to die.[30] The parliamentary and unicameral systems that are common in Europe, where political authority is less fragmented and where policy initiatives only have to be approved by one elected body, are more transparent and offer fewer opportunities for powerful special interest groups to block redistributive reforms.[31]

The American system of checks and balances causes three kinds of distortions. First, it creates an unlevel legislative playing field. The multilayered policy-making process gives an edge to wealthy donors, business interests, and other well-organized constituencies that benefit from political access, insider knowledge, and personal ties to lawmakers. Powerful lobbyists and advocacy groups have numerous opportunities to quash, or at least declaw, threatening policy measures. Congressional initiatives promising to deliver comprehensive reforms are thus progressively watered down as they wind their way through a labyrinthine legislative process.[32]

Second, the maze of checks and balances, along with other institutional and procedural obstacles to majority rule, favors slow and incremental change, creating a powerful status quo bias.[33] In the American political system, it is easier to *stop* something from happening than to *make* something happen. The legislative process in the United States is designed for small ball rather than the home run. Fundamental reforms are difficult to achieve, not only because organized interest groups possess veto power, but also because policy making is so much a product of compromise, concession, and accommodation. When lawmakers are not simply kowtowing to the interests of economic elites, legislative procedures funnel policy formation toward the moderate middle, weeding out strong measures that might really make a difference in the lives of the poor.

Third, the status quo bias in American politics is less of an obstruction when powerful business groups press for new legislation to promote deregulation, cutbacks in social programs, or tax cuts for the rich. But when a transformation in the economic environment threatens the well-being of millions of working Americans—precisely what has happened since the

1970s—political paralysis sets in with a vengeance. The result is what Jacob Hacker and Paul Pierson call "drift": the "systematic, prolonged failures of government to respond to the shifting realities of a dynamic economy." The problems of inequality and poverty have grown worse over the past several decades partly because the combination of corporate influence, political grid-lock, and an energized congressional right wing has prevented the updating of social policy to meet the new demands of a changing and increasingly insecure socioeconomic environment.[34]

The do-nothing tendency of American government advantages the big winners in the economic lottery, those who profit most from market condi-tions. Unlike the majority of ordinary Americans, the wealthy, as Charles Noble argues, have less need for "an active government on their side." They already reap huge rewards in the private economy. The political process further bolsters their dominant economic position by empowering them also to "stop other people from using government to claim their fair share." The American political structure gives privileged groups a multitude of means and opportunities to thwart legislation intended to achieve a more equitable distribution of income and wealth.[35]

Federalism

In most western democracies, the bulk of policy-making authority is vested in the central government. Political power in the United States, by contrast, is divided between federal and state governments. Under this arrangement, called "federalism," each state possesses autonomous authority on a wide range of matters, including education, welfare, taxation, and the minimum wage. Instead of having uniform laws that apply equally to everyone, citi-zens' rights and responsibilities vary according to the state in which they happen to live.[36]

Federalism impedes efforts to fight poverty and reduce inequality by reinforcing the political system's inherent probusiness and status quo biases. First, federalism diminishes the power of the national government, thus limit-ing its ability to undertake large-scale social reforms. With its fragmented lines of authority and multiple veto points, American federalism favors de-fenders of the status quo over advocates of social change. The dispersed nature of political power, with fifty states having a place at the table, makes government slow to respond to social problems, creates many points of ac-cess for corporate groups to block legislation harmful to their interests, and lessens the ability of reform-minded movements to mobilize and target their typically limited resources.[37] Second, state governments, even more so than the central government, are vulnerable to the influence of business interests. In a capitalist economy in which private business firms control investment decisions, state officials are particularly sensitive to corporate preferences and constrained to avoid legislation—including redistributive tax and spend-ing measures—that might prompt businesses to locate or relocate in another and more accommodating state. Third, state governments, the majority of which are now under Republican control, are also susceptible to corporate-backed lobbies, including the Chamber of Commerce and the Koch brothers' Americans for Prosperity. As Gordon Lafer documents in an eye-opening new book, these organizations, among others coordinated by the American Legislative Exchange Council (ALEC), bring together conservative state lawmakers and donors from the country's largest corporations. Operating in relative invisibility, ALEC has undertaken a highly successful stealth cam-paign to advance the corporate agenda by directly participating in the formu-lation of probusiness legislation at the state level. The chief objectives of this powerful corporate network include the destruction of unions, both public sector and private sector; the weakening or elimination of labor protections, including rules governing workplace safety and the use of child labor; the privatization of public services, including education; and cutbacks in social expenditures for welfare, food stamps, unemployment compensation, and health care.[38]

The typical argument in favor of federalism and "states' rights" is that government is best that governs closest to the people. This justification is heard frequently today from political operatives on the right pushing to shrink the size of the federal government and transfer an increasing number of responsibilities to state governments. But in the past few years, when "blue" cities in "red" states have enacted progressive municipal ordinances—paid parental leave laws or a minimum wage increase, for example—conser-vative state legislators, rather than embracing this expression of local control, have instead invoked "preemption" laws. These laws empower states to block or overturn legislation passed by cities—despite city governments be-ing even closer to the people than state governments. The right of employers to dictate terms to their workforce, it appears, trumps the virtue of decentral-ized government.[39]

Poverty is a structural problem, due not only to the structure of the American economic system, but also to the structure of the American political system. The persistence of poverty in the United States is partly the by-product of long-standing political institutions that amplify the power of business, under-mine the principle of majority rule, inhibit the formation of leftist political parties, and impede efforts to achieve egalitarian reforms. The very organiza-tion of the political system marginalizes the interests of poorer Americans and prevents enactment of the sort of government policies that might move us down the path toward a more equal and just society.

THE POLITICAL MOBILIZATION OF BUSINESS

The American political system has a built-in conservative bias, with policy makers largely ignoring the problem of poverty. Disadvantaged groups are not typically able to attract much attention through normal political channels. Government tends to be receptive to their needs only when, through such means as protests, strikes, demonstrations, and boycotts, they cause enough social disruption to force themselves into the political spotlight, as was the case with the civil rights movement of the 1950s and 1960s, and as is the case today in battles around the country to increase the minimum wage.

Since the 1970s the naturally rightward slant of American politics has tilted even further to the right, and government policy, marred by a long history of negligence toward the poor, has turned downright punitive. Just as the early 1970s marked an economic watershed, these years also marked a political watershed. At the same time employers were undoing the implicit social contract of the postwar years, a parallel power shift was under way in the political system. This growing imbalance of power gradually gave rise to a right turn in fiscal, tax, monetary, and regulatory policy. Over the past four decades, as a changing economy has made life harder for low-income households and riskier for most Americans, government in the United States has exacerbated the problem by pursuing a political agenda that rewards the haves and penalizes the have-nots.

Corporate America in the early 1970s found itself besieged from all sides: growing international competition; declining profits; and political setbacks at the hands of consumer, environmental, and labor groups.[40] Business leaders were alarmed by the direction the country seemed to be going. As one executive put it: "If we don't take action now we will see our own demise. We will evolve into another social democracy."[41] And take action they did. In response to what they perceived to be a heightened threat to their political and economic standing, business groups launched a well-financed and multifaceted counteroffensive.

Beginning in the 1970s, corporate leaders and wealthy individuals entered a period of sustained political activism.[42] They poured millions of dollars into "advocacy advertising" to sell the public on the virtues of big business and the evils of big government, on the merits of the free market and the malevolence of trade unions. To shore up the ideological case for the corporate agenda, they doled out truckloads of money to conservative think tanks, including the newly created Heritage Foundation.[43] Business leaders became more actively involved in electoral politics as well, increasing their financial commitment to corporate political action committees (PACs). They also adopted a more aggressive strategy for disbursing campaign contributions. Rather than playing it safe by giving money to both Democrats and Republicans, they reserved funds for candidates outspoken in their support for probusiness policies. [44] Through these means and others, corporate America sought to smash organized labor, eliminate government regulations, lower the tax burden on the rich, and reduce spending on social welfare programs. Under the Trump administration, and with the increasing "radicalization of the Republican Party," this offensive—intended "to reverse decades of economic and social policy by any means available"—continues with a renewed virulence. [45]

THE POLITICAL MARGINALIZATION OF THE WORKING CLASS AND THE POOR

The rightward power shift under way since the 1970s is due not only to the political mobilization of corporate America and its allies, but also to a concomitant decrease in the organized power and political influence of ordinary Americans. While business has become stronger, countervailing forces have become weaker. The political playing field is stacked heavily in favor of the affluent. Consider, for example, the class-skewed pattern of political participation. Compared to wealthier Americans, those on the lower end of the income distribution are less likely to vote, join political organizations, donate time and money to political campaigns, or engage in other forms of political activity. The political participation gap between the rich and the poor is large, more so in the United States than in other democratic nations, and by some measures it is growing. These "disparities in political voice," Kay Schlozman and her colleagues state, are "substantial" and "persistent," so much so that they undermine the conditions required for political equality. [46]

In recent decades a considerable number of Americans, more so those in the lower half of the income distribution, have withdrawn from political life and community affairs or have been shut out, leaving an open field for powerful business groups and special interest organizations. [47] What accounts for this rising level of political and civic disengagement? Robert Putnam proposes one answer. Americans born since the 1940s, he claims, unlike the public-spirited generation that came of age during World War II, have failed to acquire enduring habits of political involvement. Due especially to the isolating effects of television, postwar generations have come to live lives that are more private than public, more personal than political. [48] Robert Dahl cites a related factor. Americans today, he argues, prodded by advertisers to envy and emulate the rich and the famous, have abandoned a "culture of citizenship" in favor of a "culture of consumerism." [49] We talk about our possessions, not our politics, what to buy, not who to vote for. Instead of attending political meetings, we visit the shopping mall. To other critics, the current practice of journalism is the culprit. Americans have become disaffected and depoliticized by news programming geared toward sensationalism, scandals, celebrities, and feel-good human-interest stories. Reporters do a poor job of keeping citizens interested and informed. And the media's often negative and disparaging coverage of government and politicians fuels a climate of political cynicism and apathy.[50] Robert McChesney and John Nichols agree with this assessment, but they draw attention to a deeper problem: the decay of the "democratic infrastructure." A healthy democracy, they argue, cannot survive in a political climate in which elites rule, money talks, and ordinary people have no real voice. Americans have not so much withdrawn from democratic politics as they have been "expunged." The end result is a "citizenless democracy," with an increasingly disaffected public inclined—not without reason—to believe the system is rigged, politicians are untrustworthy, and government is corrupt.[51] Frederick Solt arrives at a similar conclusion. Increasing economic inequality, he argues, by enhancing the political influence of the rich and undermining political equality, causes less-affluent citizens to become disengaged from a political process in which they are deprived of any real power.[52]

The class bias in political representation and government policy is the product of a political environment that disadvantages and disempowers the working class and the poor. In what follows, I discuss in somewhat greater detail five additional changes in the political landscape since the 1970s that have contributed to the political marginalization of low-income Americans.

The Decline of Organized Labor

In 2016 only 10.7 percent of wage and salary employees in the United States were represented by a labor union, and in the private sector only 6.4 percent of workers were union members, down from more than one-third in the mid-1950s.[53] The rate of unionization is higher in most other industrialized nations. European countries also have centralized wage-setting institutions. This adds to the influence of organized labor, as wage settlements negotiated by unions also apply to much of the nonunionized labor force. By contrast, only a relatively small percentage of American workers are protected by collective bargaining agreements. The weakness of labor unions in the United States, and the correspondingly heightened imbalance of power between employers and employees, is among the chief factors explaining why problems of poverty and inequality are worse in this country than in other developed nations.[54] State-level analyses also reveal a relationship between union density and economic outcomes. States and regions in the United States with higher levels of unionization have lower rates of household poverty, higher rates of intergenerational mobility, and a larger middle class.[55]

The decline of unions is good for business, but bad for workers, and it is bad for American democracy as well. Though they have not always lived up to their promise, labor unions, especially when they are allied with civic associations and community groups, perform a variety of essential political functions. They help ensure that government is accountable to the public, serves the needs of the broad electorate, and operates according to the rule of law.[56] At their best, furthermore, labor unions draw attention to the hardships experienced by working Americans, expose mistreatment in the workplace, offer members the opportunity to develop their abilities as citizens, mobilize low-income voters typically neglected by the major political parties, provide support for left-liberal political candidates, lobby in support of a stronger welfare state, and keep economic justice issues alive on the political agenda. Because labor unions "serve as the only truly important political 'voice' of lower- and middle-status people," their presence also contributes to preserving some degree of political equality.[57] Without the backing of organized labor, working Americans lack the institutional means to express their political preferences in the public sphere. Unions constitute an indispensable counterweight, setting limits on business's ability to convert its massive economic power into political power. Indeed, in a capitalist society, in which large corporations occupy a dominant economic position, a strong labor movement is vital to the functioning of democratic government.

The weakened condition of organized labor in the United States has not only eroded workers' bargaining power in the economic system, it has also altered the configuration of political power. Unions today lack the political influence they possessed in the 1950s and 1960s, when membership levels were higher. They are less effective at turning out voters to support proworker candidates, less capable of exerting pressure through strikes or social protests, less influential within the Democratic Party, and less able to represent the interests of wage-earning Americans in the political system. With the decline of union power, business groups and their political and ideological allies have obtained a stranglehold over government policy on core economic issues. International trade, workplace health and safety, labor law, the minimum wage, and social welfare policy—on these and other issues critical to the economic well-being of ordinary people, the interests of corporate America have come to predominate over those of the working class and the poor.

The Transformation of American Liberalism

In the 1970s and after, the "class content of American liberalism underwent a profound shift," with middle-class professionals displacing blue-collar workers as the chief constituency of the Democratic Party.[58] This development was partly due to the decline of organized labor, but it resulted also from the emergence of a new constellation of liberal organizations embodying the growing concerns of the more-educated public. These organizations, including environmental and consumer groups, raised awareness on vital matters, but their ascendancy also significantly altered the legislative priorities of the

Democratic Party. According to Jeffrey Berry, the citizens' groups that have appeared on the scene since the 1970s, groups that nowadays define the liberal agenda, are "focused largely on issues unconnected to the problems of the poor, the disadvantaged, or even the working class."[59] This "new liberalism," fixated on "postmaterial" and quality-of-life issues, Berry argues, has diverted attention from problems of poverty and economic inequality.[60] In its eagerness to mobilize a constituency around the concerns of educated professionals, furthermore, the Democratic Party, as Thomas Frank argues, has conveyed a profound complacency about the trajectory of the US economy and the fate of the millions of Americans who do not have a college degree. The changing configuration of liberalism, and its blindness to issues of growing economic hardship, has left the working class and the poor underrepresented in the political system and underserved by government policy.[61]

The Transformation of American Civic Life

American "civic democracy," according to Theda Skocpol, has also undergone a transformation, one paralleling the evolution of American liberalism.[62] Since the 1970s, she argues, "membership" organizations, which facilitated the civic engagement of less-privileged Americans, have given way to a proliferation of "advocacy" groups. From veterans' groups to trade unions, membership organizations derived their strength from the active involvement of their constituents. They mobilized voters, encouraged public deliberation, and educated people in the art of citizenship. While membership organizations promoted a sort of democracy from below, opening opportunities for popular participation, advocacy organizations, including diverse business, professional, and citizens' groups, have a more elitist cast. They are organized in a "top-down" manner, typically run by a professional staff located in New York or Washington. They depend on fund-raising and the expertise supplied by full-time consultants and lawyers. They focus less on grassroots activism than on research, publicity, lobbying, and litigation. And they are "heavily tilted toward upper-middle-class constituencies." Advocacy organizations have produced benefits for many Americans, but their preeminence reinforces the class bias of political participation and government policy. This "civic transformation," Skocpol believes, has diminished "America's capacity to use government for socioeconomically redistributive purposes," and it has, even if only unwittingly, contributed to the exclusion of social justice issues from the political agenda.[63]

Voter Suppression

While many Americans have more or less voluntarily withdrawn from political life, for others, victims of an ongoing assault on the right to vote, nonparticipation in the electoral arena is a largely involuntary matter.[64] More than 6 million people in the United States, disproportionately black, are barred from voting by felony disenfranchisement laws or, as in the case of Alabama and several other states, are prohibited from voting until they pay off court fees and other "legal financial obligations."[65] Others are denied the right to cast a ballot by duplicitous efforts to suppress voter turnout, with phony warnings of voter fraud and calls for "election integrity" serving as a legitimating cover story. Governing officials in GOP-dominated states, increasingly so since 2010, have sought to bolster a partisan advantage by enacting voter laws deterring certain categories of people—particularly African Americans, but also in some cases students and the elderly—from exercising their citizenship rights. Some states require voters to show an approved photo ID or even proof of citizenship. Others have made it difficult for citizens to register, limited opportunities for early voting, restricted the use of absentee ballots, closed polling places in selective locations, reduced hours for voting, conducted partisan purges of voting rolls, or deceitfully deterred voters by getting them to falsely believe they lack a valid ID.[66] Other people are hindered from voting because they can't get away from work or can't afford to stand in line for hours waiting for their turn. Voter suppression is a partisan issue. Republicans benefit from low turnout; Democrats benefit from high turnout. We are becoming a "two-tiered democracy," Ari Berman argues, "a country where it's harder to vote in Republican-controlled states and easier to vote in Democratic ones."[67]

The Politics of Race

Racism and racial resentment, by obscuring common economic interests across racial lines, also contribute to the political weakness of the working class and the poor.[68] The enduring pattern of social and residential segregation, the persistence of racial stereotypes, the recent appeal to white identity, and the pervasive use of racially coded political rhetoric impede solidarity, causing struggling white workers to vent their anger at African Americans and immigrants rather than the plutocrats who run the country. Racism has the consequence of concealing the fact that low-income white people and low-income black people "suffer under the same regime of inequality." It serves as a "ready-made propaganda weapon for use against the aspirations of the great majority of working Americans."[69] The political ramifications of this racial divide are especially severe because African Americans and Hispanics make up a disproportionate share of the poor, and they loom even larger in the public perception of poverty. It is difficult to rally popular enthusiasm for a renewed war on poverty or a concerted drive to create a more equal society when the white majority suspects that undeserving minorities will be the primary beneficiaries. The politics of race undercuts the politics of redistribution.[70] The racial divide in the United States and the recent upsurge in white nationalism and white racial hostility, inflamed by Donald Trump both before and after his election to the presidency, make poor people, the minority poor in particular, easy targets of scapegoating; lessen the ability of ordinary citizens to band together for a common cause; and undermine support for policies to combat poverty, inequality, and injustice.[71]

The decline of unions, the changing face of liberalism, the transformation of civic life, voter suppression, and the politics of race—for these and many other reasons, the working class and the poor are unable to exert much sustained political influence, further tilting the political system in favor of business over labor. Working Americans are not totally without power, of course, and they have even managed to win some significant victories in recent years. At state and local levels, for example, campaigns to increase the minimum wage have achieved notable success. But the big story since the 1970s is how the upward redistribution of political power has intensified the class bias of government policy. This in turn has worsened the economic prospects for less-affluent Americans and has resulted in persistently high levels of inequality and poverty.

THE SYNERGY OF MONEY AND POWER

The synergy of money and power has reinforced the rightward shift in the American political system. Politics in the United States has become a cash game. To be a serious player nowadays, even just to get a seat at the table, requires a huge stack of chips. Poorer Americans are relegated to the role of spectators, and even then they rarely get to observe the big-money games. These are conducted outside the public eye, in corporate boardrooms, the offices of lobbying firms, and the proverbial smoked-filled corridors of government.

In American politics, "money talks," and since the 1970s it talks louder than ever.[72] Making matters worse, money has become a more powerful political force at the same time inequality in the distribution of income and wealth has escalated. The result is a vicious cycle. Economic inequality causes political inequality, as the rich use their money to buy political access and shape the policy agenda. Political inequality causes economic inequality, as the rich use their political influence to amass even more money. And so on. This fusion of money and power threatens to make government more than ever the servant of the wealthy and threatens to make the wealthy more than ever a dominant political class. Gary Burtless and Christopher Jencks take note of this ominous synergy in their assessment of "American inequality." The most worrisome consequence of the growing concentration of income and wealth, they conclude, is its impact "on the distribution of political influence." What are the implications for American democracy, they ask, if the rich can convert their money into political power and so manipulate government policy to increase even further their share of the nation's resources?[73]

Money talks, but what really matters is what it says. If what the wealthy want from government is more or less the same as average Americans, then the influence of big money, though contrary to the democratic ideal, is less consequential. In fact, however, the preferences and priorities of the richest Americans, the top 1 percent or the top 10 percent, differ significantly from those of the general public. On economic issues particularly, those at the top of the economic pyramid are more conservative than the larger population. Compared to other Americans, the wealthy are more in favor of deficit reduction, tax cuts, and reduced spending on social welfare programs, and they are less in favor of a higher minimum wage, government job creation, and national health insurance. To the extent money talks—and rich donors certainly think it does—then government policy on key economic issues will reflect the minority interests of economic elites rather than the majority interests of the general public.[74]

Money enters the political arena through many pathways, but two stand out. First, it takes a lot of money to run a political campaign, giving wealthy donors inordinate influence in determining who competes for elected office. Second, it takes a lot of money to lobby public officials, giving wealthy donors inordinate influence in the day-to-day formulation of government policy. As the role of money in US politics grows, opportunities shrink for meaningful participation by the poor, or even the middle class. Money undermines the democratic ideal of political equality. It empowers the rich way beyond their numbers, and it crowds out the voices of the less affluent, precluding ordinary citizens from achieving equal representation or gaining a fair hearing in the political process.

Candidates for political office who are able to raise money are not guaranteed victory, of course, but if they cannot attract wealthy donors, they cannot effectively compete. Most of the presidential hopefuls in the 2016 election, for example, were "deeply dependent on a small pool of the richest Americans." In the early phase of the campaign, prior to the nominating conventions, the *New York Times* reported that half of all contributions, $176 million, came from just 158 families, most of them "leaning right."[75] In recent decades, at all levels of government and regardless of party affiliation, politicians have become increasingly reliant on private contributions to finance their political campaigns. The price of running for office has skyrocketed as candidates have become dependent on expensive television advertising and the costly advice of polling experts, professional consultants, and public relations specialists. Over the past thirty years, consequently, money has appreciated in value more than time as a resource in political campaigns. This development exacerbates the class bias of the political process. The rich contribute far more to candidates than do less-affluent voters, and the contributions from business exceed those from labor by a ratio of 15 to 1.[76]

Since 2010 court decisions, including the *Citizens United* ruling, have struck down limits on political contributions in the form of "outside money."[77] The predictable result is a dramatic increase in the ability of the wealthy to exploit their financial advantage in the political arena. Outside money includes advocacy and campaign spending by individuals or groups that is not directly coordinated with the organization of any particular candidate. Through super PACs, for example, wealthy political investors, acting independently, can spend an unlimited amount of money on behalf of (or against) candidates of their choice.[78] The rise of super PACs and other vehicles for channeling ever-larger sums of money into the electoral process exacerbates an already present threat: the transformation of American democracy into American "dollarocracy."[79]

Money has a corrosive effect on the electoral process. It narrows the range of viable candidates, the range of issues brought before the public, and the range of voters participating in elections. Private financing of electoral contests, Jay Mandle argues, results in political platforms and debates that poorly reflect the concerns of citizens who cannot afford to make large campaign contributions. This depresses voter turnout, particularly among the low-income population, those most likely to favor and benefit from redistributive social welfare policies. In the United States and other countries where campaigns are funded privately rather than publicly, the rate of voter turnout and the level of government spending on health, education, and pensions are substantially lower. The influence of private money in the electoral process, Mandle concludes, reduces "the scope of democratic choice," limits the parameters of political debate, and engenders government policy that is "biased toward the interests of the wealthy."[80]

Money matters after elections are over, too. Even more so, in fact, if corporate political activity is any indication. For every dollar corporations contribute to political campaigns, they spend thirteen dollars on lobbying.[81] In 2016 the total number of registered lobbyists, hardly any of whom speak for the poor, exceeded eleven thousand, with countless others serving in various unofficial lobbying capacities, and the total amount of money spent on lobbying in that year was approximately $3.15 billion.[82] During the period from 1998 to 2017, the US Chamber of Commerce, contributing more than $1.35 billion, headed the list of top spenders by a wide margin, with most of the other big political investors consisting of trade organizations, business associations, and corporations.[83] From 1998 to 2012, Lee Drutman reports, "between 90 and 95 of the top 100 spending organization have been business organizations."[84] The class bias in organized political participation far exceeds the class bias in individual political participation. Organizations representing business interests, Kay Lehman Schlozman and her colleagues show, account for 72 percent of expenditures on lobbying, with unions, social welfare groups, and public interest groups combined accounting for less than 5 percent of total lobbying expenditures. In "no domain of organized interest activity," they also find, do "organizations that provide services to or political representation of the poor register more than a trace."[85] Why is there so much poverty and inequality in the United States? One reason is the skewed distribution of organized political power. In the high-stakes world of lobbying, the rich dominate and the poor are voiceless.[86]

Corporations and business groups have an army of well-informed, well-connected, and well-financed professional lobbyists to watch over their interests on a daily basis. The poorest of Americans, those most in need of government assistance, partly because they lack an organized political presence, are severely disadvantaged in the high-powered world of pressure politics. They do not have anything like a meaningful chance to participate in the policy arena, and even less do they have an equal say in the formation of government policy. In the competition to gain the ear of legislators, ordinary citizens "speak in a whisper while the most advantaged roar."[87] The result is predictable: the US political system, as one authoritative report concludes, "is a great deal more responsive to the preferences of the rich than to the preferences of the poor."[88]

Recent studies provide striking confirmation of this conclusion, while at the same time raising doubts about the reality of American democracy. In one analysis, Larry Bartels examines the voting behavior of legislators in the House (2011–2013) and the Senate (1989–1995, 2011–2013). The members of both chambers vote mainly on the basis of their political convictions, of course, with Republicans leaning conservative and Democrats leaning liberal. Legislators in the House, he finds, did show some responsiveness to the preferences of low-income voters, but they were twice as responsive to the preferences of the affluent. Senators were more responsive to their constituents, but in a markedly class-biased manner: very responsive to the views of high-income voters, but not "at all responsive to the views of poor constituents." In sum, according to Bartels, the policy preferences of "low-income citizens as a group seem to be getting little or no weight in the policy-making process, whereas the views of affluent people are getting considerable weight."[89] Martin Gilens, in a meticulous assessment of the correspondence between public preferences and policy outcomes, draws a similar conclusion. When there is a divergence between the political preferences of the affluent (the top 10 percent) and the political preferences of middle-income Americans, he finds, the affluent, despite their minority status, consistently emerge as victors in the policy arena. And when the preferences of the affluent and the poor diverge, government is entirely unresponsive to the concerns of the poor. This pattern, Gilens acknowledges—with economic elites exerting unparalleled influence over federal government policy—is consistent with the cynical judgment that the American political system is more of a *plutocracy* than a *democracy*.[90] The phenomenon of unequal democracy is also found at the state level. According to research by political scientists, the policy decisions of state governments, particularly on economic issues, are unresponsive to the political preferences of the low-income citizens. In the American political system, where money plays such an outsized role, the interests of the poor are completely neglected.[91]

Standing outside the legislative process looking in, low-income citizens exert little or no influence; nor do they have much presence *inside* the legislative process. With the rare exception, as Nicholas Carnes shows, men and women from the working class are excluded from positions of political power. Indeed, the number of millionaires in Congress far exceeds the number of those with experience as blue-collar workers. The business of running government is a job held overwhelmingly by the affluent. Of all the people who served in Congress from 1999 to 2008, he finds, only 2 percent had a career in blue-collar work before entering politics. Our unequal democracy is not just a product of which citizens speak the loudest, but also "who's doing the *listening*." The "*shortage of people from the working class in American legislatures*," Carnes argues, "*skews the policy-making process toward outcomes that are more in line with the upper class's economic interests.*"[92] The wealthy have a political advantage because they occupy a privileged position not only outside of government, but inside it as well.

POLICY CONSEQUENCES OF THE POWER SHIFT: ROBIN HOOD IN REVERSE

Individualistic theories, with their narrow focus on the alleged deficiencies of the poor, give insufficient attention to the role played by political forces in causing variations in the rate and severity of poverty. People's economic outcomes are dependent on government, and since the 1970s government policy has become increasingly skewed toward the interests of the rich. The poor are not victims of their own failings so much as they are victims of unresponsive and at times malicious lawmaking bodies. In this era of rising inequality and widespread economic insecurity, rather than stepping in to assist the millions of Americans struggling to keep their heads above water, elected officials have enacted tax, spending, trade, and regulatory measures that only make life harder for the poor and widen the gap between the haves and the have-nots. In the following pages, to illuminate the political aspect of the poverty problem, I briefly examine four important policy arenas: welfare, unemployment insurance, the minimum wage, and labor law. My objective in each case is to illustrate how government leaders over the past three or four decades have turned their backs on the working class and the poor.

Welfare Reform: The War on the Poor

The enactment of the Personal Responsibility and Work Opportunity Reconciliation Act in 1997 was one of the most significant outgrowths of the right turn in American politics. This legislation abolished Aid to Families with Dependent Children and replaced it with a new welfare program, funded by block grants to the states, entitled Temporary Assistance for Needy Families (TANF).[93] Initiated by congressional Republicans, and receiving the eventual approval of the Clinton administration, this overhaul of the welfare system was advertised to combat "welfare dependency" and promote work, marriage, and two-parent families. TANF established time limits, permitting poor mothers to receive benefits for a lifetime total of no more than sixty months, with states allowed to set even shorter limits. In 2015 Arizona reduced the lifetime limit to twelve months.[94] To facilitate a rapid transition to "economic self-sufficiency," TANF also mandated work requirements, forcing poor mothers to get jobs in exchange for their benefits, even if this meant abandoning their education or leaving their children with unreliable care providers. And as a mechanism of enforcement, TANF established a system of sanctions, including reduced-benefit penalties for noncompliance with work rules and other stipulations.[95]

The implementation of TANF resulted in a dramatic decline in the welfare rolls. The number of families receiving cash welfare payments shrank from over 5 million in the mid-1990s to 1.3 million in December 2016. Disturbingly, however, the decline in the welfare caseload continued unabated even as the rate and severity of poverty worsened. Between 2000 and 2012, a period of persistent economic weakness, the number of poor children increased by more than 4 million, the number of poor female-headed households rose by nearly 2.4 million, and the number of people in deep poverty reached a near-record high of more than 20 million.[96] And yet, despite years of increasing economic hardship, the number of families receiving TANF benefits in 2012 was lower than it was in 2000.[97]

What accounts for the seemingly paradoxical decline in the welfare caseload during a decade or so of slow growth, weak job creation, and increasing poverty? Certainly there has been no reduction in the number of needy families or in the number of poor families *eligible* for TANF. What has declined, rather, is the number of eligible families *enrolled* in TANF. In a statement to congress, Kay E. Brown, representing the Government Accountability Office, reported that almost 90 percent of the decrease in the cash assistance caseload in the decade following the enactment of TANF resulted from a decline in the number of eligible families participating in the program.[98] This outcome was largely the product of a deliberate effort on the part of state agencies—now possessing almost complete discretion in the management of the program—to reduce welfare rolls, both by discouraging entry into the program and by hurrying exit out of the program. In Mississippi, to take an extreme example, of the nearly 12,000 low-income residents who applied for TANF, only 167 were approved and enrolled.[99]

With the enactment of welfare reform, cash assistance ceased being an entitlement. Unlike Social Security, under the TANF program, eligibility does not confer a right to benefits. As a result, countless deserving families have been denied aid during difficult times.[100] In the year TANF was enacted, for every one hundred families in poverty, sixty-eight received benefits. As of 2014, that number had fallen to twenty-three.[101] Single mothers with children and without regular employment are among the neediest of the country's poor, and they are receiving the least assistance from government.[102] One tragic result is that many poor households have fallen into "extreme poverty," living on less than $2 per day per person in total cash income.[103] This brings to light the dark side of welfare reform: the government safety net for poor mothers and their children has been decimated, leaving an increasing number of low-income families to make do on their own.[104]

Not only has the number of poor families receiving TANF benefits declined, but so have benefit levels. The size of the block grant states receive from the federal government was fixed at $16.5 billion in 1996 and has not changed since, not even adjusted for inflation. In addition, since states have considerable flexibility in determining how to use their share of this grant, only part of it—approximately 25 percent—is expended on cash payments to poor families.[105] Most states, furthermore, do not adjust benefit levels to the rate of inflation, so not only are fewer families receiving cash assistance today, but the purchasing power of what little they receive has declined by approximately 20 percent since 1996. In 2015 the monthly payment for a TANF family of three in the median state was $429. And in none of the fifty states do TANF benefits bring families up to even 50 percent of the poverty line.[106]

Studies based on interviews with low-income women, including both current and former TANF recipients, point to numerous additional defects in the reformed welfare system. Poor women have not received adequate help in their efforts to reconcile work-family conflicts, secure decent housing, find affordable and reliable child care, resolve periodic transportation problems, or deal with health-care issues. Nor has the reform of the welfare system helped poor women, if they are able to find jobs at all, escape the low-wage labor market, work their way out of poverty, and attain economic self-sufficiency.[107] Leaders of both political parties, nevertheless, have judged welfare reform a success. This tells us less about the workings of welfare than about the priorities of government policy makers. If the purpose is to reduce the welfare rolls and increase the labor force participation of poor mothers, then welfare reform has been reasonably effective. But if the purpose of a welfare system is to make sure needy families have an adequate income and the opportunity to improve their lives, then welfare reform has been an abysmal failure.

Unemployment Insurance: The Fraying of the Safety Net

The Unemployment Insurance (UI) program, administered and financed jointly by the federal government and the states, was enacted as part of the Social Security Act of 1935. It is intended "to provide temporary partial wage replacement for involuntarily unemployed workers." By propping up consumer demand, it also functions to "stabilize the economy during recessions."[108] The UI program bolsters the bargaining power of workers as well. If they have an unemployment check to fall back on, laid off workers are not quite so desperate to take just any job that comes along. They are free to wait, at least for awhile, for better jobs to appear. By giving workers this modicum of leverage, the UI program contributes to the maintenance of wage standards.[109]

Due to chronic underfunding, exacerbated by the surge in claims during the Great Recession, the UI program has been in a "state of disrepair" for some time.[110] It suffers from another long-standing failing as well. Since state governments have considerable discretion over eligibility requirements and benefit levels, there are substantial inequities across the country, with workers in some states being better served by the program than workers in others.[111] Despite the differences among state programs, however, most, in varying degrees, have certain deficiencies in common.[112]

First, the wages of nonstandard workers, including part-timers, temps, seasonal workers, independent contractors, and others—a population consisting disproportionately of women, racial/ethnic minorities, and younger workers—are, with some exceptions, subject to the payroll tax. But while they may pay into the system, in many states workers employed in these alternative work arrangements are denied benefits by eligibility rules that are, in today's changing occupational world, unreasonable and outdated.[113]

Second, as a result of work-family conflicts, women are disproportionately job "leavers" rather than job "losers."[114] The demands of the caretaking role, such as tending a sick child, may cause women to withdraw temporarily from the workforce. Because they leave their jobs "voluntarily" and for "personal" reasons, women and working mothers in particular face a greater likelihood of being disqualified for unemployment benefits.[115]

Third, eligibility for UI benefits and the monetary value and duration of those benefits are dependent on the work history of the applicant. As administered in many states, this rule unfairly penalizes workers with low hourly wages. To fulfill minimum earnings requirements and qualify for benefits, lower-wage employees have to work more hours prior to losing a job than higher-wage employees. Since 1990 some states have even raised earnings requirements, thus excluding more of the working poor—precisely those most in need—from access to unemployment compensation.[116]

Fourth, workers typically receive unemployment payments for a maximum of twenty-six weeks, though that number is far lower in some states.[117] In the economy of the past couple of decades, however, as evidenced by higher rates of long-term unemployment, and especially since the 2007 recession, it takes more time for laid-off workers to find a new job. In the present economy, periods of unemployment last longer, causing an increasing percentage of UI recipients to exhaust their benefits.[118]

Fifth, benefit levels, averaging around $340 per week in 2016, with significant variation from state to state, typically replace only about half of workers' wages, far less than in most European countries. Even when they receive unemployment compensation, many families in the United States are still left below the poverty line.[119]

With Republican dominance in state governments and the unprecedented political offensive ongoing at the state level by the Chamber of Commerce, Americans for Prosperity, the ALEC, and other corporate-backed organizations, the ability of the UI program to serve its intended purposes is being deliberately undermined. Already, through the efforts of corporate advocates and conservative lawmakers, many states have passed legislation tightening eligibility requirements, cutting benefit levels, and shortening the duration for receiving compensation (currently down to twelve weeks in some states).[120]

The unemployment insurance system in the United States has failed to keep pace with an economy in which fewer and fewer workers have standard forty-hour-a-week jobs. An increasing number of wage earners, especially those most vulnerable to poverty, are denied benefits or are seeing their benefits run out. After reaching a peak of 75 percent in 1975, the recipiency rate—the percent of the officially unemployed population receiving UI benefits—hit a record low of 23.1 percent in December 2014. In thirteen states fewer than one in five jobless workers receive UI benefits, and in Florida, only one in eight do.[121] This is the essential shortcoming of the US unemployment insurance program: "American workers are more vulnerable than ever to involuntary unemployment, yet fewer are protected by UI."[122] A sizable majority of today's unemployed workers are not receiving the assistance they need. In the current economic environment, with secure and decent-paying jobs in short supply, and in the current political environment, with the antigovernment conservatives gaining the upper hand in the policy arena, elected officials have permitted, even promoted, the unraveling of the unemployment safety net, leaving millions of Americans to fend for themselves.

The Minimum Wage: Lowering the Floor

The minimum wage law was created as part of the Fair Labor Standards Act of 1938, a legislative measure intended to curtail "labor conditions detrimental to the maintenance of the minimum standard of living necessary for health, efficiency and general well-being of workers."[123] The minimum wage establishes a floor on hourly earnings. It is not indexed to the rate of inflation, however, so its real value declines over time as the cost of living goes up. This is where politics enters the picture. Whether or not the minimum wage is raised, how often, and by how much is a matter decided by Congress and by state and local legislators. The level of the minimum wage is thus an outgrowth of political struggles, usually pitting low-wage workers and labor groups, with support from the liberal wing of the Democratic Party, against the Republican Party, corporate lobbies, conservative advocates, and employers, particularly small-business owners. How much workers earn, therefore, and the likelihood of their escaping or avoiding poverty, is contingent on the balance of power between contending interests and the inevitably politicized decisions of elected officials. The severity of poverty and the magnitude of economic inequality in the United States are partly by-products of the politics of the minimum wage.[124]

The real (inflation-adjusted) value of the federal minimum wage trended upward throughout the 1950s and 1960s, rising in tandem with productivity growth. It peaked in 1968 at $9.68 per hour (in 2016 dollars), declined somewhat in the 1970s, and then in the 1980s, reflecting the rightward drift of American politics, fell rapidly, dropping almost 30 percent during the Reagan era, with Congress legislating no increase from January 1981 to April 1990. After four modest raises in the 1990s, the last in 1997, the purchasing power of the minimum wage still remained well below its 1968 level. From September 1997 until July 2007, the federal minimum wage was stuck at $5.15 per hour, the longest period without an increase since its inception. Congress finally raised the minimum by 70 cents in 2007, and it reached its current level of $7.25 per hour in 2009, still 25 percent below the 1968 peak.[125] Tipped workers, including waitresses and waiters, are even worse off. They haven't had a raise since 1991. The federal minimum wage for this large and growing category of workers, mostly women, stands at a mere $2.13 per hour.[126]

As of July 2017 twenty-nine states plus the District of Columbia had a minimum wage higher than the federal minimum. The District of Columbia had the highest minimum at $12.50 per hour, with Massachusetts and Washington tied for the highest among states at $11.00 per hour.[127] A number of municipalities around the country have passed ordinances adopting a minimum wage higher than the state minimum. Several cities in California, plus Seattle, Portland, Chicago, and others have a higher local minimum wage already in place or set to take effect at some point over the next few years.[128] Proponents of a higher minimum wage still face a difficult battle, however. Gordon Lafer documents how corporate-backed lobbyists and conservative legislators have fought tenaciously in many locations, successfully blocking cities and states from increasing the minimum wage, barring measures to peg the minimum wage to the rate of inflation, establishing exemptions and subminimum wages for certain industries and categories of workers, and otherwise creating loopholes in the application of the minimum wage law. In addition, in response to minimum wage victories in cities around the country, several Republican-dominated state governments have drawn up "preemption" laws, denying localities the legal right to set their own minimum wage.[129]

Despite rising prices for necessities, including housing, health care, and education, workers making the minimum wage today are paid substantially less than their counterparts in the 1960s and 1970s, and so are millions of other employees whose wages, though higher than the minimum, are affected by the federal standard. American minimum wage workers are also paid substantially less than their counterparts in most other developed counties.[130] Full-time workers earning the federal minimum make approximately $15,000 a year before taxes—$3,500 less than in 1968—not enough even to lift a family of two above the poverty line. They are worse off today than in the past relative to the middle class as well. The hourly wages of workers receiving the minimum in 2016 were 35 percent of the median wage for full-time workers, down from 52 percent in 1968.[131] Not surprisingly, minimum wage workers have also fallen further behind the rich. To cite just one relevant example, the earnings of top CEOs in the restaurant industry in 2013, in which many minimum wage workers are employed, were 721 times the minimum wage.[132]

According to a 2014 survey conducted by the Center for American Progress, 80 percent of respondents, including 67 percent of Republicans, expressed support (58 percent strong support) for an increase in the minimum wage. A 2015 poll also found most Americans favoring a higher minimum, with 75 percent—including 92 percent of Democrats and 53 percent of Republicans—supporting a federal minimum wage of $12.50 by 2020.[133] The many successful campaigns to raise state- and city-level minimum wages, often through ballot initiatives, also attest to public support for a higher minimum. In its continued refusal to raise the federal minimum wage, Congress is *not* responding to the wishes of the electorate. The decline in the real value of the minimum wage since the 1960s testifies to the diminished political power of organized labor, the inordinate political power of business interests in Congress and in the states, and the weakened conditioned of American democracy.

Labor Law: The Assault on Unions and Workers' Rights

Workers in the United States seeking to form unions face "an exceptionally hostile terrain," and this terrain has become even more hostile since the 1980s.[134] The main path to unionization is a National Labor Relations Board election. But prounion employees are disadvantaged in this process because employers have multiple opportunities to subvert fair and democratic elections.[135] And with the aid of union-busting consultants, they have devised an impressive array of union avoidance strategies.[136] Since the 2000s, as documented by Kate Bronfenbrenner, employers have increasingly relied on coercive, retaliatory, and intimidation tactics, including plant closing threats, harassment, and firings.[137] According to a report by John Schmitt and Ben Zipperer, the number of illegal firings of prounion workers during union organizing drives skyrocketed during the 1980s, declined somewhat in the 1990s, and then started climbing again in the 2000s. For the period from 2001 to 2007, they estimate that "union organizers and activists faced a 15 to 20 percent chance of being illegally fired."[138] Employers resort to illegal measures in resisting unionization because labor laws repeatedly go unenforced; and when they are enforced, the penalties are insufficiently costly to deter violations.[139] The combination of weak labor laws and lax enforcement has given rise to a "culture of impunity" in which employers are effectively free to deny workers the right to unionize.[140]

Corporate lobbies have also contributed to the disarming of unions by pushing state legislatures, dominated by the Republican Party since 2010, to enact "right-to-work laws," already in effect in twenty-eight states, and to undo "prevailing wage laws."[141] Right-to-work legislation makes it illegal to require employees who benefit from a union contract to join or pay dues to that union. By creating an incentive for workers to become "free riders"—take the gains from unionization but avoid the costs—right-to-work laws threaten the financial viability of unions and effectively create business-friendly, union-free zones in the states where they are enacted.[142] Prevailing wage laws require that workers employed in publicly funded construction projects receive wage and benefit compensation equivalent to the occupational standards of the local community. The purpose of such laws, currently under attack in many states, is to prevent nonunion contractors from undercutting prevailing wage levels and lowering workers' standard of living.[143]

Employees seeking union representation face daunting obstacles. But the situation is even worse for many categories of workers who are explicitly excluded from labor law protection—including agricultural workers, domestic workers, workers classified as "independent contractors," low-level supervisors, and in some states, public employees.[144] Many part-time and temporary workers, who constitute a large and growing share of the workforce, also do not have the right to unionize.[145] Even when workers, against all odds, manage to form a union, existing labor laws often prevent them from exercising any real power. They are prohibited from participating in secondary boycotts or sympathy strikes, for example, and while they cannot be legally fired for going out on strike, in what amounts to practically the same thing, their jobs can be filled by "permanent replacements."[146]

The playing field is tilted against workers also because of the rightward drift of the courts since the 1980s and at the Supreme Court level since 2005 especially, when John Roberts assumed the position of chief justice. As evident in both its rulings and the ideological convictions of its members, the Roberts Court has "become perhaps the most business-friendly court in recent history."[147] Court cases over the past couple of decades have restricted the regulatory powers of government, impeded the ability of organizers to communicate prounion information to employees, limited collective bargaining rights, made it more difficult for workers and consumers to bring suits against businesses, and denied class-action suits, such as the gender discrimination case *Walmart v. Dukes*.[148]

It is not only when workers participate in union activity that business owners violate their rights and treat them unfairly. Workers on the job, and sometimes in their personal lives as well, are subject to the dictatorial rule of their employers. Depending on the work setting, as Elizabeth Anderson shows, they are denied the right of free speech, are prevented from taking bathroom and meal breaks, face retaliation for lodging complaints against employer abuses, are pressured to support particular political candidates and causes, are subject to surveillance and searches, and are sanctioned for off-duty conduct and lifestyle choices deemed inappropriate by employers.[149] Among the most egregious violations workers experience today is wage theft. Employers steal from their employees because it is profitable to do so, because they can typically get away with it, and because the penalties are minimal if they get caught with their hands in the till. Wage theft takes many forms: paying workers below the legal minimum, denying workers overtime pay, insisting that employees work off the clock, tip stealing by supervisors or managers, illegal deductions from workers' paychecks, and refusing to pay wages earned (a problem for undocumented workers in particular). The annual amount of money stolen from workers though wage theft, as Gordon Lafer observes, is considerable, "far greater than the combined total stolen in all the bank robberies, gas station robberies, and convenience store robberies in the country."[150]

If government authorities and the courts do not support the right of workers to form unions, if they rarely enforce laws protecting workers' rights, and
if employers suffer only minimal penalties for violating the law, then to be
sure, labor laws will be broken. And they have been broken, routinely and
increasingly so over the past several decades. What is most troubling is not
that employers habitually engage in antiunion activities that violate the spirit
and letter of the law or that they are willing to resort to just about any means
to reduce labor costs. This is to be expected of self-interested, profit-max-
imizing business firms. More troubling is that a putatively democratic
government and putatively impartial legal system have become enablers of
this employer malfeasance. In the ongoing and highly successful business
offensive against organized labor and the rights of workers more generally,
government and the courts have effectively lined up against working
Americans. In the current political climate, a product of the rightward shift in
American politics, the right of employers to resist unions and exploit workers
is subject to far more legal protection than is the right of workers to form
unions and be treated fairly.

Government policy since the 1970s has become increasingly imbalanced in
favor of business over labor. This is reflected both in what policy makers
have done and in what they have failed to do. Welfare reform, unemployment insurance, the minimum wage, and labor law—in all these policy areas,
government officials have pursued an agenda that in hard times makes life
even harder for the working class and the poor. The same right-turn story,
ramped up even more since the 2016 election, could be told about tax policy,
monetary policy, and regulatory policy. The conservative, probusiness bias
in American politics is evident also in the refusal of government leaders to
pass the sort of worker- and family-friendly legislation common in most
other advanced industrialized countries, including universal health insurance,
subsidized child care, and paid parental leave.

This is not to say the US government does nothing to help working-class
families. The Earned Income Tax Credit boosts the wages of low-income
workers; food stamps and other nutrition programs help fight hunger; and
Medicaid offers health care to the poor, the disabled, and the elderly.
Contrary to the claims of antigovernment crusaders, moreover, these and
other programs, all currently under attack by the Right, show that government can make a positive difference in the lives of average Americans. In
drawing attention to the class bias of political policy, therefore, we should
not overlook the benefits many people still derive from government programs. And by the same token, we should not underestimate how much low-
income families will be harmed by the ongoing and recently intensified assault on the welfare state.

CONCLUSION

The power shift in American politics underlies the continued refusal of government officials to contemplate policies that might reduce growing inequalities and alleviate economic hardships. The American political system, even more so since the 1970s, is strongly resistant to egalitarian social reforms. This is the case, as we have seen, for an assortment of reasons. Business is exceptionally powerful, organized labor is exceptionally weak, government leaders are unresponsive to the policy preferences of low-income Americans, the working class and the poor are politically marginalized, and the synergy of money and power gives economic elites an overwhelming political advantage. The combination of these factors in a country whose political institutions lean naturally to the right explains why redistributive policies are absent from the political agenda and why levels of inequality and poverty remain so persistently high. In the current political context, poorer Americans lack equitable access to one of the most important means for improving their economic prospects: government. The working class and the poor are not only denied a fair share of the gains from increasing productivity, they are also denied a fair share of the benefits from public policy.

Chapter Seven

The Cultural System and Poverty

HEARTS AND MINDS

An ideological battle is being waged in the United States. In this ongoing culture war, activists on the right and the left are locked in a struggle for the hearts and minds of the American public. On issues ranging from abortion to gay rights, immigration to evolution, health care to climate change, antagonists fight it out in diverse venues of public discourse: the news and entertainment media; court cases; legislative hearings; political campaigns; and meetings of church groups, school boards, and civic organizations. In the trenches of everyday life, too, skirmishes arise between family members, friends, neighbors, classmates, and coworkers. This war of ideas—the expression of conflicting values, interests, and visions of society—is a dynamic force in the political culture and an influence on social policy.

On one important front in this larger culture war, opposing versions of "poverty knowledge" are pitted against one another.[1] The clash of conflicting poverty theories and policy prescriptions resounds in the public sphere, though it is louder at some times than others. Think tanks, business groups, academic experts, political pundits, labor activists, and welfare rights advocates—each weighing in on the plight of the poor—all contend to gain a hearing in the arenas of public opinion and policy formation. The stakes in this battle are high. The winning side at any particular historical moment defines the problem of poverty, sets the terms of debate, and controls the political agenda.

When individuals ponder issues of poverty, inequality, and welfare, their thinking is shaped by the larger cultural context. Ann Swidler envisions the surrounding culture as a "tool kit" of symbolic resources that individuals dip into selectively to construct meanings and devise courses of action.[2] Included

143

within this tool kit is the reigning vocabulary of poverty. Among the terms gaining prominence since the 1970s are "personal responsibility," "self-sufficiency," "family values," "illegitimacy," "underclass," "welfare dependency," "big government," and "makers and takers." These and other keywords dictate the prevailing definition of the poverty problem, the boundaries of respectable disagreement, and the policy responses deemed appropriate.

The cultural tool kit also consists of various "story lines," as Eduardo Bonilla-Silva calls them. These enable us to translate the immense complexity of the social world into commonsense principles and folk theories. The American Dream, the Horatio Alger myth, the narrative of triumph over adversity, and tales of rugged individualism and self-made men—these are among the story lines commonly invoked when Americans are prompted to wonder why some are rich and others poor. Story lines such as these are widely available. They are deposited in our cultural heritage and circulate in movies, television shows, books, magazines, and fairy tales. These story lines equip us with ready-made formulas we "use to make sense of the world, to decide what is right and wrong, true or false, important or unimportant."[3]

As in the case of the economic and political systems, the cultural system is a site of power and conflict. What transpires within this system, and which terminology and story lines win acceptance, determine whether average Americans are informed or uninformed about social issues, whether they perceive the poor as "deserving" or "undeserving," and whether they believe government should do more or less to help disadvantaged groups. The cultural system matters, as people's convictions and sentiments about poverty and welfare shape their political preferences and voting behavior.

This chapter turns the individualistic perspective on its head. In its preoccupation with the culture of the poor, the conventional view ignores the other side of the coin: how the mainstream culture, particularly through its influence on government policy, affects poor people's access to resources and opportunities. After all, a lot hinges on whether ordinary Americans respond to poverty with apathy or outrage, whether they regard the poor with hostility or empathy, and whether they view poverty as an inevitable condition or a resolvable problem. Whether we have more or less poverty and whether the hardships experienced by the poor are more or less severe depend on the temper of middle-class culture.

Because of their narrow focus on the deficiencies of the poor, individualistic theories, as we have seen, fail to recognize adequately how the rate and depth of poverty in the United States depend on power struggles within the economic and political systems. The purpose of this chapter, revealing another weakness of the individualistic perspective, is to show how the lives of the poor and their prospects for escaping poverty are also constrained by ideological forces. Poverty is not only an economic problem and a political problem; it is a cultural problem as well. We have the poverty we have in this country in part because of the ideas and attitudes prevalent among the larger population. The poor are held hostage not only to the decisions of economic and political elites, but also to the opinions and feelings of the middle class.

My objective in this chapter is to illustrate the importance of the cultural system for understanding the persistence of poverty in the United States. I pursue this by first looking at popular beliefs about inequality, mobility, poverty, welfare, and the American Dream. Americans' thinking about these and related issues, I argue, reveals the powerful, though not uncontested, influence of the dominant individualistic perspective. I then discuss how the US news media and the right-wing ideology machine reinforce this perspective, creating a cultural and political ethos favoring individualistic explanations and remedies over structural ones. I conclude by considering the rightward turn of public discourse on issues of poverty and welfare over the past half century. This cultural power shift has not only engendered a change in the language Americans use to talk about the poor, it has also, through its influence on government policy, made life harder for low income families and has moved us further away from a real solution to problems of poverty and inequality.

THE AMERICAN DREAM IN AN ERA OF INCREASING INEQUALITY

Americans underestimate the extent of inequality in the United States and overestimate the extent of social mobility. The rich possess a far greater share of the nation's wealth than what the typical American assumes, the pay of CEOs compared to workers is far greater than what the typical American assumes, and the chance of someone from the poorest quintile rising into one of the upper quintiles is far less than what the typical American assumes. Average Americans not only think the United States is a much more equal society than it really is, but they also endorse a level of equality even greater than what they incorrectly imagine already exists.[4] Reflecting on such research findings, journalist Chrystia Freeland offers this comment: "Americans actually live in Russia, although they think they live in Sweden. And they would like to live on a kibbutz."[5]

Though troubled by increasing inequality and preferring a more equitable distribution of income and wealth, most Americans still believe in the American Dream. They think the United States, uniquely, is a "land of opportunity" where individual effort pays off, where "everyone who works hard can get ahead," and where anyone can become rich.[6] Compared to Europeans, Americans are less likely to agree that "success in life is pretty much determined by forces outside our control" and more likely to agree that "hard work is very important for getting ahead in life." Americans are inclined to believe their economic fate rests in their own hands.[7] This, indeed, is the "bedrock premise" of the American Dream: "individuals have control over their own lives."[8] Even in the midst of the Great Recession, the vast majority cited hard work, ambition, and education as the most important factors promoting economic mobility, more important even than the state of the economy. Despite economic hard times, the "notion that America is a meritocracy where individuals can apply themselves and move ahead continues to endure."[9]

As the economy recovered, slowly and unevenly, from the 2007–2009 recession, opinion polls showed significant concern about the country's future and a feeling on the part of many that the economic system unfairly favors the wealthy.[10] Even so, researchers found "little indication that beliefs in individualism, the efficacy of hard work, and the potential for personal progress have been seriously eroded."[11] Though doubts about the American Dream have increased since 2000, most or many Americans, depending on the survey, still affirm the promise of upward mobility, agreeing with the statement that "most people who want to get ahead can make it if they're willing to work hard."[12]

In reflecting on the sometimes puzzling responses to opinion polls on economic inequality and the status of the American Dream, Jeff Manza and Clem Brooks argue that the public, by and large, is culturally disposed toward what they call "mobility optimism." While Americans may think the system is stacked in favor of the rich, they nevertheless remain confident about the availability of opportunities and their own chances for success. To the extent that people embrace this optimism, they are less inclined to question the legitimacy of the American political economy, even in a period of growing inequality, or support redistributive measures such as raising taxes on the wealthy or expanding programs for the poor.[13] If, however, inequality is perceived as limiting possibilities for upward mobility, if it is judged to be so extreme as to threaten the reality of the American Dream—and there is some evidence of such a shift in the thinking of the public—this could weaken people's mobility optimism and generate greater public pressure for egalitarian social policies.[14]

THE IDEOLOGY OF INDIVIDUALISM

The individualistic ideology associated with the American Dream assumes that opportunities in the United States are available for anyone motivated to succeed, economic outcomes are primarily a function of ability and effort, and existing inequalities are for the most part fair.[15] The logic of this ideology encourages its adherents to attribute poverty to the deficiencies of the poor and to favor individualistic solutions. Policy advocates, regardless of political affiliation, thus typically target the poor for reform. Conservatives recommend improving poor people through tough love and moral uplift, while liberals call for more training and education. In the US political culture, structural reforms—for example, government job creation, public investment in poor communities, or redistribution of income and wealth—rarely receive serious consideration. Measures such as these, besides facing strong opposition from powerful business groups, are a hard sell to a public schooled in the virtues of self-reliance and small government.

This individualistic belief system is sometimes said to have the status of a "dominant ideology" in the United States.[16] Even if not altogether dominant, the cultural power of the individualistic perspective outweighs that of the opposing structural perspective.[17] Americans are more frequently exposed to individualistic story lines and, like popular commercial jingles, they are highly accessible to cognition, easy to recall and apply. The entertainment media, particularly television and movies, regularly disseminate morality tales promoting and reinforcing the individualistic ideology. In an exhaustive study, Stephen Pimpare finds that American films addressing issues of poverty and homelessness, if they don't place blame on the poor themselves, leave the causes of poverty unexamined, while conveying the message that individuals "can rise above" any obstacles they might encounter. Such movies, Pimpare shows, rarely shed light on the larger "political economy context." Nor do they touch on issues of policy and power, examine in any detail the day-to-day living circumstances and experiences of the poor, or ask audiences to reflect on the political and moral implications of widespread poverty in one of the richest countries in the world. Rather than presenting a critical perspective on American social institutions, these films bolster the dominant individualistic view.[18]

According to Robert Bulman too, Hollywood films routinely tell familiar stories about how determined and hardworking individuals overcome adversity to achieve success and realize their dreams. The popular genre of urban high-school films, from *Blackboard Jungle* to *Dangerous Minds*, communicates just this message, Bullman argues, confirming what many audience members already take for granted: individual effort and a positive, can-do attitude, with a little prodding from dedicated teachers, are all that is necessary for disadvantaged teens to lift themselves out of poverty.[19] Stories of impoverished individuals pulling themselves up by their own bootstraps, trading in their rags for riches, are psychologically and emotionally compelling. They make us feel good, giving us pleasure and comfort, and they stick in our minds.

Individualism is a powerful ideology not only because it has popular allure, but also because it is the preferred ideology of the powerful, legitimating an economic and political system that perpetuates their privileged status.[20] This ideology acquires further credibility because it is thoroughly insti-

tutionalized in American culture, regularly affirmed in the educational, political, and economic arenas and in the process of family socialization.
Americans' routine exposure to ideologies of poverty and inequality is consistently skewed toward a language accentuating the efficacy of individual
striving rather than the constraint of limited opportunities. Finally, the ideology of individualism is influential not only because it proposes easily understandable and culturally sanctioned explanations for poverty, but also because it suggests straightforward and uncontroversial solutions: education,
hard work, and family values.

In the following sections I briefly review some of the research on what
Americans think about poverty, focusing also on the country's growing partisan divide, and then reconsider the relative strength of individualism and
structuralism in American political culture.

BELIEFS ABOUT POVERTY AND THE POOR

Social scientists exploring the beliefs of the American public have uncovered
two distinct theories of poverty.[21] One camp attributes poverty primarily to
individual or internal factors, such as lack of motivation, irresponsible behavior, or deviant values. The other camp attributes poverty primarily to structural or external factors, such as discrimination, substandard schools, or lack of
jobs.[22] The majority of the populace, most studies show, falls into the first
camp. James Kluegel and Eliot Smith, for example, find that Americans
"strongly endorse individual reasons for economic position, particularly for
poverty, and reject liberal and (especially) radical explanations emphasizing
structural causes."[23] Judith Chafel, in an extensive review of the literature,
draws a similar conclusion. The American public for the most part, she
states, is predisposed to "blame the victim"; perceives poverty as being "inevitable, necessary, and just"; and appears generally "content with the status
quo."[24]

The influence of the individualistic ideology is evident also from studies
of attitudes toward the poor. If the public attributes poverty to the failings of
the poor rather than to structural causes, then they are likely also to have
disparaging views of poor people. This is precisely what Catherine Cozzarelli and her colleagues discover. Based on data gathered from a sample of
college students, they show that judgments about the character traits and
personality attributes of the poor are much more negative than corresponding
opinions about the middle class. Poor people, for instance, are typically
regarded as being less hardworking, responsible, friendly, proud, family
oriented, or intelligent than middle-class people. The individualistic propen-
sity to blame the poor for their poverty goes hand in hand with the tendency
to regard poor people, in one respect or another, as inferior.[25]

Welfare recipients bear the brunt of negative stereotypes about the poor, and because they are typically thought of as black, they are subject to racial stereotypes as well. In responding to opinion polls, Americans commonly assert that women on welfare do not want to work, prefer living on the government dole, could get along without public assistance if they tried, and have babies out of wedlock to increase their monthly payments.[26] These beliefs reinforce the perception that poverty results from individual failings rather than structural constraints. Even many welfare recipients (though usually citing structural factors in their own individual cases) concur with the popular view that most women on public assistance are lazy, unmotivated, and inclined to abuse the system.[27]

Despite the ubiquitous presence of individualistic story lines in the cultural system, not all Americans think alike about issues of poverty, welfare, and inequality, nor do they all repudiate structural explanations. Beliefs about the causes of poverty vary by income, education, race, gender, religion, and other socioeconomic and demographic characteristics. Women, low income individuals, and people who are nonwhite, younger, more educated, and less religious are more likely to cite structural factors as causes of poverty.[28] Attitudes toward the poor differ also depending on the segment of the poverty population in question. For example, compared to studies of "generic" poverty, research on public views of homelessness has found stronger support for the structural viewpoint.[29] The American public also tends to have more favorable attitudes toward the white poor than the black poor,[30] women than men,[31] children than single mothers,[32] the elderly than the working-age poor,[33] and poor people who appear to be trying to get ahead than those who seem content to live off welfare.[34] In addition, as discussed below, Americans' thinking about poverty, inequality, and government is also characterized by deep partisan differences.

THE PARTISAN DIVIDE

The Great Recession and its aftermath set the stage for two populist uprisings, one on the right and one on the left: the Tea Party in 2009 and Occupy Wall Street in 2011. The latter was a prelude to the unexpected showing of Bernie Sanders in the Democratic primaries, and the former was a prelude to the even more unexpected victory of Donald Trump in the presidential election. Populists, whether right or left, align themselves with the "people" against the "elites." Who are these nefarious elites? The chief enemy for right-wing populism is the *political* elite, career politicians and corrupt government officials looking out for their own interests at the expense of the little guy. Populism on the right expresses a deep distrust of government. "By far," Guy Molyneux observes, this is "the least-appreciated factor underlying

Trump's 2016 victory."[35] The chief enemy for left-wing populism is the *economic* elite, a "billionaire class" of greedy CEOs and Wall Street financiers enriching themselves at the expense of the larger public.[36] Populism on the left expresses a deep suspicion of corporate capitalism. These two populisms, one condemning political elites, the other condemning economic elites, tell different stories about why things sometimes go wrong in the country and what we should do about it. For the Right, when business malfunctions this is typically due to the pernicious interference of big government in the workings of the private enterprise system, hence the need for deregulation. For the Left, when government malfunctions this is typically due to the pernicious interference of big business in the workings of the democratic political system, hence the need to get money out of politics.

Left-wing populism, as exemplified by the Occupy slogan, "We are the 99 percent," adopts a broad conception of the "people," so inclusive, in fact, that it papers over long-standing divisions by class, race, region, and party affiliation. Right-wing populism, with its mixture of racial resentment, nativism, and hostility toward recipients of government assistance, adopts a more exclusive conception of the "people." Besides targeting political elites, it perceives a moral schism in the nonelite population, with an aggrieved "us" confronting an undeserving "them." For the populist Tea Party wing of the Republican Party in particular, the "people," dishonored and disrespected if not entirely forgotten, consist of hardworking, taxpaying Americans unfairly squeezed by big government on the one side and assorted freeloaders and moochers on the other. Right-wing populists believe that government bureaucrats and politicians, when not preoccupied with advancing their own careers, are busy soliciting sympathy and doling out patronage for favored minorities and special interests: immigrants, refugees, Muslims, African Americans, homosexuals, feminists, and the poor.[37]

The sharp differences in political outlook between left-wing populists and right-wing populists are not surprising. Recent surveys, however, document a growing partisan divide among the public more generally. The beliefs of Democratic-leaning Americans (Dems for short) and Republican-leaning Americans (Reps for short) have become increasingly divergent on a range of issues. Reps, for example, are more likely than Dems to agree that "most people who want to get ahead can make it if they're willing to work hard" (77 percent to 49 percent). Dems are more likely than Reps to believe the economic system unfairly favors the powerful (82 percent to 46 percent), inequality is a "very big" problem (66 percent to 26 percent), "government should do more to reduce the gap between the rich and the poor" (81 percent to 34 percent), and "government should do more to help the needy" even at the risk of going deeper into debt (71 percent to 24 percent). While 76 percent of Dems say "poor people have hard lives because government benefits don't go far enough to help them live decently," 65 percent of Reps say "poor people have it easy because they can get government benefits without doing anything in return." Dems and Reps disagree also about the best strategy for reducing poverty. Dems (75 percent compared to 29 percent for Reps) favor "raising taxes on wealthy Americans and large corporations in order to expand programs for the poor." Reps (59 percent compared to 17 percent for Dems) favor "lowering taxes on wealthy people and corporations in order to encourage more investment and economic growth." This pattern of large and increasing partisan differences is evident on numerous other measures of attitudes, opinions, and political values. [38]

Analyses of the 2016 presidential election also provide some insights into American political culture and the partisan divide. Drawing on surveys of voters, Lee Drutman identifies two areas where the differences between Clinton supporters and Trump supporters are particularly strong, one pertaining to social identity issues and the other to economic issues. On the social identity front, Trump supporters, committed to traditional moral values and anxious about ongoing cultural and demographic changes, stand out in their opposition to abortion, gay marriage, and transgender bathrooms and in their negative feelings about minorities and immigrants. Clinton voters are more accepting of diversity and more liberal on social issues. On the economic front, Clinton supporters stand out in their thinking that the economic system is unfair, taxes should be raised on the wealthy, and government should play a bigger role in addressing economic problems. Trump voters are more accepting of inequality and far more negative in their attitudes toward government intervention and redistributive policies. [39]

Much of the debate about the surprising Trump victory and the current political alignment has focused on white people without a college degree. Though sometimes referred to as the white working class, many of these people are relatively well-to-do retirees and small business owners. This population, approximately 45 percent of all voters in 2016, supported Trump over Clinton by 62.5 percent to 31.6 percent, a much wider margin in favor of the Republican candidate than in the 2012 presidential election. [40] A significant percentage of this population, some of whom went for Obama in 2008 and 2012, voted for Trump not primarily because they were racists or white nationalists or diehard Republicans, though many were all of these things, but because they were frustrated by politics as usual. These "exasperated" voters, as Justin Gest calls them, are mostly residents of small towns and rural communities in the Midwest and rust belt that still haven't recovered from the Great Recession and face looming threats of further job loss due to trade and automation. [41] Disliking both candidates, they were marginal supporters of Trump only, desperately reaching out for an economic lifeline. [42] Along with the decline in turnout among African Americans, Clinton's underperformance among non-college-educated voters likely cost her the presidency. She, and the Democratic Party more generally, failed to generate sufficient enthusiasm among black voters and failed to address seriously the economic issues faced by today's working class, both white and nonwhite. Instead of firming up its minority and working-class base, the Democratic Party has instead adopted a strategy of relying on support from urban professionals, chasing after moderate Republican voters in affluent suburbs, and cozying up to Wall Street donors. [43]

As opinion surveys show, conservatives and liberals differ in their attitudes toward the poor. The former tend toward a more individualistic perspective and resent government spending on antipoverty programs. The latter tend toward a more structural perspective and have a largely favorable view of government efforts to fight poverty. These two sides are not equally matched, however. While opposition to government social programs is central to the conservative worldview and the Republican agenda, support for such programs, at least since the 1960s, is a secondary issue in the liberal worldview and the Democratic agenda. This political asymmetry gives a powerful edge to the individualistic perspective over the structural perspective in American political culture.

STRONG INDIVIDUALISM, WEAK STRUCTURALISM

Studies of public opinion on a variety of social policy issues reveal that Americans do not slavishly adhere to the principle of individualism. They hold views that are often ambiguous, uncertain, and inconsistent; they endorse and shift easily among multiple and often contradictory theories; what they presume to be true in general or as a matter of abstract principle often conflicts with what they regard as true in the concrete case of particular individuals; and their beliefs about poverty are sensitive to the manner in which the issue is framed. [44] While the individualistic ideology certainly exerts a powerful cultural influence, Americans nevertheless remain divided in their understanding of the sources of poverty, particularly along party lines, with many acknowledging the importance of structural causes. Most Americans also resist the laissez-faire policy prescriptions that follow from the individualistic ideology. Their embrace of individualism is tempered by a countervailing commitment to egalitarian values. They believe (or at least they say) that government has a responsibility to guarantee equality of opportunity and ensure the basic needs of all citizens are met. [45] Indeed, many Americans even favor increased government spending on programs to reduce poverty. [46]

Despite these findings, however, and the sometimes muddy picture that emerges from public opinion studies, there are a number of reasons to think that individualism remains a dominant ideology, at least as pertains to the issue of poverty. Particularly in the arenas of mainstream public discourse and policy formation, the individualistic perspective prevails over the structural perspective.

First, most Americans believe there are many causes of poverty, some internal, some external. Individualism and structuralism are not necessarily perceived as being incompatible. Individualists do not always deny the relevance of structural factors, and those affirming structural causes do not necessarily reject a baseline individualistic perspective.[47] African Americans and Latinos in particular, Matthew Hunt finds, strongly agree with *both* individualistic and structural explanations for poverty. Structural views, he suggests, "may be combined with, or layered on to, an existing individualistic base."[48] Survey data collected over many years provide evidence of such a bedrock individualism, showing that over 90 percent of Americans cite "lack of effort" as an important cause of poverty.[49] The general pattern, it would be fair to say, is one of widespread acceptance of individualism, with a sizable population *also* supporting structural explanations.[50] While people often agree with elements of the structural perspective, this by no means precludes them from having a more general and deeply rooted adherence to the dominant individualistic ideology.

Second, compared to their individualistic counterparts, those who support structural arguments are more ambivalent about their beliefs, less firmly tied to their position, and less likely to draw policy recommendations consistent with their structural leanings. Proponents of individualism, no doubt due in part to its greater cultural currency, are less liable to alter their opinions over time. In contrast to the "stable effects of individualism," Hunt observes, "structuralist beliefs are more variable, more responsive to group memberships, personal experiences, and the prevailing social climate."[51] In the US political tradition, the principle of individualism and the doctrine of limited government are stronger than competing humanitarian and egalitarian values that might inspire support for structural programs to combat poverty.[52] Thus, while many Americans "want the government to help the poor," they also "insist that the role be limited and not replace an individual's obligation to pursue self-reliance."[53] In contrast to individualism, which is firmly grounded in the political culture, the influence of structuralism is more uncertain and tenuous and less likely to engender a deep commitment to structural solutions.

Third, a strong structural perspective emphasizes increasing inequality in the distribution of wealth and power, the inability of the American political economy to generate enough decent-paying jobs, and the failure of American political institutions to live up to the democratic ideal. But many Americans who are perceived as falling into the structural camp endorse a weak structuralism only. What they usually have in mind when they say that poverty is caused by external circumstances is that poor people cannot get ahead because of a deprived family background or inadequate schools—because of inequality of opportunity. Consistent with the liberal human capital approach, weak structuralists favor measures designed to help the poor help themselves, including initiatives to expand education and training programs. They show much less support, however, for the redistribution of income and wealth or for policies to fight poverty and inequality through direct government expenditures.[54] In its call for modest though certainly desirable reforms, this weak structuralism affirms a traditional conception of American society as a meritocracy in the making. In contrast to a strong structuralism, the weak version does not contradict the individualistic perspective so much as it qualifies it.

Fourth, while many Americans recognize that "structural barriers" hinder poor people from escaping poverty, this is muted in its implications by being joined with the even more powerful belief that "anyone who works hard enough can overcome such barriers."[55] A majority of Americans agree with this statement: "One of the big problems in this country is that we don't give everyone an equal chance." And yet an even larger majority believes that "most people who don't get ahead should not blame the system, they only have themselves to blame."[56] In a recent interview study, Lawrence Eppard likewise finds that social work students commonly hold to some version of the idea that hard work is sufficient to overcome any barriers to success individuals might encounter.[57] The American public believes in both the efficacy of individual effort and the existence of structural barriers to achievement. But the first belief trumps the second, leaving only a watered down, weak version of structuralism.

Fifth, according to what Robinson and Bell call the "underdog principle," the poor are less likely than the rich to regard existing inequalities as just.[58] People who favor structural explanations, similarly, whether weak or strong, are generally located on the lower and less influential end of the social hierarchy. Proponents of the structural perspective, besides being less consistent in their adherence, tend to occupy the political margins. As Lawrence Bobo points out, people holding beliefs challenging the dominant ideology are more likely to be disengaged from politics, excluded from public debate, and lacking in "'effective' public opinion."[59] Even where there is significant dissent, individualism remains a powerful ideology because it is the ideology of the powerful.

Sixth, as we saw in the previous section, individualism prevails over structuralism in American political culture because, in combination with a distrust of the welfare state and government activism more generally, it is deeply embedded in the DNA of the Republican Party and an essential element of the GOP's governing philosophy. The Democratic Party leans toward the structural perspective and favors government programs for the poor, but its political identity is more diffuse and its priorities lie elsewhere. With respect to issues of poverty and inequality, the Republican Party is outspoken in its support for individualism, while the voice of the Democratic Party in defense of structuralism is barely audible. This imbalance tilts the political culture in favor of individualism over structuralism.

The ideological battle for the hearts and minds of the American public is important. What Americans think about the causes of poverty and how they feel about welfare recipients and the poor have an effect on their policy preferences. Individuals inclined toward the structural perspective favor a more generous welfare system and are more likely to support redistributive policies.[60] People's beliefs have political implications; at the very least, they establish boundaries for what at the moment is politically possible. In the United States, where individualism remains the dominant ideology, this is bad news for the poor. As long as the majority of Americans, and an even larger majority of powerful Americans, adhere to an individualistic view-point—as long as they believe poverty is the fault of the poor and govern-ment programs do more harm than good—advocates for structural reforms of the sort needed to effectively address the problem of poverty face a steep uphill battle.

THE NEWS MEDIA

Americans acquire most of their information about the world and their under-standing of social and political issues from the media, especially from televi-sion news programs. The media play a powerful role in shaping the percep-tions and opinions of the American public and fashioning the imagery and discourse surrounding issues of poverty.[61] While journalists do a good job of covering some issues, reporting on poverty is not their strong suit. News stories about the poor are infrequent, and when they do appear, they typically provide only a cursory analysis and give tacit support to the individualistic ideology. Media coverage of poverty serves less to enlighten the public or provoke genuine debate than to pass along the conventional wisdom. In this respect, the media are part of the poverty problem.

The purpose of the news media in an ideal democratic world is to supply people with the information they need to fulfill their citizenship responsibil-ities and ensure political and economic leaders are held publicly account-able.[62] Judged by this standard, the US news media are doing a miserable job. One important reason for this is that news organizations are subordinate parts of an increasingly concentrated system of corporate conglomerates. Just a handful of corporations, among them Time Warner and News Corp, own almost all of the country's major media companies. The ability of the press to serve faithfully as a watchdog in the interests of democracy is compromised by this concentration of media ownership and by the media's location within the larger corporate system.[63] The corporate entities that own and operate newspapers, news magazines, television and radio news programs, and the various online media have their own particular economic and political interests. These may intrude, directly or indirectly, on the practice of journalism and the content of the news. The political, economic, and corporate setting within which producers, publishers, editors, and reporters work creates strong resistance to news stories that might, for example, trace the causes of poverty back to the behavior of large corporations, the economic and political power of big business, or the nature of capitalism itself.

Mainstream news organizations are not just owned by large corporations, they are also commercial, profit-seeking enterprises themselves. News programs and publications in the United States, with the proliferation of competing news sources, have increasingly come under the sway of business imperatives. The news is a commercial product; it is manufactured, marketed, and sold just like any other commodity. Journalism is as much a business as it is a profession, and like any other business, its purpose is to make money. News organizations are pressured to be profitable; to restrain production costs; and to cut back, for example, on the expensive investigative reporting required to shed light on the lives of the powerful and the powerless and to reveal the otherwise hidden worlds of workplaces and corporate boardrooms, courthouses and government agencies.[64]

The news media are subject to the conservative sensibilities of their chief customers as well. Advertisers are not eager to pay for news programming that courts controversy, gives voice to dissident viewpoints, casts a negative light on the culture of consumerism, or exposes the business of America to critical scrutiny. To keep advertising revenues flowing in, the media also need to be concerned about attracting an audience—readers for newspapers and magazines, listeners for radio, and viewers for television. Caught up in a continuous scramble to improve ratings and expand audience share, news programs nowadays more than ever bow down to the "supra-ideology" of entertainment.[65] This creates an incentive to downplay hard and probing news in favor of scandals, bloodshed, car chases, puff pieces, celebrity gossip, melodramatic human interest stories, and the spectacle of opinion mongering and "outrage discourse" that has become the meat and potatoes of talk radio and the cable news networks.[66]

The news media create both noise and silence, drawing attention to some issues and diverting attention from others. They set the agenda, telling the public, by implication, what is important and what is not. The first thing that should be said about mainstream news coverage of poverty is that there is just not very much of it.[67] A FAIR study of the three major nightly news networks (CBS, NBC, and ABC) during the fourteen-month period from January 2013 through February 2014 found a total of only twenty-three segments on poverty, fewer than two a month, with many of these being "uselessly brief or even dismissive."[68] Though poverty receives little coverage, and even less in-depth coverage, inequality has attracted considerable media attention, particularly since the appearance of the Occupy Wall Street movement in 2011. But as *New York Times* reporter Jason DeParle acknowledges, the dominant theme in stories about inequality is the growing wealth of the superrich, not the continuing deprivation of the persistently poor.[69] News stories explicitly addressing the problem of poverty are sufficiently rare that, as one media critic reports, their publication "becomes a sort of 'very special episode' of journalism that we sort of roll out every so often."[70] In such stories, furthermore, the poor tend to be distanced and objectified, appearing merely as "objects of reporting," not as deserving citizens in their own right.[71] In any case, no matter how thoroughly we might read our daily newspapers, and no matter how many hours we might spend watching television news programs, listening to talk radio, or surfing the web, we are unlikely to conclude from our exposure that poverty is a serious problem in the United States, much less a structural problem. While journalists offer an occasional story about the poor, for the most part poverty is a neglected social issue. The media "have 'disappeared' the needy from the news."[72]

The second thing that should be said about mainstream news coverage is that it consistently represents poverty as an individual problem rather than a social problem, a "personal trouble" rather than a "public issue."[73] When news programs shine a light on poverty, they rarely provide much illumination. They can, at their best, offer a glimpse into the daily lives of the poor, and can even puncture stereotypes, rouse passion, and elicit sympathy. But the systemic nature of poverty falls outside the normal purview of news reporting.[74] The "very nature of journalism," Peter Parisi observes, "seems opposed to portrayals of the 'big picture.'"[75] The gaze of the news media is drawn toward the micro as opposed to the macro, to isolated cases more than recurring social patterns, personal circumstances more than social context, and the shortcomings of individuals more than the inequities of the system. Journalists provide *depictions* of the poor—people down on their luck, in need of social assistance, or victims of their own bad choices. But in the news media's efforts to capture the human drama, the less visible social forces ultimately responsible for the persistence of poverty remain hidden.

How do the news media, when they do not simply ignore the problem, manage so consistently to miss the forest for the trees? How do the constraints and conventions of news reporting lead journalists to overlook the big picture and portray poverty primarily as an individual problem? Without presuming to be comprehensive, in what follows I identify several factors pertaining to the practice of journalism and the organization of news coverage that illustrate how the media tend to obscure or misconstrue the nature of American poverty.

Framing Poverty in News Stories

The news media compose reports, and the coherence and effects of these reports derive from how they are "framed": how they are packaged or put together.[76] On the infrequent occasions when television addresses issues of poverty, news programs typically frame their reports in a manner that unwittingly induces viewers to blame poverty on the poor. Shanto Iyengar's research shows the majority of news stories about poverty employ an "episodic" as opposed to a "thematic" frame: they focus on the personal experiences of the poor rather than on broader policy issues. When television programs describe poverty in thematic terms, viewers are more likely to attribute the problem to social conditions, but when the more popular episodic frame is used, they hold poor people themselves responsible. How television news coverage presents the issue to the public, Iyengar argues, influences "what people take to be the causes and cures of poverty." By employing "episodic" rather than "thematic" frames in their stories about the poor, the news media reinforce the ideology of individualism.[77]

In another analysis of framing, Max Rose and Frank R. Baumgartner examine media coverage of poverty from 1960 to 2008, focusing specifically on the *New York Times* and four other prominent newspapers. Up until the late 1960s, with the war on poverty under way, most coverage of the poor conformed to a positive or "generous" frame. Consistent with the structural perspective, the poor were portrayed as victims of second-rate schools, resource-deprived communities, insufficient economic opportunities, and other barriers to mobility. Since the late 1960s and early 1970s, however, corresponding to a conservative resurgence, the framing of poverty has undergone a dramatic change, from positive to negative, from "generous" to "stingy." Newspaper coverage shifted from an emphasis on structural barriers to a focus on the poor as lazy, undeserving, and inclined to take advantage of the welfare system. As this unsympathetic framing of the poor took hold, Rose and Baumgartner show, the level of government spending to alleviate poverty declined, suggesting that how the poor are represented in the news media has a measurable impact on public policy.[78]

News Reporting as Storytelling

When the news media address issues of poverty or welfare, as in the case of "episodic" reports, they commonly employ a narrative structure. They tell stories, mostly stories about individuals. This way of conveying information has the advantage of being universally familiar. The story form also makes news reports easy to follow, brings out the human dimension of a topic, gives audiences a rooting or booing interest, and invites them to compare their own stories to those told in the media.

Though storytelling is an effective (and affective) means of communication, for some subject matter, including poverty, the habitual use of personal narrative produces a distorted picture. In the first place, news stories are selective; they inevitably make a long story short and a complex story simple. They also spotlight some cases rather than others. And the particular individuals featured in reports on poverty and welfare are typically chosen less because they are representative than because they are available, interesting, or conform to stereotypical notions of the poor. What makes a better story, an extreme though sensational example or an unremarkable but average case?

News reports employing a storytelling technique also place individuals at the center of attention. This puts the focus on people's personal qualities and unique circumstances, implicitly underlining the causal role these play in perpetuating poverty. If social forces are brought into the narrative at all, these are typically mentioned only in passing, leaving unquestioned the tendency to interpret social problems as individual troubles. "Personalized story frames," Parisi concludes, typically subordinate social structure to individual choice, thus lending support to the "ideology of individualism."[79]

The Welfare Poor, the Working Poor, the Newly Poor, and the Already Poor

In the period prior to the enactment of the 1996 welfare reform legislation, media coverage of poverty focused disproportionately on the welfare system and welfare recipients. The typical television news reports of the era, Maura Kelly finds, depicted welfare mothers as "childlike, hyperfertile, lazy, and bad mothers." Ange-Marie Hancock similarly shows that news coverage at the time conveyed a stock picture of the welfare recipient: a single, jobless, teenage African American mother. By promoting the image of the "welfare queen," the news media validated sexist and racist stereotypes while also diverting attention from the economic and political causes of poverty.[80]

The news media's preoccupation with the issue of welfare during these years left the erroneous impression that the poverty population and the welfare population were coterminous and that the poverty population and the working population were mutually exclusive. Explicit stories about the poor were almost always about welfare recipients, who were presumed to be nonworkers, and stories about the hardships endured by American workers seldom mentioned poverty. In the early 2000s, a period of weak economic growth, the *New York Times* published numerous revealing articles on globalization, outsourcing, downsizing, long-term unemployment, joblessness, and stagnant wages. But rarely in these articles did reporters from the *Times* underline the connection between the economic developments they documented and the continuing problem of poverty. By segregating reports on the

poor from news about economic conditions and the plight of American workers, the media obscure the structural nature of the poverty problem and foster
a false image of a divide between the "underclass" and the working class.[81]

The pattern of news coverage has changed over the past decade or so.
Welfare recipients, a diminishing fraction of the poverty population, rarely
make the headlines anymore. Nor do those whose poverty preceded the financial collapse. Instead, the media's attention today is focused on formerly
middle-class people, victims of the opioid epidemic for example, who have
fallen on hard times due to the Great Recession and the continued weakness
of the American economy. Far less attention is paid to the large segment of
the poverty population who were struggling before the recession—people
who had it bad then and have it even worse now. Sympathetic reports on the
"newly" poor, furthermore, have the effect, through invidious comparison, of
stigmatizing the "already" poor.[82] By relying on this particular story line,
Stephen Pimpare argues, the news media implicitly reinforce the distinction
between the "deserving" poor, hardworking Americans who have blameless-
ly lost their jobs, and the "undeserving" poor, work-averse freeloaders looking to live off the government dole.[83]

The Racialization of Poverty and Welfare

When Americans visualize the poor, they see black people. The media bear
much of the responsibility for this racialization of poverty. The percentage of
African Americans appearing in the pictures and footage accompanying
news stories about the poor far exceeds their percentage in the poverty population.[84] In their depictions of the poor, the news media convey the impression that poverty is primarily a black problem. The faces of African
Americans are even more prominently on display when news articles take a
negative tone, as when they address issues of welfare abuse or welfare dependency. White faces are featured more frequently in news stories that shine
a more positive light on the poor, for example articles disclosing the hardships of the working poor, the tragedy of the "newly poor," or the plight of
the elderly. Black people are overrepresented in the media's visual coverage
of poverty and welfare, and particularly so in news stories painting an unsympathetic picture of the poor.[85]

Because white Americans equate being poor with being black, their thinking about poverty is filtered through their racial attitudes, resentments, and
stereotypes. And since many white Americans have negative views of black
people, seeing them as lazy or intellectually inferior, for example, they have
negative views of the poor as well. African Americans are a segment of the
poverty population that whites perceive to be particularly blameworthy and
undeserving of public assistance.[86] The more the media associate poverty
and race, the more they strengthen disparaging attitudes toward both poor

people and African Americans. The media-induced racialization of poverty fosters a blame-the-victim mentality, perpetuates racism, dampens public enthusiasm for social programs, and makes it difficult to mobilize white support for political and economic reforms that might alleviate the hardships of the poor.[87]

Reliance on Official and Mainstream Sources

News organizations depend heavily on official sources of information and analysis, including political officeholders, corporate spokespersons, government bureaucrats, anointed experts housed in think tanks, and the representatives of public and private social service organizations. These sources are readily available and eager to offer their views; they have the appearance of being authoritative and objective, professional and nonpartisan; they are media savvy, capable of presenting their thoughts in a manner consistent with journalistic requirements; and their respectability helps ensure that news reports remain within the boundaries of acceptable opinion. Reporters return to these reliable sources again and again, enhancing their credibility.[88]

The news media's reliance on credentialed and mainstream sources diminishes the range of debate on social issues. Because they lack the official status that comes from having an "institutional seal of approval," more politically marginal groups, including poor people themselves, are denied a fair and equal hearing in the press.[89] According to the FAIR study mentioned previously, of the fifty-four sources included in the twenty-three segments of nightly news coverage about the poor from January 2013 through February 2014, only twenty-two "were people personally affected by poverty."[90] The general pattern, Charlotte Ryan explains, is for established sources to set forth the "main message" of a story, with poor people and their advocates—who are typically represented as "special interests" rather than "democratic voices"—brought in to supply the "color."[91] In her analysis of the welfare reform debate in the 1990s, for example, Ryan found that, compared to welfare recipients and their political allies, official sources were cited more frequently, more prominently, and at greater length, and they were treated with more respect and presumed to be more credible.

Putting Out the News on a Daily Basis

The organizational imperatives of publishing a daily paper or producing a nightly news broadcast, along with the built-in predilection to define news as what is new that day, distracts attention from underlying structural and historical forces. The news media are drawn by their very nature as organs of daily information to highlight today's news developments and news makers. Local television news stations, indeed, take great pride in announcing they are first on the scene or first to report a breaking story. Depth of analysis takes second seat to getting there before anyone else, and the next day the news cycle begins all over again.

With their day-to-day focus on newsworthy individuals and dramatic events, the media provide insufficient analysis of enduring social process- es.[92] The news media are limited by an attention span both narrow and short; they not only neglect social structure, but also neglect history. As Robert Entman argues, in the absence of coverage explicitly portraying poverty "as a continuing multifaceted social problem," journalists inevitably give support to the individualistic ideology.[93] The daily orientation of the media and the conception of news as what is happening now, along with the infrequent coverage of the poor, are bound to create the impression that poverty is an incidental rather than a systemic problem. Audiences might be less tempted to reduce poverty to bad choices or bad luck if the news media were more oriented toward the longer run, if they focused not just on immediate events, but on developments. Michael Schudson suggests that if "the media operated monthly or annually rather than daily," the social and historical forces that existing formats overlook might be more visible features of news coverage.[94]

The Sound Bite Bias

In broadcast media especially, and in the print media to a lesser extent, coverage of social problems is subject to severe time and space constraints. Only a small percentage of potential news stories can be fitted into the pages of the daily newspaper, and even fewer can be squeezed into a half-hour news telecast. News stories are short and getting shorter, with nightly televi- sion broadcasts nowadays pared down to "nineteen minutes of News McNuggets."[95] Even the most newsworthy events receive only a few col- umns of print or a couple of minutes of airtime. The media have the capacity to deal with news topics in only the most cursory manner and are often reduced to relaying sound bites, snippets of information and opinion. There is little time for nuance, complexity, or context. Television can portray a problem, identify victims, and reveal symptoms, but it lacks the resources to explore the complex socioeconomic causes of issues like poverty and in- equality. Time and space limitations, and financial resources as well, pre- clude in-depth reporting.

The inevitably superficial nature of news coverage works to the advan- tage of the individualistic perspective. The structural perspective offers a complicated theory of poverty, not amenable to a twenty-second summary. It is also a dissenting view in American political culture—harder to understand, more controversial, and certain to provoke resistance. To build a case for the structural viewpoint requires time and space, as this book illustrates, and this is precisely what the news media have in short supply.[96]

Focus on Technical Issues

Daniel Hallin argues that the media typically underline *technical* issues rather than *political* issues in their coverage of news stories.[97] Journalists approach the topic of poverty from a technical angle when, for example, they write stories about the measurement of poverty or when they investigate policy effectiveness. How many people are poor, and by what criteria? Are public- and private-sector efforts successful in boosting the skills of low-income workers, providing food and shelter to destitute families, or enabling single mothers to make the transition from welfare to work? By turning the spotlight on measurement issues and policy evaluation, reporters leave the comforting illusion that the powers that be are earnestly applying themselves to the resolution of pressing social problems. In pursuing such technical questions, furthermore, and skirting more controversial issues, reporters also make themselves less vulnerable to accusations of political bias.

Journalists suppress important political questions when their stories stick with technical issues. By ignoring "conflicts of interest" and "clashes over the ends and values of political life," they depoliticize the problem of poverty. By concentrating on technical issues, in addition, the news media treat the audience not as citizens, but as passive consumers of expert knowledge. This technical mode of journalism, Hallin observes, does not present news stories in a manner likely to provoke dialogue about larger social issues, raise tough ethical questions, or engender reflection about what kind of society we have or would like to have.[98]

News organizations' coverage of social problems is constrained by numerous pressures: corporate imperatives and commercial interests, competition for ratings and audience share, inadequate funds to do investigative reporting, the routine conventions and practices of professional journalism, and subtle and not-so-subtle influences emanating from the larger political and economic environment. Subject to these pressures, the news media, ultimately, are much better at producing entertainment than enlightenment, and they certainly fall well short of providing the information, analysis, and range of viewpoints Americans need to deliberate in an informed and rational way about issues of poverty, welfare, and inequality.

Media effects, of course, are not overwhelming or irresistible.[99] News consumers do not passively accept the portrait of poverty presented in the news media; audiences come away from their exposure to the news with different interpretations of what they have seen, heard, or read, and Americans do manage to acquire information about the world from sources other than the mainstream media. In the end, however, while they do not in any simple manner *cause* Americans to adopt a blame-the-victim perspective, the news media, however unwittingly, do reinforce the ideology of individualism, making it difficult for people to conceive of or embrace a coherent structural alternative.

THE RIGHT-WING IDEOLOGY MACHINE

In the early 1970s, against the backdrop of a deteriorating economy, business leaders and their intellectual allies surveyed a grim landscape. In the war of ideas, so it seemed, probusiness conservatism was on the ropes. The federal government was in thrall to the liberal agenda; the news media delivered a steady stream of unflattering reports about business and businessmen; colleges and universities had become left-wing outposts; civil rights, antiwar, feminist, consumer, and environmental movements disseminated a succession of radical challenges to the establishment worldview; and public opinion held corporate America in low regard.[100] In this hostile climate, business executives found themselves on the defensive. As the chair of Westinghouse at the time lamented: "College professors don't love us. The news media don't trust us. The government doesn't help us. . . . [I]t's so lonesome out here in business land."[101]

In 1971 Lewis F. Powell, who would subsequently be appointed by Richard Nixon to the Supreme Court, circulated a memorandum within the US Chamber of Commerce warning the business community that the "free enterprise system"—indeed, "individual freedom" itself—was under broad attack and in "deep trouble." He admonished business leaders to rise up on their own behalf, urging them to join together and take a more aggressive political and ideological stance in defense of American capitalism.[102] Irving Kristol, William Simon, and other conservative thinkers and activists echoed Powell's message throughout the 1970s, and many corporate managers, too, came to believe they faced an ideological and political crisis.[103] With their backs against the wall, business interests set out to win over public opinion, change the tenor of the media, turn the culture around, and alter the terms of political discourse. They formed powerful lobbying and advocacy organizations, launched a concerted drive to combat left-liberal inroads in the media and the universities, stepped up their attacks on big government and organized labor, and set out to transform the Republican Party into an uncompromising champion of the free-market system. This political resurgence of business yielded, as one of its products, a right-wing ideology machine that would over the course of the next four decades evolve into an imposing network of corporate sponsors, foundations, business groups, think tanks, media watchdogs, radio and television talk shows, and internet sites.[104]

Since the early 1970s, continuing into the present on an even grander scale, wealthy donors have invested heavily to advance the conservative cause, check the spread of antibusiness ideas, and propel public opinion to the right. Most of this huge sum has come from corporate contributions and conservative foundations tied to rich business families: the Bradley Foundation, the Smith Richardson Foundation, the Scaife Family Foundations, the Castle Rock Foundation (funded by the Coors family fortune), the Koch family foundations, and the John M. Olin Foundation. These institutions, with deep roots in corporate America, constitute the economic substructure of the right-wing ideology machine.[105]

Conservative think tanks, the beneficiaries of increasing corporate and foundation funding beginning in the 1970s, are the heavy artillery in the right-wing arsenal.[106] The Hoover Institution (1919) and the American Enterprise Institute (1943) grew significantly during the 1970s and afterward, thanks to an infusion of corporate money. The Heritage Foundation (1973), initially established with funding from the Coors family, the libertarian Cato Institute (1978), and the Manhattan Institute (1978) are among the most important of the newer organizations in the conservative armory.[107] According to one estimate, during the decade of the 1990s alone, right-wing think tanks spent $1 billion spreading the conservative gospel.[108] In 2012 the Heritage Foundation, closely allied with the Tea Party, spent $82 million to advance the cause of the more militant wing of the Republican Party.[109] And to ready themselves for the 2016 election, the Koch brothers and their allies accumulated a "political war chest" of nearly a billion dollars.[110]

The Right also carried the war of ideas into the very heart of the enemy stronghold: the media. Corporate leaders and conservative thinkers in the 1970s, unhappy with a public culture that seemed decidedly unfriendly to business, attributed the problem to politically biased news reporting. The unbalanced coverage of partisan media, as they saw it, tarnished the image of business and eroded public support for the free enterprise system.[111] To combat the influence of what they perceived to be antagonistic news media, the Right pursued a two-pronged strategy: intimidate the media from without and seize control from within. On the one hand, activists on the right established a number of media watchdog groups, including Accuracy in Media and the Media Research Center.[112] The "sole mission" of the latter, as tellingly stated on its website, "is to expose and neutralize the propaganda arm of the Left: the national news media."[113] With funding provided by the same corporate sources and wealthy families that subsidize right-wing think tanks, these organizations monitor news coverage, publicize instances of presumed political bias, and pressure news outlets to make room for conservative viewpoints.

Invoking the principle of "balance," the Right also launched a campaign to transform the media from within, to give a louder voice to conservative and probusiness points of view in news coverage.[114] This effort, too, met with great success, evidenced by the emergence of a powerful "right-wing media infrastructure," with Fox News at the center, and the rise of a large and highly visible right-wing "punditocracy."[115] Conservative commentators, including George Will, Michelle Malkin, Ann Coulter, David Brooks, Newt Gingrich, and William Kristol, to name a few, have attained an influential presence within the mainstream news media. Along with other like-minded men and women, they are frequent guests on CNN, MSNBC, Fox News, and Sunday morning talk programs; they make regular appearances on talk radio, a venue dominated by the Right; they operate internet sites, including the *Drudge Report* and *Breitbart News*; they write syndicated columns for newspapers across the country; they contribute to political blogs; they publish articles in the *National Review*, the *Weekly Standard*, the *American Spectator*, and other conservative political magazines; and—including such notables as Michael Savage, Mark Levin, Glenn Beck, Sean Hannity, Rush Limbaugh, Laura Ingraham, Alex Jones, and (formerly) Bill O'Reilly—they host their own television and radio programs. The public visibility and cultural influence of right-wing pundits far exceed that of their liberal counterparts.[116]

Armed with corporate and foundation money, the Right since the 1970s has attained an impressive foothold in the news industry and has gained the upper hand in the battle for the hearts and minds of the American public. Presiding over a conservative strategy session in 2003, Paul Weyrich, co-founder of the Heritage Foundation, exulted in the achievements of the movement he helped set in motion: "There are 1,500 conservative radio talk show hosts. . . . You have Fox News. You have the Internet, where all the successful sites are conservative. The ability to reach people with our point of view is like nothing we have ever seen before!"[117]

Business leaders since the 1970s, while simultaneously engaged in an aggressive struggle to shift the balance of power within the economic and political systems, have also joined in a campaign, in alliance with conservative activists, strategists, and intellectuals, to alter the ideological balance of power. This effort gave rise to a well-financed right-wing ideology machine that disgorges a continuous outpouring of high-profile books, opinion periodicals, policy reports, editorial statements, internet gossip, and television and radio commentary. This "Republican propaganda mill," as Lewis Lapham calls it, has become a powerful voice in American political culture.[118]

THE RIGHTWARD TURN IN POVERTY DISCOURSE

With renewed vigor in the 1970s, conservative business leaders and their allies set out to change the cultural climate. They advertised the virtues of free-market capitalism, small government, individual liberty, and self-reliance, and they denounced the evils of business regulation, labor unions, the welfare state, progressive taxation, and liberalism itself. In cooperation with an increasingly ideological Republican Party, they continue in this endeavor today and have gained a powerful presence in the political culture. This decades-long ideological mobilization has met with significant success. One important instance is the rightward drift of poverty discourse since the 1960s, with the war on poverty giving way to a "war against the poor" and a "war on welfare."[119] Through the tireless proselytizing of think tank intellectuals, political pundits, corporate lobbyists, business groups, and the Republican Party, and with little effective opposition from Democrats, a conservative orthodoxy has gained preeminence in the mainstream political culture, defining what counts as common sense on issues of poverty, inequality, welfare, and race.[120] To illustrate this shift in the ideological landscape, in what follows I briefly discuss four interrelated ideas that occupy a prominent position in today's poverty discourse: the perversity of the welfare state, government dependency, makers and takers, and personal responsibility.

The perversity of the welfare state. The 1970s witnessed the launching of a powerful "conservative disinformation campaign," one that continues to win converts today.[121] The gist of this campaign is the claim that government is the problem, not the solution, as Ronald Reagan famously affirmed, and that government efforts to combat poverty cause more harm than good. The welfare state, critics charge, undermines the work ethic, encourages idleness, promotes out-of-wedlock births, discourages family formation, and saps individual initiative. Charles Murray, indeed, has proposed that the poor would be better off if the entire federal welfare system for the working-age population were dismantled.[122] The incessant reference to "failed" government policies, one of the central themes of the right-wing offensive, pervades the mainstream thinking about poverty and welfare, trickling down to the larger public as well. According to a 2014 survey, nearly half of Americans and two-thirds of Republicans believe that aid to the poor "does more harm than good."[123] This "perversity thesis" has a twofold effect. First, it shifts the blame for poverty and its consequences from the labor market to big government, from corporate capitalism to liberal social programs. Second, it fuels skepticism about the efficacy of public policy, creating a reserve of ready opposition to what is, in reality, the only means possible for conducting a serious-minded war on poverty: the intervention of the federal government.[124]

Government dependency. Since the 1980s the issue of welfare dependency, broadened in recent years to include the receipt of just about any form of government assistance, has taken center stage, replacing poverty "as the main object of social policy."[125] The greatest evil, according to some sizable segment of the public, is not that people are poor, but that they are receiving a welfare check, food stamps, unemployment compensation, disability payments, or Medicaid assistance. Programs such as these, conservatives argue, however well-meaning, promote a crippling dependency, inhibiting the poor from lifting themselves out of poverty through their own individual efforts. The safety net, as Speaker of the House Paul Ryan puts it, has become an all-too-comfortable "hammock that lulls able-bodied people to lives of dependency and complacency, that drains them of their will and their incentive to make the most of their lives."[126] The rhetoric of dependency enables critics of the welfare state to change the conversation. By dramatizing the purported psychological damage resulting from the receipt of government aid, they avoid talking about the *causes* of economic deprivation—why so many low-income families cannot currently meet their needs for food, housing, medical care, and other essentials—and they avoid talking about the well-documented *benefits* of safety net programs.[127] The concept of dependency, as deployed by the Right, encourages Americans to think that the most pressing issue is not lack of opportunities for education and employment, but the moral impairment of the poor and the hazardous inducements of the welfare system.

Makers and takers. The welfare state, conservative critics argue, causes harm to its supposed beneficiaries. The even greater danger, however, is that easy access to government assistance is turning much of the country into a bunch of "freeloaders," people who get from government more than they give. This population of "takers" rather than "makers" is said to be quite large, too: 47 percent of Americans according to Mitt Romney, as stated at a fund-raiser in 2012, and as much as 60 percent according to Paul Ryan.[128] Regularly disseminated by, among other sources, Fox News, Tea Party activists, and the libertarian Right, this argument projects an image of a divided society, "us" versus "them": on the one side, hardworking, taxpaying, mostly white Americans, and on the other side a growing population of moochers and parasites, disproportionately nonwhite, living off the largesse of big government and the revenue generated by the nation's "job creators."[129] In this reverse class analysis, it is not the rich who are exploiting the poor, but the poor who are exploiting the rich.[130] The "makers" versus "takers" rhetoric, all the more persuasive due to the racialization of poverty and welfare, aggravates a situation in which it is already difficult for the poor to be seen in a sympathetic light or gain visibility as deserving recipients of government assistance.

Personal responsibility. In 1996, with bipartisan support, President Bill Clinton "ended welfare as we know it" by signing the Personal Responsibility and Work Opportunity Reconciliation Act. This piece of legislation elevated the concept of "personal responsibility," making a seemingly innocuous expression "central to our moral vocabulary" in debates about poverty, inequality, and welfare.[131] Among the value-laden implications it imparted are the following. (1) We are each responsible for our own life outcomes and should not blame outside forces if we fail to meet societal standards.[132] (2) Government has a role to play, but in a limited capacity, and only when potential beneficiaries are truly deserving—only when they exhibit consistently good behavior (e.g., demonstrate a willingness to work) and are in need of assistance for reasons beyond their own control. (3) Our duty to ensure our own self-sufficiency, our *personal* responsibility, supersedes our duty to our fellow human beings, our *social* responsibility. In this "age of responsibility," the moral imperative that each individual be self-reliant supplants the goal of establishing socioeconomic institutions that maximize opportunities for every citizen to flourish. The objective of eradicating poverty, in other words, is sacrificed to the aim of holding people accountable for their own life outcomes.[133] This conception of responsibility, in sum, is both highly individualistic, suggesting we are each largely on our own, obligated to fend for ourselves and owing nothing to society, and "deeply punitive," as Yascha Mounk argues, with the distribution of benefits predicated on judgments of moral worth.[134] It is also conservative, in the traditional sense that government is assigned only a minor role in promoting the well-being of the individual, a task, it is presumed, best left to the operation of market forces.

The language of the Right on issues of poverty and welfare, partly through sheer repetition, has carried the day.[135] Conservative intellectuals, pundits, and politicians, sometimes with tacit support from liberals, have promulgated a thoroughly individualistic ideology. They have directed public scrutiny toward the alleged pathologies of the poor while diverting attention from the failings of the American political economy. And they have ceaselessly denigrated the welfare state and government social programs, so effectively indeed that even Democrats seldom rise up in their defense. The right-wing ideology machine has been successful in propagating a view of poverty that, astonishingly, makes no reference to weak job growth, low wages, or rising inequality. Instead it offers "a substitute language, of deviance and deprivation."[136] Conservatives have managed to shift the focus of the poverty debate, inciting the public to notice one thing but not the other: to see the breakdown of the family, but not the deteriorating circumstances of American workers; to see the aberrant behavior of a ghetto "underclass," but not institutional discrimination and residential segregation; to see unwed mothers on welfare, but not work-family conflicts; to see the heroics of corporate "job creators," but not the struggles of the working poor; to see people on food stamps, but not jobs that fail to pay a living wage; to see the costs of social spending, but not the harm caused by cutbacks in government programs; and to see the nonmainstream lives of the poor, but not the irresponsible conduct of economic and political elites.

CONCLUSION

The political culture in the United States predisposes Americans toward individualistic explanations for poverty; the normal operation of the mainstream
media tacitly reinforces this tendency; and the right-wing ideology machine,
with its unrelenting attack on government, absolves the capitalist economy
from any responsibility for the existence of poverty. It is not surprising in this
cultural and intellectual environment that many Americans blame poverty on
the poor and that structural solutions are largely absent from the political
agenda.

What Americans believe about the causes of poverty and what they think
should be done to combat the problem are significant in their own right, but
also because they influence government policy. It is too simple, of course, to
think that the government simply does what the electorate wants—if it did
we would have national health care, a higher minimum wage, gun control,
and a cleaner environment. Social policy in our imperfect democracy, as we
saw in chapter 6, does not so much echo the desires of the public as it reflects
the preferences of economic elites.[137] But public opinion is a factor. It is
difficult to imagine the advent of a real war on poverty without somehow
encouraging more Americans to take the problem seriously. Terry Maguire, a
welfare rights activist based in Philadelphia, makes just this point: "You
can't end poverty without winning the hearts and minds of the people. It's a
battle of ideas, a battle of images, and ultimately a battle of stories."[138]

Chapter Eight

The Social System and Poverty

WE ARE NOT ALONE

We have relatives, friends, peers, neighbors, and coworkers. We belong to an assortment of groups, some by virtue of our race, ethnicity, or gender, others on a more voluntary basis: food co-ops, street gangs, book clubs, and social movements. We attend schools, churches, community meetings, and political rallies. We join with others at parks, basketball courts, golf courses, and music concerts. We get together for marriages and funerals, anniversaries and birthdays, weekend parties and poker games. We interact with a variety of officials, functionaries, and service professionals: principals and teachers, cops and judges, priests and therapists, bankers and lawyers, real estate and insurance agents, welfare caseworkers and medical personnel. We are also tied to others through our location in social space. We reside in a particular state and region, in an urban or rural area, in the city or the suburbs. We live in a "good" neighborhood or a "bad" neighborhood. In all these ways and more, we are connected to other people, and not just through market mechanisms, not just as self-interested buyers and sellers. Yet these distinctly *social* connections have significant *economic* consequences.

Individualistic theories imagine that we each chart our own course. Our economic destinies are conditioned only by our personal attributes: our choices and preferences, motivations and aspirations, abilities and talents, knowledge and skills, attitudes and values. Proponents of this perspective seem to envision economic life as a series of competitive races, with all contestants beginning from the same starting point and subject to the same rules and regulations. Noncontestants in any particular event are observers only. While they might stand on the sidelines and cheer for their favorites, they do not intervene in the competition. And because such contests take place on a level playing field, how individuals fare is entirely a matter of their own prowess and determination.

In reality, however, the race of life is far from fair. Not everyone begins from the same place, the rules do not apply equally to all contestants, and merit is by no means the only determinant of success. In real-life competition, furthermore, we do not arrive at the starting gate or make our way from the starting gate to the finish line on our own. We sometimes rely on the kindness of strangers, and we often get a little help from our friends. Other people are not just spectators; they make a difference in how well or how poorly we perform. If we are fortunate, the people we know will keep us informed about where and when important races are run, see to it we get entered into the most prestigious competitions, introduce us to the race officials, make sure we get a favorable starting position, and supply us with the skills and equipment we need to compete successfully. And once the race commences, they will provide aid along the way, guiding us toward the inside track, giving us a helpful boost now and then, subverting the efforts of our competitors, and even sometimes carrying us along on their shoulders. If we are not so fortunate, on the other hand, if we are not surrounded by people who are in a position to shower us with assistance, the race of life can be arduous, just finishing difficult, and victory doubtful. In real-world competitions, without the benefit of a strong supporting cast, even people who possess a natural gift for running may find themselves left behind.

An individual's place in the social structure exerts a powerful influence on his or her economic prospects. Some are advantaged and others disadvantaged by their location in the network of social statuses, social relations, and social institutions. People's ability to acquire valuable cultural and human capital and the availability of opportunities to convert that capital into a good job and a decent life are profoundly affected by the characteristics and composition of their social relationships and group affiliations, their institutional ties and interpersonal networks, and their neighborhoods and communities. The individualistic perspective fails to provide an adequate understanding of inequality and poverty precisely because it neglects this crucial relationship between social structure and economic mobility. As Glen Loury observes: "The merit notion that, in a free society, each individual will rise to the level justified by his or her competence conflicts with the observation that no one travels that road entirely alone." The social system has relevance for an analysis of poverty because people's economic outcomes are shaped by their social contexts, and these produce differences in "what otherwise equally competent individuals can achieve."[1]

The individualistic perspective, as we have seen, offers a faulty analysis because it fails to recognize adequately how economic, political, and cultural forces contribute to the persistence of poverty. This chapter examines a further limitation of individualistic theories. In explaining why some people are more vulnerable to poverty than others, these theories place too much emphasis on the deficiencies of individuals and too little on the deficiencies of their social environment. With its narrow focus on individual attributes, the individualistic perspective ignores the independent influence of people's social location on their life chances.

My objective in this chapter is to illustrate the importance of social system variables for understanding poverty. I pursue this by discussing three phenomena that have received considerable attention in the social sciences: group memberships, neighborhood and place-based effects, and social networks. In each case my purpose is to demonstrate the inadequacy of individualistic explanations and to show, in support of a structural perspective, that people's economic outcomes are contingent on social forces outside their immediate control.

GROUP MEMBERSHIPS

The characteristics of the groups to which we belong influence our economic prospects. Group memberships matter in two ways. First, they contribute to the formation of what we normally think of as individual traits: our interests, preferences, beliefs, and abilities. Second, they determine our access to tangible resources, including opportunities for education and employment. Group affiliations shape our aspirations and the means available to realize those aspirations. They affect both who we are and what we do with our lives.

Groups differ in how they are formed and in their characteristics and composition. Individuals become group members through some combination of choice and constraint. Some group affiliations, along with the social identities they confer, derive from ascribed statuses, as in the case of groupings based on gender, nationality, race, and ethnicity. Some groups, including those made up of friends, peers, and cohorts, are by-products of social processes that sort people into neighborhoods, schools, and jobs. And some memberships are more voluntary, such as when a parent participates in the PTA, a student pledges a sorority, or an employee joins a labor union or professional organization.

However they originate, groups exert an independent effect on individuals' economic lives, helping some and hurting others. People's prospects for accumulating wealth or avoiding poverty depend on their group memberships, not just their native abilities, achievement motivations, or human capital endowments. The outcomes people attain thus depart from what would be expected if individual attributes were the sole determinants of economic achievement. Due to their group memberships, as studies of race and gender consistently show, otherwise equivalent workers may differ significantly in their earnings and occupational trajectories. Because groups matter, life chances are not reducible to individual-level characteristics.

Steven Durlauf, acknowledging the significance of group affiliations to economic attainment, proposes a "memberships theory" of poverty and inequality.[2] This theory "shifts the emphasis in a causal explanation of poverty from individual characteristics . . . to memberships and group influences that constrain individual outcomes."[3] Durlauf identifies a number of avenues through which memberships influence individual achievement, including peer group effects, adult role model effects, and labor market connections.[4] The influence of peers, for example, might explain why some adolescents are drawn toward sports while other are more academically oriented, why some are politically engaged while others are apathetic, or why some hew to the straight and narrow while others are drawn toward delinquency and crime. Young people may be influenced by the experiences and examples of their elders as well. By observing adults in their circle of acquaintances, adolescents make inferences about the payoff for education, the likelihood of getting a good job, and the viability of the American Dream. Adult role models, wittingly or not, affect adolescents' aspirations and their vision of how best to make a life for themselves. Group affiliations matter also because they provide members with connections of varying quality that might be exploited to aid educational advancement or find employment. In these ways and others, group differences result in individual inequalities. The characteristics of the groups to which a person belongs, independent of individual and family characteristics, "condition the range of the individual's life economic prospects."[5]

A recurring theme in the literature on poverty concerns the potentially detrimental influence the group memberships of the poor have on their norms and behaviors. But whether or not this occurs, as Durlauf emphasizes, depends on the surrounding material conditions. The cultural theory of poverty frequently overlooks this important point when it posits an autonomous "underclass" subculture. Peer groups and role models typically promote patterns of deviant or seemingly self-destructive behavior only when the social and economic foundations are already weak and when conventional avenues of achievement are closed off. A group norm usually emerges and induces conformity when it has a genuine reality quotient, when it appears reasonably appropriate given the availability of opportunities and the experiences of group comembers. Adolescents are more likely to think education is a sham when schools are run down, teachers have low expectations, and graduates fail to move up the occupational ladder. They are more apt to be persuaded of the benefits of illicit employment when legitimate jobs are scarce, demeaning, or dead end. And they are more liable to fall into a pattern of deviant, defiant, or rebellious behavior when they perceive a bleak future or inhabit a plainly unjust social milieu.[6]

Group memberships affect economic outcomes not only because comembers influence each other's aspirations, norms, and behaviors, but also because groups vary in their status and prestige. Some groups occupy a more privileged position than others: men compared to women, whites compared to nonwhites, natives compared to immigrants, professionals compared to hourly workers. As a result of normal psychological processes, furthermore, individuals exhibit a preference for and have a more positive view of group comembers. They are psychologically inclined to perceive people who look, talk, and live the way they do as more intelligent, competent, and worthy than people who are different. Individuals also tend to adopt stereotypical views of those outside their group and exhibit bias in evaluating their behavior and performance. The predisposition to categorize people into in-groups and out-groups, a cognitive process often operating beneath the level of awareness, is an important cause of discrimination, one with particularly significant consequences in educational and occupational settings. Group memberships, due to such social psychological mechanisms, can either facilitate or impede economic attainment. They are relevant because the members of some groups are regarded more highly and treated more favorably than the members of other groups. The benefits of belonging to a privileged group, moreover, as in the case of white males, often flow automatically and invisibly to members, regardless even of whether they explicitly identify with the group. The members of less-privileged groups, on the other hand, because they are judged more negatively and subject to prejudice and discrimination, encounter substantial obstacles to achievement and are more vulnerable to poverty.[7]

Group memberships are relevant to individual attainment also because groups, not just individuals, are actors in the competitive struggle for access to resources and opportunities, often act in a deliberate manner to promote their members' interests, and vary in their capacity to secure desirable ends. The life outcomes of individuals are not just a matter of their own personal attributes and endowments; they are tied also to the relative status and power of the groups to which they belong, including groups based on race and gender.[8] Other kinds of groups matter as well. As Kim Weeden shows, for example, explicitly challenging individualistic explanations of economic inequality, some occupational groups, professional groups in particular— through such means as licensing, certification, and credentialing—are able to boost the earnings of their members by limiting competition. By contrast, members of occupational groups who lack the power to implement such "social closure" practices, including most low-end service workers, are fully subject to the leveling effect of market forces. Workers' earnings thus imperfectly reflect their human capital, as individuals' wages depend also on whether or not they belong to occupational groups able to set favorable rules governing the operation of their particular labor market.[9]

Groups differ in broader dimensions of social power as well, in their ability to secure economic rewards, influence the course of government policy, and shape the imagery and messages disseminated by the cultural apparatus. Dominant groups, as Charles Tilly argues in his theory of "durable inequality," are able to exploit subordinate groups and hoard opportunities. Because social institutions favor powerful groups, and because groups tend to channel resources to comembers, individuals belonging to privileged groups enjoy undeserved advantages, while those belonging to less-privileged groups suffer undeserved disadvantages. People's economic fate is not simply a function of their personal traits; it depends also on the status and power of their group memberships.[10]

GEOGRAPHICAL DISPARITIES AND NEIGHBORHOOD EFFECTS

Over the past couple of decades, geography has emerged as an important variable in the study of economic inequality: the city versus the country, coastal areas versus the heartland, highly populated states versus sparsely populated states, the urban northeast versus the rural south. Because resources and opportunities vary by location, where people live is a significant determinant of economic outcomes. In some places success is easier to achieve; in other places poverty is harder to avoid.

The national figures on unemployment, poverty, and other measures of economic well-being conceal significant variations among communities, cities, states, and regions. Since 2000, and especially since the Great Recession, "place-based disparities" in economic well-being have become increasingly visible. According to a 2017 report by the Economic Innovation Group, 52.3 million people, approximately 17 percent of the US population, live in economically "distressed" communities, with another 57.2 million people living in "at-risk" communities. A community is counted as distressed based on measures of educational attainment, housing occupancy, labor force participation, poverty rate, and median income, plus two other particularly revealing trend measures: the percent change in the number of jobs and the percent change in the number of business establishments. Between 2011 and 2015 communities identified as distressed, located disproportionately in the urban North and the rural South, experienced a 6.0 percent decline in employment and a 6.3 percent decline in business establishments, compared to a 9.4 percent increase in employment and a 4.2 percent increase in business establishments for the country as a whole. For hundreds of communities across the United States, to put it differently, the Great Recession has not come to an end, and many are likely to experience continued economic stagnation for years to come.[11] Economic recovery has also been much slower in small cities than in big ones, a worrying sign that low-population metro areas may have a difficult economic future.[12] The lesson is clear: place matters. What is good for the country as a whole is not equally good everywhere, and for some zip codes is not good at all. It follows, furthermore, that how well individuals do in their lives—whether they end up prosperous or poor—is dependent not just on their cognitive ability, work ethic, or education, but also on where they happen to reside.

Studies of the geography of inequality over the past several decades have focused especially on neighborhoods. This is understandable. For most people, the neighborhood is their most immediate and salient environment. Some neighborhoods, as we all know, are better than others, and whether a neighborhood is "good" or "bad" has profound consequences for the lives of its residents. Neighborhoods differ most importantly in their class and racial composition. Income segregation, largely a by-product of rising economic inequality, has been on an upward trajectory since the 1970s. The result is a growing chasm between wealthy communities at one end and impoverished communities at the other, with a shrinking share of the population living in middle-income communities. More so than at any other time in recent American history, rich families and poor families—especially those with children—occupy increasingly separate and vastly different social worlds, each invisible to the other. The experiences and opportunities of children in the United States, which have long been among the most unequal in the developed world, are becoming even more unequal.[13]

Racial residential segregation has declined somewhat since the 1970s, though African Americans and Hispanics, particularly those residing in large metropolitan areas, continue to live apart from non-Hispanic whites.[14] High-poverty neighborhoods, reflecting the intersection of class and race, are also often "ghettos" or "barrios," populated primarily by people of color.[15] But many poor racial/ethnic minorities also reside in high-poverty pockets located in the rural South, along the Mexican border, on reservations out West, or in declining suburban communities.[16] The number of Americans living in these "extremely poor" neighborhoods—census tracks with a rate of poverty exceeding 40 percent—has more than doubled since 2000, with a large number of African American and Hispanic households isolated in areas of concentrated poverty.[17]

This pattern of residential segregation is among the most consequential and disturbing features of American society. It not only violates the ideal of integration, but it also establishes *place* as a fundamental dimension of social stratification. The experiences and life outcomes of two otherwise identical individuals vary greatly depending on where they happen to live. Regardless of their abilities and how hard they might try to get ahead, kids growing up in the South Bronx, one of the poorest communities in the country, do not have anything like the same life chances as kids raised in wealthy Connecticut suburbs. The inhabitants of different neighborhoods encounter "fundamentally different opportunities."[18] This is especially true at the extremes—for the growing number of people who live in either very impoverished, "low-opportunity neighborhoods," or very affluent, "high-opportunity neighborhoods."[19] The undeniably deep disparities between poor communities, disproportionately black and Hispanic, and rich communities, disproportionately white, have only grown larger since the Great Recession.[20] The effects of such geographical inequities on the educational and economic life chances of residents undermine the principle of equality of opportunity, the central tenet of the American Dream.

Neighborhood inequalities magnify household inequalities, with particularly adverse consequences for the poor. The misfortune of living in a poor neighborhood compounds the misfortune of living in a poor family. Individuals lacking in family resources, if they reside in high-poverty neighborhoods, encounter a "double burden"; they are deprived of community resources as well.[21] Poor families located in segregated and impoverished neighborhoods—"opportunity deserts," as Eddie Glaude Jr. calls them—are not only isolated from the mainstream of society, but they are also commonly stuck with crowded and dysfunctional schools, inferior housing, inadequate public facilities, and an unhealthy and sometimes dangerous residential environment.[22] Reflecting the connection between neighborhood conditions and economic mobility, the residents of impoverished neighborhoods are also likely to pass along their poverty to their children.[23] The social, economic, and political mechanisms channeling affluent families into affluent neighborhoods and poor families into poor neighborhoods yield cumulative advantages for the former and cumulative disadvantages for the latter. The dearth of social resources in poor communities penalizes poor families, making it harder for them to provide for their children's future. The abundance of social resources in rich communities rewards rich families, making it easier for them to ensure a privileged life for their offspring. The geographical distribution of social resources—stratification by place—underlies the self-perpetuating nature of poverty and inequality.[24]

The concept of "neighborhood effects" refers to the influence of neighborhood conditions on life outcomes over and beyond the effects of individual and family characteristics.[25] Research has focused especially on how the attributes of neighborhoods affect the life chances of children, adolescents, and young adults. Among the issues most commonly addressed in this literature are social and cognitive development, physical and mental health, school readiness and performance, educational attainment, sexual behavior and fertility, family formation, delinquency and crime, and, for adults, employment and earnings. Compared to their middle-class counterparts, and to poor children in low-poverty neighborhoods as well, children who grow up in impoverished neighborhoods are significantly handicapped. They have higher rates of infant mortality, child abuse, and low birth weight. They are less prepared when they begin school, perform less well in the classroom, score lower on educational achievement tests, are more likely to drop out, and are less likely to attend college. They have a greater risk of teenage and nonmarital births and a higher incidence of social, behavioral, and emotional problems. They are more likely to engage in delinquent and criminal behavior, use drugs, drink alcohol, and suffer from psychological distress and depression.[26] Children growing up in poor communities have hard lives and are deprived of opportunities for personal development, a decent education, and a secure economic future. And as Patrick Sharkey documents, drawing attention to the intergenerational inheritance of both place and poverty, the prospects for such children are even bleaker if their parents, as is the case for many African Americans, were also raised in poor communities.[27]

Neighborhood environments influence life outcomes because they shape people's values, attitudes, and aspirations and determine their access to resources and opportunities. But how precisely do high-poverty areas yield adverse effects, and through what specific processes, mechanisms, or path ways do residential contexts limit the life chances of the poor? I present below a brief overview of five characteristics of poor neighborhoods that have been hypothesized to play a causal role in producing adverse neighborhood effects.[28] This is intended to illustrate how and why location matters, illuminate some of the fundamental differences between the living circumstances of the rich and the poor, and suggest why some poor communities might be better off than others.[29]

Institutional Resources

Neighborhoods vary in the quantity and quality of their institutional resources: schools, libraries, child-care providers, recreational centers, youth programs, parks and playgrounds, medical facilities, grocery stores, transportation systems, and social service agencies.[30] Community resources are a vital element of a healthy neighborhood landscape. They play a significant role in the process of socialization; afford opportunities for safe and enriching activities; supply essential goods and services; contribute to the acquisition of psychological, cultural, and human capital; and function to stimulate political awareness and promote political solidarity. Affluent communities, rich in institutional resources, provide their residents with a multitude of benefits, augmenting the ability of privileged families to transmit advantages to their children. Institutional resources in high-poverty neighborhoods, on the other hand, are typically unavailable, inaccessible, unaffordable, and of low quality.[31] To supply their children with vital services, poor parents are often forced to compensate by pursuing various "resource-seeking strategies," including costly searches and commutes outside their neighborhoods.[32] The absence of community resources is an especially severe problem for poor families because they have a greater need for the support such resources offer and are less able to purchase equivalent resources in the private market. The weakness of institutional resources in poor neighborhoods makes it difficult for already hard-pressed parents to ensure their children receive a healthy upbringing, are adequately prepared for school, and have a reasonable opportunity for upward mobility.

Labor Market Conditions

The state of the labor market in poor communities is another potential cause of disadvantaging neighborhood effects. In the 1970s and 1980s, William Julius Wilson argues, poor urban communities were wracked by a series of "structural economic changes": "the shift from goods-producing to service-producing industries, the increasing polarization of the labor market into low-wage and high-wage sectors, technological innovations, and the relocation of manufacturing industries out of the central cities." This economic restructuring worsened an already weak central-city labor market, giving rise to a "new urban poverty" characterized by high levels of joblessness.[33] An uneven recovery since the Great Recession has brought increasing business creation and job growth to prosperous neighborhoods, but since 2010 the economic prospects for residents in poorer communities have only deteriorated, and even middle-class neighborhoods are barely holding their own.[34] Adolescents and young adults in high-poverty neighborhoods, besides facing the barrier of job discrimination, have few local opportunities to learn the ropes of the work world, gain experience and training, build up a record of stable employment, or cultivate labor market contacts.[35] Jobs in the community, if available at all, are usually low paying, dead end, insecure, and rife with frustration and conflict—as Daniel Dohan says about barrio jobs, "more a source of ongoing difficulty than a source of manifest opportunity."[36] The characteristics of local labor markets severely constrain poor people's employment prospects and their later-life economic outcomes. Adolescents who grow up in high-poverty neighborhoods, whether located in big cities or the rural countryside, and people who reside there as adults, pay a high price. They have lower wages, work fewer hours, and spend more time below the poverty line than otherwise equivalent workers.[37]

Political Power

The concentration of disadvantaged Americans in impoverished areas and of advantaged Americans in prosperous areas generates geographical disparities in political power. Poor people, already susceptible to political marginalization, are further handicapped, as Amy Widestrom argues, because their communities tend to be lacking in political resources. They typically have a shortage of voluntary associations, civic organizations, and "safe neighborhood spaces" where residents can gather to express their grievances, forge bonds of political solidarity, cultivate political skills, and gain experience in political activism. This weakness in the "civic environment" depresses political participation, diminishes the capacity of residents to organize for political purposes, and reduces the community's political clout. In highly distressed neighborhoods, where almost everyone is struggling to get by, people lose confidence in their "political capacity." Poor neighborhoods suffer politically also because they are far less likely to receive positive attention from officeholders and political candidates, who generally have more to gain by catering to voters in affluent districts. Given their lack of political leverage, high-poverty communities, not surprisingly, are victims of government neglect and inadequate public investment. The political powerlessness of poor communities, in turn, because they are unable to get their share of scarce social resources, exacerbates the adversities caused by other neighborhood effects.[38]

Collective Socialization

Family members socialize children, but their upbringing is influenced by a variety of community agents as well, including adult neighbors, peer groups, role models, mentors, and social institutions. Neighborhoods differ in the prevalence of these bearers of "collective socialization" and in their effectiveness at promoting norms and behaviors conducive to educational and occupational achievement. In neighborhoods characterized by concentrated poverty, residential segregation, and social isolation, processes of collective socialization may be inadequate or even detrimental. The influence of delinquent peers and the paucity of positive mentors and adult role models, some research suggests, leave poor adolescents alienated from mainstream norms. They are also propelled into illicit behaviors by hostile treatment at the hands of external authorities (e.g., the police), by the brute reality of limited opportunities, and by perceptions of relative deprivation: the recognition of how daunting the obstacles are that they face as compared to more affluent teenagers. Adolescents growing up under these harsh circumstances are bound to find it difficult to envision a successful future or believe that "playing by the rules" is a surefire recipe for avoiding poverty.[39]

Social Disorganization

A community exhibits social organization when residents are bound together through frequent interactions, social ties, and shared norms. Social organization, according to Robert Sampson and his colleagues, promotes "collective efficacy."[40] Residents trust and help one another, they monitor the behavior of children in the neighborhood, and they are willing and able to intervene to enforce community norms and pursue common goals. Because high-poverty neighborhoods, deprived of essential resources, are often lacking in collective efficacy, patterns of trust and informal social control are weaker. Children who grow up in such communities, accordingly, are more likely to get caught up in socially undesirable behaviors and in turn experience poor educational and employment outcomes. Social disorganization at the neighborhood level adds to the difficulties people face in their efforts to cope with or escape from poverty.[41]

The scholarship on neighborhood effects introduces a structural dimension to the study of poverty and inequality by shifting the focus from individual characteristics to community characteristics and also to the "wider spatial environment" within which particular communities themselves are located.[42] The insight that residential location, particularly at the extremes, is a powerful determinant of life chances presents a significant challenge to the prevailing moral calculus. People "don't want believe in the importance of neighborhoods," Nancy Denton states. If they did, they would have to acknowledge the problem of spatial inequality, admit that getting ahead is not simply a matter of individual effort, and even entertain the idea that society bears some responsibility for remedying what is a patently unjust distribution of resources and opportunities.[43]

SOCIAL NETWORKS AND SOCIAL CAPITAL

People are not only members of groups and residents of neighborhoods; they are also nodes in social networks.[44] The life of any particular individual intersects at various points with the lives of any number of other individuals. The term "social network" is commonly used to denote the pattern of these recurrent interpersonal relationships. An individual's social network consists of the people he or she is connected to in one capacity or another: family members; friends; acquaintances; coworkers; and diverse "institutional agents," including teachers, child-care providers, social service workers, and criminal justice personnel.[45] The sum of these networks is sociologically significant because the ties binding people together and connecting individuals to organizations perform a variety of important social functions. They channel information, convey cultural messages, create social solidarities, forge expectations and obligations, facilitate the enforcement of social norms, engender relations of mutual trust, serve as sources of social support, and operate as conduits of power and influence. In the performance of these functions, furthermore, social networks shape the distribution of resources and opportunities, advantaging some and disadvantaging others.

Social scientists have coined the term "social capital" to refer to the distinctly *social* resources embedded in social networks. Unlike financial capital and human capital, properties of individuals located respectively in their "bank accounts" and "inside their heads," social capital is a uniquely structural resource. It "inheres in the structure of relations between actors and among actors." Social capital consists of the benefits people derive from their personal interactions and social relations. If we have ties to others, we are not solely dependent on our own personal resources. We can draw on our connections to family members, friends, and acquaintances to help us achieve our goals. The concept of social capital, by drawing attention to the importance of *social* as distinct from *personal* resources, challenges the premise that individuals are the solitary authors of their own lives. People's economic fate is shaped in a multitude of ways by their connections to others and by an assortment of more or less helping or hindering hands.[46]

Individuals sometimes even make investments in social capital, strategically cultivating contacts ("networking") with the expectation of reaping rewards down the road from knowing the "right" people. Most social connections, however, do not originate from economic motives or self-interested calculations, but arise routinely as by-products of ordinary social behavior or through people's involvement in organizations—child-care centers, for example, as Mario Small illustrates.[47] However formed, these connections can be accessed and mobilized for instrumental purposes. Through their networks, for example, individuals might acquire knowledge about housing, job openings, business opportunities, or government programs; they might transmit information to prospective employers about their availability and qualifications; they might procure letters of introduction, referrals, recommendations, or even job offers; they might obtain loans, investment tips, or other forms of financial assistance; they might receive advice, counseling, or emotional and psychological support; and they might get help in dealing with problems of child care, transportation, or spousal abuse. The luckiest people in the world are not necessarily people who *need* people, as Barbra Streisand sings, but people who *know* people.

The social science literature on social networks and social capital is highly relevant to the study of poverty and inequality.[48] Individuals vary in the extent and composition of their social ties and in their concomitant access to information and influence.[49] Some are implicated in "resource-rich" networks consisting of well-placed contacts and conveying timely, reliable, and useful information, while others are implicated in "resource-poor" networks.[50] As a result, individuals differ in the quantity and quality of their social capital, their stock of social resources. These differences have consequences for people's economic lives, particularly because social connections are so important in matching workers to jobs. Employers regularly use networks to recruit employees, and job seekers frequently rely on connections with friends and acquaintances to find employment. The quality of our social networks thus plays a significant, though often unacknowledged, role in determining whether we are employed or unemployed, have a good job or a bad job, rise to the top or remain stuck at the bottom. The distribution of social resources results in enhanced opportunities for some and diminished opportunities for others. Differences in social capital, even when individuals are otherwise comparable, generate unequal economic outcomes. This focus on social network and social capital inequalities underscores the relevance of yet another set of social system variables affecting the economic fate of individuals.

The empirical research on the relationship between economic status and social resources supports three broad conclusions. First, people who are weak in social networks and social capital are vulnerable to poverty. Second, people who are poor tend to be weak in social networks and social capital. Third, poor families are not uniformly lacking in social connections, and their ability to cope with or rise out of poverty is dependent on the configuration and quality of their social ties and the effectiveness of their strategies for tapping social resources. The concept of social networks can thus be usefully employed to illuminate the causes of poverty, the consequences of poverty, and why some people manage to escape poverty while others remain poor.

The poor are not all alike in their social networks, nor are they all equally deficient in social resources. In general, however, the social networks typical of the poor differ from those of the affluent, and these differences help explain why poor people are sometimes trapped in poverty. In what follows, I discuss some of the key social network characteristics of the poor, though briefly and only for the purpose of illustrating a key point: we cannot understand adequately the circumstances, struggles, and prospects of the poor if we attend only to their individual traits and neglect their social network and social capital characteristics.

Size of Social Networks

The social networks of the poor are less extensive than those of the affluent. The most impoverished among the poor, including the homeless, the long-term unemployed, residents of high-poverty neighborhoods, and the elderly, often have few enduring ties to other people.[51] This is partly because the poor are deficient in individual resources, including financial, cultural, and political capital. Since they have so little to share, they are not valued network partners. Their poverty makes it difficult for them to provide assistance to others or fulfill the obligations that social networks entail. They do not have money to lend, contacts to get a friend a job, a car to help neighbors with transportation problems, or political leverage to secure favors from elected officials. Poor people who are short of resources from which others might benefit are susceptible to being excluded from social networks. They might also disengage voluntarily, cutting themselves off from contact with others out of concern about becoming a burden, forfeiting their independence, disappointing personal contacts, or being unable to reciprocate.[52] Even those who do have a modicum of resources might choose to withdraw from demanding networks so as not to deplete their own limited stock or might perceive greater costs than rewards from their network relations.[53] In any case, the resource constraints of the poor often leave them with impoverished social connections.

Social Isolation

The social world of a sizable segment of the poverty population, racial and ethnic minorities in particular, consists mainly of other poor people. As a result of economic restructuring, residential segregation, and housing discrimination, many of the poor, particularly African Americans in high-poverty urban ghettos, are geographically isolated and, with the notable exception of personnel in the criminal justice system, have limited contact with people outside their neighborhoods. While they may have close ties with each other, the "truly disadvantaged" among the poor have minimal interaction with "individuals and institutions that represent mainstream society."[54] This "social isolation," Wilson argues, amplifies the problem of poverty because it diminishes access to positive role models, mentors, job contacts, employment information, and connections in the labor market.[55] Unemployed workers in high-poverty neighborhoods are embedded in social networks consisting disproportionately of other people who are also jobless and thus a poor source for tips about employment opportunities. The socially isolated jobless are vulnerable to network "congestion": their connections include too few people who can provide useful job information and too many people who are in need of such information.[56]

The poor also disproportionately belong to negatively stereotyped outgroups: African Americans, Latinos, immigrants, welfare recipients, and single mothers. Even if they are not geographically isolated because of residential segregation, poor people may still experience social isolation. Since people tend to confine their networks to others similar to themselves, and since privileged groups tend to hoard their privileges, poor minorities have limited access to the valuable social resources that in-groups possess. Thus, nonwhite job seekers are disadvantaged in the labor market because they lack influential connections in their own circle of acquaintances and are excluded from more resource-rich white networks.[57] Deirdre Royster shows, for example, how racially exclusive social networks, by enabling white graduates from a vocational school to monopolize desirable blue-collar jobs, left equally, if not more, qualified black workers unemployed or underemployed.[58]

Difficulty in Mobilizing Social Networks

Even when they are not socially isolated, the poor cannot necessarily count on getting help from their labor market connections. Sandra Smith, drawing on interviews with 105 low-income African Americans, found they were often unwilling to assist job-seeking friends and acquaintances.[59] They were particularly wary about using their influence when they had doubts about a person's reliability or work ethic and were concerned about their own often-insecure employment status. "Overwhelmingly," Smith reports, "respondents were fearful of making bad referrals that might tarnish their own reputations and threaten their labor market stability." As one of her interviewees explained, "If they going to use my name, I don't want them messing around. I don't want nobody messing up under my name."[60] Poor job seekers are disadvantaged not only because they lack influential social ties, Smith's study suggests, but also because their labor market contacts, due to their own precarious status, are sometimes reluctant to offer assistance.

Preponderance of Strong Ties

The poor participate in social networks composed more of "strong ties," ties to relatives and friends, than "weak ties," ties to acquaintances.[61] Strong ties have their strengths; close friends are available, motivated to provide assistance, and willing perhaps to go out on a limb.[62] But, as Mark Granovetter emphasizes, weak ties also have certain strengths. Unlike people we know well, who tend to be very much like ourselves, people we know casually often differ from us, move in separate circles, and know people we do not know. The unique strength of weak ties is that they establish connections to individuals located in social space other than our own. Weak ties thus create more expansive networks, which are more likely to provide participants with access to "novel" rather than "redundant" information, such as about job opportunities.[63] While all ties put us in the loop, weak ties put us in a bigger loop, supplying us with a wider range of interpersonal resources. The poor are disadvantaged because their networks consist more of strong ties than of resource-rich weak ties.[64]

Reliance on Disposable Ties

Matthew Desmond's research shows that many of the urban poor are lacking even in the strong ties associated with kinship networks. They do not have close and lasting relations with people they can count on for either emotional or material support. Instead of relatives or longtime friends, they rely on acquaintances for assistance in helping them to secure food, shelter, and child care, for example. These ties, Desmond finds, tend to be "emotionally intense," "demanding" and "suffocating," contrary to what is normally the case for weak ties. But they are also typically short-lived, unstable, and character-ized by low levels of trust. And while such "disposable" ties may provide services that enable poor people to survive on a day-to-day basis, they are not a source of lasting support and do not yield the sort of resources that might help the poor escape their poverty.[65]

Homogeneous Social Networks

Social networks, according to Patricia Kelly, are particularly valuable if they are "composed of persons with differing social status, linked in a variety of ways, who play multiple roles in several fields of activity."[66] Weak ties are strong, but they are even stronger if they are diverse, if they are composed of people from different social and cultural backgrounds and include well-placed connections.[67] People implicated in networks consisting of weak *and* varied ties, including links to high-status contacts, have a greater chance of securing useful information, obtaining valuable referrals and recommenda-tions, and otherwise extracting benefits from their social connections. The poor are disadvantaged because their networks, even if they include weak ties, tend to be more homogeneous and horizontal, consisting of people of the same social status as themselves, rather than varied and vertical. Thus, even when the poor successfully exploit their connections to find employment, they typically end up being routed into low-wage, dead-end jobs, achieving lateral mobility but not upward mobility.[68] Because poor people lack influen-tial contacts, their social ties, whether weak or strong, exhibit weakness rather than strength.

Lack of Productive Social Capital

Social capital, Pierre Bourdieu observes, "exerts a multiplier effect."[69] Social connections facilitate the acquisition of human, cultural, and political capital and increase the value of these as well. Poor families are susceptible to persistent poverty in part because their lack of social capital impedes their ability to accumulate other forms of capital. Whether in the form of intimate family ties or ties between families and schools, strong social networks im-prove the educational performance of children.[70] Because of the quality of their ties to teachers and school administrators, middle-class parents are able to ensure their children have access to scarce educational resources, includ-ing the attention of teachers.[71] Other research illustrates how mentors aug-ment the human capital of new entrants into the labor force. Silvia Domínguez and Celeste Watkins document how low-income mothers gained valuable training and experience through their connections to higher-status coworkers.[72] Poor people who lack social capital, on the other hand, who do not have helpful ties into schools and labor markets or within the workplace, are disadvantaged in their ability to acquire education, training, and skills.

Social connections facilitate the formation of cultural capital as well, at least when such connections cut across class and race boundaries. Having ties to an assortment of individuals with diverse backgrounds and experiences and to a variety of social institutions enhances people's opportunities to acquire knowledge about the workings of organizations, learn how to navigate their way in otherwise alien social environments, and gain a feeling of comfort and confidence in mainstream social settings. Low-income mothers, according to one study, reported significant benefits from their ties to higher-status people. The latter not only opened access to jobs, but also imparted valuable cultural capital by exposing poor women to subtle rules of the game and by offering "lessons about how to get ahead and function successfully in the work world."[73] Poor people deprived of social capital are likely to be inadequately informed about how to apply for jobs, create a favorable impression at interviews, conduct themselves in the workplace, and negotiate their way in the labor market. Because they lack quality social capital, poor people are liable to be deficient in cultural capital as well.

Preponderance of Social Support Ties

The social networks typical of the poor, particularly those located in high-poverty urban neighborhoods, are smaller and consist more of strong ties than weak ties; they are made up of people who mainly know each other, networks that are tight knit and insular rather than dispersed and diversified; and they are homogeneous, composed mostly of other poor people. These networks embody valuable social resources. For example, they may facilitate the participation of low-income mothers in the low-wage labor market by providing them with access to child care and transportation assistance.[74] But as Xavier de Souza Briggs argues, such networks engender a form of social capital that better serves the purpose of "social support," enabling the poor to "get by," than of "social leverage," enabling the poor to "get ahead."[75] The predominance of social support networks among the poor is due not only to the configuration of their social ties, but also to their limited personal resources and to the circumstance of poverty itself, in which day-to-day demands by necessity take precedence. Of course, to "get ahead" one must first "get by," but there is also a certain trade-off involved, as the pressures of daily survival sap a limited supply of social resources. Domínguez and Watkins explore this conflict in the case of African American and Latin American low-income mothers. They show how pressures from supportive ties inhibit women from making effective use of social leverage networks.[76] According to Sharon Hicks-Bartlett, similarly, many poor black mothers are caught "between a rock and a hard place." Their social support obligations, including the stressful demands of parenting in impoverished and unsafe communities, leave them unable to make a full-time commitment to the paid labor force.[77] These studies reveal how difficult it is for poor women, especially due to burdensome caregiving responsibilities, to create a balance between efforts to "get by" and efforts to "get ahead."

Negative Social Capital

The social capital of the poor leaves them doubly disadvantaged. Their networks are less likely to consist of resources conducive to upward mobility and more likely to impose costs on their members.[78] The affluent are hardly immune from the harmful consequences that can arise from human relationships, of course. But the circumstances of the poor increase the probability that their networks will generate "negative social capital."[79] For example, the social networks of the poor, because they are tight knit and their members have such pressing needs, are likely to be particularly "greedy," eliciting "omnivorous" demands.[80] Such networks, and the obligations they create, can drain the time, energy, and resources of their members. They produce anxiety and stress for both "givers," who may become overloaded with responsibilities, and "receivers," who may worry about their ability to reciprocate. Such networks also engender tension and conflict as individuals struggle to balance the needs of their immediate family members and the needs of extended kin, friends, and neighbors.[81]

Social networks, Alejandro Portes and others argue, also generate negative social capital if the ties binding people together are so strong they produce an oppressive conformity. Social connections can impede individual mobility as well if the pressure to remain loyal to the group inhibits individuals from pursuing conventional avenues of educational and occupational advancement.[82] Young people in Harlem, for example, according to Katherine Newman, had to steel themselves against ridicule from their peers if they chose to work at low-status fast-food restaurants.[83]

The social network characteristics of the poor are by-products of their poverty and contribute to the persistence of that poverty as well. The poor are deficient in social ties that might help them escape poverty, and in a self-perpetuating cycle their poverty in turn gives rise to impoverished social ties. The social networks of the poor enable them to "get by" in one fashion or another but not to "get ahead." Their social capital facilitates survival but does not generate human, cultural, or political capital conducive to economic mobility. Because they lack weak and varied ties, in addition, the poor are at a competitive disadvantage in the labor market. They do not hear about job openings, and employers, many of whom rely on networks to recruit employees, do not include them in the applicant pool. Because they are exclusionary

and because "who you know is constrained by disadvantage," social networks, as Charles Kadushin observes, are "essentially unfair."[84] The problem
faced by the poor is not simply a lack of individual resources, not simply a
merit deficiency, as individualistic theories would have us believe, but a lack
of social resources. The poor are impeded in their ability to get ahead not
only because they are starting from so far behind, but also because, in
contrast to their more well-connected counterparts, they are hobbled by their
membership in networks lacking valuable social resources.

CONCLUSION

We all occupy a location in the social system. We are, among other things,
members of groups, residents of neighborhoods, and participants in social
networks. People's place in society, over and above their individual characteristics, has consequences for their economic outcomes. One individual belongs to the "right" groups, lives in a "good" neighborhood, and is a member
of a resource-rich network. A second individual belongs to the "wrong"
groups, lives in a "bad" neighborhood, and is a member of a resource-poor
network. Blessed with a multitude of advantages, the first person, even if he
is untalented and lazy, has a good chance of attaining a middle-class life.
Burdened with a multitude of disadvantages, the second person, even if she is
able and determined, has a good chance of experiencing poverty. As a result
of differences in their social location, these two individuals compete on a
playing field that is anything but level. The first swims with the tide; the
second swims against it.

The unequal distribution of social resources gives some individuals and
groups a competitive edge over others. People who are rich in social resources—whether these originate from their groups, their neighborhoods, or
their networks—have the inside track when it comes to getting a good education, landing a decent job, and securing a career-making promotion. On the
flip side of their good luck, however, is the bad luck of those who are poor in
social resources.[85] The gains enjoyed by advantaged groups come at the
expense of disadvantaged groups. In a context in which desirable positions
are scarce, such as the labor market, success for the former is a *cause* of
failure for the latter. If people from favored groups exploit their social connections to get good jobs, this is not just a happy result for them; it is also an
unhappy result for their less-favored, less-well-connected, but equally qualified competitors. We take note of the lucky people who rise to the top, and
we sometimes even register the unlucky people who remain trapped at the
bottom, but we rarely acknowledge the causal connection between the good
fortune of the first and the bad fortune of the second.

People who are members of out-groups, reside in high-poverty neighborhoods, and participate in impoverished social networks are particularly vulnerable to poverty. Their poverty in turn exacerbates the adversities that arise from their disadvantaged social location. The social system variables discussed in this chapter provide a perspective, one superior to that put forward by individualistic theories, that adds to our understanding of why certain groups—African Americans and Hispanics, women and single mothers, immigrants and people born into working-class families—have disproportionately high rates of poverty. But while social location certainly matters, it determines who is susceptible to poverty; it does not explain why there is poverty at all or why poverty exists to the extent it does. In the current system, if anyone is going to be poor, it is going to be those people who are members of out-groups, reside in impoverished neighborhoods, and lack social connections. But why is anyone poor? This question cannot be answered by reference to social system variables. To understand why poverty exists in the first place, and why there is so much of it, we would have to return to a consideration of the economic and political systems. Poverty, fundamentally, is a problem of the political economy, not the social system. The rate and severity of poverty are primarily functions of the quantity and quality of available jobs and the level and composition of government spending. These political economy variables determine how many people are going to suffer from poverty at any point in time; social system variables determine who among the population will be doing the suffering.

But while poverty cannot be effectively combated through social system reforms in themselves, changes in the rules governing access to neighborhoods, schools, and jobs, including, for example, antidiscrimination legislation and affirmative action programs, can create a less-segregated and more equitable society, one in which opportunities for avoiding poverty are more fairly distributed and group memberships, neighborhood conditions, and social networks, along with race, gender, and class background, do not play such a prominent role in shaping life chances. Policies designed to achieve equality of opportunity hold out the promise of reducing the influence of group membership, residential location, and social connections on people's prospects for educational and occupational advancement.[86] Such policies would benefit persistently disadvantaged groups, making it possible for them to compete on a more equal footing. This would certainly be a desirable outcome, one well worth fighting for, but in the absence of more far-reaching changes in the political and economic systems, such reforms, though a step in the right direction, would not eradicate poverty. On the other hand, it might be more difficult to ignore the problem of poverty if opportunities were more equalized and the composition of the poverty population—by race, gender, and class background—more closely resembled the composition of the population as a whole. If poverty were more clearly a problem for "us" as well as "them," then we might be more strongly motivated to do something about it.

Part III

A Structural Perspective on Poverty — Ten Obstacles

Chapter Nine

Structural Obstacles and the Persistence of Poverty (I)

The problem of poverty in the United States is rooted in economic, political, cultural, and social forces outside the immediate control of the individual. These forces have created a harsh environment for poorer Americans. There are not enough decent-paying jobs to accommodate the supply of potential workers. Government programs provide insufficient assistance to low-income households. The mainstream news media downplay the seriousness of the poverty problem and obscure its structural sources. And millions of people remain vulnerable to poverty because they belong to disadvantaged groups, reside in impoverished neighborhoods, and are members of resource-poor social networks. The rate of poverty remains high in the United States because the poor are socially excluded, culturally stigmatized, politically marginalized, and deprived of opportunities to earn a living wage.

I continue to make the case for a structural perspective in this part of the book, but I shift the focus from distant "systems" forces, often operating beyond the level of everyday awareness, to the more immediate and pressing day-to-day difficulties experienced by the poor. Specifically, I examine ten obstacles or institutional problems commonly encountered by low-income households. Indicative of the deep inequalities in access to essential goods and services, these obstacles impose daily hardships on the poor and obstruct their efforts to cope with or escape from the condition of poverty. In this chapter I discuss racial and ethnic discrimination, residential segregation, housing, education, and transportation. In chapter 10 I address sex discrimination, child care, health and health care, retirement insecurity, and legal deprivation. Resulting ultimately from the failings of the American political economy, these ten problems, along with others, are both causes and effects. They are consequences of poverty, and they contribute to the persistence of poverty as well, increasing the likelihood of people getting trapped at the bottom of society and passing along their economic status to their children.

Proponents of individualistic theories, when they acknowledge such problems, ascribe them to people's own deviant values and bad choices. If the poor experience difficulties or suffer hardships, this is due mainly to their own irresponsible conduct: they refuse to take care of their homes and neighborhoods, fail to socialize their children, care little about education, don't save for the future, embrace an unhealthy lifestyle, get in trouble with the law, and rather than working hard to get ahead, complain about discrimination. Poverty would cease to be a problem, from this standpoint, if only poor people would behave properly and take responsibility for their lives.

In contrast, I argue, the problems experienced by the poor, including those discussed here, are not self-inflicted, nor are they incidental "personal troubles" affecting a mere "scatter of individuals." They are systemic, rooted in the normal operation of dominant social institutions, and they create genuine adversities for millions of Americans, not just the poor. These are "public issues of social structure."[1] They originate from and are perpetuated by an increasingly unequal distribution of economic and political power and by an unfairly skewed allocation of resources and opportunities.

RACIAL AND ETHNIC DISCRIMINATION

Poverty is not an equal opportunity problem. In 2016 the rates of poverty for African Americans and Hispanics, the two largest minority groups, were 22.0 and 19.4 percent respectively, substantially higher than the 8.8 percent for non-Hispanic whites. Though they make up about one-quarter of the total population, African Americans and Hispanics constitute somewhat more than half the poor.[2] They have lower levels of education, homeownership, income, and wealth. They have higher rates of unemployment, incarceration, single parenthood, and poor health. Not only are African Americans and Hispanics more likely to be poor, but their poverty is also more severe than that of poor whites: deeper, more concentrated, more isolating, and longer lasting. They are burdened by their own poverty, and because they are more likely to live in high-poverty communities, they are burdened by the poverty of their neighbors and neighborhoods as well.[3]

Despite the accomplishments of the civil rights movement, vast inequalities by race and ethnicity persist into the twenty-first century, with black people specifically, as Ta-Nehisi Coates observes, still "found at the bottom of virtually every socioeconomic metric of note."[4] Today's racial inequality is partly the consequence of the long history of American racism and the enduring effects of past discrimination.[5] Since before the nation was founded and continuing on into the present, the lion's share of the gains from economic growth has gone to white people, with each new generation building on its ancestors' good fortune. Government policy has also rendered "cumulative advantages" to whites and "cumulative disadvantages" to minorities.[6] During the New Deal era of the 1930s, extending into the 1940s and 1950s—a period when "affirmative action was white"—a succession of landmark social policies subsidized the birth of today's white suburban middle class. These measures legislated retirement and unemployment insurance, established the minimum wage, affirmed the right to unionize, created federally guaranteed home mortgages, and expanded access to higher education. To ensure the continued subordination of the black population, however, powerful southern legislators demanded local control over the new programs and insisted that agricultural and domestic occupations, in which most black people were employed, be excluded from New Deal provisions.[7] African Americans living in northern cities, subject to pervasive employment and housing discrimination, were also denied opportunities. So while government legislation from the 1930s into the 1960s set millions of white families on the path toward the American Dream, in both the South and the North racial and ethnic minorities—still barred from good neighborhoods, good schools, and good jobs—shared little in the general prosperity.[8]

The blatant racism of the past has by no means disappeared, and as evidenced by the growing public presence of the white supremacist "alt-right," it may even be resurgent. But present-day prejudice and discrimination are often of a more subtle kind, arising from racial biases that are implicit and unconscious.[9] Because it is less conspicuous, perhaps, many whites deny that racism today constitutes a significant barrier to achievement. A growing body of research, however, offers persuasive evidence that minorities continue to face costly racial discrimination, stemming from some combination of individual prejudice, institutional practices, and government policies.[10]

In one recent study, a team of researchers sent out email inquiries soliciting information about opening hours and other minor matters to more than nineteen thousand local public institutions all across the country, including sheriffs' and county clerks' offices, school districts, jobs centers, and libraries. Emails signed with distinctly black-sounding names were less likely to receive a response or a response with a "cordial tone" than emails signed with distinctly white-sounding names. If black people are subject to discrimination in these relatively innocuous cases, the authors emphasize, then it is likely they will also be treated unfavorably in more high-stakes encounters with public authorities.[11] In a similarly designed study testing for employment discrimination, Marianne Bertrand and Sendhil Mullainathan submitted hundreds of responses to help-wanted ads placed in Boston and Chicago newspapers. Applications bearing conventionally white names received 50 percent more interview offers than those bearing conventionally black names. Having a strong résumé, furthermore, did not help "black" applicants nearly as much as it did "white" applicants, suggesting that education and training cannot solve the racial employment gap.[12] Lending support to this conclusion, another study using the same procedure found that black job applicants with degrees from elite universities fared no better than white applicants with degrees from less-prestigious institutions.[13]

Evidence from field experiments (or audit studies) using matched pairs of white and nonwhite job seekers also discloses a clear pattern of employment discrimination.[14] Equally qualified minority applicants are less likely than their white competitors to advance to the interview stage or be offered a job, and if hired they are more likely to be steered into lower-paying, dead-end positions.[15] In one eye-opening study, Devah Pager finds that black men without criminal records stand no better chance of getting a callback after submitting a job application than do equally qualified white men *with* criminal records.[16] Being black is at least as much of a liability in the labor market as being an ex-offender, and employment opportunities for black ex-offenders are exceedingly scarce.[17] A recent analysis of all pertinent audit studies since 1989, furthermore, finds no evidence of any diminishment in the discrimination experienced by African Americans in the hiring process over the past quarter century.[18] The persistence of the black-white wage gap, even accounting for education, experience, and hours worked—and the growth of this gap since 2000—also point to the continued presence of discrimination in the labor market and the workplace.[19]

Employers discriminate, in part, because they harbor derogatory stereotypes about racial and ethnic minorities. They judge black men in a particularly negative light, regarding them as lazy, unreliable, disobedient, and criminally inclined.[20] While African American males may have the requisite skills, they are alleged to "create tensions in the workplace" and have bad attitudes and a poor work ethic.[21] Particularly in the low-wage sector of the economy, employers perceive black workers, compared to immigrants, for example, as being insufficiently "manageable, obedient, and pliable."[22] Racial bias is even more likely to affect hiring decisions in today's service economy, where the emphasis is on "soft" people skills rather than more objectively measurable "hard" skills.[23] Subjective judgments inevitably come into play in assessing soft skills, leaving more room for employers' appraisal of job candidates to be influenced, if only unconsciously, by prejudice and stereotypes. Research showing that employment discrimination is more prevalent in the "social skills" sector of the economy than in the technical skills sector supports this conclusion.[24]

Black and Hispanic job seekers are also disadvantaged in the labor market because many businesses have moved to predominantly white suburbs, and because employers use recruitment strategies that, whether by design or default, exclude minorities from the applicant pool. They announce job openings in local newspapers with a primarily white readership, rather than in metropolitan newspapers; they solicit applicants from suburban and Catholic schools, bypassing inner-city public schools; and they rely on racially exclusive informal networks to fill job vacancies.[25] Employers discriminate when they refuse to hire qualified minority applicants, but they also discriminate when their methods of recruitment deny racial and ethnic minorities a fair opportunity to compete for a job.

As a result of employment discrimination, African Americans and Hispanics have unequal access to jobs and less chance of reemployment after a job loss, and they are more likely to drop out of the labor force and less likely to achieve economic success.[26] Within the workplace, they are sometimes subject to harassment, mistreatment by supervisors, and arbitrary firing. They also tend to be segregated into lower-status occupations, where they receive less on-the-job training, fewer opportunities for advancement, and lower wages.[27] Reflecting the accumulation of labor market disadvantages, the lifetime earnings of racial and ethnic minorities are substantially lower than those of white workers.[28]

The adversities experienced by racial and ethnic minorities in the labor market also affect their housing options. Black and Hispanic families have less money to invest in homeownership, and reflecting the legacy of past discrimination, they are less likely than otherwise equivalent white families to have relatives who can afford to help out with the down payment.[29] But in addition to the financial constraints, they also encounter discriminatory barriers in the housing market. They are not free to live just anywhere they wish. One obstacle is hostility, harassment, and other forms of "move-in violence" by the residents of predominantly white communities.[30] In one Chicago neighborhood, William Julius Wilson and Richard P. Taub report, white residents "generally viewed the arrival of even a few minorities as a threat to their well-being."[31] And as Judith DeSena shows in her study of Greenpoint, New York, white property owners employ a variety of strategies to prevent minorities from moving into "their" neighborhoods. They circumvent the open market by filling housing vacancies through personal referrals and word of mouth; they apply pressure on neighbors to make sure they do not sell or rent to African American and Hispanic families; and they use their local political influence to combat initiatives promoting residential integration.[32] Racial and ethnic minorities, along with low-income whites, are also kept out of middle-class communities by zoning laws that ban apartment buildings, exclusionary land use regulations, and minimum lot size requirements. These measures make housing in desirable neighborhoods sufficiently expensive to exclude less-affluent families, a policy disproportionately affecting minority households.[33]

Studies of housing discrimination, including audit studies similar to those used in testing for employment discrimination, also reveal that racial and ethnic minorities, when looking to rent or purchase, are commonly subject to discriminatory treatment by real estate agents, landlords, and property owners. They are shown fewer units than equally qualified whites, for example, and their inquiries receive a less-positive response.[34] Other research confirms that sales and rental agents sometimes withhold information about housing availability, offer minorities less-favorable terms, and steer whites to predominantly white neighborhoods and nonwhites to predominantly nonwhite neighborhoods.[35]

Discrimination by lenders and insurers also limits housing options. When they make inquiries to mortgage lending institutions about financing, African Americans and Hispanics receive less information, assistance, encouragement, and follow-up.[36] Compared to white customers with similar characteristics, they are less likely to be approved for housing loans or mortgage refinancing.[37] Redlining has reemerged in recent years as well, with banks restricting lending to African Americans and Hispanics by "deliberately placing branches, brokers and mortgage services outside minority communities."[38] One result is that people of color are more likely to be drawn into the subprime lending market, where they pay higher fees and interest rates; are vulnerable to predatory lending practices; and face a greater risk of foreclosure, bad credit records, and debilitating indebtedness. And because of discrimination in the property insurance market, minorities are also forced to pay higher premiums or are denied the housing insurance required to qualify for a home loan.[39]

Housing discrimination is a key factor underlying racial and ethnic inequality and the high rates of poverty experienced by African Americans and Hispanics. And as Fred Freiberg of the Fair Housing Justice Center has observed, despite the Trump administration's law and order rhetoric, there is no reason to believe it will "vigorously enforce fair housing and human rights law."[40] Discrimination in the housing market is also a serious and consequential matter. It restricts prospects for education, employment, social mobility, and a safe and healthy residential environment.[41] And because homeownership is the largest investment for most families, housing discrimination also limits wealth accumulation. Racial and ethnic minorities are more likely to be confined to the rental market, and if they do manage to purchase a home, they benefit less from appreciation in property values.[42] This partly explains the massive racial wealth gap. In 2016 the median white family was worth $171,000, the median black family was worth $17,600, and the median Hispanic family was worth $20,700. Put differently, black families have about 10 cents and Hispanic families about 12 cents for every dollar of wealth possessed by the typical white family.[43] Racial and ethnic minorities thus have fewer assets they can draw on to stave off poverty during hard times, move to a better neighborhood, provide their children with a decent education, finance their retirement, or otherwise achieve a secure standard of living. Disparities in wealth contribute to the reproduction of racial and ethnic inequality and to the intergenerational transmission of poverty.

These are hard times for working Americans, and for racial and ethnic minorities, due to the cumulative and ongoing effects of segregation and discrimination, the hard times are even harder. African Americans and Hispanics are not only *uniquely* disadvantaged, but as Tommie Shelby argues with reference specifically to ghetto poverty, they are *unfairly* disadvantaged. The institutional structure and system of power in American society sanction a racially skewed distribution of resources and opportunities that is contrary to any reasonable standard of social justice.[44]

RESIDENTIAL SEGREGATION

In the mainstream political discourse and news media, the striking phenomenon of rich and poor, whites and nonwhites inhabiting geographically separate and vastly unequal worlds goes largely unnoticed, or at least unmentioned. With the United States now well into the new millennium, residential segregation endures as a skeleton in the closet.

The spatial divide between the rich and the poor has widened since the 1970s, with the result that both poverty and affluence have become increasingly concentrated: the rich live among the rich, the poor among the poor.[45] On the racial front, data from the 2010 census show a slow and modest decline in black-white segregation since the 1970s. African Americans still experience far more segregation than other minority groups, however, and in "America's Ghetto Belt"—northeastern and midwestern cities with large African American populations—the level of black-white segregation remains exceedingly high.[46] Disturbing also is the rising number of high-poverty census tracks and the increasing geographical concentration of minority poverty. Since 2000 the number of people residing in extremely poor neighborhoods (census tracts with a rate of poverty exceeding 40 percent) has almost doubled. Several million African American and Hispanic households live in severely impoverished, socially isolated, and politically neglected ghettos and barrios.[47] With the growth in concentrated poverty, an increasing number of the poor, minority children in particular, live under conditions of profound disadvantage and injustice, denied even a remotely fair chance to make a good life for themselves.[48]

Contrary to popular impression, residential segregation, with reference specifically to black-white segregation, is not the result of people being naturally inclined to live among "their own kind." Individual choice matters, but the pattern of racially segregated neighborhoods is the expression of white preferences more than black preferences, and it is the product of racial fears and stereotypes more than in-group favoritism.[49] Motivated by some

combination of antiblack prejudice and calculations of self-interest, white
people desire racially homogeneous communities; they are unwilling to enter
neighborhoods with more than a token black presence; and as suggested by
the concept of "white flight," they are quick to leave when minorities start
moving in.[50] African Americans are more strongly committed to racial integration, but many have grown wary of white neighborhoods. They have
realistic concerns about being unwelcome and resented, and they are reluctant to make themselves targets of hostility, harassment, and "move-in violence."[51] White racial prejudice, as Camille Zubrinsky Charles observes, is a
"double whammy." It undermines integration not only through its influence
on white people's residential decisions, but also on the residential choices of
black people.[52] In the face of white prejudice and housing discrimination,
even many solidly middle-class African American families end up living in
or near majority-black neighborhoods.[53]

White housing preferences are all the more important because they are
embodied in and reinforced by a long history of government policy—federal,
state, and local—that has deliberately promoted racial segregation and by the
discriminatory behavior of property owners, landlords, neighborhood associations, realtors, mortgage lenders, and home insurers. Even where these seg-
regationist policies and practices have been discontinued or diminished, the
system of residential segregation they produced, the massive inequalities
they caused, and the problems they created persist into the present—with
Ferguson, Missouri, being a case in point.[54] Nor has there ever been any
concerted effort in the country to remedy the wrongs of housing segregation
or compensate African Americans for the resources and opportunities denied
them through discriminatory policies purposefully enacted and enforced by
the US government.[55]

Where people live exerts a powerful influence on their cultural, social,
and economic prospects. Residential location shapes opportunities for education, housing, transportation, employment, and economic mobility. It affects
health and safety; exposure to crime, violence, and environmental hazards;
the availability of stores and services, libraries and parks; the characteristics
of friends, peers, and acquaintances; the quality of social contacts and
networks; and political influence. Social processes that sort people into
neighborhoods by class and race aggravate existing inequalities. For the privileged, residential segregation confers benefits, enabling them to hoard valuable resources, including superior public amenities and the highest-quality
schools. But for minorities and the poor, residential segregation piles hardship on top of hardship, multiplying and magnifying the disadvantages of
race and poverty.

Residential segregation is a troubling reality not only because it promotes
the concentration of poverty, but also because it reinforces educational inequalities. For more than a decade now, due to the decline of federal over-

sight and the discontinuation of court-ordered desegregation efforts, American schools have been undergoing a process of resegregation. For example, in what Emmanuel Felton calls the "succession movement in education," some predominantly white communities, such as Gardendale, Alabama, are creating their own separate and more racially exclusive school districts, splitting off from county school districts with larger minority populations.[56] Under the Trump administration, with Jeff Sessions as attorney general and Betsy DeVos as secretary of education, there is every reason to believe that the integrationist legacy of *Brown v. Board of Education* (1954) will continue to unravel.

Two recent reports document a rapid increase over the past two or three decades in the percentage of K–12 public schools—closing in on 20 percent—in which the student body is mostly poor and mostly nonwhite.[57] Poor minority kids are increasingly relegated to high-poverty schools, where the educational needs and challenges are great and resources are scarce, facilities run down, and teachers less qualified.[58] Because of residential segregation and the growing economic divide between poor and affluent neighborhoods, along with the lax response of government officials, American children are offered separate and unequal educational experiences. Described by Sheryll Cashin as the "great inequalizer," the segregated school system in the United States aggravates the problem of poverty and adds to the disadvantages faced by poor and minority children.[59]

Residential segregation is also a barrier to employment and a cause of racial earnings inequality. First, the labor market for urban minorities since the 1970s has deteriorated as high-wage manufacturing jobs have disappeared and as business firms have relocated from northern cities to the suburbs and to nonunion states in the South and Southwest.[60] The distance between where poor and minority workers live and where the available jobs are located has grown. Because of this "spatial mismatch," urban workers may not hear about job openings; they may not apply, figuring employers would be reluctant to hire them; and in any case, they may be unable to get to suburban jobs, either because commuting costs are unaffordable or because job sites are not accessible via public transportation.[61]

Second, residential segregation limits employment opportunities by reinforcing "social network segregation."[62] Most poor adults, if they live in impoverished and segregated communities, are acquainted mainly with people like themselves: disadvantaged minorities. Their social circles seldom include experienced mentors, influential job contacts, or persons of power and prestige. Poor African Americans and Hispanics residing in segregated neighborhoods are cut off from potentially valuable sources of employment information, and they lack the connections, referrals, and references often needed to gain entrée to good jobs.[63]

Third, as a result of residential segregation, neighborhoods acquire reputations. Whether a neighborhood is judged good or bad, safe or dangerous
depends heavily on its racial composition. African Americans and Hispanics
are not only susceptible to *race* discrimination, but to *place* discrimination as
well. Perceptions of neighborhood quality influence employers' decisions
about business location and employee recruitment. They draw inferences
about the competence and dependability of job candidates based on where
they live. Employers' inclination to use "space" as a "signal" of workers'
reliability disadvantages minority job seekers, particularly if they reside in
neighborhoods that are commonly thought of as "ghettos."[64] As Elijah Anderson observes, however, the stigmatizing "shadow of the ghetto" follows
black people wherever they go, not just those who happen to live in areas of
concentrated poverty.[65]

Residential segregation also disadvantages African Americans and Hispanics through a twofold effect on the operation of the housing market. On
the one hand, prospective minority renters and homeowners tend to be
steered or driven away from white neighborhoods and are thus denied opportunities for quality housing, social mobility, and asset accumulation. They
are not altogether free to "move on up" by purchasing homes or renting
apartments in better neighborhoods with better schools. As a consequence,
they are less able than whites to benefit from the appreciation of housing
values, build a reserve of wealth, and secure a prosperous middle-class life
for themselves and their children. On the other hand, white people typically
do not search for housing in predominantly black neighborhoods. Because
reduced demand suppresses housing values, black homeowners pay a significant "segregation tax"; they are penalized by a lower return for their housing
investment.[66] African Americans and many Hispanics as well are thus less
able than whites to accumulate wealth through homeownership and convert
their human capital and hard work into the American Dream.

Residential segregation and housing discrimination, combined with the
oppressive legacy of the past, contribute to a "racial wealth gap."[67] Racial
wealth disparities far exceed racial income disparities. While median income
for black and Hispanic families is about 60 percent of that received by white
families, the median net worth of black and Hispanic households is, respectively, only about 10 percent and 12 percent of the median net worth of white
households.[68] More than a third of both African American and Hispanic
households have zero or negative net worth, nearly twice the figure for white
households.[69] Many minority families, accordingly, are "asset poor."[70] They
have little wealth to fall back on to cushion the effects of unemployment,
cover the costs of a medical emergency, or help their children pay for college. Even middle-class African American and Hispanic families, because
they have few assets, are just a paycheck or two away from poverty. Residential segregation deters wealth accumulation, and racial minorities as a result

have a weak personal safety net and are less able to protect their children from downward mobility.

Residential segregation contributes not only to the social and economic marginalization of the poor, but also to their political marginalization. Because they are impoverished, poor communities are lacking in civic resources and political leverage and are thus able to exert little influence on state and local government policy. Because they are spatially isolated, they also have few shared interests on the basis of which they can forge coalitions with more politically powerful white and suburban residents. The interests of people living in predominantly white neighborhoods and people living in predominantly black neighborhoods are more likely to collide than coalesce, particularly during an era of government retrenchment and fiscal austerity. The urban poor are in desperate need of government assistance to improve the quality of local schools and services, provide job training, and expand employment opportunities. White suburbanites, however, are resistant to both tax increases and redistributive policies, and they prefer that scarce public resources flow in their direction. The political isolation of the urban poor and their status as occupants of ghettos and barrios makes them vulnerable to racist scapegoating and a convenient target for government cutbacks.[71]

Residential segregation is not the inevitable product of human nature or market forces. It is the result of racial prejudice, individual and institutional discrimination, and government policy. And it is harmful in its consequences. It not only frustrates the dream of an integrated and truly democratic society, it also undermines equality of opportunity, limits the life chances of people already burdened with multiple disadvantages, and thwarts the efforts of the poor to survive and escape their poverty.

HOUSING

Despite working two jobs, Alpha Manzuelta cannot afford her own apartment. For the past three years she has been living in a homeless shelter. "I feel stuck," she remarks.[72] Low-wage workers like Manzuelta are caught in a vicious mismatch between what jobs pay and what housing costs. It is difficult for poorer Americans to find a comfortable place to live and harder still to find a place that is reasonably priced and conveniently located. Nor are they likely to receive any help from woefully underfunded government housing programs. The unhappy result is that low-income households typically end up spending more than they can afford for substandard housing in undesirable neighborhoods with a long commute to work.[73] They are stuck with last-resort options: housing that is unsafe and unhealthy, infested by rodents and insects, too cold in the winter and too hot in the summer, and equipped with broken appliances and faulty plumbing. Some housing even lacks running water, flush toilets, and a shower or a bathtub.[74] Many of the poor are also vulnerable to "housing instability." Whether due to foreclosures, evictions, rent increases, intolerable conditions, or housemate conflicts, it is not uncommon for low-income families to move from one place to another, never able to settle down in a single location.[75] This can be particularly hard on children. "It's the stability I worry about," a mother of five says. "They've got to start off fresh, get new friends, new neighbors. It might not show now, but maybe later in life."[76] More than a half million poor people face an even more severe housing problem. On any given night in 2016, 549,928 Americans were homeless, including more than 120,000 children. About one-third of this homeless population lives in unsheltered locations: cars, parks, under bridges, or on the streets.[77]

Housing is not only the largest item in most household budgets, it is a priority item as well. People need a place to live before just about anything else. Because "rent eats first," many low-income Americans don't have enough money to cover other expenses.[78] They suffer from what Michael Stone calls "shelter poverty." A family is shelter poor "if it cannot meet its nonhousing needs at some minimum level of adequacy after paying for housing."[79] According to the National Low Income Housing Coalition, the number of shelter-poor renters in 2017 exceeded 20 million.[80] These families, disproportionately minority and female headed, live stressful lives. Forced into desperate trade-offs and undesirable sacrifices just to get by, they subsist by going without medical attention, doing without a car, limiting spending on clothes, and even skimping on food. The challenge of navigating shelter poverty contributes to "an atmosphere of instability," with constant fears of "hunger, utility shut-offs, and evictions."[81]

Housing is a necessity, but also an amenity. More than a roof over our heads, it is an essential ingredient of our quality of life. We need dependable housing to be safe and secure, to be physically and psychologically healthy, and to achieve a sense of comfort and personal well-being. A home of our own serves as a private sanctuary and a setting for friendship and family relations. A place to call home fulfills "fundamental human needs," and without it, "everything else falls apart."[82]

Housing is essential, necessary for both physical and mental health, but also expensive, and getting more expensive over time even as income for the typical household is stagnant or declining.[83] Millions of Americans are stuck with excessive mortgage or rental payments. A typical household, according to policy experts, can afford to spend no more than 30 percent of its total income on housing. Households are classified as having a "moderate" cost burden if they pay more than 30 percent and a "severe" cost burden if they pay more than 50 percent. In 2015, 38.9 million households, including both owners and renters, had at least a moderate cost burden, including 18.8

million households with a severe cost burden, up 3.7 million since 2001. For low-income families, unaffordable housing is the norm. Over 70 percent of households with annual income less than $15,000 are severely burdened by their housing costs, and another 32 percent earning between $15,000 and $29,999 also pay more than half their income for housing. Families so overwhelmed by rental and mortgage payments live perilous lives, only a paycheck or two away from foreclosure or eviction.[84]

Homeownership is the centerpiece of the American Dream. Yet the rate of homeownership among Americans—down sharply especially for African Americans—hit a low of 63.4 percent in 2016. This is due partly to the lingering fallout from the Great Recession and the foreclosure crisis. It also reflects the low rate of home purchases on the part of younger households, many of whom have not yet found a foothold in today's economy. With builders eyeing the higher end of the market, there has also been a shift in the pattern of new construction toward larger, more luxurious, and more expensive homes.[85] Priced out of the ownership market, many families, both low income and middle class, have abandoned or deferred the dream of homeownership, moving instead into the increasingly crowded rental market.[86]

There is no escaping the crisis of affordable housing though. For would-be renters, problems of availability and cost are bad and getting worse. In 2014 Shaun Donovan, then secretary of housing and urban development, declared that the country was in the midst of "the worst rental affordability crisis that this country has ever known."[87] This crisis is still with us. Rental costs are rising faster than earnings, particularly for households in the bottom income quintile, but also for many middle-class households. In 2015 nearly half of all renters were cost burdened, with 26 percent severely cost burdened. For low-income and minority renters, the figures were even higher.[88] The number of "worst case housing needs"—low-income renters lacking housing assistance and being severely rent burdened or living in substandard housing (or both)—has skyrocketed since 2007, rising from 5.9 million to a peak of almost 8.5 million in 2011 and then, with an improving economy, falling to 7.7 million in 2013.[89] Though the "worst cases" have it worse, even many moderate-income people have trouble paying the monthly rent. A full-time worker in 2017 would have to earn an hourly wage of $21.21, almost three times the federal minimum, to afford a two-bedroom rental home, and an hourly wage of $17.14 to afford a one-bedroom rental home. And in no place in the country, including states and cities with a minimum wage higher than the federal minimum, can a full-time minimum wage worker "afford a modest two-bedroom rental home."[90]

In his book *Evicted* and in other publications, Matthew Desmond has brought public attention to the rental affordability crisis. Because of the shortage of inexpensive rental units and the corresponding imbalance of power between landlords and tenants, low-income renters, he argues, are vulnerable to both exploitation and eviction. Between 2009 and 2011, one in eight renters in Milwaukee, not an atypical city, experienced a "forced move," and nationwide the number of evictions each year is in the millions. In low-income neighborhoods, evictions are common, especially for black women. Losing their homes, poor renters are pushed into even worse housing and worse neighborhoods, and in the turmoil of being kicked out of one place and struggling to find another, they are vulnerable to job loss as well. The consequences of eviction are destructive and destabilizing—to individuals, families, and communities. The lack of affordable housing and the experience of eviction, Desmond observes, have the effect of aggravating the material deprivation, psychological stress, and employment problems of the poor.[91] Gretchen Purser, the author of another important study, agrees. Evictions, she says, are a "mechanism for the reproduction of poverty."[92]

The lack of affordable rental housing is partly due to increasing demand, as many people have exited the homeownership market. In 2016 a record number of households were renters, 43.1 million, including most black and Hispanic households. New construction of rental units has been on the rise in recent years, but as in the case of new home construction, it is targeted to more affluent consumers. Rental prices have also been driven up by the entry of private equity firms into the housing market. These financial giants, including the Blackstone Group, have become the new slumlords, buying up rent-controlled apartments, forcing tenants out, and then reaping huge profits by raising rents.[93] For the foreseeable future, low-income households will continue to experience great difficulty locating a place to live. In 2017 there were only thirty-five "available and affordable rental homes" for every one hundred "extremely low income renter households."[94] In what is perhaps not such an unusual example, Desmond cites the case of a woman who called ninety landlords before finally finding an acceptable rental unit.[95]

Though poorer Americans, mostly renters, are the primary victims of the nation's housing problems, affluent homeowners are the primary beneficiaries of government housing policy. "It's a classic upside-down subsidy," one tax expert explains, "it goes to all the wrong people."[96] Totaling $190 billion in 2015, federal housing spending is tilted against those most in need. The chief beneficiaries are high-income households rather than low-income households and homeowners rather than renters. About 60 percent of federal government expenditures for housing went to households with incomes over $100,000, mainly in the form of tax deductions for mortgage interest payments and property taxes. The cost of these housing-related tax expenditures far exceeds housing assistance outlays for the poor, including "Section 8" housing vouchers. Indeed, the average benefit received by households with incomes of $200,000 or more was four times that received by households with incomes of $20,000 or less. And though the proportion of renters has been on the rise for a decade, as have their housing needs, homeowners received more than 70 percent of all federal spending on housing subsidies.[97]

Low-income housing programs are not only less generous, but also less widely available.[98] Approximately 5 million poor families currently benefit from housing assistance, with households generally subsidized at a level that reduces their housing costs to no more than 30 percent of their total income. But unlike tax expenditures, which are distributed to every qualified household, housing subsidies for low-income renters are allotted only until the money runs out. And there is nowhere near enough funding to provide assistance to every eligible household. Countless low-income families are thus placed on long waiting lists, and in some cities, waiting lists have been closed indefinitely, leaving needy families to fend for themselves in an increasingly inhospitable housing market. In 2015 only about 25 percent of eligible households received rental assistance. The near-term housing problems for poorer Americans are likely to get worse. The Trump administration, with Ben Carson installed as the new head of the Department of Housing and Urban Development, has promised to cut HUD's already austere budget by at least $6 billion, which could translate into the elimination of 250,000 rental vouchers.[99]

Whether or not people have reasonable access to housing in the United States today is primarily dependent on market forces, meaning that people get the housing they can pay for. The continued adherence to a market-driven housing policy is precisely the problem. In the absence of government measures explicitly designed to raise wages, expand subsidies, and increase the supply of affordable housing, low-income Americans are destined to suffer a "permanent housing crisis."[100]

EDUCATION

All mothers and fathers want their kids to get a good education. Because their children's futures are so uncertain, this may be especially true for poor parents. They cannot assume their sons and daughters will obtain adequate schooling or are destined for success. Middle-class parents worry too, of course, and they sacrifice and scrape, anticipating the day they will send their children off to college. For low-income families, however, especially if they live in segregated and high-poverty neighborhoods, the attainment of normal educational aspirations, if not out of reach entirely, requires extraordinary effort and an abundance of good luck. The poor encounter a different and much harsher educational universe, with the odds stacked against them. They are lacking in the financial assets, political leverage, social networks, insider knowledge, and institutional support necessary to ensure their children receive the quality education that has become a minimal prerequisite for achieving the American Dream.

Poverty begins at home, from the very moment of conception, and it has lasting effects on children's life outcomes, including their educational performance.[101] First, poverty is unhealthy. Children raised in poor families are susceptible to an assortment of physical and mental ailments, including low birth weight, malnutrition, lead poisoning, and chronic stress. These hit particularly hard during infancy and preschool years, hindering learning and impairing children's cognitive, behavioral, and emotional development.[102] Second, poverty is depriving. Poor parents have limited resources to invest in their children's upbringing—less money to spend on clothing, toys, games, music lessons, and educational materials. Since the 1970s, furthermore, the gap in child-enrichment expenditures between families at the top and the bottom of the income distribution has increased enormously, creating ever-wider disparities in the childhood experiences of the haves and the have-nots.[103] Third, children born into poverty generally receive less cognitive stimulation in their home environments. They may be disadvantaged by the educational level and child-rearing practices of their parents; a lack of "literacy-related activities"; and a more limited exposure to computers, books, reading, conversation, and intellectually engaging experiences.[104] Fourth, the early educational environment of poor children is less favorable also because their parents are forced to rely on neighbors, friends, and relatives rather than more costly certified providers to meet their child-care needs. Low-income parents cannot afford to enroll their kids in expensive preschool and early-education programs, and the facilities within their means offer only substandard care and instruction.[105] As a consequence of these and other factors, poor children, even before they begin kindergarten, are well behind their more affluent peers in math and verbal skills and overall school readiness. By virtue of the circumstances of their birth, they suffer from a variety of starting-gate inequalities, and by many measures these have worsened over the past few decades. And because social, educational, and economic policies do so little to remedy or compensate for preschool handicaps, the lack of family resources casts "a long shadow over children's life trajectories," undermining the principle of equality of opportunity.[106]

Poor children enter the educational system already disadvantaged by their home and neighborhood environments. And then, in defiance of any sense of fair play, the neediest of the nation's kids are crowded into the country's worst schools. Their educational opportunities are limited by the enduring pattern of residential and school segregation, the shortage of teachers and staff, and disparities in per-pupil spending. Public schools depend heavily on money from local property taxes, and since impoverished communities have a less substantial tax base, spending for poor and minority students, precisely those most in need, is generally lower than for more affluent students. State spending on education can compensate for inadequate local funds, but whether it does or not depends on how state resources are distributed to school districts. Over the past decade the trend has been one of rich schools getting more and poor schools getting less. In 2014 funding was "progressive" in only twelve states (more money allocated to poorer schools), down from sixteen the previous year and down from a high of twenty in 2008, and it was "regressive" in twenty-one states (less money allocated to poorer schools), up from fourteen the previous year. [107]

The federal government plays a role too, currently contributing about 10 percent of total spending on public education. The Trump administration, however, has proposed a $9 billion reduction in funding for the Department of Education. At the same time, Trump's educational agenda, with Betsy DeVos at the helm as education secretary, and that of "red" state legislators as well, favors local control, increased spending on charter schools and school choice programs, and ultimately the privatization of public schools. The overall aim is to shift responsibility for financing education from government to parents themselves, an outcome that can only further limit the educational opportunities of children from low-income families. [108]

Not only do schools in rich neighborhoods typically get more public resources, they get more private resources as well. Parents in wealthy communities, through fund-raising efforts and nonprofit organizations, are able to channel extra money into their children's school districts to pay for computers, art and music classes, extracurricular activities, and other educational enhancements. [109] This combination of unequal private investment and unequal public investment has produced a profoundly inequitable educational system. In the United States, indeed, and in contrast to other developed countries, more money and resources are devoted to the education of affluent children than to the education of less-affluent children, and sometimes a lot more. [110] The problem runs even deeper, however. To compensate for early childhood disadvantages and create something approximating a level playing field, children from poor families need *more* resources than middle-class children. Even equal funding is not adequate funding. [111]

School segregation and funding disparities, on top of inequalities in family resources and neighborhood conditions, yield highly unequal educational experiences and outcomes. Poor and minority students attend schools that are inferior in many respects: substandard physical structures, crowded classrooms, lower teacher expectations, and fewer supplies and facilities, including computers, Internet access, and science labs. Teachers in schools serving low-income students have a higher turnover rate, and they tend to have less training, experience, and subject knowledge. Poorer schools are deficient also in the availability of gifted and advanced placement classes; in the size and expertise of the support staff, including guidance counselors and school psychologists; and in the overall level of student safety, comfort, and well-being. Not all these disparities, taken individually, are large, but they bunch together, with good schools good in many ways (especially the best of the good) and bad schools bad in many ways (especially the worst of the bad). School inequalities also "add up," and they have a cumulative effect over time: "Some students experience a long string—maybe even twelve consecutive years—of 'bad' schools, while others may get a long string of 'good' schools." Rather than equalizing opportunities, the existing educational system reinforces "the transmission of low socioeconomic status from parents to children."[112]

Students in the United States encounter an educational system that is not only unequal, but separate as well.[113] Low-income and minority children are packed into high-poverty schools or slotted into low-achievement tracks in middle-class schools. Poor schools differ not only because they receive less money and are generally unequal in instructional quality, but also because the student body is disproportionately disadvantaged. According to one recent report, 40 percent of low-income children attend schools with a poverty rate of at least 75 percent, a level of segregation that has been on the upswing since the 1970s.[114] This concentration of poverty in the classroom creates a detrimental learning environment for children and an unfairly demanding educational setting for teachers who are already strapped for time and resources. It is also liable to leave students with the impression they are being warehoused by an uncaring system.[115] Segregated and high-poverty schools perpetuate a multitude of inequalities, undermining the educational achievement and life chances of low-income and minority students. As long as the school system remains divided by class and race, poor children will not have anything like an equal opportunity to realize their educational potential.[116]

Politicians and pundits across the political spectrum can be found intoning the familiar higher education mantra whenever issues of poverty and inequality arise. American colleges and universities are not equal opportunity institutions, however, and their doors are not as wide open to the poor and the working class as they are to students from high-income families. Children from affluent households are much more likely to attend college than children from low-income households. In 2014, 80 percent of eighteen- to twenty-four-year-olds from the top income quartile but only 45 percent of those from the bottom income quartile were enrolled in college. Since 2008, moreover, the percentage of low-income students entering college right after high school has declined by 10 percent. Differences in graduation are even greater than those for enrollment. Of people with a college degree by the age of twenty-four, most (54 percent) were from the top income quartile, with only 10 percent from the bottom income quartile.[117]

Rather than being the great equalizer, higher education in the United States serves largely as a training ground for the privileged, and the higher up one goes in the academic hierarchy, the more this is true. The race and class composition of the student body at the most prestigious colleges and top professional schools—"the pipelines to our principal corridors of power"—is highly skewed.[118] According to a *New York Times* analysis, black and Hispanic students are more underrepresented in the country's top colleges today than they were thirty-five years ago.[119] These same elite colleges, another recent study finds, enroll more students from the top 1 percent of the income distribution than from the entire bottom half.[120] These disparities in college attendance cannot be explained fully by differences in academic preparation or intellectual ability. Indeed, as Robert Putnam observes, high-achieving poor kids are no more likely to graduate from college than are low-achieving rich kids.[121] This is partly the result of poor recruitment practices on the part of selective colleges. But affluent students possess numerous advantages in the application process as well. They have greater access to knowledgeable and well-connected high school guidance counselors; they can afford to enroll in expensive SAT prep courses; they receive valuable assistance, sometimes even from professional consultants, in writing résumés, preparing for interviews, and navigating complicated financial aid forms; they benefit from early admissions programs and in some cases from their status as "legacies" and children of wealthy donors; and they can more easily draw on the first-hand experience of parents, siblings, and friends.[122]

Money, too, remains a significant barrier to higher education for students from low-income families. The distribution of income and wealth has reached record levels of inequality, working-class earnings have been stagnant for years, states have cut spending on higher education, financial aid has failed to keep pace with the rising price of a college degree, and tuition costs have soared.[123] Between 1971 and 2011, according to Suzanne Mettler, the cost of attending a four-year public university increased from 6 percent to 9 percent of family income for those in the wealthiest quintile and from 42 percent to 114 percent for those in the poorest quintile.[124] Depending on the institution, children from low-income families who get a degree do reasonably well in their later-life outcomes, but colleges with a record of boosting the mobility of such students have become increasingly unaffordable.[125]

Rather than seeking remedies for an inequitable situation, government lawmakers and college administrators have made the problem worse. First, the share of college costs covered by Pell grants, the principal federal aid program for needy students, has been shrinking since the mid-1970s, from a high of 67 percent down to 27 percent.[126] Second, the composition of government aid to higher education has shifted, from scholarship grants, a crucial resource for working-class students, to guaranteed loans and tax credits aimed at more affluent families.[127] Third, with state legislatures cutting funding for higher education, public universities have become more and more reliant on tuition revenue. In response, universities today are catering more to higher-paying out-of-state and foreign students, enticing applicants by equipping their campuses with luxury dormitories, swimming pools, top-of-the-line food services, and other amenities. Meanwhile, for children from low-income families, facing heightened competition from out-of-state residents and rising in-state tuition costs, a college education even at a public school has become increasingly out of reach. [128] Fourth, with an eye on their national rankings, many colleges and universities, eager to enroll high SAT applicants, have reshuffled their admissions priorities, replacing need-based aid with merit-based aid. [129]

Affluent students today are claiming a larger slice of a shrinking financial assistance pie, while poorer students "are getting killed on the aid side, and they are getting killed on the tuition side." [130] Many high-performing low-income students, as a consequence, forgo college, settle for a less-expensive college, enroll in a two-year community college, gamble on getting a degree from a for-profit university, work long hours to cover their tuition costs, or go deep into debt. In any case, money has become an increasingly important determinant of who goes to college, what college they attend, whether or not they graduate, and how long it takes to complete a degree.

People who lack a good education are vulnerable to poverty, and they would certainly benefit from a more equitable educational system. But even far-reaching educational reform is not enough to compensate for the larger societal effects of class disadvantage, racial discrimination, and residential segregation. Problems of poverty and inequality are fundamental; the problem of education is symptomatic. Creating more equal *schools*, though unlikely in the current political environment, would be a step in the right direction. But only by creating a more equal *society*—with a more equitable foundation for children's upbringing—can we achieve any substantial decrease in the gap between the educational achievement of the rich and the poor and their respective opportunities for social mobility. [131]

TRANSPORTATION

Not only are the jobs available to the poor lousy, but it is hard to get to them as well. Unable to find employment near her home, Intesar Museitef, a single mother with a six-year-old son, travels four hours every workday to a $7-an-hour job as a home health-care aide. There is little else she can do. "If I leave this job," she explains, "I have nothing." Atlanta resident Stacy Calvin also has a four-hour commute—two trains and a bus ride everyday—spending nearly as much time on the road as she does at her part-time job. James Robertson commutes on foot. For ten years after his car broke down he has walked twenty-one miles back and forth to work at a factory job in the Detroit area, leaving time for only about two hours of sleep each weeknight. Because of rising housing costs, low-wage workers with jobs in Manhattan have been forced to relocate further and further from their worksites. A four-hour daily commute is not unusual, and more than 750,000 New Yorkers, mostly low income, commute at least two hours every workday.[132]

Millions of low-end workers are similarly squeezed by scarce job prospects, stagnant wages, rising housing costs, and inadequate transportation. With limited residential choices, they are relegated to impoverished neighborhoods isolated from employment opportunities. Because they cannot always afford to live near work or are unwelcome in the community, they are stuck with long and costly daily commutes. The arduous trek from home to work and back consumes precious hours, at the expense of family, friends, leisure, and sleep. Low-income workers, hindered by the lack of reliable transportation, are caught in a time trap that not only lessens the quality of their everyday lives, but also impedes their efforts to escape poverty and limits their opportunities for achieving a better future.[133]

Transportation problems loom large in the lives of the poor. In their study of industrial restructuring in South Bend, Indiana, Charles Craypo and David Cormier report that undependable transportation was among the hardships most frequently mentioned by the low-wage workers they interviewed.[134] The immediate obstacle for many low-income households is that they do not have the money to purchase, insure, and maintain a car. According to one report, approximately 20 percent of the poor live in households with no access to an automobile.[135] Without a car, they are reliant on public transportation, limited in the jobs they can search for and choose from, face longer commutes, and sometimes miss work or arrive late. Access to an automobile is a key determinant of whether the poor are employed or unemployed, leave welfare for work, or are able to climb out of poverty.[136] Owning a car presents its own difficulties, however. "It's either your tires or extra gas or a part tearing up," laments one welfare recipient. "I can never really get ahead."[137] Even those who have a functioning vehicle confront tough choices. To keep the gas tank filled for the drive to work, they limit family outings and visits to friends and cut back expenditures on other items, including food and leisure. One mother of three young children quit using her car, relying instead on a combination of trains and shuttles, but now it takes her more than twice as long to get to work. What she saves in money, she loses in time. "It's a nightmare," she says.[138]

Many poorer Americans, African Americans and Hispanics in particular, are dependent on public transportation.[139] In New York City and elsewhere, however, buses and subways, due to rising fare prices, have for many people become unaffordable.[140] Buses are also often slower than cars and have numerous other drawbacks as well. They do not always get passengers where they want to go, leaving long distances to travel by foot or other means; they do not always get passengers to their destinations when they need to be there; and service is frequently erratic, with travelers sometimes left in the lurch.

But even when public transportation is right on time, riders are still often stuck with long commutes. A Brookings study found that just 22 percent of all low- and middle-skill jobs in the typical metropolitan area are accessible by public transit within ninety minutes.[141] From 2000 to 2012, moreover, the number of jobs in big cities near residential areas decreased, with the largest declines for high-poverty and majority-minority neighborhoods, where the availability of reliable public transportation is already severely limited.[142]

Partly due to residential segregation, many job seekers, particularly African Americans and Hispanics, reside in neighborhoods far removed from where jobs are located. A study by economists David Phillips finds that such workers, living in poor neighborhoods and having long commutes, are subject to "discrimination by distance." Looked upon less favorably by employers, they receive fewer callbacks than similarly qualified applicants living closer to the job location.[143] Interviews show that employers are inclined to believe that bus and subway riders are less desirable hires, in part because they are presumed to "have much more of a problem with consistency to getting to work." Suburban employers sometimes even cite the unreliability of public transportation as an explanation for why they do not advertise jobs in metropolitan newspapers. "It seems prejudiced sometimes to say you don't want to hire them," a supervisor at an Atlanta construction firm remarked, but "we've got to have people that are flexible and can get to jobs everywhere and be there on time and not worry about set schedules for getting back and forth to work."[144] Pointing to a durable pattern of *systemic* inequality, the research cited here reveals that racial and ethnic minorities are disadvantaged by an interlocking combination of factors—residential segregation, employment discrimination, and transportation inequities—each feeding on the other.

Even if suburban employers were willing to hire city workers, many of the available jobs do not pay enough to compensate for the time and monetary costs of a long commute. Whether through choice or constraint, therefore, inner-city residents in the labor force are typically employed in or around the larger urban area.[145] They do not normally have great distances to travel, but they do have to venture outside their neighborhoods for employment. And because they are reliant on public transportation, their trips to work can still be long and inconvenient, even if they do not journey all the way out to the suburbs.[146] Some research suggests, indeed, that for many of the poor the real problem is less a "spatial mismatch" than an "automobile mismatch." Low-income workers spend more time getting to and from their jobs not necessarily because their commute *distance* is so great, but because their commute *mode*, public transportation, is slow and unreliable.[147] In either case, whether measured in miles or minutes, the distance between where workers live and where jobs are located diminishes the quality of people's lives.

The public transportation system in the United States, underfunded and inequitable, does not mesh well with the needs of poor families and the low-income workforce. Jobs in the growing service economy are geographically dispersed, sometimes located in out-of-the-way places not served by existing bus lines. Thousands of workers, including nannies, home health-care aides, and house cleaners, for example, are employed in people's homes, off the main thoroughfares.[148] Many low-wage workers in the expanding 24/7 economy have nonstandard hours as well and are sometimes on the job in the middle of the night, when public transportation is not readily available.[149] And because their work schedules often vary unpredictably from day to day and week to week, service workers cannot always plan in advance to meet their transportation requirements. Nor is the transportation system designed for parents running errands with children in tow, pushing strollers; carrying diapers, toys, juice boxes, and snacks; and laden with bags of groceries.[150] The elderly too, particularly those who live in poorer neighborhoods or less comfortably situated retirement homes, are not well served by the current system of public transportation. Many seniors, hindered by physical limitations, cannot get to and from bus stops and subway stations. If they don't have family and friends who can drive them around and can't afford to spend money on taxis or other forms of private transportation, they "become prisoners in their own homes," isolated from the outside world. "They eat, sleep, watch TV, and take medicine, but can't go anywhere."[151]

Rural residents face particularly severe transportation problems. They often reside miles from employment sites, welfare offices, schools, medical facilities, day-care centers, grocery stores, and voting booths. Many of the rural poor, like their urban counterparts, do not have the money to purchase a vehicle or keep it running. And more than a third of rural Americans live in areas where there is no public transportation at all.[152] Most of the city jobs that are available, as one Iowa resident reported, "won't even pay for gas driving back and forth." In rural Alabama, a state with no funding for public transportation, a local authority reports that hiring a ride to the nearest city, about an hour away, costs "at least $50."[153] Jennifer Mosher, a resident of rural Delaware County in New York, was fortunate enough to buy a cheap car—her "greatest blessing"—so she could get back and forth to work. But due to monthly loan payments, high gas costs, and the expense of constant repairs, car ownership also turned out to be her "biggest headache."[154] Lacking their own means of transportation, people are forced to improvise. For nine months, an Oregon woman hitchhiked fifty-five miles each way to a job in Eugene.[155]

Inadequate transportation, by limiting freedom of mobility, also causes low-income families a variety of non-work-related hardships. They are restricted to local restaurants and stores, where goods and services are often expensive and of lesser quality. Parents are unable to travel outside their immediate neighborhoods to provide their children with enriching experiences and public services, including trips to museums, zoos, libraries, and parks. And they have a greater likelihood of missing appointments with medical personnel, welfare caseworkers, and other service professionals. Transportation is also a major expense for low-income families, more costly than anything other than housing. It eats up nearly 16 percent of total income, far more than for middle- and upper-income households, and far more also than low-income households spent just four years ago. [156]

Spurred by political activists and the dictates of welfare reform, many local public and private agencies have implemented modest initiatives to alleviate the transportation problems of the poor. [157] But in recent years transit policies around the country, especially in big cities like Los Angeles, have threatened to make the problem worse by reallocating transportation resources from the urban poor to the suburban middle class. Partly because of concerns about air pollution and traffic congestion, transit agencies, as Mark Garrett and Brian Taylor argue, have focused more on increasing the availability of public transportation for suburban commuters, who would otherwise drive to work, than on upgrading services for low-income city residents, many of whom are already "transit dependent." [158] Thus in many cities funding priorities have shifted from the expansion and improvement of bus operations to the development of new rail projects. [159] This changing pattern of public investment promotes an increasingly unequal two-tiered transit system, with heavily subsidized facilities serving more higher-income riders and resource-starved bus lines serving mostly poor, minority riders. Garrett and Taylor attribute this disparity to the political, economic, and racial divide that separates cities and suburbs and to the strong aversion to redistributive social programs on the part of policy makers and the middle-class public. Their analysis draws attention to the role played by politics and power in creating a mismatch between the disbursement of public funds and the transportation needs of the poor. [160]

Transportation inequity is a consequence of poverty and powerlessness, and it is an obstacle to surviving and overcoming poverty as well. This is not an isolated problem that can be solved on its own. It is nested in an assortment of other structural problems: low-wage work, residential segregation, racial discrimination, and unaffordable housing. The lack of access to reliable transportation for poorer Americans is a by-product of the larger phenomenon of rising economic and political inequality. Inadequate transportation is more than a social problem; it is "a social justice issue." [161]

Chapter Ten

Structural Obstacles and the Persistence of Poverty (II)

SEX DISCRIMINATION

As of 2015, 42 percent of mothers were sole or primary breadwinners (supplying at least half of total family income) and another 22.4 percent were co-breadwinners (supplying 25–49 percent of family income).[1] Despite their increasing presence in the paid economy, women, especially when they are mothers and even more so when they are single mothers, are disproportionately vulnerable to poverty. In 2016, 13.4 percent of working-age women (ages eighteen to sixty-four) were poor, compared to 9.7 percent for working-age men.[2] Women face a greater risk of poverty because their earnings lag behind those of men. This gender wage gap results from differences between women and men in how much they work, what jobs they have, and how much they are paid.

For full-time, year-round workers, women's annual earnings as a percentage of men's crossed the 70 percent threshold for the first time in 1990. In 2016, more than a quarter century later, women hit a new mark, with earnings reaching 80.5 percent of men's. Progress, yes, but the pace is slow. African American and Hispanic women fare less well than women on average, bringing home only 63.3 percent and 54.4 percent respectively of white male earnings.[3] Compared to men, working women are also more likely to be paid at or below the minimum wage and more likely to be among the working poor.[4] Nevertheless, women have made genuine gains. Since 2000, full-time working women on average have seen an increase of approximately $3,000 in their annual earnings, even picking up some ground on men. This narrowing of the gender wage gap, however, is due partly to the persistent stagnation of men's earnings going all the way back to 1975. Women's pay has been catching up to men's pay in part because men's pay has been flat for decades.[5]

The gender disparity is greater if we consider all workers, and not just full-timers. A significant number of women, 26.5 percent compared to 13.4 percent for men, work part-time, and the hourly pay for part-time jobs is typically less than for full-time jobs. Women are disadvantaged not only because they work fewer hours than men, but also because the pay they receive is lower for each hour they work.[6] Including part-time workers yields a gender wage gap of 73 percent instead of 80.5 percent.[7] The disparity is greater still if we consider long-term earnings and not just annual earnings. Stephen Rose and Heidi Hartmann find that measured across a fifteen-year period, 1983 to 1998, women earned only 38 percent of what men earned, far less than when the pay gap is calculated on a yearly basis.[8] According to one estimate, the gender earnings gap, which tends to increase with age, costs the average working woman more than $530,000 over the course of her life-time.[9]

Women earn less than men in part because they do the bulk of society's unpaid labor. Household responsibilities and caregiving duties limit their participation in the labor market and the kinds of jobs they can take. The demands on women's time in both the workplace and the family have increased as well, exacerbating the difficulty of juggling paid and unpaid labor. On the one hand, more jobs today require employees to work long hours or be available on a moment's notice; on the other hand, the prevailing norm of "intensive mothering" calls for women to devote themselves fully to the care of their children.[10] Working women with children—pressed to be both ideal mothers and ideal workers—face a nearly impossible challenge.

Even when employed full time women often work a "second shift" at home in addition to their regular jobs.[11] They do most of the cooking, cleaning, and other household chores, and if they are mothers they also handle the bulk of the child-care duties, a pattern that seems highly "resistant to change."[12] Men are doing more nowadays, but still considerably less than women. The progress in attitudes regarding the household division of labor and men's and women's roles has hit a plateau, partly due to the continued pressure couples feel to accommodate to gendered norms and expectations still prevalent in most workplaces.[13] Since the mid-1990s, indeed, support for "gender egalitarianism" has ceased its "upward trend."[14]

Many women work a "third shift" on top of their "second shift." They engage in a variety of caregiving activities beyond mothering: tending aging parents, sick friends and relatives, or needy neighbors. Though undervalued compared to other kinds of labor, unpaid care work is vital to the functioning of society. But because it may force women out of the labor force altogether, leave others with less time for paid work, and result in career interruptions, caretaking substantially reduces women's labor market earnings.[15]

If they are mothers, women in the workforce encounter an additional obstacle: they make less money than comparable nonmothers, with low-wage working women, those who can least afford it, enduring the highest cost. Women with children pay a "motherhood penalty," and the more children they have, the more they are penalized.[16] This penalty partly reflects the difficulties women have balancing work responsibilities and child-care duties, but some of it is also due to employer discrimination. Mothers are generally perceived as lacking in competence and work commitment, and their job applications are less likely to elicit callbacks from employers than those of otherwise equivalent nonmothers.[17] Employers are wary of hiring women with children on the assumption that being a mother is incompatible with being a good worker. For some employers, indeed, the status of motherhood is itself "a marker of unreliability."[18]

Men predominate in some employment fields, women in others. For example, men are overrepresented by a wide margin in mining, construction, manufacturing, and software development, and in managerial positions in architecture, engineering, computers, and information systems. Women are overrepresented among nurses, elementary and middle-school teachers, event planners, social workers, paralegals, and librarians.[19] A significant portion of the gender pay gap, as much as half according to one estimate, is due to industry and occupational differences in employment and the devaluation of women's work.[20] Though employment sex segregation declined from the 1960s at least up until the 1990s, women are still consigned to lower-paying and less-desirable "women's jobs," while men are channeled into more rewarding and prestigious "men's jobs." Even when occupations have similar educational and skill requirements, jobs in which women predominate pay less and have fewer opportunities for advancement than jobs in which men predominate, and the higher the proportion of women in a particular occupation, the lower the pay.[21]

Whether they are mothers or not, women's employment opportunities are obstructed by deep-rooted stereotypes about their attributes and capabilities and by cultural conceptions of what constitutes gender-appropriate work.[22] Women are commonly believed to be less rational, competent, and authoritative than men and more emotional, expressive, and nurturing. They are thus presumed to be better equipped for some jobs than others. Gender stereotypes such as these, transmitted through the process of socialization, may even enter into the self-evaluations and employment preferences of men and women themselves, and they certainly come into play when workplace gatekeepers make decisions about recruitment, hiring, pay, promotion, training, and work assignments.[23] Women who do cross over into predominantly male occupations are commonly paid less than their male counterparts. They may also be met with not-so-welcome reminders of their outsider status: their femininity may be questioned; they may be subject to ridicule, harassment, or ostracism; and they may encounter other forms of hostility and resistance from male coworkers.[24] Because of the sexist culture of many male-dominated occupations, Francine Blau suggests, women may be discouraged from seeking entry into nontraditional jobs, resulting in diminished career prospects.[25]

Though sex discrimination in the labor market is less pervasive and blatant than in the past, it is still a significant cause of gender inequality. Such discrimination operates partly through unconscious gender biases, but it also originates from explicit cultural beliefs about gender differences.[26] Discrimination is difficult to uncover, and even when perceived or suspected it often goes unchallenged. But the evidence is clear that a significant portion of the gender earnings gap results from the inequitable treatment of women in the labor market and the workplace.[27] Consider just a few examples. (1) Male nurses, a 2015 study found, make more than $5,000 a year on average than comparable female nurses.[28] (2) Almost seventy thousand current and former female employees of Sterling Jewelers, where complaints about sexual harassment had gone unanswered for years, joined a class action suit in 2017 charging the company with pay and promotion discrimination.[29] (3) With evidence they were paid less, given less-desirable job assignments, and scheduled for fewer hours than their male counterparts, female managers and cashiers won a $100,000 settlement in a lawsuit against a Checkers fast-food franchise.[30] (4) In an audit study conducted by David Neumark and his colleagues, matched pairs of women and men applied for jobs as waiters and waitresses at dozens of Philadelphia restaurants. Despite equivalent qualifications, men were significantly favored over women in expensive restaurants, where wages and tips were substantially higher.[31] (5) In another audit study, published in 2012, science faculty were asked to rate the application materials for fictitious "male" and "female" candidates for a laboratory management position. Regardless of whether evaluators themselves were men or women, applicants designated with a "male" name were judged more competent than applicants designated with a "female" name.[32]

Because they are often barred from more lucrative blue-collar jobs and because of their caretaking responsibilities, working-class women, particularly women of color, are found disproportionately in the service sector, where unions are uncommon, wages low, working conditions poor, and opportunities for mobility scarce. They are employed as child-care and health-care providers, waitresses, cashiers, receptionists, and housecleaners. These jobs typically lack health insurance, retirement benefits, sick leave, vacation time, and standardized work schedules. The prospects for these "undervalued and underpaid" workers have deteriorated in recent decades, moreover, as a changing economy has undermined the life chances of people without a college education. With the shrinking number of jobs in manufacturing and mining, many less-educated men also are experiencing economic hardship.

In their struggles to make ends meet in the precarious low-wage service economy, however, women have shouldered more than their fair share of the costs resulting from economic restructuring and rising inequality. [33]

The challenge of combining motherhood and paid work is hard enough for middle-class women. For single mothers forced to manage on their own, solely responsible for both bringing home the bacon and taking care of the kids, the difficulties are compounded, especially if they are trapped in the low end of the labor market. Because many single women with children are African American or Hispanic, they are not only penalized for being women and mothers, they are susceptible to discrimination on the basis of race and ethnicity as well. Single motherhood is also more prevalent among less-educated women, those with no more than a high school degree. They face a difficult struggle trying to support a family by themselves in an economic environment increasingly unfavorable to workers without a college education. And to make matters worse, single mothers, especially welfare recipients, are also denigrated and stigmatized in the larger culture. The 1996 overhaul of the welfare system and the subsequent cutback in cash assistance for low-income women has only increased the economic and psychological strains associated with single motherhood. The adversities of this harsher environment are felt not only by mothers, of course, but also by their children, with potentially detrimental effects on later-life outcomes. [34]

The absence of sensible social policies is another reason women in the United States have lower earnings than men and face a higher risk of poverty. Compared to other industrialized countries, government in the United States provides relatively little assistance to low-income families. Tax policies are less redistributive, and welfare programs less generous. And while citizens in most other developed nations benefit from comprehensive child-care subsidies and paid parental-leave rights, families in the United States—mothers in particular—are expected to carry the burden of raising children on their own. [35]

CHILD CARE

Among the many changes in American society since World War II, few have been more far-reaching than the remarkable growth in the labor force participation of women, especially wives and mothers. In 1947 only 18.6 percent of women with children under age eighteen and only 12 percent with preschool children were in the labor force. As recently as the 1960s, the rate of employment for women with children under six was still less than 30 percent. By March 2015, 69.9 percent of women with children under eighteen were in the labor force, including 63.9 percent of mothers with children under six and 61.4 percent with children under three. [36] Regardless of the age of their children, most mothers are also paid workers. In 2016, 66.5 percent of mothers in married-couple households and 72.5 percent of mothers in female-headed households were employed.[37] The model of the family celebrated on television sitcoms of the 1950s—a male breadwinner, a stay-at-home mother, and children reared solely by their parents—has become the exception. The norm today is a paying job for mom and child care for the kids.

Approximately 12 million preschool children are in some kind of child-care arrangement on a regular basis. Among the different forms of child care available for preschoolers, the three types currently most in use, ranked from most to least expensive, are (1) center-based care, including preschools, nurseries, and day-care centers; (2) family day care, consisting of independent providers offering child-care services out of their homes; and (3) relative or kin care, often supplied by grandmothers or aunts, either in their own or in parents' homes.[38] While affluent families rely more on center-based care, low-income families, single and minority mothers in particular, depend more heavily on relatives, primarily because of cost considerations, but also because kin care is relatively trustworthy, convenient, and flexible.[39]

Poor families are severely constrained in their options because child care, an inherently labor-intensive practice, is expensive, and high-quality care is very expensive. The average annual cost of full-time care for a child age four and below is $9,589, higher than the average cost of in-state college tuition and nearly as high as the average cost of rent.[40] Child care is costly for any family, and for low-income families it is a major budget item, eating up a large share of total earnings. In many states, a minimum-wage worker with two children in a day-care center would have nothing left over after paying the bill. For single mothers working low-wage jobs without substantial government assistance, child care in a licensed center with a well-trained staff is far beyond their financial means.[41]

Even if they can scrape up the money, finding quality child care is not a simple matter. About half of American children live in "child-care deserts": "areas with little or no access to quality care."[42] Parents in such areas are left with limited options. They can seek out child-care facilities beyond their immediate community. But this requires that they have reliable transportation, not always the case for low-income households. It means more of their day spent on the road as well, traveling from home to day care to work and then back again. Even this is only possible if parents have jobs with stable and predictable working hours. Leaving the labor force altogether and becoming a full-time caregiver is another option, though the downside is a loss of earnings and a loss of potential retirement benefits. The conflict between child care and work is very real, with parents having to choose between undesirable alternatives. In 2016, 2 million parents of young children "had to quit a job, not take a job, or greatly change their job because of problems with child care."[43]

Parents need affordable child care, but they would also like to have quality child care.[44] Even costly care, however, is not necessarily quality care. Child-care arrangements, beyond the requirement of keeping children safe, qualify for a high rating only if they are educationally enriching. This is particularly important in the case of children in their formative first five years.[45] By this criterion, according to one estimate, most "child care settings do not rank high on quality." Over 80 percent are merely "fair."[46] At a minimum, quality child care requires a well-paid and well-trained staff. In the United States, however, caring for children is practiced as a low-wage job, not a respected profession. Caregivers are among the poorest paid workers in the country. In 2015 the average hourly wage for "child-care workers" varied from a high of $12.66 in Massachusetts to a low of $8.88 in Mississippi, not a level of earnings likely to attract or retain the most qualified people or even enable care providers themselves to avoid poverty or meet their own child-care needs.[47] Staff members in child-care centers do not typically receive extensive training, and the rate of turnover is high, making it difficult for children to establish a close relationship with caretakers. Many child-care centers are also understaffed, with a ratio of caregivers to children well below what is necessary to maintain quality treatment. In Florida, for example, Sharon Lerner reports, "one child care provider can legally look after as many as eleven 2-year-olds, fifteen 3-year-olds, or twenty 4-year-olds," and even these shocking ratios, she observes, "are routinely violated."[48] Family day care and relative care, both of which are unregulated and unlicensed in most states, also typically fail the quality test. In neither arrangement are caretakers supervised or trained, and in both they serve mainly in a custodial or babysitting capacity, rarely providing children with the kind of learning environment and educational experience they need in their early years.[49] In sum, according to Suzanne Helburn and Barbara Bergmann, there is "a distressing amount of poor care" in the United States and "a paucity of good care." Most child care is "mediocre," they argue, and a "substantial number" of infants "receive care that is unacceptable." Inferior child care is not just a problem for the poor by any means. But children from low-income families, precisely those most in need of a boost up during their preschool years, rarely receive good care, and, as Helburn and Bergmann conclude, they are "more likely than not to receive care that is less than even minimally adequate."[50]

The federal government provides child-care subsidies to low-income families, but the funds are limited and available to only a fraction of those in need. The Child Care and Development Block Grant (CCDBG) is the primary federal program designed to assist low-income working families with children.[51] The level of funding for this program is woefully insufficient, however, and increasingly so because spending has failed to keep pace with the rate of inflation. The number of children served by the CCDBG has been on the decline since 2007, hitting a record low of 1.4 million in 2015. Only about 10 to 15 percent of eligible households currently receive child-care assistance.[52] Thousands of needy families and needy children, if they are not simply turned away, are placed on waiting lists, in some states longer than twenty thousand. Even those lucky enough to receive a subsidy may be saddled with high copayments.[53] For poor children without a subsidy and no set child-care arrangement, life is a "kaleidoscope of caretakers." One mother on a waiting list in Virginia was reduced to letting her eleven-year old daughter spend her after-school hours riding around on a city bus driven by the girl's grandmother.[54] Ultimately, government-funded child-care subsidies and the supply of good and affordable facilities are insufficient to meet the needs of American families. And with projected budget cuts from the Trump administration, the near-term challenges confronting low-income families with children are certain to get worse.

In their efforts to manage child care, poor families, including those headed by single mothers, face an assortment of daunting problems. They have to find competent and responsible providers, available at the right place, the right time, and for the right price. Because of their limited resources and irregular work schedules, they are often forced to cobble together multiple child-care arrangements, relying on one primary caretaker during most of the day or week and then one or two secondary caretakers to fill in the gaps.[55] These arrangements are often unstable: a day-care provider ceases operations, a relative becomes unavailable, or the quality of care proves unsatisfactory. Periodic disruptions in care, besides the considerable inconvenience they cause, create an insecure and inconsistent early-life experience for young children.[56] Parents, mothers in particular, also have to live with the guilt they may feel for not always being available when their children need them, and they also have to deal with the stigma of not always complying with middle-class ideals of a "good mother" and a "good worker." And if they are single mothers, they have to struggle with all these everyday challenges on their own, typically with little help from the government and little sympathy from employers.[57]

The problems low-income parents encounter in their daily lives are all the more difficult to resolve because many have nonstandard jobs in the 24/7 service economy.[58] They work evenings, graveyard shifts, and weekends. They are sometimes on call, like many Walmart employees, expected to come into work on a moment's notice. Their hours are often unpredictable, with changing work schedules from week to week, making it difficult to plan child-care arrangements in advance. Their lives are unstable and stressful, tough on both parents and children. The child-care industry, moreover, which typically operates on a daytime, Monday through Friday schedule, is not designed to serve the needs of nonstandard workers. Low-income families thus have little choice but to fall back on informal and sometimes ad hoc arrangements. These can be difficult to organize, however, particularly when parents have no control over their working hours. Nor can they count on relatives, friends, and neighbors being readily available or always willing to watch over their children.

Poor families face extraordinary difficulties managing child care, and the problems they experience, as Julie Press argues, decrease their likelihood of avoiding or escaping poverty. Child-care demands perpetuate poverty by limiting the time parents can devote to work, training, and education, thus reducing their earnings in both the short term and the long term. As Press shows, poor parents with child-care problems, mothers more so than fathers, are less likely to be in the labor force, they work fewer hours when they are employed, and they are more susceptible to periodic bouts of unemployment. They are also more likely to work part time, be tardy or absent, quit a job, or be fired as a result of child-care issues, and to refuse a promising opportunity for the sake of a job with an accommodating boss or family-friendly hours. For parents whose employment options are limited to the low-wage sector, furthermore, it simply may not pay to keep a job. The costs of child care and other work-related expenses, including transportation, may exceed potential earnings. Poor parents lacking affordable child care, because of its effects on work effort, are trapped in poverty. Their continued poverty, in turn, means they cannot afford quality child care, with adverse effects on their children's educational development and later-life economic prospects. In this manner, the poverty of the parents is passed along to the children.[59]

Poverty exacerbates the problem of child care, and the lack of quality child care exacerbates the problem of poverty. This vicious cycle is the product of a system in which individual families are expected to shoulder the bulk of the financial burden for the care and education of their young children. There could not be a better recipe for perpetuating the gap between the haves and the have-nots. Child care in the United States is a commodity, not a public good, and like any other commodity, consumers get what they pay for. Less-affluent parents, unfortunately, cannot pay for much. In the absence of a more stringently regulated, well-funded, and equitable public child-care system—of the sort available in other industrialized nations—the children of low-income families, compared to the lucky children born into wealthy families, are bound to receive inferior care and an inferior preschool education. Because of these early life inequalities, they are also likely to experience greater hardships as adults.[60]

HEALTH AND HEALTH CARE

Poverty is bad for your health. The share of Americans in the bottom third of the income distribution who report just fair or poor health is much higher than the share in the top third—38.2 percent compared to 12.3 percent. In a thirty-two-nation study, only two countries, Portugal and Chile, had a larger income-based health gap.[61] Lower-income Americans don't just imagine they are less healthy, either. They really are. They have a higher incidence of asthma, heart disease, hypertension, high blood pressure, diabetes, cancer, and low birth weight.[62] Poverty is not just unhealthy; it is deadly. As Michael Reisch observes, it "steals years from one's life."[63] According to a study by Raj Chetty and his collaborators, the lower people's income, the shorter their lives. The life expectancy difference between Americans in the top 1 percent and the bottom 1 percent is fifteen years for men and ten for women, a death gap that has been trending upward since 2001.[64] Health disparities by socio-economic status are a universal phenomenon, but in the United States the degree of health inequality is unusually high, and the "association between low income and poor health" is unusually strong.[65]

The relationship between economic status and health has drawn consider-able attention recently with the opioid epidemic and the rising death rate among less-educated white Americans. Though not fully understood, these "deaths of despair," due primarily to drug overdose, alcohol abuse, and sui-cide, appear to be rooted in declining economic opportunities for people without a college degree and the destabilizing effects of economic hardship on marriage and family life. White working-class Americans have been par-ticularly susceptible to such deaths. This is the case, according to one inter-pretation, because their economic circumstances and prospects are so much worse than the preceding generation and because their lives, as judged by traditional expectations, have gone so far off course. These comparative metrics heighten people's consciousness of their relative deprivation, prompting feelings of distress and hopelessness. Whatever the precise causal mechanisms, however, these "deaths of despair" testify to the influence of socioeconomic conditions on health outcomes.[66]

Spending on health care in the United States, whether measured per capita or as a percentage of GDP, is much higher than elsewhere in the industrial-ized world. But compared to that of ten European countries, the overall performance of the American health-care system, calculated by scores on seventy-two indicators, is dead last. The United States, for examples, ranks at the bottom on measures of affordability, timely access to medical care, life expectancy, and infant mortality.[67] This paradox—high spending and poor performance—is due partly to inequities in health-care provision. People who can pay the price or have good health insurance typically receive excel-lent medical attention. If they are really rich, they can pay lofty fees, as much as $80,000 a year, to guarantee on-call medical care by "concierge" or "bou-tique" doctors.[68] Millions of Americans, by contrast, including those most likely to suffer from illness, disease, and injury, are lacking in even the most basic access to medical care. Money is one factor. The provision of medical care in this country, more so than in other developed nations, is organized on a primarily for-profit basis.[69] The poor, along with many of those above the poverty line, are often forced by cost considerations to refrain from or delay purchasing prescription drugs or getting medical and dental treatment.[70]

Insurance is another factor. The current system, with health coverage tied to employment, is rapidly unraveling. The percentage of private-sector workers with employment-based health insurance has been on the decline for three decades, with low-wage workers least likely to have coverage. Between 1991 and 2012 the share of all private-sector workers with access to employment-based health insurance declined from 77.3 percent to 70.2 percent. The share of low-wage (bottom quartile) and part-time workers with coverage in 2012 was 30.8 and 23.7 percent respectively.[71] Even if they have insurance, low-income workers face escalating costs: higher premiums, co-payments, and deductibles. Health care is extraordinarily expensive in the United States. Whether insured or not, many Americans cannot afford to get the care they need or end up burdened by exorbitant medical bills. Some are even forced into bankruptcy by their physical and mental ailments.[72]

The enactment of the Affordable Care Act (ACA) and the expansion of Medicaid coverage in thirty-two of the fifty states have resulted in improved performance of the American health-care system and a decline in the uninsured population to a record low of 10.9 percent in 2016. Though progress has been made, the percentage of those without health insurance is still higher in the United States than in other comparable countries.[73] The Trump administration and congressional Republicans have been unable so far to legislate the repeal of the ACA, but they are currently endeavoring to undermine the program by other means: (1) limiting advertisement and outreach to people needing to sign up for insurance; (2) making it difficult for consumers to acquire information and obtain assistance and counseling as they try to assess their enrollment options; (3) opening the door to substandard "association health plans"—cheaper plans with limited coverage—which could destabilize the ACA marketplaces by drawing off healthier consumers; (4) cutting subsidies to insurance companies that enable them to sell reduced-cost plans to low-income households; and (5) abolishing the individual mandate requiring everyone to purchase health insurance.[74] In addition to their assault on the ACA, congressional Republicans are also contemplating eliminating the tax deduction for medical expenses, a move that would be very costly for the elderly and the chronically ill; and they have thus far refused to extend funding for the Children's Health Insurance Program (CHIP), which provides health-care services to approximately 9 million children from low-income families.[75] How all this will play out, as of mid-December 2017, is uncertain.

Poor people do not receive the medical attention or insurance coverage they need, but this is not the main cause of their health problems. Even if they had unlimited access to medical care, the poor would still have higher rates of morbidity and mortality. The real culprit is poverty. As Helen Epstein says, poverty is "enough to make you sick."[76] What is it precisely about poverty that is so unhealthy? First, the condition of poverty is not conducive to healthy living.[77] The poor inhabit a social environment—their homes, neighborhoods, schools, and workplaces—in which the pursuit of a healthy lifestyle is not an easy option. They are more likely to smoke cigarettes and are less likely to eat nutritious food, exercise daily, be well-informed about health issues, or visit a doctor on a regular basis. Most cannot afford the basics of a healthy life: a wholesome diet, proper clothing, adequate shelter, enriching leisure activities, a safe and comfortable living environment, and quality child care.

Second, the poor experience more everyday hardships and live more stressful lives than the rich, especially if they are subject to "structural racism" and residential segregation.[78] They also have a shortage of coping resources, including the legal aid necessary to compel fair treatment from landlords, employers, lenders, police officers, and others.[79] The type of stress the poor have, furthermore—"the chronic and continual stress that come from experiencing constant shocks due to circumstances beyond individuals' control"—is more harmful than the achievement-oriented stress of their more affluent counterparts.[80] People on the lower end of the class structure encounter a multitude of daily insecurities, including uncertainties about food, transportation, housing, child care, health care, and regular employment. These insecurities are often accompanied by feelings of anxiety and hopelessness, with effects that accumulate over time, inducing a "generalized susceptibility" to illness and disease.[81] The effects are also lasting. A history of early childhood poverty has persistently detrimental health consequences, even for those who subsequently manage to escape the ranks of the poor. People who experience economic adversity and chronic stress during their preschool years are vulnerable to health problems as adults.[82]

Third, millions of poor households, disproportionately black and Hispanic, not only contend with their own personal health issues, but also encounter environmental risks stemming from unsafe and unhealthy neighborhood conditions.[83] Poor and racially segregated communities have higher levels of crime and violence. They are often lacking in police, fire, and sanitation services, health-care centers, and medical personnel. They rarely feature running tracks, bicycle paths, or health clubs. And while many poor neighborhoods are "food deserts"—"lacking ready access to fresh, healthy, and affordable food"—what they do have in abundance are fast-food restaurants, convenience marts, and liquor stores.[84] They also have lower levels of social integration and cohesion, such that individuals have fewer resources for acquiring health information and social support, and they have correspondingly higher levels of social isolation, increasing the likelihood they will be forced to cope with their illnesses on their own.[85] People living in poor and racially segregated neighborhoods—Flint, Michigan, to take one notorious example—have a higher exposure to pollution, toxic waste, and lead poisoning as well.[86] And because high-poverty neighborhoods are stressful places to live, residents are also susceptible to depression, anxiety, and other psychological disorders.[87]

Fourth, poverty is unhealthy because many poor people, 2.5 million according to one estimate, live in overcrowded and physically inferior housing, with inadequate ventilation, pest infestation, and faulty plumbing and heating.[88] Poor children are commonly exposed to mold and mildew, rats and mice, cockroaches and dust mites, all of which increase the risk of infectious disease and asthma. Children living in older housing are also in danger of lead poisoning, particularly harmful because it can impair cognitive development. Substandard housing also increases the likelihood of fire and other residential accidents, one of the leading causes of injury and death among children, and it is detrimental to their emotional and behavioral well-being.[89] Decrepit housing, as Matthew Desmond observes, is also a potential hazard to psychological health: "not only because things like dampness, mold, and overcrowding" might cause depression, "but also because of what living in awful conditions" tells "you about yourself."[90] The high cost of housing in the United States impairs the health of low-income families as well because less money is left over after paying the rent to cover necessities essential to healthy living, including nutritious food and regular medical care.[91]

Fifth, the working conditions of less-educated Americans contribute to higher rates of sickness, injury, and early death.[92] In today's economy, where working-class jobs are often unfulfilling, if not downright perilous—hard on the body and the mind—the "social experience" of employment "translates into poor health."[93] Low-wage workers are sometimes penalized for taking a sick day or being absent from work to care for a family member; in some cases, they are forced to work despite health problems or risk getting fired.[94] Often treated unfairly and compensated unjustly, low-wage workers commonly endure a demoralizing disconnect between effort and reward. They have little control over their workplace circumstances, and in many jobs the strain from being subject to continuous monitoring and harsh supervision takes a physical and psychological toll. Employees with irregular hours, unpredictable work schedules, and night shifts also tend to experience health problems, such as sleeping disorders, and their children's health and well-being too are adversely affected by the parents' nonstandard hours.[95]

Many service-sector and blue-collar workers, in addition, are exposed to toxic substances and unsafe work environments, and they are at greater risk of workplace illnesses, accidents, and fatalities. Those who work outdoors may also be vulnerable to hazardous weather, extremes of cold and heat.[96] In 2015, according to the latest report from the AFL-CIO, nearly 5,000 workers were killed on the job, another 50,000–60,000 died from occupational diseases, and nearly 3.7 million reported work-related illnesses and injuries, with perhaps another 7 to 11 million injuries unreported.[97] These grim numbers are likely to get worse in the near future, with industry groups having a prominent presence in the business-friendly Trump administration. Already many workplace safety rules and regulations have been loosened or repealed, including a rule requiring employers to maintain a public record of workplace injuries.[98]

Poor health adversely affects people's economic outcomes, but the bigger part of the story is how poverty adversely affects people's health. Poor people are unhealthy because they are economically deprived. But poverty causes ill health also because it inhibits individuals from achieving "autonomy, empowerment, and human freedom."[99] These are no less crucial to personal well-being than are food, shelter, and clothing. People experience chronic stress and stress-related health problems when basic human needs go unfilled: when they have little control over their own lives, whether in their homes, workplaces, or communities; are excluded from the social and economic mainstream, unable to participate as full-fledged members of society; are subject to disparaging cultural stigmas and looked down upon; are treated unfairly and denied opportunities for living a decent life; and are on the bottom looking up, with those on the top continually receding from view. The poor, under normal conditions, are powerless, exploited, and marginalized. This perhaps more than anything else is what makes poverty a health hazard. Only by attacking the fundamental economic and political inequalities at the root of poverty can we make significant progress in addressing the health problems of disadvantaged Americans.

RETIREMENT INSECURITY

The rate of poverty for the elderly fell from over 35 percent in 1959 to 15 percent in 1975. Over the next two decades it continued to decline, though more slowly, leveling off toward the end of the 1990s. In 2016 the poverty rate for the sixty-five and older population was 9.3 percent. The dramatic reduction in elderly poverty over the past half century has been one of the great success stories of the American welfare state. Even so, the picture for seniors is far from rosy. The number of elderly poor is still substantial, 4.6 million in 2016.[100] It may even be much larger. A highly regarded alternative measure, the Supplemental Poverty Measure, estimates a rate of poverty for seniors of 14.6 percent, much higher than the official estimate of 9.3 percent.[101] Many of the elderly, and not just those below the poverty line, endure real hardships. According to a recent study by Helen Levy, 20 percent of those over age sixty-five, those with poor health especially, report experiencing at least one of five material hardships: "food insecurity, skipped meals, medication cutbacks, difficulty paying bills, and dissatisfaction with one's financial situation."[102] One-third of older adults, including 54 percent of elderly renters, are "cost burdened," meaning they pay more than 30 percent of their income on housing and are in danger of having too little money left over to cover other expenses. The problem of housing for the aged is projected to become increasingly severe over the next two decades.[103]

Some of the elderly are doing quite well, of course, but many others—varying by class, race, and gender—are barely scraping by. Aging, as Corey Abramson observes, is a "stratified process."[104] The rates of poverty for older African Americans and Hispanics remain exceptionally high, 18.5 percent and 17.4 percent respectively, more than twice the rate for non-Hispanic whites.[105] Because they live longer, earn less during their working years, and receive correspondingly less retirement income, the rate of poverty for women over sixty-five is significantly higher than for men, 10.6 percent compared to 7.6 percent.[106] Despite the notable progress achieved during the 1960s and 1970s, moreover, the incidence of poverty among the aged in the United States is still much greater than elsewhere in the industrialized world, and double the level of many European countries.[107]

The economic status of the elderly and those destined to become elderly is bound to a retirement system that fails to provide adequate income security for millions of older Americans. This system is often described as a stool composed of three legs—Social Security, personal savings, and employment-based retirement savings. For poorer Americans, even in the best of times, these three legs have never been all that sturdy. Workers with low lifetime earnings, disproportionately women and racial/ethnic minorities, receive commensurately smaller Social Security checks; few manage to accumulate significant assets or savings during their working years; and many do not have a private pension plan to augment their retirement income. This three-legged retirement stool has become even more wobbly since the 1980s, with dire implications for low-wage workers as they approach their retirement years.

From its very inception up to the present, Social Security has been under attack, with right-wing critics denouncing it as a "Ponzi scheme" and calling for individual retirement accounts instead ("privatization").[108] Others, proclaiming an urgent need to reduce entitlement costs, have proposed raising the retirement age. Given the growing life expectancy gap between higher-income Americans and lower-income Americans, however, this would effectively mean a sizable transfer of social welfare benefits from the shorter-lived poor to the longer-lived rich.[109] What is worth considering, however, is the role played by increasing inequality in contributing to the impending shortfall of Social Security revenue. The payroll tax, which funds Social Security, is capped at around $120,000. In an era of rising earnings inequality, with high earners slicing off an increasingly large piece of the economic pie, a growing share of total earnings is exempt from the payroll tax. The result is less money being collected to pay for Social Security. By raising the cap—Bernie Sanders recommends a cut-off line of $250,000—and by strengthening policies to increase the earnings of average Americans and thus payroll tax revenue, the solvency of the Social Security system could be ensured without inflicting additional pain on poorer Americans.[110]

Despite alarmist and politically motivated warnings about its future, Social Security is the most durable component of the retirement system, and certainly the most essential. It is the single largest source of income for two-thirds of women and one-half of men sixty-five and over, and it is the *only* source of income for nearly 30 percent of elderly women and 20 percent of elderly men. Black and Hispanic men and women and people of all races over the age of seventy-five are even more reliant on Social Security.[111] A large and growing share of the elderly population, reduced to hobbling around on just one feeble retirement leg, is almost entirely dependent on monthly Social Security checks.

Social Security is critical to the survival of all but the most affluent retirees. It is also the nation's most effective antipoverty program. Compared to public pension systems in other industrialized countries, Social Security benefit levels are relatively low, certainly not generous enough to lift all the elderly above the poverty line.[112] In the absence of Social Security, however, nearly 15 million people would be added to the poverty numbers, increasing the rate of poverty for the older population from the current level of 9.3 percent to nearly 50 percent. Social Security is particularly vital to the economic well-being of elderly women, who both live longer and are less likely to have other sources of income. Without Social Security, two-thirds of all unmarried women over sixty-five would be poor.[113]

The elderly population is reliant on Social Security partly because the personal savings leg of the retirement system is woefully inadequate. Relatively few retirees have substantial savings or income from assets, and this is especially true for racial/ethnic minorities and households in the bottom half of the income distribution. The elderly in recent years have become increasingly debt burdened as well. The number of Americans sixty and over with student debt, mostly from borrowing for their children's or grandchildren's education, has quadrupled since 2005, and the average amount of that debt has doubled over the same time period.[114] The percentage of older families with mortgage debt has also grown sharply, as has the value of that debt.[115] Credit card debt among the elderly has increased too, more than doubling since the Great Recession.[116] With millions of working Americans enduring stagnant or declining earnings, with affordable housing in short supply, and with the rising cost of health care and higher education, it is unrealistic to imagine that future retirees will be any more able than current retirees to build up a retirement nest egg through personal savings.

Older Americans can achieve a comfortable retirement only if they have a private pension to supplement their Social Security benefits. The employer-sponsored pension is now the wobbliest leg of the retirement system and is missing entirely for most low-end workers. As of 2014, fewer than two-thirds of private-sector workers had access to an employment-based retirement plan; even fewer, 48 percent, participated in one; and 31 percent of workers had no retirement savings at all.[117] For the bottom quintile, only 10 percent of workers were enrolled in a retirement plan, and only 8 percent had any retirement account savings.[118] The existing employment-based retirement system leaves many future retirees, including most low-income workers, without a pension leg to stand on and likely to end up dependent entirely on Social Security.

Millions of currently working-age Americans face the prospect of retirement insecurity—"not being able to maintain their standard of living in retirement"—and "that problem is growing worse over time."[119] This looming retirement crisis is due in large part to the changing nature of the private pension system. During the "golden age" of the post–World War II era, employees were typically covered by a "defined-benefit" (DB) pension plan. Similar to Social Security, these traditional pensions guaranteed workers a fixed and lifelong monthly payment upon retirement. Since the 1980s, however, employers by the droves have ceased offering DB plans or have frozen those already in existence and have replaced them, if at all, with "defined contribution" (DC) plans instead, mostly of the 401(k) type.[120] These plans offer employees the option of contributing pretax income to their own individual investment accounts, sometimes with matching funds from employers. In 2013, of households covered by an employment-based retirement plan, about 60 percent were DC plans only, up from 33 percent in 1989.[121]

This shift from DB plans to DC plans has increased the risk of retirement insecurity for working Americans. Under the new system, workers' contributions are voluntary rather than mandatory; employees rather than employers have primary responsibility for funding and managing their retirement accounts; the payout for retirees is uncertain, dependent on the vicissitudes of the stock market; the investment risk is borne entirely by employees, with employers freed from any long-term financial obligations to their workers; and DC plans, unlike DB plans, are not insured by the federal government.[122] Many upper-tier workers, riding the wave of soaring stock prices in the 1990s, benefited from the introduction of DC plans. But for the vast majority of workers, particularly those lower down in the earning distribution, the demise of DB plans has reduced their potential retirement income. Not surprisingly, the rate of poverty for elderly householders without a DB pension is about nine times greater than for those with a DB pension. The rise of the defined-contribution system and the demise of the defined-benefit system have diminished the likelihood of a secure retirement for millions of working Americans.[123]

Experts in the field believe that households are "at risk" if they cannot be expected to maintain their preretirement standard of living once they enter their retirement years. According to one "middle ground" estimate, the percentage of at-risk households was 52 percent in 2013, up from 31 percent in 1983.[124] Nari Rhee and Ilana Boivie, in a study for the National Institute on Retirement, report that the average working household "has virtually no retirement savings." "The hope of retirement security," they conclude, "is out of reach for many Americans in the face of a crumbling retirement infrastructure."[125]

An increasing number of the elderly, 18.8 percent, up from 12.8 percent in 2000—"more than at any time since the turn of the century"—are still working, with more of them working full time as well. Some are continuing to work because they can and want to, but many others simply cannot afford to retire; "they hold onto their jobs not because they cherish them, but because they lack alternative income."[126] Holding down three part-time jobs, sixty-two-year-old Susan Zimmerman says: "I will probably be working until I'm 100." But with the combination of weak employment growth and age discrimination, getting a job, however necessary, is not always easy for older workers, particularly if they are reentering the labor market after being laid off. Getting a good job is even harder. Some are funneled into low-paying "old-person jobs," and some are unable to find work at all.[127] Since the Great Recession, older women reentering the labor market have had a particularly hard time. As one fifty-eight-year-old woman fruitlessly searching for work explained: "Now I'm on the other side of the rainbow, and it's not pretty over here."[128] Though no longer in the paid workforce, other seniors, mostly women, many over seventy-five, are working nevertheless as unpaid caregivers—"the old taking care of the old"—tending to their spouses, siblings, friends, and sometimes even their own parents.[129]

The retirement outlook for younger workers is even grimmer, especially for those trapped in the low-wage sector, but also for many middle-class young adults saddled with student debt and still trying to find a steady job. For poorer workers especially, victimized by low wages and the constant pressure of immediate expenses, there is little they can do on their own to improve their retirement prospects. Frugality is not the answer for people who make barely enough money to live on. In the absence of significant reforms—to raise the earnings of low-end workers, increase the payout from Social Security, and overhaul a private pension system that largely excludes low-wage workers—the poverty experienced by millions of adults during their working years is bound to be reproduced as they cross the threshold into old age.

LEGAL DEPRIVATION

Equal justice for all—this is the bedrock principle of the American legal system. The reality, however, falls well short of the ideal. The poor and the working class, racial and ethnic minorities in particular, are frequent victims of injustice. They are vulnerable to employment and housing discrimination, police misconduct, exploitative behavior by employers, and predatory lending practices. If they are consumers or employees, they may be compelled to sign binding arbitration agreements, relinquishing their right to join class action suits, take grievances to court, or otherwise seek legal recourse when their rights are violated.[130] If they work as nannies, agricultural laborers, home health-care aides, or day laborers—categories of employment not covered by labor laws—they are susceptible to wage theft, as are workers in the restaurant and retail industries.[131] If they are private sector workers of just about any kind, once they cross the threshold into the workplace, as Elizabeth Anderson documents, they fall under the dictatorial power of their employers, are denied the right to free speech, and are subject to surveillance, invasions of privacy, and countless other infringements on their individual freedoms.[132] And sometimes just being poor is sufficient to be thought of as a criminal, or at least as an inferior, unworthy, and undeserving person.[133]

Millions of Americans do not receive adequate medical assistance because they cannot afford it, and for the same reason, millions of Americans do not receive adequate legal assistance. In civil law, unlike criminal law, there is no right to counsel. People only get the legal representation they can pay for. This unequal "access to lawyers" undermines the principle of equal "access to justice." Indeed, as one law professor argues, by virtue of the billions of dollars large corporations spend each year in legal fees, they, not ordinary citizens, have "the greatest access to justice."[134] Because low-income Americans, and many middle-class Americans, don't have the money to pay for costly legal help, they are unable to safeguard their rights in cases concerning, for example, child custody, domestic violence, consumer fraud, housing and employment discrimination, eviction, and foreclosure. They are likewise disadvantaged in their disputes with employers, landlords, creditors, merchants, utility companies, social service agencies, and other private and public authorities. Instead of "justice for all," we have "justice for some"—namely, people with money.[135]

The Economic Opportunity Act of 1964, which inaugurated the war on poverty, was amended in 1966 and 1967 to include federal funding for legal services for the poor. This measure signaled recognition of government's responsibility for guaranteeing access to legal assistance and for redressing inequities in the justice system. The advent of the legal services program, by assembling a corps of lawyers prepared to defend the rights of the poor and advocate on their behalf, altered the American legal environment, anticipating the possibility that equal justice would become a reality. [136]

In 1974 Congress consolidated the patchwork of legal aid under the authority of the Legal Services Corporation (LSC), a private, nonprofit, government-funded organization. [137] The LSC expanded throughout the 1970s, and by 1981 it had offices in all fifty states and had reached a modest "minimum access" goal of two lawyers for every ten thousand people under the poverty line. Over the next two decades, however, beginning with Ronald Reagan's election to the presidency in 1980 and followed by Republican victories in the 1994 congressional elections, legal services became the target of a reinvigorated right-wing campaign. While failing to abolish the LSC, the conservative assault did result in a substantial reduction in funding and the imposition of numerous restrictions on the practices of legal services lawyers. They were, for example, prohibited from representing prisoners or undocumented immigrants, acting on behalf of the poor through political activism or legislative lobbying, participating in class action suits or cases concerning legislative redistricting, and a host of other activities. [138]

Even in 1981, when its budget reached its peak, the LSC had nowhere near the resources necessary to provide adequately for all those wanting help with their legal problems. Since then the level of funding has declined steadily, even as the number of people eligible for assistance has increased. Adjusted for inflation, the budget for the LSC in 2015, despite support from the Obama administration, was less than half the 1980 level. [139] Today, with only about one legal aid attorney for every ten thousand Americans living in poverty, approximately 80 percent of poor people's legal needs go unmet. [140] As a result of this "justice gap," many people, despite their lack of qualifications and knowledge of legal procedures, have no choice but to serve as their own representatives in court. [141] And when they do, such as in foreclosure and eviction cases, they are far more likely to lose than when represented by a lawyer. [142]

By international standards the "justice gap" in the United States is unusually large. According to the most recent report from the World Justice Project, the United States ranks a meager twenty-eighth in its ability to deliver civil justice in an accessible, affordable, and timely manner—a lower ranking than nearly every other developed nation. [143] Among thirty-one of the world's "richest" countries, another study shows, the United States ranks thirtieth in its provision of "access to justice" for low-income people in civil cases. The United States talks a good game where the ideal of "justice for all" is concerned but refuses to put its money where its mouth is. Due largely to the shrinking budget for the LSC, the United States spends considerably less on civic legal aid than other industrialized countries. [144] "In this vital area of equal access to justice," legal scholar and jurist Early Johnson states, "we are truly an 'underdeveloped country.'"[145] And with the election of Donald

Trump, we appear to be on our way to becoming even more underdeveloped. The Trump administration proposes to eliminate all federal funding for the LSC.[146] This plan has provoked a storm of criticism, including protests from more than 160 law school deans, corporate attorneys for 185 companies, the heads of 150 major law firms, and even a handful of congressional Republicans.[147] Most poor Americans are already denied access to legal assistance. The ending of federal funding for the LSC would widen an already disgracefully large justice gap.

The inequities within the criminal justice system are even more disturbing, with particularly harsh and sometimes deadly consequences for racial and ethnic minorities. Recent investigations of policing and court practices in Ferguson, Missouri, and Baltimore, Maryland, disclose a deplorable record of racism and unconstitutional conduct. Law enforcement in Ferguson, the Justice Department found, prioritized raising revenue through tickets, fines, and fees over ensuring public safety, and the police department, specifically targeting African Americans, exhibited a blatant pattern of racial stereotyping, racial bias, and "discriminatory intent." In Baltimore, similarly, the Justice Department revealed multiple examples of police misconduct, including discrimination against African Americans, excessive use of force, and "unconstitutional stops, searches, and arrests."[148] Racial inequities in the practice of criminal justice are not, of course, unique to Ferguson and Baltimore. Throughout the country, in fact, low-income Hispanics and African Americans, especially young black men, encounter disparities at every stage in the criminal justice process: who falls under the suspicion of law enforcement and how they are treated, who gets stopped and questioned by the police, who gets arrested and charged with a crime, who is found or pleads guilty, who gets incarcerated and for how long, who gets paroled, and what happens to them once they are released from prison.[149] And according to a recent report from the National Registry of Exonerations, black people also make up a disproportionate share of those found to be wrongfully convicted of murder, sexual assault, and drug crimes.[150]

As criminal defendants, the poor do at least have a constitutional right to legal counsel, but this by no means guarantees equal justice. A major impediment is the "crisis in indigent defense," with nowhere near enough public defenders to meet the needs of low-income people facing criminal charges.[151] In too many cases, the lawyers assigned to poor defendants are unqualified, inexperienced, overburdened, and underpaid, and few have the time or resources to do the investigative work necessary to provide clients with a proper defense.[152] Budgetary cutbacks in many states have overwhelmed the public defender system, effectively denying low-income defendants their constitutional right to legal counsel.[153] In Florida and many other states, even when found not guilty, low-income defendants are required to pay public defender fees and other court costs, and if unable to do so, since failure to pay is a crime, they may be thrown in jail.[154] In Louisiana, despite the presumption of innocence, poor people arrested for crimes and unable to pay bail are routinely imprisoned, marking time behind bars until their names rise to the top of waiting lists to see a lawyer.[155] This phenomenon—people spending time in jail, weeks and months even, because they are too poor to post bail—is a common experience throughout the country, with harmful consequences, including family disruption and job loss.[156]

As the 1960s wound down, a halfhearted war on poverty gave way to a full-blown war on crime, one fought mainly with the weapons of aggressive policing and mass incarceration.[157] The ensuing "law and order" regime led to a dramatic increase in the number of people behind bars. Relatively stable throughout most of the twentieth century, the size of the prison population began a steep upward climb in the mid-1970s, increasing by more than 500 percent over the next four decades, a trend only weakly related to crime rates.[158] In 2015 the number of adults in prison or jail was nearly 2.2 million, trending down slightly from previous years, with another 4.65 million on probation or parole.[159] African Americans and Hispanics make up a dispro-portionate share of the incarcerated population, almost 60 percent of those serving time in state and federal prisons.[160]

Along with the broader war on crime, the war on drugs also bears some responsibility for the rising rate of incarceration. Between 1980 and 2015 the number of drug offenders in prisons (federal and state) and jails increased by over 1,000 percent, from 41,000 to 470,000.[161] This is a lot of people, but still only about 20 percent of the prison population. It is important to keep in mind, however, that drug offenders have shorter sentences than those ar-rested for violent crimes. And while comprising a relatively modest percent-age of prisoners at any point in time, they make up a larger share, more than 30 percent, of those circulating into and out of the prison system. They consequently make up a sizable portion of the nonimprisoned population forced to deal with the stigma of a felony conviction and a prison record, reducing their chances of obtaining housing or employment and in many states costing them the right to vote.[162] And just as racial and ethnic minor-ities have borne the brunt of the war on crime, so too have they been dispro-portionately singled out by the war on drugs, despite being no more likely than non-Hispanic whites to use or sell illegal substances. Because inner cities are prime targets of policing and not, for example, college campuses, and because of harsher penalties for the use of crack versus powdered co-caine, the war on drugs has not only increased the number of those passing through the prison system, it has contributed to the skewed racial composi-tion of that population as well.[163]

Prosecutors have a great deal of discretion in whether or not to file charges against someone who is arrested, what charges to file (e.g., misde-meanor or felony), and whether those pronounced guilty are put away behind bars. In a political environment in which "tough on crime" rhetoric resonates with voters and severe sentencing laws are the norm, prosecutors, as John Pfaff argues, have becoming increasingly aggressive in the exercise of their authority, particularly in the arena of plea agreements, where the vast majority of criminal cases are settled. From the standpoint of prosecutors, plea bargains are *efficient*, allowing them to process cases in a matter of days and without the surprises that sometime arise in a trial, and they are *effective*, giving them a strategic advantage vis-à-vis low-income defendants, those without counsel, of course, but also those assigned public defenders too strapped for resources to put up much of a fight. While members of the larger public sometimes imagine that plea agreements enable defendants to serve less time in prison than they deserve, the opposite is closer to the truth. Even when their cases are weak, prosecutors are in a position to convince defendants to plead guilty to felony charges with significant prison time by withholding information and by threatening them with even longer prison terms should they go to trial. Since the 1970s, as a result, a greater percentage of those arrested for crimes are admitted to prisons. This, according to Pfaff, is the primary cause of rising incarceration. To underline once again a key point: prosecutors are able to prevail in plea deals and send more arrestees to prison not only because of their discretionary power, but because they are able to *use* that power, and they are able to use it to such effect in part because low income defendants lack "meaningful legal representation."[164]

Justice is neither cheap nor color-blind, and racial minorities and the poor are doubly penalized. In the area of civil law, they are not helped by the legal system as much as they have a right to be, and in the area of criminal law, they are harmed by the legal system more than they deserve to be. Because people are poor, they are victims of injustice; because they are victims of injustice, they remain poor. The "poor get prison," Jeffrey Reiman quips, but it is also true that the imprisonment of millions of young, mostly minority men exacerbates the problem of poverty.[165]

CONCLUSION

"Poverty or near poverty is not a problem," David Shipler observes. "It is an array of interlocking problems."[166] These problems are cumulative, reinforcing, and causally interrelated. Racial discrimination promotes residential segregation, and residential segregation, besides intensifying racial prejudice, gives rise to a dual housing market and a separate and unequal school system. Adverse neighborhood conditions and substandard housing cause health problems; health problems not only eat up money that might be spent on better housing, higher quality child care, or a new car, they also perpetuate poverty by limiting the work effort of adults and the educational attainment of children. Transportation problems make it difficult for poor families to manage child care; child-care problems reinforce sex discrimination; and the combination of sex discrimination, child-care problems, and transportation problems makes it nearly impossible for parents, especially single mothers, to find and keep a good job. These problems, in turn, cause high levels of stress and anxiety, with poor people as a result becoming inordinately susceptible to illness and disease. And the cycle goes on, with endless permutations and combinations.

Most poor people confront several of these and other obstacles simultaneously. Black and Hispanic households, partly because they are subject to discrimination and are more likely to reside in areas of high or extreme poverty—increasingly so since 2000—are particularly vulnerable to multiple and overlapping disadvantages.[167] To conceive poverty as simply a lack of income or focus attention on just a single problem, such as housing, or even a series of problems examined sequentially, as I have done here, is bound to leave a misleading picture of the lives of the poor and the difficulties they face. Low-income households experience problems in bunches, with one exacerbating another, and when they find a solution to one, this often comes at the expense of aggravating others or creating entirely new troubles. Compared to the nonpoor, the poor encounter hardships and emergencies more regularly and are less financially prepared to deal with them.[168] Struggling just to keep their heads above water, they find themselves worrying constantly about money, just one bad decision, one mistake, away from sinking. What's more, the difficulties experienced by the poor, particularly since 2000, are getting worse, and they are getting worse precisely during a period when the safety net is being shredded and low-income people, in the name of "personal responsibility," are increasingly forced to deal with their problems on their own.[169]

The poor are often accused of making bad choices, but the real problem is that their circumstances so often force them to choose between altogether undesirable alternatives. They encounter a series of harsh dilemmas: go to work or stay home with a sick child; repair the car or fix the plumbing and heating; choose among eye care, dental care, or prescription drugs; put food on the table or pay the rent on time; accumulate credit card debt or deny their kids a present, a new article of clothing, or a night out at the movies; take on a second job, attend to the educational needs of their children, or get involved in local politics; try to find a better house in a better neighborhood or save for retirement. These dilemmas are not unique to the poor, of course, but the needs of low-income households are more pressing, their resources more limited, and their trade-offs more severe.

The obstacles identified here, along with many others, constrain the life chances of the poor, limit their options, and make it difficult for them to cope with their poverty and ensure a decent future for their children. This country faces serious problems in the areas of health care, discrimination, retirement security, education, child care, housing, and all the rest, and for the poor, these problems have reached an immediate crisis level. These are not isolated social problems, however, and they cannot be remedied as such. They originate from deeply rooted economic and political disparities. We cannot hope to address effectively the many social problems endured by the poor without confronting the underlying inequalities in wealth and power that are ultimately responsible for the persistence of poverty.

Chapter Eleven

Conclusion

POVERTY AND POWER

We need to change how we think about poverty in the United States. We need to shift the focus from the characteristics of the poor to the dynamics of the larger political economy, from the deficiencies of individuals to the failings of social institutions. Instead of attributing poverty to the presumably self-defeating values and behaviors of the poor, I propose an alternative structural perspective. Today's poverty problem, I argue, originates from deep-rooted disparities in income, wealth, and power. No program for combating poverty can be successful without confronting these underlying economic and political inequalities. Poverty is a structural problem, and it demands a structural solution.

A structural perspective maintains that poverty is caused by circumstances external to the poor—by economic, political, cultural, and social forces beyond the immediate control of the individual. These forces determine whether the rate of poverty goes up or down, whether the conditions of the poor get better or worse, and who among the population is most at risk. They shape the options available to people, their access to resources, their quality of life, and their prospects for social mobility. At the same time, by allocating advantages and disadvantages, these forces generate inequalities, enriching some and impoverishing others. Whether we have more or less poverty cannot be explained by reference to individual ability and effort. Larger structural forces are at play, including the state of the economy, the contour of government policy, the climate of public opinion, and the pattern of social relations.

The structural perspective proposed in this book, as the title suggests, underlines the connection between poverty and power. Steven Lukes defines power as "the capacity to bring about outcomes."[1] This capacity plays a causally significant role in the allocation of resources and opportunities. It is deployed, for example, when employers move their operations overseas, hire union avoidance consultants to fend off collective bargaining, and replace full-time workers with independent contractors and temps. It is deployed when political officeholders enact tax policies favorable to big business, dismantle environmental and workplace regulations, and reduce spending on social programs targeted to low-income families. It is deployed when the news media, wittingly or not, lead the public to believe poverty results from personal misfortune, low-income Americans are more than adequately cared for by a generous welfare state, and the presence of widespread poverty is unrelated to the increasing wealth of the top 1 percent. And it is deployed when privileged groups conspire to maintain the exclusivity of their neighborhoods, schools, and social networks. This capacity is deployed also when citizens in cities and states mount campaigns to raise the minimum wage; people gather at town hall meetings to voice their opposition to government policies; activists mobilize to challenge white supremacists or protest racial injustice; unionized workers strike for better wages and working conditions; and mayors, in response to outraged constituents, establish sanctuaries for undocumented immigrants threatened by deportation.

Power is the servant of interests and ideologies, and the exercise of power typically engenders resistance from individuals and groups upholding competing interests and ideologies. Where there is power there is conflict, and where there is conflict there are winners and losers. Power is also unequally distributed. Because the wealthy possess vast resources and occupy the country's political, economic, and cultural "command posts," they are far more able than others to overcome opposition and bring about desired outcomes,[2] even more so in recent years. Over the past three or four decades, as we have seen, there has been a significant upward redistribution of economic, political, and ideological power—to the benefit of employers over employees, business over labor, the Right over the Left. The persistent class, race, and gender inequalities we observe in society, along with the widening gap between the rich and the poor, do not result from inexorable social processes or neutral market forces. These inequalities are by-products of a growing imbalance of power between the haves and the have-nots. This power shift, under way since the 1970s, accounts for the seeming paradox of so much poverty in a country with so much wealth.

A structural perspective implies a particular conception of the poverty problem. Poor people lack money, of course, but they also lack power. This may be the more fundamental issue. Poverty persists in large part because the ability to call the shots—to make economic and political policy, allocate costs and rewards, and control the flow of information and ideas—has become increasingly concentrated at the upper end of the class system, leaving the working class and the poor all the more marginalized and vulnerable. Under normal circumstances, ordinary Americans do not have the resources or leverage to demand higher wages and better working conditions; influence political leaders and government policy; alter the cultural discourse and imagery; or eradicate barriers to mobility caused by discrimination, segregation, and social exclusion. Poverty is not just a matter of income; it is also a matter of power. And no theory of poverty and inequality can be taken seriously if it fails to bring power fully into the picture.[3]

PROGRAMS AND POWER

There is no shortage of good ideas for fighting poverty. Recent reports from The Center for American Progress and the Economic Policy Institute include many worthy proposals.[4] Books by academics and activists also contain valuable compilations of strategies and programs for creating a more equal and just society.[5] Given the wealth of material already available, there is no need for another detailed survey of policy recommendations. No book on poverty would be complete, however, without at least some thoughts about how to fix the problem. So, borrowing mainly from the works referred to above and without presuming to be comprehensive, I present here a list of policy ideas and objectives that would help reduce poverty and inequality and create a better and more just society. The specifics of how these might be designed and administered can be found in the sources cited here and elsewhere. Some of the remedies proposed below are modest in their purposes, but others, heeding Michelle Jackson's call to think big, are more ambitious and radical, aiming not just to ameliorate poverty but to eradicate it.[6] To bring some order to this overview, I sort these policies into four somewhat overlapping categories, distinguished by the particular aspect of the poverty/inequality problem they address. Following this, in the final segment of this chapter, I return once again to the issue of power.

Income Support Policies

The policy proposals included in this category reduce the incidence and severity of poverty by putting more money into the hands of the poor, directly or indirectly, lifting them above, or at least closer to, the poverty line.

- Create jobs in the public sector to achieve a true full-employment economy, with government serving as an employer of last resort.
- Establish a universal basic income to ensure minimal living standards and provide a measure of guaranteed economic security for all Americans, while also lessening people's dependence on a persistently weak labor market.

- Establish a higher minimum wage, indexed to the rate of inflation, the rate of productivity, or median earnings.
- Increase the Earned Income Tax Credit for low-wage families and expand coverage to include childless workers.
- Increase unemployment insurance benefit levels to prevent people who are laid off from falling into poverty and to provide better coverage for the growing population of female, immigrant, low-wage, part-time, and contingent workers.
- Create a more dependable safety net by expanding eligibility and benefit levels for public assistance programs and by establishing uniform eligibility and benefit standards across states.
- Increase the payroll tax cap to ensure the financial stability of Social Security and strengthen the public and private pension systems to reduce retirement insecurity.
- Promote asset accumulation through government-financed trust funds for children and government matching contributions to savings accounts for low-income families.
- Change the Federal Reserve's monetary policy to prioritize the goal of low unemployment over the goal of low inflation.
- Pass progressive tax reform to make the wealthy shoulder more of the burden of raising government revenues.

Public Goods Policies

The policy proposals in this category would not increase the income of the poor but would improve their quality of life. Low-income families would receive vital resources and services not solely as private commodities, but in the form of government-provided or -subsidized public goods. This would also leave poor families with more money to cover other expenses. Though it would not lower the official rate of poverty, the provision of public goods would diminish the level of material hardship, make income poverty more tolerable, and alleviate some of its more harmful consequences. [7]

- Provide universal health insurance along with accessible and affordable medical care.
- Provide high-quality child-care assistance.
- Increase the supply of affordable housing and make housing vouchers available to all households below a specified income threshold.
- Improve and expand public transportation systems, with subsidies for low-income passengers.
- Increase spending in poor neighborhoods on street cleaning, garbage pick-up, libraries, internet services, public spaces, and other amenities.

Equal Opportunity Policies

Some Americans are disproportionately vulnerable to poverty, including racial and ethnic minorities, immigrants, single mothers, and children. The policy proposals in this category, though they would not necessarily reduce the aggregate level of poverty, would make poverty more of an equal opportunity affliction, less likely to fall so heavily on those already suffering multiple disadvantages.

- Strengthen antidiscrimination legislation, including more rigorous enforcement mechanisms and more costly penalties.
- Maintain and extend affirmative action and comparable-worth programs to combat race and sex discrimination.
- Implement measures to reduce residential and educational segregation, including restrictions on zoning exclusions and stronger enforcement of fair housing laws.
- Establish universal preschool programs to ensure that all children are adequately prepared when they enter kindergarten and are able to achieve their full developmental potential throughout their subsequent school years.
- Channel additional funding and educational resources into public schools in poor neighborhoods to guarantee that all children, regardless of class, race, and residence, have an equal opportunity to receive a quality education.
- Increase funding for Pell Grants and incentives for colleges, particularly selective colleges, to enroll and graduate more African American and Hispanic students and more students from working-class families.
- End the war on drugs and reduce reliance on incarceration as the principal means for dealing with criminal offenders.
- Abolish the money bail system.
- Reform immigration to create a path to citizenship for undocumented immigrants.
- Combat stereotypical portraits of the working poor, welfare recipients, single mothers, and racial and ethnic minorities in the media.
- Make workplaces more family friendly by requiring paid sick leave, paid parental leave, a right to predictable schedules, and more equitable treatment for part-time workers.

Empowerment Policies

While some policies fight poverty by putting more money into the hands of the poor, the measures in this final category work on a deeper level. They are intended to put more power into the hands of the poor, giving them a stronger economic and political voice. Policies of this kind are particularly important because without increased empowerment and activism on the part of working-class and low-income Americans, it is unlikely that any new war on poverty will get very far off the ground.

- Introduce more democracy, not only in the increasingly oligarchic political system, but in the functioning of corporations and private businesses as well.[8]
- Protect workers' right to collective bargaining and their right to be treated in a safe, dignified, and humane manner within the workplace.
- Impose harsher penalties on employers who use illegal tactics to prevent unionization and who otherwise violate workers' rights.
- Reform campaign finance, including fully funded public financing, to reduce the corrupting influence of money in politics.
- Abolish felony disenfranchisement laws.
- Simplify the voter registration process and strengthen prohibitions against voter intimidation and suppression tactics.
- Loosen the grip of the two-party system by reforming electoral arrangements to create alternative voting procedures, including proportional representation, that might facilitate multiparty competition.
- Support educational efforts and cultural change to encourage higher levels of political awareness, participation, and activism.
- Reform the corporate-dominated mainstream media system and support alternative news media more fully committed to the goal of promoting informed citizenship and democratic deliberation.
- Reform immigration to guarantee that all workers, including undocumented immigrants, have sufficient civil and citizenship rights to protect themselves from exploitative treatment by employers.
- Increase funding for legal aid services to overcome the gross inequity of a justice system in which millions of Americans in both civil and criminal cases are denied access to competent and dedicated legal representation.

Viewed from within the severely constricted universe of mainstream American politics, the policies listed above might seem to have a pie-in-the-sky quality. And no doubt they will be difficult to achieve, some more so than others. But they are feasible. Most of these policies, after all, are already in place in other industrialized countries. If Europe and Canada can do it, we can do it too. Though it would require higher taxes on the wealthy, many, perhaps even the majority, of Americans, and not just the poor, would benefit from the implementation of these policies, so there may even be a potentially sizable constituency prepared to support such reforms.

These measures have another selling point. They are necessary if we hope to realize long-standing American ideals: a just economic system in which opportunities are available to everyone and rewards are distributed equitably; a genuinely democratic political system in which the preferences of ordinary Americans, not the dictates of big business, determine the course of government policy; an enlightened political culture in which informed citizens actively participate in the public discourse; and a social system in which access to opportunities for education, housing, and employment are not dependent on class, race, or gender.

Good programs and lofty ideals are not enough, however. If they were, the problem of poverty would have been solved a long time ago. We have the know-how, but we lack the political will and the political means necessary to put that knowledge into effect. This point takes us back to the central theme of this book: the connection between poverty and power. Poverty is not so much an intellectual or technical problem as it is a political problem. Policy experts are less crucial to the fight against poverty than are political activists. Poverty endures not because extraordinary ingenuity is required to invent solutions, but because the power to enact needed reforms is lacking. The problem of poverty cannot be effectively remedied without coming to grips with the problem of power—and this means organization, confrontation, and political conflict. As Joe Soss reminds us, only through a willingness to fight for it can a victory against poverty be won.[9]

MOVEMENTS AND POWER

Poverty is a stubbornly persistent condition. We might even be tempted to throw up our hands in the face of this seemingly intractable problem: "That's just the way things are." But there is nothing inevitable about millions of Americans living below the poverty line, and the changes needed to reduce poverty, including those cited in the previous section, are within our grasp. We only have to look at the example of other developed nations to see this. Human beings have assembled the structures that perpetuate poverty, and through human intervention these structures can be disassembled, reassembled, or replaced.

It is true, however, that no single person can do much about low-wage work, racial discrimination, inferior schools, residential segregation, inadequate health care, or an unresponsive government. But as the civil rights movement, the women's movement, and other examples of collective action show, if people band together and take a stand, they can transform the basic norms and institutions of society. They may not have much influence through normal political channels, clogged up by money; they may not have much of a voice in the larger political culture, dominated by a commercialized media system; and they may be lacking in wealth, prestige, connections, and other power resources. But they are not altogether powerless. Ordinary Americans, including the poor, as Frances Fox Piven argues, have considerable "potential power." As workers, consumers, tenants, students, welfare recipients, and community residents, we are all enmeshed in a web of cooperative activities, arrangements, and interdependencies whose continued existence depends on our ongoing participation and implicit consent. By withholding our contributions, refusing to play our assigned roles, and strategically violating the rules of the game, we can obstruct the normal workings of social institutions. This "disruptive power," manifest in civil disobedience, strikes, boycotts, demonstrations, protests, sit-ins, walkouts, and other forms of contentious political behavior, gives otherwise powerless people real leverage. By skillfully exploiting this power to threaten or create disorder, poorer Americans and their allies can conceivably extract concessions from business owners, government officials, and other decision-making authorities and can potentially generate momentum for more far-reaching reforms. [10]

Poverty is created and maintained through the exercise of power, and it can be eradicated only through a countervailing or oppositional mobilization of power. This requires an upsurge of "organized people power," a democratic resurgence played out not just in voting booths, but also in workplaces, public bureaucracies, communities, and the streets. This might seem hopelessly idealistic, but in fact thousands of advocacy groups, community and student activists, labor organizers, progressive intellectuals, and working Americans—based in what Earl Wysong, Robert Perrucci, and David Wright call "alternative power networks"—have been or currently are engaged in battles on many fronts to promote progressive social change. [11] Consider just a few examples. The Democratic Socialists of America (DSA) is an activist organization that for many years now has been fighting to create a more democratic, equal, and humane society. [12] Family Values @ Work, Forward Together, and MomsRising, along with other similarly focused organizations, have been at the forefront in battles over pay equity, health care, child care, sick leave, parental leave, and more flexible, family-friendly workplaces. [13] Founded in 1968, the Center for Community Change is a grassroots activist group committed to the organization and empowerment of low-income people, particularly people of color, around issues of social and economic justice. [14] Immigrant organizations, including the Washington Immigrant Solidarity Network, have helped revitalize the labor movement in Los Angeles and elsewhere, pressing not only for better wages but also for immigration reform and citizenship rights. [15] Activists in the environmental justice movement have exposed the pattern of hazardous waste and pollutants being disproportionately located near poor and minority communities, and they have organized opposition to racist environmental, transportation, and development policies. [16] The Black Lives Matter (BLM) movement was sparked by the killing of Trayvon Martin in Sanford, Florida, in 2012, followed by the acquittal of his killer, George Zimmerman, in 2013, as well as by the police killing of Michael Brown in Ferguson, Missouri, in 2014. Though police brutality and racism in the criminal justice system are central issues in the BLM agenda, the platform of The Movement for Black Lives affirms a more encompassing vision, calling for, among other things, economic justice, community control, and political self-determination.[17]

The fate of poorer Americans is closely tied especially to the state of working-class activism. Though on the defensive since the 1970s, the labor movement, including both unionized and nonunionized workers, is still the most potent expression of "people power" and the only force ultimately capable of challenging the economic, political, and cultural dominance of business.[18] Due to weak labor laws and lax enforcement, along with the determined opposition of employers, union organizing today is a daunting challenge. With little immediate prospect of unionization, many low-wage workers have forged innovative grassroots organizations separate from, though sometimes intersecting with, organized labor.[19] These workers—including "domestic workers, day laborers, restaurant workers, taxi drivers, guestworkers, garment workers, nail salon workers, farmworkers and more"—are often aided in their efforts by "worker centers," more than two hundred of which have appeared throughout the country since the early 1990s.[20] Including the New York Taxi Workers Alliance, the National Domestic Workers Alliance, and the Coalition of Immokalee Workers, worker centers are community-based institutions that, along with other services, advocate on behalf of low-wage workers, provide legal assistance, draw media attention, build local coalitions, and help organize demonstrations and direct action engagements.[21] One example is the Restaurant Opportunities Centers United (ROC). Through such tactics as the "public shaming" of targeted restaurants, ROC has helped workers in the food industry achieve higher pay and a more humane workplace environment.[22]

The Fight for $15 campaign, which labor expert Ruth Milkman calls "the single most important initiative on the labor front in the last few years," is one of today's more visible expressions of "people power."[23] Fight for $15 began in 2012 when several hundred fast-food workers in New York City walked off their jobs to protest low wages, bad working conditions, and mistreatment at the hands of managers. Workers at McDonald's have been among the core activists in this campaign since its inception, but the movement has expanded to include workers in retail establishments, home health-care and child-care industries, airport workers, and others. Through nationwide one-day strikes and sit-ins, with support from religious groups, Black Lives Matter, community organizations, and sympathetic politicians, demonstrators have drawn public attention to the injustice of immensely profitable corporations paying their workers poverty level wages. "This movement is changing our political debate," says Mary Kay Henry, president of the Service Employees International Union, which has provided financial backing for the Fight for $15. "The movement is changing what employers think they can get away with. The movement is making cities and states raise the minimum wage."[24]

Out of necessity, unions today, compared to those of the past, serve more directly as vehicles for fighting poverty. With the decline of jobs in the manufacturing sector, union organizing efforts are targeting low-wage service workers, including custodians, hotel and restaurant employees, workers in the health-care industry, and other segments of the working poor. The Justice for Janitors movement, composed largely of Hispanic immigrants, is a case in point, epitomizing today's "new unionism," in which unions, especially "poor workers' unions," composed disproportionately of women, immigrants, and racial and ethnic minorities, look more like social movements than bureaucratic organizations.[25] For proponents of this new unionism, the labor movement is a dynamic force for social change, but only when it taps the collective power of the larger working class and emphasizes not just bread-and-butter union issues, but more fundamental "demands for democracy and equality."[26] This social-movement unionism requires organized labor to establish closer ties between local unions and their communities, including the nonunion population of low-wage workers, the unemployed, welfare recipients, and other disadvantaged groups.[27] It also requires the labor movement to reinvent itself by pursuing a partnership or "fusion" with other progressive social movements, including those organized around issues of race, gender, sexuality, the environment, globalization, and peace.[28] These coalition-building strategies, besides creating a substantial oppositional power base, hold out the promise of a narrow workplace unionism being transformed into a broader movement for social and economic justice.

A reinvigorated labor movement, with a stronger economic and political presence, can win benefits for the working class and the poor: higher wages, better working conditions, a more generous welfare state, and worker-friendly government policies. Beyond this, however, labor activism is a democratizing force. It opens opportunities for political participation and self-determination on the part of otherwise marginalized people and empowers poorer Americans, enhancing their capacity for collective action and equipping them for future struggles. Today's labor movement, reconfigured as a genuine social movement, in conjunction with other social justice movements, has the ability to oppose a structure of power that has become dangerously imbalanced. The example of these movements offers up a vision of how poor and working-class Americans can mobilize their potential power to promote social change.

It is sometimes said that poor people should pull themselves up by their own bootstraps. This is good advice. But for such efforts to be successful, they must be collective rather than individual undertakings, political rather than purely personal endeavors. Only a broad-based mobilization of power can bring about the economic and political changes needed to eradicate poverty. A collective bootstraps strategy, with poorer Americans taking the lead, joined together through labor unions, worker centers, community groups, and grassroots organizations, and with the support of sympathetic political office-holders, is the best hope for a successful war against poverty. While poverty and powerlessness normally go hand in hand, the social justice movements on the scene today testify to the potential power possessed by poorer Americans. Only by more fully realizing this potential is there any chance of achieving the ambitious goal enunciated by Martin Luther King Jr. fifty years ago: "the total, direct and immediate abolition of poverty."[29]

Appendix

The Individualistic Perspective and the Structural Perspective

Individualistic Perspective	Structural Perspective
Poverty is an individual problem, the result of the failings of the poor.	Poverty is a social problem, the result of the failings of society.
The source of poverty and the causes of its persistence are located in the values, attitudes, and behaviors of poor people themselves.	The source of poverty and the causes of its persistence are located in the economic, political, cultural, and social institutions of society.
Poverty derives from the inadequacies, weaknesses, and deficiencies of the poor.	Poverty derives from inequalities in the distribution of power, opportunities, and resources.
Poverty is due to the inability or unwillingness of the poor to take advantage of the opportunities available to them.	Poverty is due to the inability of economic and political systems to provide sufficient opportunities.
Poor people suffer from bad life decisions.	Poor people suffer from limited options.
The primary obstacles to economic achievement are internal, located within individuals themselves.	The primary obstacles to economic achievement are external, located within the larger societal environment.

The problem of poverty is one of lazy, low-skilled, poorly educated workers.

The problem of poverty is one of lousy, low-paying, dead-end jobs.

Poverty is a cultural and moral problem, resulting from the weakening of family values and the decline of the work ethic.

Poverty is an economic and political problem, resulting from the economic exploitation and marginalization of the poor.

The poor and the middle class are similar in the opportunities available to them, but differ fundamentally in their values and aspirations.

The poor and the middle class are similar in their values and aspirations, but differ fundamentally in the opportunities available to them.

Equality of opportunity is the predominant reality in the United States; individuals compete on a roughly equal playing field, with everyone having a reasonable chance to achieve economic success.

Inequality of opportunity is the predominant reality in the United States; individuals compete on an unequal playing field, and many people are denied a reasonable chance to achieve economic success.

Prejudice and discrimination on the basis of race/ethnicity and gender no longer constitute significant barriers to economic achievement.

Prejudice and discrimination on the basis of race/ethnicity and gender continue to constitute significant barriers to economic achievement.

Individual choice matters more than environmental constraints in explaining people's economic outcomes.

Environmental constraints matter more than individual choice in explaining people's economic outcomes.

Poverty is an outcome of the decisions and choices made by poor people themselves.

Poverty is an outcome of the decisions and choices made by economic and political elites.

Market outcomes are efficient and fair, and government intervention to alleviate poverty is generally unnecessary and undesirable.

Market outcomes are inefficient and unfair, and government intervention to alleviate poverty is necessary and desirable.

Poverty can best be combated by reforming and resocializing the poor to provide them with the skills, attitudes, and motivations necessary to compete successfully in the labor market.

Poverty can best be combated by reforming and restructuring the labor market to create better job opportunities and boost the earnings of low-wage workers.

The allocation of valued resources in society is a by-product of individual striving and the distribution of ability.

The best strategy for the poor to overcome poverty is to improve their skills and exert greater individual effort.

The allocation of valued resources in society is a by-product of social conflict and the distribution of power.

The best strategy for the poor to overcome poverty is to participate in collective political action to achieve a more equitable distribution of social resources.

Notes

1. POVERTY AS A SOCIAL PROBLEM

1. Adam Johnson, "45 Million Americans Live in Poverty, But You Wouldn't Know It from Watching 2016 Coverage," *Alternet*, January 5, 2016, http://www.alternet.org/election-2016/45-million-americans-live-poverty-you-wouldnt-know-it-watching-2016-coverage.

2. Binyamin Appelbaum, "Poor Seem Far Down the List on the Candidates' Agendas," *New York Times*, August 12, 2016; "Not Yet Talking About Poverty," unsigned editorial, *New York Times*, September 14, 2016.

3. Jeff Shesol, "The 'P' Word: Why Presidents Stopped Talking about Poverty," *New Yorker*, January 9, 2014, http://www.newyorker.com/news/news-desk/the-p-word-why-presidents-stopped-talking-about-poverty.

4. Nicholas Kristof, "Growing Up Poor in America," *New York Times*, October 30, 2016.

5. Martin Luther King Jr., *Where Do We Go from Here: Chaos or Community?* (New York: Harper & Row, 1967), 166.

6. Tim Wise, *Under the Affluence: Shaming the Poor, Praising the Rich, and Sacrificing the Future of America* (San Francisco: City Lights Books, 2015), 115–19; and Melissa Boteach and Donna Cooper, "What You Need When You're Poor: Heritage Foundation Hasn't a Clue," Center for American Progress, August 2011, https://www.americanprogress.org/issues/poverty/news/2011/08/05/10063/what-you-need-when-youre-poor/.

7. Wise, *Under the Affluence*, 110–15; Michelle Goldberg, "Poverty Denialism," *The Nation*, November 25, 2013, 6–8; and Rebecca Vallas, "It's Not Just Climate Change Anymore. Meet the Right-Wing Poverty Deniers," Moyers and Company, June 20, 2016, http://billmoyers.com/story/not-just-climate-change-anymore-meet-right-wing-poverty-deniers/.

8. Pew Research Center, *The Partisan Divide on Political Values Grows Even Wider* (October 5, 2017), 16, http://assets.pewresearch.org/wp-content/uploads/sites/5/2017/10/05162647/10-05-2017-Political-landscape-release.pdf.

9. Cited in Philip N. Cohen, "No, Poverty Is Not a Mysterious, Unknowable, Negative Spiral Loop," *Family Inequality* (blog), December 7, 2015, https://familyinequality.wordpress.com/2015/12/07/no-poverty-is-not/.

10. Gordon Lafer, *The Job Training Charade* (Ithaca, NY: Cornell University Press, 2002), 11.

11. See David Brady and Lane M. Destro, "Poverty," in *Oxford Handbook of U.S. Social Policy*, ed. Daniel Béland, Kimberly J. Morgan, and Christopher Howard (New York: Oxford University Press, 2014), 585–602.

12. Mark R. Rank, "Toward A New Paradigm for Understanding Poverty," in *The Oxford Handbook of the Social Science of Poverty*, ed. David Brady and Linda M. Burton (New York: Oxford University Press, 2016), 866–83; and Alice O'Connor, *Poverty Knowledge: Social Science, Social Policy, and the Poor in Twentieth-Century U.S. History* (Princeton, NJ: Princeton University Press, 2001).

13. Jessica L. Semega, Kayla R. Fontenot, and Melissa A. Kollar, *Income and Poverty in the United States: 2016*, US Census Bureau, Current Population Reports, P60-259, September 2017, 44–55, tables B-1 and B-2, https://www.census.gov/content/dam/Census/library/publications/2017/demo/P60-259.pdf.

14. Semega, Fontenot, and Kollar, *Income and Poverty in the United States: 2016*, 17, table 5.

15. Semega, Fontenot, and Kollar, *Income and Poverty in the United States: 2016*, 43.

16. John Halpin and Karl Agne, *50 Years After LBJ's War on Poverty: A Study of American Attitudes about Work, Economic Opportunity, and the Social Safety Net* (Washington, DC: Center for American Progress, January 2014), 8, https://cdn.americanprogress.org/wp-content/uploads/2014/01/WOP-PollReport2.pdf.

17. Elise Gould, Tanyell Cooke, and Will Kimball, "What Families Need to Get By: EPI's 2015 Family Budget Calculator," Economic Policy Institute, August 26, 2015, 1–2, 6, http://www.epi.org/files/2015/epi-family-budget-calculator-2015.pdf.

18. Timothy M. Smeeding, "Government Programs and Social Outcomes: Comparison of the United States with Other Rich Nations," in *Public Policy and Income Distribution*, ed. Alan J. Auerbach, David Card, and John M. Quigley (New York: Russell Sage, 2006), 162, table 4.2.

19. Lawrence Mishel et al., *The State of Working America*, 12th ed. (Ithaca, NY: Cornell University Press, 2012), 450, figure 7W.

20. See Timothy M. Smeeding, "Poverty Measurement," in Brady and Burton, *Oxford Handbook of the Social Science of Poverty*, 32–36.

21. Timothy M. Smeeding and Lee Rainwater, "Comparing Living Standards Across Nations: Real Incomes at the Top, the Bottom, and the Middle," in *What Has Happened to the Quality of Life in the Advanced Industrialized Nations*, ed. Edward N. Wolff (Northampton, MA: Edward Elgar, 2004), 153–85.

22. See Lyle Scruggs and James P. Allan, "The Material Consequences of Welfare States: Benefit Generosity and Absolute Poverty in 16 OECD Countries," *Comparative Political Studies* 39, no. 7 (September 2006): 880–904.

23. Alberto Alesina and Edward L. Glaeser, *Fighting Poverty in the U.S. and Europe: A World of Difference* (Oxford: Oxford University Press, 2004), 47.

24. Mishel et al., *State of Working America*, 450–52, figures 7X and 7Y; see also Janet C. Gornick and Markus Jäntti, "Child Poverty in Cross-National Perspective: Lessons from the Luxembourg Income Study," *Children and Youth Services Review* 34 (2012): 558–68.

25. United Nations Children's Fund (UNICEF), *Building the Future: Children and the Sustainable Development Goals in Rich Countries*, Innocenti Report Card No. 14 (June 2017), 9–25, https://www.unicef-irc.org/publications/pdf/RC14_eng.pdf.

26. Tim Smeeding, "Cash Matters and Place Matters: A Child Poverty Plan That Capitalizes on New Evidence," *Pathways* (Spring 2017): 14–20, http://inequality.stanford.edu/sites/default/files/Pathways_Spring2017_Cash-Place.pdf.

27. Semega, Fontenot, and Kollar, *Income and Poverty in the United States: 2016*, 44, table B-1.

28. Mishel et al., *State of Working America*, 437–40.

29. Matthew Desmond, "Severe Deprivation in America: An Introduction," *Journal of the Social Sciences* 1, no. 1 (2015): 3–4.

30. Semega, Fontenot, and Kollar, *Income and Poverty in the United States: 2016*, 18–19, table 6.

31. Mishel et al., *State of Working America*, 427–28; and Semega, Fontenot, and Kollar, *Income and Poverty in the United States: 2016*, 17, table 5.

32. Kathryn J. Edin and H. Luke Shaefer, *$2.00 A Day: Living on Almost Nothing in America* (Boston: Mariner Books, 2015), xv; and H. Luke Shaefer and Kathryn Edin, "The Rise of Extreme Poverty in the United States," *Pathways* (Summer 2014): 28–32.

33. Edin and Shaefer, *$2.00 A Day*, 1–63, 159.

34. Patricia Ruggles, *Drawing the Line: Alternative Poverty Measures and Their Implications for Public Policy* (Washington, DC: Urban Institute, 1990), 39–52.

35. Amartya Sen, *Social Exclusion: Concept, Application, and Scrutiny*, Social Development Papers No. 1 (Asian Development Bank, June 2000), https://www.adb.org/sites/default/files/publication/29778/social-exclusion.pdf; and Brian Nolan and Ive Marx, "Economic Inequality, Poverty, and Social Exclusion," in *The Oxford Handbook of Economic Inequality*, ed. Wiemer Salverda, Brian Nolan, and Timothy M. Smeeding (Oxford: Oxford University Press, 2009), 315–41.

36. Mary Corcoran and Jordan Matsudaira, "Is It Getting Harder to Get Ahead? Economic Attainment for Two Cohorts," in *On the Frontier of Adulthood: Theory, Research, and Public Policy*, ed. Richard A. Settersten Jr., Frank F. Furstenberg Jr., and Ruben C. Rumbaut (Chicago: University of Chicago Press, 2005), 356–95.

37. Annette Bernhardt et al., *Divergent Paths: Economic Mobility in the New American Labor Market* (New York: Russell Sage, 2001), 111, 171, 166.

38. Fatih Guvenen, Greg Kaplan, Jae Song, and Justin Weidner, "Lifetime Incomes in the United States over Six Decades," April 21, 2017, https://fguvenendotcom.files.wordpress.com/2014/04/gks_lifetime_history_2017_apr_nber.pdf; and Michael D. Carr and Emily E. Wiemers, "The Decline in Lifetime Earnings Mobility in the U.S.: Evidence from Survey-Linked Administrative Data" (working paper, Washington Center for Equitable Growth, August 2016), http://cdn.equitablegrowth.org/wp-content/uploads/2016/05/03113002/carr_wiemers_2016_earnings-mobility1.pdf.

39. Roberta Rehner Iversen and Annie Laurie Armstrong, *Jobs Aren't Enough: Toward a New Economic Mobility for Low-Income Families* (Philadelphia, PA: Temple University Press, 2006), 13–20.

40. Miles Corak, "Economic Mobility," *Pathways: The Poverty and Inequality Report 2016* (Stanford Center on Poverty and Inequality), 51–57, http://inequality.stanford.edu/sites/default/files/Pathways-SOTU-2016-Economic-Mobility-3.pdf.

41. Mishel et al., *State of Working America*, 151–54; Miles Corak, "Income Inequality, Equality of Opportunity, and Intergenerational Mobility," *Journal of Economic Perspectives* 27, no. 3 (Summer 2013): 79–102.

42. Raj Chetty et al., "The Fading American Dream: Trends in Absolute Income Mobility Since 1940," National Bureau of Economic Research, Working Paper 22910 (December 2016), http://www.equality-of-opportunity.org/papers/abs_mobility_paper.pdf.

43. See Timothy M. Smeeding, "Gates, Gaps, and Intergenerational Mobility: The Importance of an Even Start," in *The Dynamics of Opportunity in America: Evidence and Perspectives*, ed. Irwin Kirsch and Henry Braun (New York: Springer, 2016), 255–95.

44. William J. Collins and Marianne H. Wanamaker, "Up From Slavery? African American Intergenerational Economic Mobility Since 1880," National Bureau of Economic Research, Working Paper 23395 (May 2017), http://www.nber.org/papers/w23395.pdf.

45. Edward Rodrigue and Richard V. Reeves, "Five Bleak Facts on Black Opportunity," *Social Mobility Memos* (blog), Brookings, January 15, 2015, https://www.brookings.edu/blog/social-mobility-memos/2015/01/15/five-bleak-facts-on-black-opportunity/.

46. See Laura Lein et al., "Social Policy, Transfer Programs, and Assistance," in Brady and Burton, *Oxford Handbook of the Social Science of Poverty*, 733–50.

47. I discuss these developments more fully and with accompanying references in chapters 6, 9, and 10.

48. Executive Office of the President of the United States, Office of Management and Budget, *Major Savings and Reforms Budget of the U.S. Government Fiscal Year 2018* (2017), https://www.whitehouse.gov/sites/whitehouse.gov/files/omb/budget/fy2018/msar.pdf; and Justin Miller, "The Freedom Caucus's Man on the Inside," *American Prospect*, Fall 2017, 58–63.

49. Robert Pear, "Thousands Could Lose Food Stamps as States Restore Pre-Recession Requirements," *New York Times*, April 2, 2016; and Stephanie Land, "The New Right-Wing War on Food Stamps," *Alternet*, March 30, 2016, http://www.alternet.org/economy/new-right-wing-war-food-stamps.

50. Executive Office, *U.S. Government Fiscal Year 2018*, 125; Rachel West and Melissa Boteach, "House Republican Cuts to Nutrition Assistance Would Harm Families in Every State," Center for American Progress, August 2017, https://www.americanprogress.org/issues/poverty/news/2017/08/08/437168/house-republican-cuts-nutrition-assistance-harm-families-every-state/.

51. Alice Ollstein, "Trump's HHS Unveils Medicaid Overhaul That Will Mean Fewer People Covered," Talking Points Memo, November 7, 2017, http://talkingpointsmemo.com/dc/medicaid-work-verma-cms-hhs.

52. Pavlina R. Tcherneva, "Trump's Bait and Switch: Job Creation in the Midst of Welfare State Sabotage," *Real-World Economic Review* 78 (March 2017): 155, 158, http://www.paecon.net/PAEReview/issue78/Tcherneva78.pdf.

53. See Jared Bernstein, "Real Tax Reform: What It Is and What It Isn't," *American Prospect*, Fall 2017, 52–57; Kate Zernike and Alan Rappeport, "New Objective: Cutting the Safety Net," *New York Times*, December 3, 2017; and Josh Bivens and Hunter Blair, "Common Tax 'Reform' Questions, Answered," Economic Policy Institute, October 3, 2017, http://www.epi.org/files/pdf/136165.pdf.

54. Melissa Boteach, Rebecca Vallas, and Eliza Schultz, "A Progressive Agenda to Cut Poverty and Expand Opportunity," Center for American Progress, June 2016, 2–3, https://cdn.americanprogress.org/wp-content/uploads/2016/06/03081022/RoadmapOpportunity-report.pdf.

55. Mark Robert Rank, *One Nation, Underprivileged: Why American Poverty Affects Us All* (New York: Oxford University Press, 2004), 92–95.

56. Mark R. Rank and Thomas A. Hirschl, "The Likelihood of Experiencing Relative Poverty Over the Life Course," *PLOS ONE*, July 22, 2015, http://journals.plos.org/plosone/article?id=10.1371/journal.pone.

57. Jonathan Morduch and Rachel Schneider, *The Financial Diaries: How American Families Cope in a World of Uncertainty* (Princeton, NJ: Princeton University Press, 2017), 158–62.

58. Mark Robert Rank, Thomas A. Hirschl, and Kirk A. Foster, *Chasing the American Dream: Understanding What Shapes Our Fortunes* (Oxford: Oxford University Press, 2014), 77.

59. Rank, *One Nation, Underprivileged*, 88, 107; and Mark Robert Rank, "As American as Apple Pie: Poverty and Welfare," *Contexts* 2, no. 3 (Summer 2003), 41–49.

60. Gabriel Zucman, "Wealth Inequality," *Pathways: The Poverty and Inequality Report 2016* (Stanford Center on Poverty and Inequality), 39–44, http://inequality.stanford.edu/sites/default/files/Pathways-SOTU-2016-Wealth-Inequality-3.pdf.

61. Jesse Bricker et al., "Changes in U.S. Family Finances From 2013 to 2016: Evidence from the Survey of Consumer Finances," *Federal Reserve Bulletin* 103, no. 3 (September 2017): 10, https://www.federalreserve.gov/publications/files/scf17.pdf; see also Emmanuel Saez, "Striking It Richer: The Evolution of Top Incomes in the United States (Updated with 2015 Preliminary Estimates)," June 30, 2016, https://eml.berkeley.edu/~saez/saez-UStop incomes-2015.pdf.

62. Bricker et al., "Changes in U.S. Family Finances from 2013 to 2016," 10–11; Matt Breunig, "New Fed Data: Top 10% Now Own 77% of the Wealth," People's Policy Project, September 27, 2017, http://peoplespolicyproject.org/2017/09/27/new-fed-data-the-top-10-now-own-77-of-the-wealth/; see also Edward N. Wolff, "Household Wealth Trends in the United States, 1962 to 2013: What Happened Over the Great Recession?" *Journal of the Social Sciences* 2, no. 6 (October 2016): 24–43.

63. On the concept, measurement, and incidence of "asset poverty," see Edward N. Wolff, *A Century of Wealth in America* (Cambridge, MA: Belknap Press of Harvard University, 2017), 492–550.

64. Wolff, *A Century of Wealth in America*, 527, table 11.9; and Kasey Wiedrich et al., *The Steep Climb to Economic Opportunity for Vulnerable Families* (Corporation for Enterprise Development, January 2016), 7–8, http://assetsandopportunity.org/assets/pdf/2016_Scorecard_Report.pdfp.

65. Morduch and Schneider, *Financial Diaries*, 73.

66. Board of Governors of the Federal Reserve, *Report on the Economic Well-Being of U.S. Households in 2016* (Federal Reserve, May 2017), 25–29, https://www.federalreserve.gov/publications/files/2016-report-economic-well-being-us-households-201705; see also Neal Gabler, "My Secret Shame," *Atlantic Monthly*, May 2006, 53–63.

67. Bricker et al., "Changes in U.S. Family Finances from 2013 to 2016," 13; see also Thomas Shapiro, "Wealth," *Pathways: The Poverty and Inequality Report 2017* (Stanford Center on Poverty and Inequality), 36–38, http://inequality.stanford.edu/sites/default/files/Pathways_SOTU_2017_wealth.pdf; and Amy Traub et al., "The Asset Value of Whiteness: Understanding the Racial Wealth Gap," Demos and Institute on Assets and Social Policy, February 13, 2017, http://www.demos.org/sites/default/files/publications/Asset%20Value%20of%20Whiteness.pdf.

68. Wolff, *A Century of Wealth in America*, 529–31; and Dedrick Asante-Muhammed et al., "The Ever-Growing Gap: Without Change, African-American and Latino Families Won't Match White Wealth for Centuries," Institute for Policy Studies, August 2016, 8, http://www.ips-dc.org/wp-content/uploads/2016/08/The-Ever-Growing-Gap-CFED_IPS-Final-2.pdf.

69. Paul Kiel, "Debt and the Racial Wealth Gap," *New York Times*, January 3, 2016.

70. Thomas M. Shapiro, *Toxic Inequality: How America's Wealth Gap Destroys Mobility, Deepens the Racial Divide, and Threatens Our Future* (New York: Basic Books, 2017), 22.

71. Economic Policy Institute, State of Working America Data Library, "Wages by Percentile," 2017, http://www.epi.org/data/#?subject=wage-percentiles.

72. Rakesh Kochhar et al., *The American Middle Class Is Losing Ground* (Washington, DC: Pew Research Center, December 9, 2015), http://assets.pewresearch.org/wp-content/uploads/sites/3/2015/12/2015-12-09_middle-class_FINAL-report.pdf.

73. Rakesh Kochhar et al., *Middle Class Fortunes in Western Europe* (Washington, DC: Pew Research Center, April 24, 2017), http://assets.pewresearch.org/wp-content/uploads/sites/2/2017/04/30145550/ST_2017.04.24_Western-Europe-Middle-Class_FINAL.pdf.

74. Alex Rowell and David Madland, "New Census Data Show Household Incomes Are Rising Again, But Share Going to Middle Class Is at a Record Low," Center for American Progress, September 12, 2017, https://www.americanprogress.org/issues/economy/news/2017/09/12/438778/new-census-data-show-household-incomes-rising-share-going-middle-class-record-low/; David Leonhardt and Kevin Quealy, "U.S. Middle Class No Longer World's Richest," *New York Times*, April 23, 2014; and Steven Pressman, "The Fall of the US Middle Class and the Hair-Raising Ascent of Donald Trump," *Real-World Economics Review* 78 (March 2017): 112–24, http://www.paecon.net/PAEReview/issue78/whole78.pdf.

75. Federal Reserve, "Report on the Economic Well-Being of U.S. Households in 2016," 7.

76. Thomas Piketty, Emmanuel Saez, and Gabriel Zucman, "Economic Growth in the United States: A Tale of Two Countries," Washington Center for Equitable Growth, December 6, 2016, 3–4, http://equitablegrowth.org/research-analysis/economic-growth-in-the-united-states-a-tale-of-two-countries/; and Thomas Piketty, Emmanuel Saez, and Gabriel Zucman, "Distributional National Accounts: Methods and Estimates for the United States," July 6, 2017, https://eml.berkeley.edu/~saez/PSZ2017.pdf.

77. Kerry A. Dolan, "Forbes 2017 Billionaires List: Meet the Richest People on the Planet," *Forbes*, May 20, 2017, https://www.forbes.com/sites/kerryadolan/2017/03/20/forbes-2017-billionaires-list-meet-the-richest-people-on-the-planet/#65e8a2ba62ff; and Michelle Chen, "Bill Gates, Jeff Bezos, and Warren Buffet Own More Wealth Than the Entire Poorest Half of the US Population," *The Nation*, November 13, 2017, https://www.thenation.com/article/bill-gates-jeff-bezos-and-warren-buffett-own-more-wealth-than-the-entire-poorest-half-of-the-us-population/.

78. Alisha Coleman-Jensen et al., *Household Food Security in the United States in 2016*, US Department of Agriculture, Economic Research Report No. 237, September 2017, https://www.ers.usda.gov/webdocs/publications/84973/err-237.pdf?v=42979.

79. Matthew Desmond, *Evicted: Poverty and Profit in the American City* (New York: Crown, 2016), 313; on poverty as injustice, see also Tommie Shelby, *Dark Ghettos: Injustice, Dissent, and Reform* (Cambridge, MA: Belknap, Harvard University Press, 2016).

2. THE BIOGENETIC THEORY OF POVERTY
AND INEQUALITY

1. I borrow the term "biogenetic" as a label for this theory from Peter Knapp et al., *The Assault on Equality* (Westport, CT: Praeger, 1996).

2. Richard J. Herrnstein and Charles Murray, *The Bell Curve: Intelligence and Class Structure in American Life* (New York: Free Press, 1994).

3. Two book-length studies of *The Bell Curve* deserve to be singled out: Knapp et al., *The Assault on Equality*; and Claude S. Fischer et al., *Inequality by Design: Cracking the Bell Curve Myth* (Princeton, NJ: Princeton University Press, 1996). For valuable compilations, see Bernie Devlin et al., eds., *Intelligence, Genes, and Success: Scientists Respond to "The Bell Curve"* (New York: Copernicus, Springer-Verlag, 1997); Steven Fraser, ed., *The Bell Curve Wars: Race, Intelligence, and the Future of America* (New York: Basic Books, 1995); Kenneth Arrow, Samuel Bowles, and Steven N. Durlauf, eds., *Meritocracy and Economic Inequality* (Princeton, NJ: Princeton University Press, 2000); Russell Jacoby and Naomi Glauberman, eds., *The Bell Curve Debate: History, Documents, Opinions* (New York: Times Books, 1995); and Joe L. Kincheloe, Shirley R. Steinberg, and Aaron D. Gresson III, eds., *Measured Lies: The Bell Curve Examined* (New York: St. Martin's Press, 1996).

4. Herrnstein and Murray, *Bell Curve*, 25.

5. Herrnstein and Murray, *Bell Curve*, 25–27.

6. On the "democratization of higher education" and "cognitive partitioning by occupation," see Herrnstein and Murray, *Bell Curve*, chapters 1 and 2.

7. Herrnstein and Murray, *Bell Curve*, 91.

8. Herrnstein and Murray, *Bell Curve*, 117, 386.

9. Herrnstein and Murray, *Bell Curve*, 3–4, 14, 105.

10. On the multidimensional nature of intelligence, see Howard Gardner, *Frames of Mind: The Theory of Multiple Intelligences* (New York: Basic Books, 1983); and Robert J. Sternberg, *The Triarchic Mind: A New Theory of Human Intelligence* (New York: Penguin, 1988).

11. On the influence of the test situation on test performance, see Claude M. Steele and Joshua Aronson, "Stereotype Threat and Test Performance of Academically Successful African Americans," in *The Black-White Test Score Gap*, ed. Christopher Jencks and Meredith Phillips (Washington, DC: Brookings Institution Press, 1998), 401–27.

12. Christopher Jencks, "Racial Bias in Testing," in Jencks and Phillips, *Black-White Test Score Gap*, 55–85.

13. See Fischer et al., *Inequality by Design*, 42–43; and Melvin L. Kohn, "Two Visions of the Relationship between Individual and Society: The Bell Curve versus Social Structure and Personality," in *A Nation Divided: Diversity, Inequality, and Community in American Society*, ed. Phyllis Moen, Donna Dempster-McClain, and Henry A. Walker (Ithaca, NY: Cornell University Press, 1999), 34–51.

14. Keith E. Stanovich, *What Intelligence Tests Miss: The Psychology of Rational Thought* (New Haven: CT: Yale University Press, 2009); and Richard E. Nisbett, *Mindware: Tools for Smart Thinking* (New York: Farrar, Straus and Giroux, 2015), 14.

15. See Michael Daniels, Bernie Devlin, and Kathryn Roeder, "Of Genes and IQ," in Devlin et al., *Intelligence, Genes, and Success*, 45–70; and Marcus W. Feldman, Sarah P. Otto, and Freddy B. Christiansen, "Genes, Culture, and Inequality," in Arrow, Bowles, and Durlauf, *Meritocracy and Economic Inequality*, 61–85.

16. Bernie Devlin, Michael Daniels, and Kathryn Roeder, "The Heritability of IQ," *Nature* 388 (July 31, 1997): 468–71; and Robert Plomin, "Genetics and General Cognitive Ability," *Nature* 402 (December 2, 1999): C25–C29.

17. Eric Turkheimer et al., "Socioeconomic Status Modifies Heritability of IQ in Young Children," *Psychological Science* 14, no. 6 (November 2003): 623–28; and Richard E. Nisbett et al., "Intelligence: New Findings and Theoretical Developments," *American Psychologist* 67, no. 2 (March 2012): 130–59.

18. Daniels, Devlin, and Roeder, "Of Genes and IQ," 64–65; Bruce Bradbury et al., *Two Many Children Left Behind: The U.S. Achievement Gap in Comparative Perspective* (New

York: Russell Sage, 2015), 41; and Timothy M. Smeeding, "Gates, Gaps, and Intergenerational Mobility: The Importance of an Even Start," in *The Dynamics of Opportunity in America: Evidence and Perspectives*, ed. Irwin Kirsch and Henry Braun (New York: Springer, 2016), 261–64.

19. Herrnstein and Murray, *Bell Curve*, 389, 416 (italics added).

20. James J. Heckman, "Lessons from the Bell Curve," *Journal of Political Economy* 103, no. 3 (October 1995): 1110–11.

21. Douglas Wahlsten, "The Malleability of Intelligence Is Not Constrained by Heritability," in Devlin et al., *Intelligence, Genes, and Success*, 71–87; see also Richard E. Nisbett, *Intelligence and How to Get It: Why Schools and Culture Count* (New York: W. W. Norton, 2009), 21–38.

22. On the efficacy of interventions to raise intelligence, see Fischer et al., *Inequality by Design*, ch. 7; and Richard Nisbett, "Race, IQ, and Scientism," in Fraser, *Bell Curve Wars*, 44–48.

23. Wahlsten, "The Malleability of Intelligence," 71.

24. Daniels, Devlin, and Roeder, "Of Genes and IQ," 66.

25. Nisbett, *Intelligence and How to Get It*, 119–52.

26. Orley Ashenfelter and Cecilia Rouse, "Schooling, Intelligence, and Income in America," in Arrow, Bowles, and Durlauf, *Meritocracy and Economic Inequality*, 111.

27. Herrnstein and Murray, *Bell Curve*, 127, 135.

28. For a detailed analysis of the AFQT, see Fischer et al., *Inequality by Design*, 40–42, 55–69.

29. Janet Currie and Duncan Thomas, "The Intergenerational Transmission of 'Intelligence': Down the Slippery Slopes of *The Bell Curve*," *Industrial Relations* 38, no. 3 (July 1999): 297–330.

30. See Douglas S. Massey, "Review Essay," *American Journal of Sociology* 101, no. 3 (November 1995): 752; and Stephen Jay Gould, "Curveball," in Fraser, *Bell Curve Wars*, 19.

31. Kohn, "Two Visions," 39. For overviews of the conceptual, measurement, and statistical problems with Herrnstein and Murray's index of SES, see Fischer et al., *Inequality by Design*, chapter 4; and Knapp et al., *Assault on Equality*, appendix 1.

32. Herrnstein and Murray, *Bell Curve*, 386.

33. See Fischer et al., *Inequality by Design*, chapter 4.

34. See, for example, Sanders Korenman and Christopher Winship, "A Reanalysis of *The Bell Curve*," Working Paper No. 5230 (Washington, DC: National Bureau of Economic Research, 1995).

35. Herrnstein and Murray, *Bell Curve*, appendix 4. On the weak correlations reported by Herrnstein and Murray, see Gould, "Curveball," 18–20; and Howard Gardner, "Cracking Open the IQ Box," in Fraser, *Bell Curve Wars*, 26–27.

36. Herrnstein and Murray, *Bell Curve*, 101.

37. John Cawley et al., "Cognitive Ability, Wages, and Meritocracy," in Devlin et al., *Intelligence, Genes, and Success*, 180, 190. See also John Cawley, James Heckman, and Edward Vytlacil, "Meritocracy in America: Wages Within and Across Occupations," *Industrial Relations* 38, no. 3 (July 1999): 250–96.

38. Herrnstein and Murray, *Bell Curve*, 117; see Fischer et al., *Inequality by Design*, 242n12.

39. On the "individualistic bias" of *The Bell Curve*, see Knapp et al., *The Assault on Equality*, 15–16, 219–21.

40. Herrnstein and Murray, *Bell Curve*, 511–12; for a critique, see Knapp et al., *The Assault on Equality*, chapter 3.

41. Peter Sacks, *Tearing Down the Gates: Confronting the Class Divide in American Education* (Berkeley: University of California Press, 2007), 115.

42. For a recent study documenting how class, race, and gender affect achievement, even controlling for ability as measured by early childhood test scores, see Alex Bell et al., "Who Becomes an Inventor in America? The Importance of Exposure to Innovation: Executive Summary," The Equality of Opportunity Project, December 2017, http://www.equality-of-opportunity.org/assets/documents/inventors_summary.pdf.

43. Cawley et al., "Cognitive Ability, Wages, and Meritocracy," 180; see also Cawley, Heckman, and Vytlacil, "Meritocracy in America," 250–96.

44. On issues of gender and race, see Fischer et al., *Inequality by Design*, 88–91, 171–203.

45. Charles Tilly, *Durable Inequality* (Berkeley: University of California Press, 1998).

46. Fischer et al., *Inequality by Design*, 180–81.

47. On the confusion between causation and correlation in Herrnstein and Murray's analysis of the relationship between IQ and poverty, see Knapp et al., *The Assault on Equality*, 213, 218–19; Leon J. Kamin, "Lies, Damned Lies, and Statistics," in Jacoby and Glauberman, *Bell Curve Debate*, 81–105; and K. C. Cole, "Innumeracy," in Jacoby and Glauberman, *Bell Curve Debate*, 73–80.

48. Kohn, "Two Visions," 46.

49. Fischer et al., *Inequality by Design*, 18.

50. Turkheimer et al., "Socioeconomic Status Modifies Heritability"; Nisbett et al., "Intelligence," 135–37; and David C. Berliner, "Our Impoverished View of Educational Research," *Teachers College Record* 108, no. 6 (June 2006): 949–95.

51. Herrnstein and Murray, *Bell Curve*, 52.

52. See Knapp et al., *Assault on Equality*, 82–85, 219–20; Kohn, "Two Visions," 36. For an especially valuable discussion of this problem in *The Bell Curve*, see Fischer et al., *Inequality by Design*, 7–10 and ch. 5.

53. See Mark Robert Rank, *One Nation, Underprivileged: Why American Poverty Affects Us All* (New York: Oxford University Press, 2004), 50. Rank underlines the important distinction between two separate questions: "Who loses out at the economic game?" and "Why does the game produce losers in the first place?"

54. The 10 percent estimate comes from Fischer et al., *Inequality by Design*, 14.

3. THE CULTURAL THEORY OF POVERTY
AND INEQUALITY

1. On the origins and development of the cultural theory of poverty (or culture of poverty theory), see Alice O'Connor, *Poverty Knowledge: Social Science, Social Policy, and the Poor in Twentieth-Century U.S. History* (Princeton, NJ: Princeton University Press, 2001), 99–123, 196–210; and Michael Katz, *The Undeserving Poor: America's Enduring Confrontation with Poverty*, 2nd ed. (New York: Oxford University Press, 2013), 9–29, 50–68.

2. Michael Harrington, *The Other America: Poverty in the United States* (New York: Macmillan, 1993 [1962]). Lewis presented his version of the culture (or subculture) of poverty theory in a series of books and articles. See Oscar Lewis, "The Culture of Poverty," in *Explosive Forces in Latin America*, ed. John J. TePaske and Sydney Nettleton Fisher (Columbus: Ohio State University Press, 1964), 149–73; Oscar Lewis, "The Culture of Poverty," *Scientific American*, October 1966, 19–25; Oscar Lewis, *La Vida: A Puerto Rican Family in the Culture of Poverty—San Juan and New York* (New York: Vintage, 1966), xlii–lii; and Oscar Lewis, "The Culture of Poverty," in *On Understanding Poverty: Perspectives from the Social Sciences*, ed. Daniel Patrick Moynihan (New York: Basic Books, 1968), 187–200.

3. William Ryan, *Blaming the Victim*, rev. and upd. ed. (New York: Vintage, 1976).

4. On how the "vocabulary of poverty" has changed since the 1960s, see Michael Katz, *The Undeserving Poor: From the War on Poverty to the War on Welfare* (New York: Pantheon, 1989), 3–8.

5. Edward C. Banfield, *The Unheavenly City Revisited* (Boston: Little, Brown, 1974), 54, 235.

6. Banfield, *Unheavenly City Revisited*, 61, 72, 234–35.

7. Banfield, *Unheavenly City Revisited*, 143, 238, 269–70.

8. William A. Kelso, *Poverty and the Underclass: Changing Perceptions of the Poor in America* (New York: New York University Press, 1994), 170, 164.

9. Lawrence M. Mead, "A Biblical Response to Poverty," in *Lifting Up the Poor: A Dialogue on Religion, Poverty, and Welfare Reform*, ed. Mary Jo Bane and Lawrence M. Mead (Washington, DC: Brookings Institution Press, 2003), 70.

10. Mead, "A Biblical Response to Poverty," 67; and Lawrence M. Mead, "A Reply to Bane," in Bane and Mead, *Lifting Up the Poor*, 121-22.

11. Cited in Yamiche Alcindor, "Comments on Poverty Start Uproar," *New York Times*, May 26, 2017.

12. Mead, "A Biblical Response to Poverty," 62–66; and Lawrence M. Mead, *The New Politics of Poverty: The Nonworking Poor in America* (New York: Basic Books, 1992), 110–32.

13. Charles Murray, "The Hallmark of the Underclass," *Wall Street Journal*, September 29, 2005.

14. Myron Magnet, *The Dream and the Nightmare: The Sixties' Legacy to the Underclass* (New York: William Morrow, 1993), 38–39.

15. Magnet, *Dream and the Nightmare*, 16.

16. "Race, Class, and Culture: A Conversation with William Julius Wilson and J. D. Vance," Brookings Institution, September 5, 2017, https://www.brookings.edu/events/race-class-and-culture-a-conversation-with-william-julius-wilson-and-j-d-vance/.

17. J. D. Vance, *Hillbilly Elegy: A Memoir of a Family and Culture in Crisis* (New York: HarperCollins, 2016), 1–2.

18. But see Vance, *Hillbilly Elegy*, 47–59.

19. Economic Innovation Group, "The 2017 Distressed Community Index," http://eig.org/wp-content/uploads/2017/09/2017-Distressed-Communities-Index.pdf.

20. Vance, *Hillbilly Elegy*, 7, 146–48, 255–56.

21. Betsy Rader, "I Was Born in Poverty in Appalachia: 'Hillbilly Elegy' Doesn't Speak for Me," *Washington Post*, September 1, 2017, https://www.washingtonpost.com/opinions/i-grew-up-in-poverty-in-appalachia-jd-vances-hillbilly-elegy-doesnt-speak-for-me/2017/08/30/734abb38-891d-11e7-961d-2f373b3977ee_story.html?utm_term=.a7c1f9b5df38.

22. Vance, *Hillbilly Elegy*, 21.

23. Daniel Patrick Moynihan, *The Negro Family: The Case for National Action*, US Department of Labor, Office of Policy Planning and Research (Washington, DC: Government Printing Office, March 1965), 29, 5, 30, 47. The full text of this report, with the original pagination, is included in Lee Rainwater and William L. Yancey, eds., *The Moynihan Report and the Politics of Controversy* (Cambridge, MA: MIT Press, 1967). For an illuminating analysis of the Moynihan report and the controversy it has generated up to the present, see Daniel Geary, *Beyond Civil Rights: The Moynihan Report and Its Legacy* (Philadelphia: University of Pennsylvania Press, 2015).

24. Mead, *New Politics of Poverty*, 149; see also Lawrence E. Harrison, *Who Prospers? How Cultural Values Shape Economic and Political Success* (New York: Basic Books, 1992), 207–11.

25. Dinesh D'Souza, *The End of Racism: Principles for a Multiracial Society* (New York: Free Press, 1995), 24, 100, 477–524.

26. Magnet's *The Dream and the Nightmare* offers the most fully developed rendition of this thesis; see also Kelso, *Poverty and the Underclass*, 154–56; and Joel Schwartz, *Fighting Poverty with Virtue: Moral Reform and America's Urban Poor, 1825–2000* (Bloomington: Indiana University Press, 2000), 145–49.

27. Magnet, *Dream and the Nightmare*, 17, 19–20.

28. Kelso, *Poverty and the Underclass*, 34, 155–56.

29. The most influential example of this argument is Charles Murray, *Losing Ground: American Social Policy, 1950–1980* (New York: Basic Books, 1984).

30. George Gilder, *Wealth and Poverty* (New York: Basic Books, 1981), 69.

31. Harrison, *Who Prospers*, 211.

32. Cited in Charles M. Blow, "Poverty Is Not a State of Mind," *New York Times*, May 19, 2014.

33. Gilder, *Wealth and Poverty*, 68–70.

34. Schwartz, *Fighting Poverty with Virtue*.

35. Kelso, *Poverty and the Underclass*, 181.

36. For a nuanced analysis of the practical problems and ethical questions raised by the moral reform strategy, see Tommie Shelby, "Liberalism, Self-Respect, and Troubling Cultural Patterns in Ghettos," in *The Cultural Matrix: Understanding Black Youth*, ed. Orlando Patterson, with Ethan Fosse (Cambridge, MA: Harvard University Press, 2015), 498–532; see also Tommie Shelby, *Dark Ghettos: Injustice, Dissent, and Reform* (Cambridge, MA: Belknap, Harvard University Press, 2016).

37. Dick Armey, *The Freedom Revolution* (Washington, DC: Regnery Publishing, 1995), 228–33.

38. Marvin Olasky, *The Tragedy of American Compassion*, preface by Charles Murray (Washington, DC: Regnery Gateway, 1992); Marvin Olasky, *Renewing American Compassion*, foreword by Newt Gingrich (New York: Free Press, 1996); and Marvin Olasky, *Compassionate Conservatism: What It Is, What It Does, and How It Can Transform America*, foreword by George W. Bush (New York: Free Press, 2000).

39. Newt Gingrich, "A Citizen's Guide for Helping the Poor," foreword to Olasky, *Renewing American Compassion*, ix–xiv.

40. Lawrence M. Mead, "The Rise of Paternalism," in *The New Paternalism: Supervisory Approaches to Poverty*, ed. Lawrence M. Mead (Washington, DC: Brookings Institution Press, 1997), 11, 20.

41. For a critique, based on longitudinal data from the Panel Study of Income Dynamics, challenging all of these claims, see Mary Corcoran et al., "Myth and Reality: The Causes and Persistence of Poverty," *Journal of Policy Analysis and Management* 4, no. 4 (Summer 1985): 516–36.

42. Anuj K. Shah, Sendhil Mullainathan, and Eldar Shafir, "Some Consequences of Having Too Little," *Science* 338 (November 2012): 682–85; and Matthew Desmond, *Evicted: Poverty and Profit in the American City* (New York: Crown, 2016), 216–226.

43. Jens Ludwig and Susan Mayer, "'Culture' and the Intergenerational Transmission of Poverty: The Prevention Paradox," *The Future of Children* 16, no. 2 (Fall 2006): 175–96.

44. Mark Robert Rank, *One Nation, Underprivileged: Why American Poverty Affects Us All* (Oxford: Oxford University Press, 2004), 88–95, 106–7; see also Jonathan Morduch and Rachel Schneider, *The Financial Diaries: How American Families Cope in a World of Uncertainty* (Princeton, NJ: Princeton University Press, 2017).

45. For an excellent discussion of this point, see Michael Zweig, *The Working Class Majority: America's Best Kept Secret* (Ithaca, NY: Cornell University Press, 2000), 77–93.

46. See Jessi Streib et al., "Life, Death, and Resurrections: The Culture of Poverty Perspective," in *The Oxford Handbook of the Social Science of Poverty*, ed. David Brady and Linda M. Burton (New York: Oxford University Press, 2016), 247–69, esp. 252–54.

47. Bradley R. Schiller, *The Economics of Poverty and Discrimination*, 9th ed. (Upper Saddle River, NJ: Pearson Prentice Hall, 2004), 65.

48. See, for example, Morduch and Schneider, *Financial Diaries*.

49. For critiques of the underclass label, see Herbert J. Gans, *The War against the Poor: The Underclass and Antipoverty Policy* (New York: Basic Books, 1995); and Leslie Inniss and Joe R. Feagin, "The Black 'Underclass' Ideology in Race Relations Analysis," *Social Justice* 16, no. 4 (Winter 1989): 13–34.

50. Mike Rose, "The Inner Life of the Poor," *Dissent* (Summer 2013): 71.

51. Magnet, *Dream and the Nightmare*, 38–55.

52. Mead, *New Politics of Poverty*, 148; Banfield, *Unheavenly City Revisited*, 235; and Magnet, *Dream and the Nightmare*, 38–39.

53. Jacquelin W. Scarbrough, "Welfare Mothers' Reflections on Personal Responsibility," *Journal of Social Issues* 57, no. 2 (Summer 2001): 261–76.

54. William Julius Wilson, *When Work Disappears: The World of the New Urban Poor* (New York: Alfred A. Knopf, 1996), 180.

55. Jennifer L. Hochschild, *Facing Up to the American Dream: Race, Class, and the Soul of the Nation* (Princeton, NJ: Princeton University Press,1995), 55–88; and Alford A. Young Jr., *The Minds of Marginalized Black Men: Making Sense of Mobility, Opportunity, and Future Life Chances* (Princeton, NJ: Princeton University Press, 2004), 107–55.

56. Sandra L. Barnes, "Achievement or Ascription Ideology? An Analysis of Attitudes about Future Success for Residents in Poor Urban Neighborhoods," *Sociological Focus* 35, no. 2 (May 2002): 207–25.

57. Naomi Farber, "The Significance of Aspirations among Unmarried Adolescent Mothers," *Social Service Review* 63, no. 4 (December 1989): 523.

58. Rachel K. Jones and Ye Luo, "The Culture of Poverty and African-American Culture: An Empirical Assessment," *Sociological Perspectives* 42, no. 3 (1999): 454.

59. Young, *Minds of Marginalized Black Men*, 157.

60. On Ryan, see Charles M. Blow, "Paul Ryan, Culture and Poverty," *New York Times*, March 22, 2014.

61. See, for example, Wilson, *When Work Disappears*, 179–81, 251.

62. Roberta Rehner Iversen and Naomi Farber, "Transmission of Family Values, Work, and Welfare among Poor Urban Black Women," *Work and Occupations* 23, no. 4 (November 1996): 437–60.

63. Marta Tienda and Haya Stier, "Joblessness and Shiftlessness: Labor Force Activity in Chicago's Inner City," in *The Urban Underclass*, ed. Christopher Jencks and Paul E. Peterson (Washington, DC: Brookings Institution, 1991), 151.

64. Daniel Dohan, *The Price of Poverty: Money, Work, and Culture in the Mexican American Barrio* (Berkeley: University of California Press, 2003), 64.

65. See, for example, Haya Stier and Marta Tienda, *The Color of Opportunity: Pathways to Family, Welfare, and Work* (Chicago: University of Chicago Press, 2001), 157–62; Mark Robert Rank, *Living on the Edge: The Realities of Welfare in America* (New York: Columbia University Press, 1994), 111–27; and Alejandra Marchevsky and Jeanne Theoharis, *Not Working: Latina Immigrants, Low-Wage Jobs, and the Failure of Welfare Reform* (New York: New York University Press, 2006).

66. Iversen and Farber, "Transmission of Family Values," 446.

67. Stephen M. Petterson, "Are Young Black Men Really Less Willing to Work?," *American Sociological Review* 62, no. 4 (August 1997): 605–13; see also Stier and Tienda, *Color of Opportunity*, 205–12.

68. Sarah Maslin Nir, "8-Day Wait in the Heat for a Career in Carpentry," *New York Times*, August 16, 2016.

69. John Schmitt, *Low-Wage Lessons* (Washington, DC: Center for Economic and Policy Research, January 2012), http://cepr.net/documents/publications/low-wage-2012-01.pdf.

70. Bureau of Labor Statistics, "Labor Force Statistics," 2018, https://data.bls.gov/time series/LNS12032194.

71. Cited in Sam Pizzigati, "Mulvaney Corrects Jesus," Portside, May 24, 2017, http://www.portside.org/2017-05-27/mulvaney-corrects-jesus.

72. See, for example, Richard B. Freeman, "Employment and Earnings of Disadvantaged Young Men in a Labor Shortage Economy," in Jencks and Peterson, *Urban Underclass*, 103–21; and Paul Osterman, "Gains from Growth? The Impact of Full Employment on Poverty in Boston," in Jencks and Peterson, *Urban Underclass*, 122–34.

73. Lawrence Mishel, Jared Bernstein, and Sylvia Allegretto, *The State of Working America, 2004/2005* (Ithaca, NY: Cornell University Press, 2005), 315.

74. Patricia Cohen, "With Pay Rising, Millions Climb Out of Poverty," *New York Times*, September 26, 2016.

75. See L. Randall Wray and Marc-Andre Pigeon, "Can a Rising Tide Raise All Boats? Evidence from the Clinton-Era Expansion," *Journal of Economic Issues* 34, no. 4 (December 2000): 811–45.

76. See Ronald B. Mincy, ed., *Black Males Left Behind* (Washington, DC: Urban Institute Press, 2006); and Peter Edelman, Harry J. Holzer, and Paul Offner, eds., *Reconnecting Disadvantaged Young Men* (Washington, DC: Urban Institute Press, 2006).

77. Alford A. Young Jr., "On the Outside Looking In: Low-Income Black Men's Conception of Work Opportunity and the Good Job," in *Coping with Poverty: The Social Contexts of Neighborhood, Work, and Family in the African-American Community*, ed. Sheldon H. Danziger and Ann Chic Lin (Ann Arbor: University of Michigan Press, 2000), 141–71; and Andrew

L. Reaves, "Black Male Employment and Self-Sufficiency," in Danziger and Lin, *Coping with Poverty*, 172–97.

78. See Devah Pager, "The Mark of a Criminal Record," *American Journal of Sociology* 108, no. 5 (March 2003): 937–75; and Bruce Western, Jeffrey R. Kling, and David F. Weiman, "The Labor Market Consequences of Incarceration," *Crime and Delinquency* 47, no. 3 (July 2001): 410–27.

79. See, for example, Scarbrough, "Welfare Mothers' Reflections on Personal Responsibility," 261–76; Kathryn Edin and Laura Lein, *Making Ends Meet: How Single Mothers Survive Welfare and Low-Wage Work* (New York: Russell Sage, 1997), 60–142; and Sandra Danziger et al., "Barriers to the Employment of Welfare Recipients," in *Prosperity for All? The Economic Boom and African Americans*, ed. Robert Cherry and William M. Rodgers III (New York: Russell Sage, 2000), 245–78.

80. Daniel T. Lichter, Christie D. Batson, and J. Brian Brown, "Welfare Reform and Marriage Promotion: The Marital Expectations and Desires of Single and Cohabiting Mothers," *Social Service Review* 78, no. 1 (March 2004): 21.

81. Kathryn Edin and Maria Kefalas, *Promises I Can Keep: Why Poor Women Put Motherhood Before Marriage* (Berkeley: University of California Press, 2005), 6.

82. Naomi Farber, "The Significance of Race and Class in Marital Decisions among Unmarried Adolescent Mothers," *Social Problems* 37, no. 1 (February 1990): 54.

83. Robin L. Jarrett, "Living Poor: Family Life among Single Parent, African American Women," *Social Problems* 41, no. 1 (February 1994): 36.

84. Edin and Kefalas, *Promises I Can Keep*; Elijah Anderson, *Code of the Street: Decency, Violence, and the Moral Life of the Inner City* (New York: W. W. Norton, 1999), 142–78.

85. William Julius Wilson, *The Truly Disadvantaged: The Inner City, the Underclass, and Public Policy* (Chicago: University of Chicago Press, 1987), 95–106; Andrew Cherlin, *Labor's Love Lost: The Rise and Fall of the Working-Class Family in America* (New York: Russell Sage, 2014); and David Autor, David Dorn, and Gordon Hansen, "When Work Disappears: Manufacturing Decline and the Falling Marriage-Market Value of Men," National Bureau of Economic Research, Working Paper No. 23173 (February 2017), https://economics.mit.edu/files/12736.

86. Farber, "Significance of Race and Class," 58.

87. Jarrett, "Living Poor," 38.

88. Edin and Kefalas, *Promises I Can Keep*, 71–103, 111–19, 125–28; and Wilson, *When Work Disappears*, 98–99, 102–5.

89. Edin and Kefalas, *Promises I Can Keep*, 47–49.

90. Edin and Kefalas, *Promises I Can Keep*, 106–7, 111–12, 119–24, 130.

91. For a look at the same set of issues from the standpoint of poor single fathers, see Kathryn Edin and Timothy J. Nelson, *Doing the Best I Can: Fatherhood in the Inner City* (Berkeley: University of California Press, 2013).

92. Mario Luis Small, David J. Harding, and Michèle Lamont, "Reconsidering Culture and Poverty," *American Academy of Political and Social Science* 629 (May 2010): 6–27; and Orlando Patterson, with Enthan Fosse, eds., *The Cultural Matrix: Understanding Black Youth* (Cambridge, MA: Harvard University Press, 2015).

93. See Michael Rodríguez-Muñiz, "Intellectual Inheritances: Cultural Diagnostics and State of Poverty Knowledge," *American Journal of Cultural Sociology* 3, no. 1 (2015): 89–122; and Stephen Steinberg, "Poor Reason: Culture Still Doesn't Explain Poverty," *Boston Review*, January 13, 2011, http://bostonreview.net/steinberg.php.

94. Zweig, *Working Class Majority*, 91.

95. Schwartz, *Fighting Poverty with Virtue*, 137.

96. Schwartz, *Fighting Poverty with Virtue*, xiv.

97. For evidence that upper-class people are less empathetic, altruistic, and ethical than lower-class people, see Paul K. Piff et al., "Higher Social Class Predicts Increased Unethical Behavior," *Proceedings of the National Academy of Sciences* 109, no. 11 (March 2012): 4086–91.

98. Fred Block, "A Moral Economy," *Nation*, March 20, 2006, 16–19.

4. THE HUMAN CAPITAL THEORY OF POVERTY AND INEQUALITY

1. Bradley R. Schiller, *The Economics of Poverty and Discrimination*, 9th ed. (Upper Saddle River, NJ: Prentice-Hall, 2004), 2.

2. E. Michael Foster, "Labor Economics and Public Policy: Dominance of Constraints or Preferences?," in *Labor Economics: Problems in Analyzing Labor Markets*, ed. William Darity Jr. (Boston: Kluwer, 1993), 269–94; Stephen A. Woodbury, "Culture and Human Capital: Theory and Evidence or Theory versus Evidence," in Darity, *Labor Economics*, 239–67; and Stephen Steinberg, "Human Capital: A Critique," *Review of Black Radical Political Economy* 14, no. 1 (Summer 1985): 67–74.

3. Jon Elster, *Sour Grapes: Studies in the Subversion of Rationality* (Cambridge, UK: Cambridge University Press, 1983), 109–40.

4. Many economists nowadays also question the individualistic assumptions of their discipline, calling instead for a perspective that gives greater weight to social forces and power differentials in explaining people's investment choices and economic outcomes. See, for example, Eric A. Schutz, *Inequality and Power: The Economics of Class* (New York: Routledge, 2011); and Robert Chernomas and Ian Hudson, *Economics in the Twenty-First Century: A Critical Perspective* (Toronto: University of Toronto Press, 2016).

5. Katherine Boo, "After Welfare," *New Yorker*, May 14, 2001, 98.

6. See Bruce Bradbury et al., *Too Many Children Left Behind: The U.S. Achievement Gap in Comparative Perspective* (New York: Russell Sage, 2015).

7. See Peter Cappelli, *Will College Pay Off? A Guide to the Most Important Financial Decision You Will Ever Make* (New York: PublicAffairs, 2015); and Teresa Kroeger and Elise Gould, "The Class of 2017," Economic Policy Institute, May 4, 2017, http://www.epi.org/files/pdf/124859.pdf.

8. See Stephen J. McNamee and Robert K. Miller Jr., *The Meritocracy Myth*, 3rd ed. (Lanham, MD: Rowman & Littlefield, 2014); and Robert Reich, *Saving Capitalism: For the Many, Not the Few* (New York: Knopf, 2015), 89–96.

9. Josh Bivens and Lawrence Mishel, "Understanding the Historic Divergence Between Productivity and a Typical Worker's Pay," Economic Policy Institute, September 2, 2015, http://www.epi.org/publication/understanding-the-historic-divergence-between-productivity-and-a-typical-workers-pay-why-it-matters-and-why-its-real/.

10. See Adam Dean, "Power Over Profits: The Political Economy of Workers and Wages," *Politics & Society* 43, no. 3 (2015): 333–60; and Christopher Kollmeyer, "Market Forces and Workers' Power Resources: A Sociological Account of Real Wage Growth in Advanced Capitalism," *International Journal of Comparative Sociology* 58, no. 2 (2017): 99–119.

11. Yasemin Besen-Cassino, "Cool Stores Bad Jobs," *Contexts* 12, no. 4 (Fall 2013): 42–47.

12. Dalton Conley, *The Pecking Order: A Bold New Look at How Family and Society Determine Who We Become* (New York: Vintage, 2004), 125; see also Paulo R. A. Loureiro, Adolpho Sachsida, and Mário Jorge Cardoso de Mendonça, "Links Between Physical Appearance and Wage Discrimination: Further Evidence," *International Review of Social Sciences and Humanities* 2, no. 1 (2011): 249–60.

13. Elise Gould, "8 Years of the Lilly Ledbetter Fair Pay Act," *Working Economics Blog*, Economic Policy Institute, January 27, 2017, http://www.epi.org/blog/8-years-of-the-lilly-ledbetter-fair-pay-act/.

14. See Vincent J. Roscigno, *The Face of Discrimination: How Race and Gender Impact Work and Home Lives* (Lanham, MD: Rowman & Littlefield, 2007).

15. Pierre Bourdieu, "The Forms of Capital," in *Handbook of Theory and Research for the Sociology of Education*, ed. John G. Richardson (New York: Greenwood Press, 1986), 243–45.

16. Lauren A. Rivera, *Pedigree: How Elite Students Get Elite Jobs* (Princeton, NJ: Princeton University Press, 2015), 7–8, 316n31; and McNamee and Miller, *The Meritocracy Myth*, 17, 77, 85–89.

17. Michèle Lamont and Annette Lareau, "Cultural Capital: Allusions, Gaps and Glissandos in Recent Theoretical Developments," *Sociological Theory* 6 (Fall 1988): 153–68.

18. See Annette Laureau, "Cultural Knowledge and Social Inequality," *American Sociological Review* 80, no. 1 (February 2015): 1–27.

19. Rivera, *Pedigree*, 270.

20. See Gordon Lafer, *The Job Training Charade* (Ithaca, NY: Cornell University Press, 2002), 67–77; George Farkas, "Cognitive Skills and Noncognitive Traits and Behaviors in Stratification Processes," *Annual Review of Sociology* 29 (2003): 541–62; and James J. Heckman, "Hard Evidence on Soft Skills," *Focus* 29, no. 2 (Fall/Winter 2012-13): 3–8.

21. Peter Cappelli, "Is the 'Skills Gap' Really About Attitudes?," *California Management Review* 37, no. 4 (Summer 1995): 108–24.

22. Richard C. Edwards, "Individual Traits and Organizational Incentives: What Makes a 'Good' Worker?," *Journal of Human Resources* 11, no. 1 (Winter 1976): 58–59.

23. Roger Waldinger and Michael I. Lichter, *How the Other Half Works: Immigration and the Social Organization of Labor* (Berkeley: University of California Press, 2003), 15.

24. Barbara Ehrenreich, *Nickel and Dimed: On (Not) Getting By in America* (New York: Henry Holt, Metropolitan, 2001), 110–11; for a compelling account of modern workplaces as dictatorships, see Elizabeth Anderson, *Private Government: How Employers Rule Our Lives (and Why We Don't Talk About It)* (Princeton, NJ: Princeton University Press, 2017).

25. See Margaret M. Zamudio and Michael I. Lichter, "Bad Attitudes and Good Soldiers: Soft Skills as a Code for Tractability in the Hiring of Immigrant Latina/os Over Native Blacks in the Hotel Industry," *Social Problems* 55, no. 4 (November 2008): 573–89.

26. The concept of "cheerful robot" comes from C. Wright Mills, *The Sociological Imagination* (New York: Oxford University Press, 1959), 175.

27. Ehrenreich, *Nickel and Dimed*, 210–11.

28. Samuel Bowles and Herbert Gintis, "Does Schooling Raise Earnings by Making People Smarter?," in *Meritocracy and Economic Inequality*, ed. Kenneth Arrow, Samuel Bowles, and Steven N. Durlauf (Princeton, NJ: Princeton University Press, 2000), 125; see also Samuel Bowles, Herbert Gintis, and Robert Szarka, "Escalating Differences and Elusive 'Skills': Cognitive Abilities and the Explanation of Inequality," in *Race, Poverty, and Domestic Policy*, ed. Michael Henry (New Haven, CT: Yale University Press, 2004), 431–48.

29. Samuel Bowles and Herbert Gintis, "Schooling in Capitalist America Revisited," *Sociology of Education* 75, no. 1 (January 2002): 12–14.

30. Nan Lin, "Inequality in Social Capital," *Contemporary Sociology* 29, no. 6 (November 2000): 787.

31. William Julius Wilson, *The Truly Disadvantaged: The Inner City, the Underclass, and Public Policy* (Chicago: University of Chicago Press, 1987), 60.

32. Katherine Newman, *No Shame in My Game: The Working Poor in the Inner City* (New York: Alfred A. Knoff, 1999), 77–85, 161–74.

33. Deirdre A. Royster, *Race and the Invisible Hand: How White Networks Exclude Black Men from Blue-Collar Jobs* (Berkeley: University of California Press, 2003), 115.

34. Karl Alexander, Doris Entwisle, and Linda Olson, *The Long Shadow: Family Background, Disadvantaged Urban Youth, and the Transition to Adulthood* (New York: Russell Sage, 2014), esp. chapter 8.

35. William Lazonick, Philip Moss, Hal Salzman, and Öner Tulum, "Skill Development and Sustainable Prosperity: Cumulative and Collective Careers versus Skill-Biased Technical Change," Institute for New Economic Thinking, December 8, 2014, https://www.inet economics.org/uploads/papers/Skill-Development-and-Sustainable-Prosperity-20141208.pdf.

36. Andrew Weiss, *Efficiency Wages: Models of Unemployment, Layoffs, and Wage Dispersion* (Princeton, NJ: Princeton University Press, 1990); and Anthony B. Atkinson, *Inequality: What Can Be Done* (Cambridge. MA: Harvard University Press, 2015), 250–52.

37. For in-depth criticism of the theory of skill-biased technological change, see Lazonick et al., "Skill Development and Sustainable Prosperity"; Peter H. Cappelli, "Skill Gaps, Skill Shortages, and Skill Mismatches: Evidence and Arguments for the United States," *ILR Review* 68, no. 2 (March 2015): 251–90; and Lawrence Mishel, Heidi Shierholz, and John Schmitt, "Don't Blame the Robots: Assessing the Job Polarization Explanation of Growing Wage Inequality," Economic Policy Institute, November 19, 2013, http://s3.epi.org/files/2013/tech nology-inequality-dont-blame-the-robots.pdf.

38. Thomas Piketty, *Capital in the Twenty-First Century*, trans. Arthur Goldhammer (Cambridge, MA: Belknap Press, 2014), 304–8, 314.

39. Lazonick et al., "Skill Development and Sustainable Prosperity"; and Cappelli, *Will College Pay Off?*, 156–57.

40. Lawrence Mishel et al., *The State of Working America*, 12th ed. (Ithaca, NY: Cornell University Press, 2012), 286–91.

41. Lazonick et al., "Skill Development and Sustainable Prosperity," 6; see also Facundo Alverado et al., "The Top 1 Percent in International and Historical Perspective," *Journal of Economic Perspectives* 27, no. 3 (Summer 2013): 3–20.

42. Jay Shambaugh et al., "Thirteen Facts about Wage Growth," The Hamilton Project (September 2017), 3, figure 3b, http://www.hamiltonproject.org/assets/files/thirteen_facts_wage_growth.pdf.

43. Mishel et al., *State of Working America*, 211–16; and Edward N. Wolff, *Does Education Really Help? Skill, Work, and Inequality* (Oxford: Oxford University Press, 2006), 12–14.

44. Peter Gottschalk, "Inequality, Income Growth, and Mobility: The Basic Facts," *Journal of Economic Perspectives* 11, no. 2 (Spring 1997): 30.

45. Daron Acemoglu and David Autor, "What Does Human Capital Do? A Review of Goldin and Katz's *The Race between Education and Technology*," *Journal of Economic Literature* 50, no. 2 (2012): 444; Shambaugh et al., "Thirteen Facts about Wage Growth," 3, figure 3A; Mishel et al., *State of Working America*, 216, 178, figure 4A, 302–5; and Paul Beaudry, David A. Green, and Benjamin M. Sand, "The Great Reversal in the Demand for Skill and Cognitive Tasks," *Journal of Labor Economics* 34, no. 1, pt. 2 (January 2016): S199–S247.

46. US Department of Labor, Bureau of Labor Statistics, *Employment Projections—2014–24*, December 8, 2015, table 6, https://www.bls.gov/news.release/pdf/ecopro.pdf; see also Mishel et al., *State of Working America*, 305–9.

47. Jared Bernstein and Lawrence Mishel, "Seven Reasons for Skepticism about the Technology Story of U.S. Wage Inequality," in *Sourcebook of Labor Markets: Evolving Structures and Processes*, ed. Ivar Berg and Arne L. Kalleberg (New York: Kluwer, 2001), 414.

48. Lafer, *Job Training Charade*, 61.

49. Ruy A. Teixeira and Lawrence Mishel, "Whose Skills Shortage—Workers or Management?," *Issues in Science and Technology* 9, no. 4 (Summer 1993): 69.

50. See, for example, Lafer, *Job Training Charade*, 19–44.

51. D. W. Livingstone, *The Education-Jobs Gap: Underemployment or Economic Democracy* (Boulder, CO: Westview Press, 1998); see also D. W. Livingtone, ed., *Education and Jobs: Exploring the Gaps* (Toronto: University of Toronto Press, 2009).

52. Frederic L. Pryor and David L. Schaffer, *Who's Not Working and Why: Employment, Cognitive Skills, Wages, and the Changing U.S. Labor Market* (New York: Cambridge University Press, 1999), 74.

53. Stephen Vaisey, "Education and Its Discontents: Overqualification in America, 1972–2002," *Social Forces* 85, no. 2 (December 2006): 835–64. Vaisey's high estimate counts workers as overqualified if they have at least one year of education beyond that required for the job; his low estimate uses a three-year benchmark. See also Arne L. Kalleberg, *The Mismatched Worker* (New York: W. W. Norton, 2007), 69–98.

54. Richard Vedder, Christopher Denhart, and Jonathan Robe, "Why Are Recent College Graduates Underemployed? University Enrollments and Labor-Market Realities," Center for College Affordability and Productivity, January 2013, esp., 12–24; see also Jaison R. Abel, Richard Deitz, and Yaqin Su, "Are Recent College Graduates Finding Good Jobs?," *Current Issues in Economics and Finance* 20, no. 1 (2014): 1–8.

55. Pew Research Center, *The State of American Jobs* (October 2016), 76, http://assets.pewresearch.org/wp-content/uploads/sites/3/2016/10/ST_2016.10.06_Future-of-Work_FINAL4.pdf.

56. Pryor and Schaffer, *Who's Not Working and Why*, 4; Beaudry, Green, and Sand, "Great Reversal."

57. Harvey Kantor and Robert Lowe, "Educationizing the Welfare State and Privatizing Education: The Evolution of Social Policy Since the New Deal," in *Closing the Opportunity*

Gap, ed. Prudence L. Carter and Kevin G. Welner (New York: Oxford University Press, 2013), 25–39.

5. THE ECONOMIC SYSTEM AND POVERTY

1. Rachel Swarns, "A Growing Economic Recovery Bypasses Low-Wage Workers and Their Tables," *New York Times*, December 15, 2014; Rachel Abrams, "Another Blow for a Battered Work Force," *New York Times*, June 26, 2017; Binyamin Appelbaum, "The Vanishing Male Worker, Waiting It Out," *New York Times*, December 12, 2014; and Abby Goodnough, "Insurance Dropouts Present a Challenge for Health Law," *New York Times*, October 12, 2015.

2. Harold Meyerson, "The Forty-Year Slump," *American Prospect* (September/October 2013): 20–33.

3. Robert J. Gordon, *The Rise and Fall of American Growth: The U.S. Standard of Living Since the Civil War* (Princeton, NJ: Princeton University Press, 2016), 613; and Sheldon H. Danziger and Robert H. Haveman, "The Evolution of Poverty and Antipoverty Policy," in *Understanding Poverty*, ed. Sheldon H. Danziger and Robert H. Haveman (New York: Russell Sage; Cambridge, MA: Harvard University Press, 2001), 13.

4. Alan B. Krueger, "Land of Hope and Dreams: Rock and Roll, Economics and Rebuilding the Middle Class," June 12, 2013, 9–10, https://obamawhitehouse.archives.gov/sites/default/files/docs/hope_and_dreams_-_final.pdf.

5. David M. Gordon, *Fat and Mean: The Corporate Squeeze of Working Americans and the Myth of Managerial "Downsizing"* (New York: Martin Kessler Books, Free Press, 1996), 5–8, 61–94; and David M. Kotz, *The Rise and Fall of Neoliberal Capitalism* (Cambridge, MA: Harvard University Press, 2015), 26-29, 43-44.

6. Michael D. Giandrea and Shawn A. Sprague, "Estimating the U.S. Labor Share," *Monthly Labor Review*, February 2017, https://www.bls.gov/opub/mlr/2017/article/estimating-the-us-labor-share.htm.

7. Josh Bivens, "The Decline in Labor's Share of Corporate Income Since 2000 Means $535 Billion Less for Workers," Economic Policy Institute, September 10, 2015, http://www.epi.org/publication/the-decline-in-labors-share-of-corporate-income-since-2000-means-535-billion-less-for-workers/.

8. Thomas Piketty, Emmanuel Saez, and Gabriel Zucman, "Distributional National Accounts: Methods and Estimates for the United States," July 6, 2017, 3–4, https://eml.berkeley.edu/~saez/PSZ2017.pdf.

9. Economic Policy Institute, "The Productivity-Pay Gap," August 2016, http://www.epi.org/productivity-pay-gap/.

10. Lawrence Mishel and Jessica Schieder, "CEO Pay Remains High Relative to the Pay of Typical Workers and High-Wage Earners," Economic Policy Institute, July 20, 2017, http://www.epi.org/files/pdf/130354.pdf; and Sorapop Kiatpongsan and Michael I. Norton, "How Much (More) Should CEOs Make: A Universal Desire for More Equal Pay," *Perspectives on Psychological Science* 9, no. 6 (2014): 587–93.

11. Matthew Goldstein, "Compensation Is Swelling Again, the Rules Are in Play, and C.E.O.s Have the President's Ear," *New York Times*, May 28, 2017.

12. Steven Greenhouse, "As Factory Jobs Disappear, Ohio Town Has Few Options," *New York Times*, September 13, 2003.

13. Jefferson Cowie and Joseph Heathcott, "Introduction: The Meanings of Deindustrialization," in *Beyond the Ruins: The Meanings of Deindustrialization*, ed. Jefferson Cowie and Joseph Heathcott (Ithaca, NY: Cornell University Press, 2003), 2.

14. Barry Bluestone and Bennett Harrison, *The Deindustrialization of America: Plant Closings, Community Abandonment, and the Dismantling of Basic Industry* (New York: Basic Books, 1982), 6.

15. Catherine Ruckelshaus and Sarah Leberstein, "Manufacturing Low Pay: Declining Wages in the Jobs That Built America's Middle Class," National Employment Law Project, November 2014, http://www.nelp.org/content/uploads/2015/03/Manufacturing-Low-Pay-

Declining-Wages-Jobs-Built-Middle-Class.pdf; and Ken Jacobs et al., "Producing Poverty: The Public Cost of Low-Wage Manufacturing," UC Berkeley Center for Labor Research and Education, May 2016, http://laborcenter.berkeley.edu/pdf/2016/Producing-Poverty.pdf.

16. *The Economic Report of the President*, January 2017, table B-14, 580, https://www.gpo.gov/fdsys/pkg/ERP-2017/pdf/ERP-2017.pdf.

17. The "goods-producing" sector includes mining, construction, and manufacturing, both durable and nondurable. The "service-providing" sector includes utilities, trade, information, financial activities, professional and business services, education and health services, leisure and hospitality, and other services. Self-employment, agricultural employment, and government employment are separate categories. See Bureau of Labor Statistics, "Employment by Major Industry Sector," December 2015, https://www.bls.gov/emp/ep_table_201.htm.

18. *Economic Report of the President*, table B-14, 580–81; Bureau of Labor Statistics, "Employment by Major Industry Sector."

19. Bluestone and Harrison, *Deindustrialization of America*, 6.

20. Steve Fraser, *The Age of Acquiescence: The Life and Death of American Resistance to Organized Wealth and Power* (New York: Little, Brown, 2015), 223–31.

21. John Russo and Sherry Lee Linkon, "The Social Costs of Deindustrialization," in *Manufacturing a Better Future for America*, ed. Richard McCormack (New York: Alliance for American Manufacturing, 2009), 183–215.

22. Charles Craypo and David Cormier, "Job Restructuring as a Determinant of Wage Inequality and Working Poor Households," *Journal of Economic Issues* 34, no. 1 (March 2000): 21–42.

23. Ruckelshaus and Leberstein, "Manufacturing Low Pay."

24. Ruth Milkman, *Farewell to the Factory: Auto Workers in the Late Twentieth Century* (Berkeley: University of California Press, 1997), 43, 22–50.

25. See Françoise Carré and Chris Tilly, *Where Bad Jobs Are Better: Retail Jobs Across Countries and Companies* (New York: Russell Sage, 2017); and Lawrence Mishel et al., *The State of Working America*, 12th ed. (Ithaca, NY: Cornell University Press, 2012), 247–48.

26. Dani Rodrik, *The Globalization Paradox: Democracy and the Future of the World Economy* (New York: W. W. Norton, 2011), 9.

27. See Robert W. McChesney and John Nichols, *People Get Ready: The Fight Against a Jobless Economy and a Citizenless Democracy* (New York: Nation Books, 2016), 131–39.

28. The World Bank, "Imports of Goods and Service (% of GDP)," http://data.worldbank.org/indicator/NE.IMP.GNFS.ZS?locations=US.

29. Mishel et al., *State of Working America*, 254–55; and Richard B. Freeman, "Globalization and Inequality," in *The Oxford Handbook of Economic Inequality*, ed. Wiemer Salverda, Brian Nolan, and Timothy M. Smeeding (Oxford: Oxford University Press, 2009), 582.

30. Freeman, "Globalization and Inequality," 577–79; and Dani Rodrik, *Has Globalization Gone Too Far?* (Washington, DC: Institute for International Economics, 1997), 11–27.

31. David H. Autor, David Dorn, and Gordon H. Hansen, "The China Shock: Local Labor Market Effect of Import Competition in the United States," *American Economic Review* 103, no. 6 (October 2013): 2121–68; and Daron Acemoglu et al., "Import Competition and the Great US Employment Sag of the 2000s," *Journal of Labor Economics* 34, no. 1, pt. 2 (2015): S141–S198.

32. "Jobs and Trade on the Campaign Trail," unsigned editorial, *New York Times*, April 3, 2016.

33. The format of my analysis here and some of the specific arguments borrow from Mishel et al., *State of Working America*, 253–54.

34. Louis Uchitelle, "Made in the U.S.A. (Except for the Parts)," *New York Times*, April 8, 2005.

35. Ralph Blumenthal, "As Levi's Work Is Exported, Stress Stays Home," *New York Times*, October 19, 2003.

36. Charles Duhigg and Keith Bradsher, "How the U.S. Lost Out on iPhone Work," *New York Times*, January 22, 2012.

37. Freeman, "Globalization and Inequality," 579–80; and Alan Blinder, "Offshoring: The Next Industrial Revolution?," *Foreign Affairs* 85, no. 2 (March/April 2006): 113–28.

38. Adrian Wood, "How Trade Hurts Unskilled Workers," *Journal of Economic Perspectives* 9, no. 3 (Summer 1995): 67.

39. Eduardo Porter, "In U.S. Groves, Cheap Labor Means Machines," *New York Times*, March 22, 2004.

40. Mishel et al., *State of Working America,* 254; and Josh Bivens, "Adding Insult to Injury: How Bad Policy Decisions Have Amplified Globalization's Costs for American Workers," Economic Policy Institute, July 11, 2017, http://www.epi.org/files/pdf/130569.pdf.

41. Kate Bronfenbrenner, "Uneasy Terrain: The Impact of Capital Mobility on Workers, Wages, and Union Organizing" (Cornell University ILR School, September 6, 2000), 18, 46–47, 53, http://digitalcommons.ilr.cornell.edu/cgi/viewcontent.cgi?article=1002&context=reports.

42. Alan Greenspan, cited in Jim Stanford, "Power, Employment, and Accumulation," introduction to *Power, Employment, and Accumulation: Social Structures in Economic Theory and Practice*, ed. Jim Stanford, Lance Taylor, and Ellen Houston (Armonk, NY: M. E. Sharpe, 2001), 5.

43. Steven Greenhouse, "Falling Fortunes of the Wage Earner," *New York Times*, April 12, 2005.

44. Steven Greenhouse, "Employers Take a United Stand in Insisting on Labor Concessions," *New York Times*, July 11, 2003.

45. Joseph E. Stiglitz, *The Price of Inequality: How Today's Divided Society Endangers Our Future* (New York: W. W. Norton, 2012), 61–62, 80.

46. James Crotty, "The Case for International Capital Controls," in *Unconventional Wisdom: Alternative Perspectives on the New Economy*, ed. Jeff Madrick (New York: Century Foundation Press, 2000), 279.

47. Dan Clawson, *The Next Upsurge: Labor and the New Social Movements* (Ithaca, NY: Cornell University Press, 2003), 131–63; and Rodrik, *Globalization Paradox*, xvii, 184-200.

48. Rodrik, *Globalization Paradox*, 190–200.

49. On this last point, see especially Robert Driskill, "Deconstructing the Argument for Free Trade: A Case Study of the Role of Economists in Policy Debates," *Economics and Philosophy* 28, no. 1 (March 2012): 1–30.

50. See Jay R. Mandle, *Democracy, America, and the Age of Globalization* (New York: Cambridge University Press, 2008).

51. Eduardo Porter, "At the Polls, Choose Your Capitalism," *New York Times*, October 31, 2012.

52. Martin Ford, *Rise of the Robots: Technology and the Threat of a Jobless Future* (New York: Basic Books, 2015), ch. 1 and 4; Steven Hill, *Raw Deal: How the "Uber Economy" and Runaway Capitalism Are Screwing American Workers* (New York: St. Martin's Press, 2015), 148–155; Claire Martin, "Salad-Making Robot May Cut Germs, and Jobs," *New York Times*, October 8, 2017; Claire Cain Miller, "Service with an Impersonal Touch," *New York Times*, September 9, 2015; and Alex Marshall, "A.I. Is Actual Music to Some Ears," *New York Times*, January 23, 2017.

53. Carl Benedikt Frey and Michael A. Osborne, "The Future of Employment: How Susceptible Are Jobs to Computerization?," September 17, 2013, 44, http://www.oxfordmartin.ox.ac.uk/downloads/academic/The_Future_of_Employment.pdf.

54. James Manyika et al., *A Future That Works: Automation, Employment and Productivity*, McKinsey Global Institute, January 2017, 29, 33, http://www.mckinsey.com/global-themes/digital-disruption/harnessing-automation-for-a-future-that-works.

55. Melanie Arntz, Terry Gregory, and Ulrich Zierahn, "The Risk of Automation for Jobs in OECD Countries," OECD Social, Employment and Migration Working Papers, no. 189 (2016), http://www.oecd-ilibrary.org/docserver/download/5jlz9h56dvq7-en.pdf?expires=1501618654&id=id&accname=guest&checksum=73B7B30567F0F343341D46A73AF1EEAA.

56. Richard Berriman and John Hawksworth, "Will Robots Steal Our Jobs? The Potential Impact of Automation on the UK and Other Major Economies," in *UK Economic Outlook* (PwC, March 2017), 30–49, http://www.pwc.co.uk/economic-services/ukeo/pwc-uk-economic-outlook-full-report-march-2017-v2.pdf.

57. Aaron Smith and Janna Anderson, *AI, Robotics, and the Future of Jobs* (Washington, DC: Pew Research Center, August 2014), http://assets.pewresearch.org/wp-content/uploads/sites/14/2014/08/Future-of-AI-Robotics-and-Jobs.pdf.

58. See Ford, *Rise of the Robots*, ch. 2; and Melissa S. Kearney, Brad Hershbein, and David Body, "The Future of Work in the Age of the Machine," Hamilton Project, February 2015, http://www.hamiltonproject.org/assets/legacy/files/downloads_and_links/Work_in_Machine_Age_February_2015_FINAL.pdf.

59. Daron Acemoglu and Pascual Restrepo, "Robots and Jobs: Evidence from US Labor Markets," October 15, 2016, http://economics.mit.edu/files/12154; for a critique of this study, see Lawrence Mishel and Josh Bivens, "The Zombie Robot Argument Lurches On: There Is No Evidence That Automation Leads to Joblessness or Inequality," Economic Policy Institute, May 24, 2017, http://www.epi.org/files/pdf/126750.pdf.

60. Liz Hamel, Jamie Firth, and Mollyann Brodie, Kaiser Family Foundation/New York Times/CBS News Non-Employed Poll, December 2014, http://kff.org/other/poll-finding/kaiser-family-foundationnew-york-timescbs-news-non-employed-poll/.

61. McChesney and Nichols, *People Get Ready*, 104.

62. Ford, *Rise of the Robots*, xii–xiii; Erik Brynjolfsson and Andrew McAfee, *The Second Machine Age: Work, Progress, and Prosperity in the Time of Brilliant Technologies* (New York: W.W. Norton, 2014), ch. 3; and Kevin Drum, "You Will Lose Your Job to a Robot—And Sooner Than You Think," *Mother Jones*, November/December 2017, http://www.motherjones.com/politics/2017/10/you-will-lose-your-job-to-a-robot-and-sooner-than-you-think/.

63. Ford, *Rise of the Robots*, 72–73, 80, 176; and Brynjolfsson and McAfee, *Second Machine Age*, 75–77.

64. Frey and Osborne, "Future of Employment," 19.

65. McChesney and Nichols, *People Get Ready*, 95–97.

66. Cited in Thomas L. Friedman, "Hillary, Jeb, Facebook and Disorder," *New York Times*, May 20, 2015.

67. Ford, *Rise of the Robots*, 27, 121.

68. Eduardo Porter and Farhad Manjoo, "Competing Visions for a Post-Work Future," *New York Times*, March 9, 2016.

69. See Zeynep Tufekci, "The Machines Are Coming," *New York Times*, April 19, 2015.

70. McChesney and Nichols, *People Get Ready*, 105.

71. Cited in Ford, *Rise of the Robots*, 12

72. See McChesney and Nichols, *People Get Ready*, 113–14.

73. On policy responses to the threat of technological unemployment, see, for example, Darrell M. West, "What Happens If Robots Take the Jobs? The Impact of Emerging Technologies on Employment and Public Policy," Brookings Institution, October 2015, https://www.brookings.edu/wp-content/uploads/2016/06/robotwork.pdf.

74. My discussion of financialization throughout this section is informed especially by the following sources: Rana Foroohar, *Makers and Takers: The Rise of Finance and the Fall of American Business* (New York: Crown, 2016); Mike Konczal and Nell Abernathy, "Defining Financialization," Roosevelt Institute, 2015, http://rooseveltinstitute.org/wp-content/uploads/2015/10/Defining_Financialization_Web.pdf; and J. W. Mason, "Disgorge the Cash: The Disconnect Between Corporate Borrowing and Investment," Roosevelt Institute, 2015, http://rooseveltinstitute.org/wp-content/uploads/2015/09/Disgorge-the-Cash.pdf.

75. Gerald Epstein and Juan Antonio Monecino, *Overcharged: The High Cost of High Finance* (New York: Roosevelt Institute, 2016), 5–8, http://rooseveltinstitute.org/overcharged-high-cost-high-finance/.

76. Foroohar, *Makers and Takers*, 152–78; Ken-Hou Lin and Donald Tomaskovic-Devey, "Financialization and U.S. Income Inequality, 1970–2008," *American Journal of Sociology* 118, no. 5 (March 2013): 1291–94; and Greta R. Krippner, "The Financialization of the American Economy," *Socioeconomic Review* 3 (2005): 182–86.

77. Gerald F. Davis, "After the Corporation," *Politics & Society* 41, no. 2 (2013): 288–89; and Eric Posner, Fiona Scott Morton, and Glen Weyl, "A Monopoly Trump Can Pop," *New York Times*, December 7, 2016.

78. Gerald F. Davis, *Managed by the Market: How Finance Reshaped America* (New York: Oxford University Press, 2009), 72–77.

79. William Lazonick, "Labor in the Twenty-First Century: The Top 0.1% and the Disappearing Middle-Class," Institute for New Economic Thinking, February 2015, 15–18, https://www.ineteconomics.org/uploads/papers/Lazonick-INET-National-Strategies-Value-Creation.pdf.

80. Mason, "Disgorge the Cash," 11–14; and Davis, *Managed by the Market*, 81–96.

81. Davis, "After the Corporation," 283–308; Davis, *Managed by the Market*; see also Neil Irwin, "The Great American Janitor Test," *New York Times*, September 3, 2017.

82. Konczal and Abernathy, "Defining Financialization," 19–21; and William Lazonick, "Innovative Enterprise or Sweatshop Economics? In Search of Foundations of Economic Analysis," *Challenge* 59, no. 2 (March 2016): 103–4.

83. Foroohar, *Makers and Takers*, 107.

84. Lazonick, "Labor in the Twenty-First Century," 15–18.

85. Mason, "Disgorge the Cash," 3, 11, 13; and Davis, *Managed by the Market*, 96.

86. Lazonick, "Innovative Enterprise or Sweatshop Economics?," 102.

87. William A. Galston and Elaine C. Kamarck, "Against Short-Termism," *Democracy: A Journal of Ideas* 38 (Fall 2015): 10–24; Gerald Epstein, *Financialization: There's Something Happening Here* (Amherst, MA: Political Economy Research Institute [PERI], August 2015), 9, https://www.peri.umass.edu/publication/item/684-financialization-there-s-something-happening-here; and William Lazonick, "Profits Without Prosperity," *Harvard Business Review* 92, no. 9 (September 2014): 49.

88. Foroohar, *Makers and Takers*, 4.

89. Davis, "After the Corporation"; Lin and Tomaskovic-Devey, "Financialization and U.S. Income Inequality"; Donald Tomaskovic-Devey, Ken-Hou Lin, and Nathan Meyers, "Did Financialization Reduce Economic Growth?," *Socio-Economic Review* (May 2015):1–24; and Jiwook Jung, "Shareholder Value and Workforce Downsizing," *Social Forces* 93, no. 4 (June 2015): 1335–68.

90. See Josh Bivens, "A 'High-Pressure Economy' Can Help Boost Productivity and Provide Even More 'Room to Run' for the Recovery," Economic Policy Institute, March 10, 2017, http://www.epi.org/files/pdf/118665.pdf; and J. W. Mason, "What Recovery: The Case for Continued Expansionary Policy at the Fed," Roosevelt Institute, July 10, 2017, http://rooseveltinstitute.org/wp-content/uploads/2017/07/Monetary-Policy-Report.pdf.

91. Hiroko Tabuchi, "Next Goal for Walmart Workers: More Hours," *New York Times*, February 26, 2015; see also Caroline Fredrickson, *Under the Bus: How Working Women Are Being Run Over* (New York: Free Press, 2015), 107–17; and Lonnie Golden, "Still Falling Short on Hours and Pay: Part-Time Work Becoming the New Normal," Economic Policy Institute, December 5, 2016, http://www.epi.org/files/pdf/114028.pdf.

92. Bureau of Labor Statistics, "The Employment Situation—November 2017," news release, December 8, 2017, 1–2, 5, table A, https://www.bls.gov/news.release/pdf/empsit.pdf.

93. Bureau of Labor Statistics, "The Employment Situation," table A-1; and Edward Fullbrook, "'Unemployment': Misinformation in Public Discourse and Its Contribution to Trump's Populist Appeal," *Real-World Economics Review* 79 (2017), 160–61, http://www.paecon.net/PAEReview/issue79/Fullbrook79.pdf; and Flavia Dantas and L. Randall Wray, *Full Employment: Are We There Yet*, Levy Economics Institute of Bard College, Public Policy Brief No. 142, 2017, 6–7, http://www.levyinstitute.org/pubs/ppb_142.pdf.

94. Bureau of Labor Statistics, "Labor Force Participation Rate," https://data.bls.gov/timeseries/LNS11300000; and Bureau of Labor Statistics, "Employment-Population Ratio—25–54 Yrs," https://data.bls.gov/timeseries/LNS12300060.

95. Patricia Cohen, "Payrolls Expand, Even as Pay Lags," *New York Times*, July 8, 2017.

96. Michael Hout, "Employment," *Pathways: The Poverty and Inequality Report 2017* (Stanford Center on Poverty and Inequality), 5–8, http://inequality.stanford.edu/sites/default/files/Pathways_SOTU_2017.pdf.

97. Emily Badher, "Why New York and the Bay Area Are Missing Millions of Workers," *New York Times*, December 8, 2017.

98. See Dantas and Wray, "Full Employment"; Jesse Rothstein, "The Great Recession and Its Aftermath: What Role for Structural Changes," *Journal of the Social Sciences* 3, no. 3 (April 2017): 22–49; and Lawrence H. Summers, "U.S. Economic Prospects: Secular Stagnation, Hysteresis, and the Zero Lower Bound," *Business Economics* 49, no. 2 (2014): 65–73.

99. Irene Tung, Yannet Lathrop, and Paul Sonn, "The Growing Movement for $15," National Employment Law Project, November 2015, 1, http://www.nelp.org/content/uploads/Growing-Movement-for-15-Dollars.pdf; Ken Jacobs et al., "Producing Poverty: The Public Cost of Low-Wage Manufacturing"; and David Cooper, "Balancing Paychecks and Public Assistance," Economic Policy Institute, February 3, 2016, http://www.epi.org/files/2015/balancing-paychecks-and-public-assistance.pdf.

100. Badher, "Why New York and the Bay Area Are Missing Millions of Workers"; Alana Semuels, "The Barriers Stopping Poor People from Moving to Better Jobs," *Atlantic*, October 12, 2017, https://www.theatlantic.com/business/archive/2017/10/geographic-mobility-and-housing/542439/; and Joan C. Williams, *White Working Class: Overcoming Class Cluelessness in America* (Boston: Harvard Business Review Press, 2017), 35–41.

101. Alan B. Krueger and Orley Ashenfelter, "Theory and Evidence on Employer Collusion in the Franchise Sector," Princeton University, Working Paper no. 614 (September 28, 2017), http://dataspace.princeton.edu/jspui/bitstream/88435/dsp014f16c547g/3/614.pdf; and Rachel Abrams, "Trapped in Fast Food's Slow Lane," *New York Times*, September 28, 2017.

102. Cited in Conor Dougherty, "How Noncompete Clauses Keep Workers Locked In," *New York Times*, June 9, 2017, https://www.nytimes.com/2017/05/13/business/noncompete-clauses.html.

103. Office of Economic Policy, US Department of the Treasury, "Non-Compete Contracts: Economic Effects and Policy Implications," March 2016, https://www.treasury.gov/resource-center/economic-policy/Documents/UST%20Non-competes%20Report.pdf; Council of Economic Advisors, "Labor Market Monopsony: Trends, Consequences, and Policy Responses," (issue brief, October 2016), https://obamawhitehouse.archives.gov/sites/default/files/page/files/20161025_monopsony_labor_mrkt_cea.pdf; and Orly Lobel, "Isn't Competition a Workers' Right?" *New York Times*, May 4, 2017.

104. *Economic Report of the President* (2017), table B-14, 580–81; and Patricia Cohen, "Public Sector Jobs Vanish, Blacks Take Blow," *New York Times*, May 25, 2015.

105. Jerry Davis, "Capital Markets and Job Creation in the 21st Century," Center for Effective Public Management at Brookings, December 2015, 6–8, https://www.brookings.edu/wp-content/uploads/2016/07/capital_markets.pdf.

106. Bureau of Labor Statistics, "Food Services and Drinking Places: NAICS 722," https://www.bls.gov/iag/tgs/iag722.htm#workforce; and Derek Thompsons, "Restaurants Are the New Factories," *The Atlantic*, August 9, 2017, https://www.theatlantic.com/business/archive/2017/08/restaurant-jobs-boom/536244/.

107. Davis, "Capital Markets and Job Creation," 8.

108. Irwin, "The Great American Janitor Test"; Arindrajit Dube and Ethan Kaplan, "Does Outsourcing Reduce Wages in the Low-Wage Service Occupations? Evidence from Janitors and Guards," *Industrial and Labor Relations Review* 63, no. 2 (January 2010): 287–306; and J. Adam Cobb and Ken-Hou Lin, "Growing Apart: The Changing Firm-Size Wage Effect and Its Inequality Consequences," https://faculty.wharton.upenn.edu/wp-content/uploads/2017/02/fswe_orgsci-v3.3.pdf.

109. David Weil, *The Fissured Workplace: Why Work Became So Bad for So Many and What Can Be Done to Improve It* (Cambridge, MA: Harvard University Press, 2014); and David Weil, "Income Inequality, Wage Determination, and the Fissured Workplace," in *After Piketty: The Agenda for Economics and Inequality*, ed. Heather Boushey, J. Bradford DeLong, and Marshall Steinbaum (Cambridge, MA: Harvard University Press, 2017), 224.

110. Arne Kalleberg, *Good Jobs, Bad Jobs: The Rise of Polarized and Precarious Employment Systems in the United States, 1970s to 2000s* (New York: Russell Sage, 2011), 75–77; and Arne L. Kalleberg, "Job Quality and Precarious Work: Clarifications, Controversies, and Challenges," *Work and Occupations* 39, no. 4 (2012): 427–48.

111. Robert Kuttner, "The Task Rabbit Economy," *American Prospect* (September/October 2013): 47.

112. Lance Morrow, "The Temping of America," *Time*, March 29, 1993, 40–41.

113. Lawrence F. Katz and Alan B. Krueger, "The Rise and Nature of Alternative Work Arrangements in the United States, 1995–2015," National Bureau of Economic Research, Working Paper 22667 (September 2016), 6–7, http://www.nber.org/papers/w22667.

114. Katz and Krueger, "Alternative Work Arrangements," 7-8 (italics in original).

115. See Abel Valenzuela Jr., "Day Labor Work," *Annual Review of Sociology* 29 (2003): 307–33; and Gretchen Purser, "'Still Doin' Time:' Clamoring for Work in the Day Labor Industry," *Journal of Labor and Society* 15, no. 3 (September 2012): 397–415.

116. Hill, *Raw Deal*, 21–28; Fredrickson, *Under the Bus*, 133–37.

117. Hill, *Raw Deal*, 5–6, 12–13, 24–25, 70–100; Fredrickson, *Under the Bus*, 137–47; Françoise Carré, "(In)dependent Contractor Misclassification," Economic Policy Institute, June 8, 2015, http://www.epi.org/files/pdf/87595.pdf; Steven Greenhouse, "On Demand, and Demanding Their Rights," *American Prospect*, Summer 2016, 41–47; and Steven Greenhouse, "The Uber Challenge," *American Prospect*, Winter 2016, 30–37.

118. Katz and Krueger, "Alternative Work Arrangements," 11, 25; US Government Accountability Office, "Contingent Workforce: Size, Characteristics, Earnings, and Benefits," GAO-15-168R, April 2015, 3, 5–6, http://www.gao.gov/assets/670/669766.pdf.

119. Katz and Krueger, "Alternative Work Arrangements," 20–22.

120. Bob Sheak and Melissa Morris, "The Limits of the Job Supply in U.S. Capitalism," *Critical Sociology* 28, no. 3 (2002): 389–415.

121. Alexander Burns, Binyamin Appelbaum, and Neil Irwin, "Trump Vows to Create 25 Million Jobs if Elected, but Offers Few Details," *New York Times*, September 16, 2016.

122. On Trumponomics, see, for example, Gerald Epstein, "Trumponomics: Should We Just Say 'No?'" *Challenge* 60, no. 2 (2017): 104–21; and Pavlina R. Tcherneva, "Trump's Bait and Switch: Job Creation in the Midst of Welfare State Sabotage," *Real-World Economics Review*, 78 (2017): 148–58, http://www.paecon.net/PAEReview/issue78/whole78.pdf.

123. See Neera Tanden et al., "Toward a Marshall Plan for America: Rebuilding Our Towns, Cities, and the Middle Class," Center for American Progress, May 16, 2017, https://cdn.americanprogress.org/content/uploads/2017/05/17073805/PathForward_MarshallPlan-report1.pdf; and Mark Paul et al., "Returning to the Promise of Full Employment: A Federal Job Guarantee in the United States," Research Brief, Vol. 2 (Insight: Center for Community Economic Development, June 2017), https://insightcced.org/wp-content/uploads/2017/06/insight_fjg_brief_2017.pdf.

6. THE POLITICAL SYSTEM AND POVERTY

1. For an insightful critique of the individualistic perspective from a "strongly political" standpoint, see David Brady, *Rich Democracies, Poor People: How Politics Explain Poverty* (Oxford: Oxford University Press, 2009), 3–19; and on the various pathways through which government influences levels of poverty and inequality, see David Brady, Agnes Blome, and Hanna Kleider, "How Politics and Institutions Shape Poverty and Inequality," in *The Oxford Handbook of the Social Science of Poverty*, ed. David Brady and Linda M. Burton (New York: Oxford University Press, 2016), 127–29.

2. Organisation for Economic Co-operation and Development, *Society at a Glance 2016: OECD Social Indicators*, 8th ed. (Paris: OECD, 2016), 102–3.

3. Timothy M. Smeeding, "Poor People in Rich Nations: The United States in Comparative Perspective," *Journal of Economic Perspectives* 20, no. 1 (Winter 2006): 69–90; and Brady, *Rich Democracies, Poor People*, 45–69.

4. OECD, *Society at a Glance 2016*, 104–5. The poverty line in this report is set at 50 percent of median disposable income (after transfers and taxes).

5. Jonathan Fisher and Timothy M. Smeeding, "Income Inequality," *Pathways: The Poverty and Inequality Report 2016* (Stanford Center on Poverty and Inequality), 32–38, http://inequality.stanford.edu/sites/default/files/Pathways-SOTU-2016-Income-Inequality-2.pdf.

6. OECD, *Society at a Glance 2016*, 109; OECD Data, *Social Spending*, 2016, https://data.oecd.org/socialexp/social-spending.htm.

7. Richard B. Freeman, *America Works: The Exceptional U.S. Labor Market* (New York: Russell Sage, 2007), 7–19; Alberto Alesina and Edward L. Glaeser, *Fighting Poverty in the U.S. and Europe: A World of Difference* (Oxford: Oxford University Press, 2004), 37–44; and Dan Zuberi, *Differences That Matter: Social Policy and the Working Poor in the United States and Canada* (Ithaca, NY: Cornell University Press, 2006), 86–107.

8. Zuberi, *Differences That Matter*, 67–85; Janet C. Gornick and Marcia K. Meyers, *Families That Work: Policies for Reconciling Parenthood and Employment* (New York: Russell Sage, 2005), 41, table 2.1, 121–46, 185–235; and Sheila B. Kamerman, "Europe Advanced While the United States Lagged," in *Unfinished Work: Building Equality and Democracy in an Era of Working Families*, ed. Jody Heymann and Christopher Beem (New York: New Press, 2005), 310–24, 327–39.

9. See Lane Kenworthy, *Social Democratic America* (Oxford: Oxford University Press, 2014), 63–68 and figure 3.6.

10. David B. Grusky, Marybeth J. Mattingly, and Charles E. Varner, "Executive Summary," *Pathways: The Poverty and Inequality Report 2016* (Stanford Center on Poverty and Inequality), 6, http://inequality.stanford.edu/sites/default/files/Pathways-SOTU-2016.pdf.

11. Janet C. Gornick and Markus Jäntti, "Poverty," *Pathways: The Poverty and Inequality Report 2017* (Stanford Center on Poverty and Inequality), 15–23, http://inequality.stanford.edu/sites/default/files/Pathways-SOTU-2016.pdf.

12. Karen Jusko, "Safety Net," *Pathways: The Poverty and Inequality Report 2017* (Stanford Center on Poverty and Inequality), 25–31, http://inequality.stanford.edu/sites/default/files/Pathways-SOTU-2016.pdf.

13. Lawrence Mishel et al., *The State of Working America*, 12th ed. (Ithaca, NY: Cornell University Press, 2012), 452–54.

14. Charles Murray, *Losing Ground: American Social Policy, 1950–1980* (New York: Basic Books, 1984).

15. Lane Kenworthy, "Do Social-Welfare Policies Reduce Poverty? A Cross-National Assessment," *Social Forces* 77, no. 3 (March 1999): 1119–39.

16. Cited in Jason DeParle, "In Debate on U.S. Poverty, 2 Studies Fuel an Argument on Who Is to Blame," *New York Times*, October 29, 1991.

17. Robert A. Dahl, *How Democratic Is the American Constitution?* (New Haven, CT: Yale University Press, 2002), 3; see also Sanford Levinson, *Our Undemocratic Constitution: Where the Constitution Goes Wrong (And How We the People Can Correct It)* (New York: Oxford University Press, 2006).

18. Alfred Stepan and Juan J. Linz, "Comparative Perspectives on Inequality and the Quality of Democracy in the United States," *Perspectives on Politics* 9, no. 4 (December 2011): 841–56.

19. On the characteristics of proportional representation systems, see Douglas J. Amy, *Behind the Ballot Box: A Citizen's Guide to Voting Systems* (Westport, CT: Praeger, 2000), 65–106, and for a convincing argument in favor of this system, see Douglas J. Amy, *Real Choices/New Voices: How Proportional Representation Elections Could Revitalize American Democracy*, 2nd ed. (New York: Columbia University Press, 2002).

20. Alesina and Glaeser, *Fighting Poverty*, 81–87.

21. On the characteristics and operation of single-member-district, winner-take-all systems, and on their strengths and weaknesses, see Amy, *Behind the Ballot Box*, 27–63.

22. Steven Hill, *Fixing Elections: The Failure of America's Winner Take All Politics* (New York: Routledge, 2002), 279.

23. Torben Iverson and David Soskice, *Electoral Institutions, Parties, and the Politics of Class: Why Some Democracies Redistribute More Than Others* (Berkeley, CA: Institute of Government Studies, 2005), http://repositories.cdlib.org/cgi/viewcontent.cgi?article=1092&context=igs.

24. On the importance for poverty reduction of a strong left-wing political presence, see Stephanie Moller et al., "Determinants of Relative Poverty in Advanced Capitalist Democracies," *American Sociological Review* 68, no. 1 (February 2003): 22–51; and David Brady, "The

Politics of Poverty: Left Political Institutions, the Welfare State, and Poverty," *Social Forces* 82, no. 2 (December 2003): 557–82.

25. These figure are derived from The World Population Review, "State Populations 2017," http://worldpopulationreview.com/states/.

26. Stepan and Linz, "Comparative Perspectives on Inequality," 844.

27. This paragraph draws on an unpublished manuscript by political scientist Douglas Amy. See also E. J. Dionne Jr., Norman J. Ornstein, and Thomas E. Mann, *One Nation After Trump: A Guide for the Perplexed, the Disillusioned, the Desperate, and the Not-Yet Deported* (New York: St. Martin's Press, 2017), 29–30.

28. Dionne et al., *One Nation After Trump*, 30–31, 259–61; David Daley, *Ratf**cked: The True Story Behind the Secret Plan to Steal America's Democracy* (New York: Liveright, 2016), xix, xxii; and Jane Mayer, *Dark Money: The Hidden History of the Billionaires Behind the Rise of the Radical Right* (New York: Anchor Books, 2017), 298–99, 410–34.

29. See Jules Lobel, "The Political Tilt of Separation of Powers," in *The Politics of Law: A Progressive Critique*, 3rd ed., ed. David Kairys (New York: Basic Books, 1998), 591–616.

30. Francis Fukuyama, *Political Order and Political Decay: From the Industrial Revolution to the Globalization of Democracy* (New York: Farrar, Straus, and Giroux, 2014), 488ff.; see also Stepan and Linz, "Comparative Perspectives on Inequality."

31. Alesina and Glaeser, *Fighting Poverty*, 90–93; and Charles Noble, *Welfare as We Knew It: A Political History of the American Welfare State* (New York: Oxford University Press, 1997), 27, 31–33.

32. For an illustration of this process showing how corporate lobbyists and industry insiders managed to dictate the course of health-care reform, ensuring the priority of their interests over those of the general public, see Kevin Young and Michael Schwartz, "Healthy, Wealthy, and Wise: How Corporate Power Shaped the Affordable Care Act," *New Labor Forum* 23, no. 2 (May 2014): 30–40.

33. See Howard Rosenthal, "Politics, Public Policy, and Inequality: A Look Back at the Twentieth Century," in *Social Inequality*, ed. Kathryn M. Neckerman (New York: Russell Sage, 2004), 864–65.

34. Jacob S. Hacker and Paul Pierson, *Winner-Take-All Politics: How Washington Made the Richer Richer—And Turned Its Back on the Middle Class* (New York: Simon & Schuster, 2010), 43, 53, 83–85.

35. Charles Noble, *The Collapse of Liberalism: Why America Needs a New Left* (Lanham, MD: Rowman & Littlefield, 2004), 27.

36. My analysis of federalism in this and the following paragraph draws on an unpublished manuscript by political scientist Douglas Amy.

37. Alesina and Glaeser, *Fighting Poverty*, 87–90; Noble, *Welfare as We Knew It*, 28–30.

38. Gordon Lafer, *The One Percent Solution: How Corporations Are Remaking America One State at a Time* (Ithaca, NY: Cornell University Press, 2017).

39. See Marni von Wipert, "City Governments Are Raising Standards for Working People—And State Legislators Are Lowering Them Back Down," Economic Policy Institute, August 26, 2017, http://www.epi.org/files/pdf/133463.pdf; David A. Graham, "Red State, Blue City," *The Atlantic*, March 2017, 24-26; Abby Rapoport, "Blue Cities, Red States," *The American Prospect*, Summer 2016, 28–33; and Emily Badger, "Red States and Blue Cities: A Partisan Battle Intensifies," *New York Times*, July 6, 2017.

40. On the predicament of US business in the early 1970s, see Thomas Byrne Edsall, *The New Politics of Inequality* (New York: Norton, 1984), 112–14; Hacker and Pierson, *Winner-Take-All Politics*, 116–18; and Dan Clawson and Mary Ann Clawson, "Reagan or Business? Foundations of the New Conservatism," in *The Structure of Power in America: The Corporate Elite as a Ruling Class*, ed. Michael Schwartz (New York: Holmes and Meier, 1987), 201–4.

41. Cited in Leonard Silk and David Vogel, *Ethics and Profits: The Crisis of Confidence in American Business* (New York: Simon and Schuster, 1976), 72.

42. On the political mobilization of business in the 1970s and after, see Edsall, *New Politics*, 107–40; Hacker and Pierson, *Winner-Take-All Politics*, 118–36; and Dan Clawson, Alan Neustadtl, and Mark Weller, *Dollars and Votes: How Business Campaign Contributions Subvert Democracy* (Philadelphia, PA: Temple University Press, 1998), 146–66.

43. Clawson and Clawson, "Reagan or Business?," 205–7; and John Micklethwait and Adrian Wooldridge, *The Right Nation: Conservative Power in America* (New York: Penguin, 2004), 76–80.

44. Clawson, Neustadtl, and Weller, *Dollars and Votes*, 150–54.

45. Thomas E. Mann and Norman J. Ornstein, *It's Even Worse Than It Looks: How the American Constitutional System Collided with the New Politics of Extremism* (New York: Basic Books, 2016), xvi, 132.

46. Kay Lehman Schlozman, Sidney Verba, and Henry E. Brady, *The Unheavenly Chorus: Unequal Political Voice and the Broken Promise of American Democracy* (Princeton, NJ: Princeton University Press, 2012), 5–6, 117–262.

47. For a particularly informative analysis of class-based changes in political participation, see Joe Soss and Lawrence R. Jacobs, "The Place of Inequality: Non-Participation in the American Polity," *Political Science Quarterly* 14, no. 1 (2009): 95–125.

48. Robert D. Putnam, *Bowling Alone: The Collapse and Revival of American Community* (New York: Simon and Schuster, 2000), 216–75.

49. Robert Dahl, *On Political Equality* (New Haven, CT: Yale University Press, 2006), 87–91; see also Steve Fraser, *The Age of Acquiescence: The Life and Death of American Resistance to Organized Wealth and Power* (New York: Little Brown, 2015), 302–23.

50. Thomas E. Patterson, *The Vanishing Voter: Public Involvement in an Age of Uncertainty* (New York: Vintage, 2003), 63–98.

51. Robert W. McChesney and John Nichols, *People Get Ready: The Fight Against a Jobless Economy and a Citizenless Democracy* (New York: Nation Books, 2016), 28–34, 115–17.

52. Frederick Solt, "Economic Inequality and Democratic Political Engagement," *American Journal of Political Science* 52, no. 1 (January 2008): 48–60.

53. US Department of Labor, Bureau of Labor Statistics, "Union Members—2016," January 26, 2017, https://www.bls.gov/news.release/pdf/union2.pdf. For analyses of the decline of organized labor, see Jake Rosenfeld, *What Unions No Longer Do* (Cambridge, MA: Harvard University Press, 2014); and Ruth Milkman and Stephanie Luce, "Labor Unions and the Great Recession," *Journal of the Social Sciences* 3, no. 3 (April 2017): 145–65.

54. Josh Bivens et al., "How Today's Unions Help Working People," Economic Policy Institute, August 24, 2017, http://www.epi.org/files/pdf/133275.pdf; and Bruce Western and Jake Rosenfeld, "Unions, Norms, and the Rise in U.S. Wage Inequality," *American Sociological Review* 76, no. 4 (August 2011): 513–37.

55. Jake Rosenfeld and Jennifer Laird, "Unions and Poverty," in Brady and Burton, *The Oxford Handbook of the Social Science of Poverty*, 801–7; David Brady, Regina S. Baker, and Ryan Finnigan, "When Unionization Disappears: State Level Unionization and Working Poverty in the United States," *American Sociological Review* 78, no. 5 (October 2013): 872–96; and Richard Freeman et al., "How Does Declining Unionism Affect the American Middle Class and Intergenerational Mobility?," National Bureau of Economic Research, Working Paper No. 21638 (October 2015), http://www.nber.org/papers/w21638.

56. David Madland and Nick Bunker, *Unions Make Democracy Work* (Center for American Progress, January 2012), https://cdn.americanprogress.org/wp-content/uploads/issues/2012/01/pdf/unions_middleclass.pdf; and Cheol-Sung Lee, "Labor Unions and Good Governance: A Cross-National Comparative Analysis," *American Sociological Review* 72, no. 4 (August 2007): 585–609.

57. Benjamin Radcliff and Patricia Davis, "Labor Organizations and Electoral Participation in Industrial Democracies," *American Journal of Political Science* 44, no. 1 (January 2000): 133.

58. Nelson Lichtenstein, *State of the Union: A Century of American Labor* (Princeton, NJ: Princeton University Press, 2002), 234–35.

59. Jeffrey M. Berry, *The New Liberalism: The Rising Power of Citizen Groups* (Washington, DC: Brookings Institution Press, 1999), 57; see also Jeff Manza, "Unequal Democracy in America: The Long View," in *The New Gilded Age: The Critical Inequality Debates of Our Time*, ed. David B. Grusky and Tamar Kricheli-Katz (Stanford, CA: Stanford University Press, 2012), 151–53.

60. Berry, *New Liberalism*, 55–60.

61. Thomas Frank, *Listen Liberal, or What Ever Happened to the Party of the People* (New York: Metropolitan Books, 2016).

62. Theda Skocpol, "Civic Transformation and Inequality in the Contemporary United States," in Neckerman, *Social Inequality*, 729–67; Theda Skocpol, "Voice and Inequality: The Transformation of American Civic Democracy," *Perspectives on Politics* 2, no. 1 (March 2004): 3–20; Theda Skocpol, "Advocates Without Members: The Recent Transformation of American Civic Life," in *Civic Engagement in American Democracy*, ed. Theda Skocpol and Morris P. Fiorina (Washington, DC: Brookings Institution, 1999), 461–509; and Theda Skocpol, *Diminished Democracy: From Membership to Management in American Civil Life* (Norman: University of Oklahoma Press, 2003).

63. Skocpol, "Advocates Without Members," 462, 471, 499–500; and Skocpol, "Civic Transformation and Inequality," 741–46, 758–59.

64. Dionne, Ornstein, and Mann, *One Nation After Trump*, 247–55; Andrea Flynn et al., *The Hidden Rules of Race: Barriers to an Inclusive Economy* (New York: Cambridge University Press, 2017), 145–55; Zachary Roth, *The Great Suppression: Voting Rights, Corporate Cash, and the Conservative Assault on Democracy* (New York: Crown, 2016); and Liz Kennedy, "Voter Suppression Laws Cost Americans Their Voices at the Polls," Center for American Progress, November 11, 2016, https://www.americanprogress.org/issues/democracy/reports/2016/11/11/292322/voter-suppression-laws-cost-americans-their-voices-at-the-polls/.

65. Connor Sheets, "Too Poor to Vote: How Alabama's 'New Poll Tax' Bars Thousands of People from Voting," *Guardian*, October 4, 2017, https://www.theguardian.com/us-news/2017/oct/04/alabama-voting-poll-tax.

66. Michael Wines, "Bitter Struggle Over the Purging of Voting Rolls," *New York Times*, November 26, 2017; and Michael Wines, "Wisconsin Law Deterred Voters, Study Finds," *New York Times*, September 26, 2017.

67. Ari Berman, "A Tale of Two States," *The Nation* (July 18/25, 2016), 31.

68. Keeanga-Yamahtta Taylor, *From #Black Lives Matter to Black Liberation* (Chicago: Haymarket Books, 2016), esp. 211–16.

69. Karen E. Fields and Barbara J. Fields, *Racecraft: The Soul of Inequality in American Life* (London: Verso, 2012), 270, 283.

70. Sean McElwee, "Racism Hurt Democrats in 2016," *Contexts* 16, no. 2 (Spring 2017): 22–23.

71. See Nicholas Confessore, "Trump Mines Grievances of Whites Who Feel Loss," *New York Times*, July 14, 2016; and Carol Anderson, "The Policies of White Resentment," *New York Times*, August 6, 2017.

72. Dan Clawson, Alan Neustadtl, and Denise Scott, *Money Talks: Corporate PACs and Political Influence* (New York: Basic Books, 1992).

73. Gary Burtless and Christopher Jencks, "American Inequality and Its Consequences," in *Agenda for the Nation*, ed. Henry J. Aaron, James M. Lindsay, and Pietro S. Nivola (Washington, DC: Brookings Institution Press, 2003), 98.

74. Benjamin I. Page, Larry M. Bartels, and Jason Seawright, "Democracy and the Policy Preferences of Wealthy Americans," *Perspectives on Politics* 11, no. 1 (March 2013): 51–73; see also Martin Gilens, "Preference Gaps and Inequality in Representation," *PS: Political Science and Politics* 42, no. 2 (April 2009): 335–41; and Jeffrey A. Winters and Benjamin I. Page, "Oligarchy in the United States," *Perspectives on Politics* 7, no. 4 (December 2009): 731–51.

75. Nicholas Confessore, Sarah Cohen, and Karen Yourish, "A Wealthy Few Lead in Giving to Campaigns," *New York Times*, August 2, 2015; and Nicholas Confessore, Sarah Cohen, and Karen Yourish, "From Only 158 families, Half the Cash for '16 Race," *New York Times*, October 11, 2015.

76. Schlozman, Verba, and Brady, *Unheavenly Chorus*, 158–62; Jay R. Mandle, *Democracy, America, and the Age of Globalization* (New York: Cambridge University Press, 2008), 52–58; and Center for Responsive Politics, "Business-Labor-Ideology Split in PAC & Individual Donations to Candidates, Parties, Super PACs and Outside Spending Groups," https://www.opensecrets.org/overview/blio.php.

77. For a valuable overview of recent legal decisions governing political contributions, see Earl Wysong, Robert Perrucci, and David Wright, *The New Class Society: Goodbye American Dream?*, 4th ed. (Lanham, MD: Rowman & Littlefield, 2014), 145–62.

78. Center for Responsive Politics, "Super PACs," https://www.opensecrets.org/pacs/superpacs.php.

79. John Nichols and Robert W. McChesney, *Dollarocracy: How the Money and Media Election Complex Is Destroying America* (New York: Nation Books, 2013).

80. Jay Mandle, "The Politics of Democracy," *Challenge* 47, no. 1 (January–February 2004): 53.

81. Lee Drutman, *The Business of America Is Lobbying: How Corporations Became Politicized and Politics Became More Corporate* (New York: Oxford University Press, 2013), 16.

82. Center for Responsive Politics, "Lobbying Database," https://www.opensecrets.org/lobby/.

83. Center for Responsive Politics, "Lobbying: Top Spenders," https://www.opensecrets.org/lobby/top.php?showYear=a&indexType=s.

84. Drutman, *Business of America*, 12–13.

85. Schlozman, Verba, and Brady, *Unheavenly Chorus*, 430–32, 442.

86. See Wysong, Perrucci, and Wright, *New Class Society*, 163–87.

87. Task Force on Inequality and American Democracy, *American Democracy in an Age of Rising Inequality* (Washington, DC: American Political Science Association, 2004), 11, http://www.apsanet.org/imgtest/taskforcereport.pdf.

88. Larry M. Bartels et al., "Inequality and American Governance," in *Inequality and American Democracy: What We Know and What We Need to Learn*, ed. Lawrence R. Jacobs and Theda Skocpol (New York: Russell Sage, 2005), 127.

89. Larry M. Bartels, *Unequal Democracy: The Political Economy of the New Gilded Age*, 2nd ed. (New York: Russell Sage; Princeton, NJ: Princeton University Press, 2016), 244, 259.

90. Martin Gilens, "Inequality and Democratic Responsiveness," *Public Opinion Quarterly* 69, no. 5 (2005): 788; and Martin Gilens, *Affluence and Influence: Economic Inequality and Political Power in America* (New York: Russell Sage; Princeton, NJ: Princeton University Press, 2012), 81–85, 234.

91. See Patrick Flavin, "Income Inequality and Policy Representation in the American States," *American Politics Research* 40, no. 1 (January 2012): 29–59; and Elizabeth Rigby and Gerald C. Wright, "Political Parties and Representation of the Poor in the American States," *American Journal of Political Science* 57, no. 3 (July 2013): 552–65.

92. Nicholas Carnes, *White-Collar Government: The Hidden Role of Class in Economic Policy Making* (Chicago: University of Chicago Press, 2013), 19–20, 11–12.

93. On the development and implementation of welfare reform, see Sharon Hays, *Flat Broke with Children: Women in the Age of Welfare Reform* (Oxford: Oxford University Press, 2003).

94. Eduardo Porter, "A Party's Strategy to Ignore Poverty," *New York Times*, October, 28, 2015.

95. Hays, *Flat Broke with Children*, 41–42; and Ellen Reese, *Backlash Against Welfare Mothers: Past and Present* (Berkeley: University of California Press, 2005), 6–12.

96. Carmen DeNavas-Walt, Bernadette D. Proctor, and Jessica C. Smith, *Income, Poverty, and Health Insurance Coverage in the United States: 2012*, US Census Bureau, Current Population Reports, P60-245 (Washington, DC: Government Printing Office, 2013), 58, table B-2, 52, table B-1, 18, table 5.

97. Office of Family Assistance, TANF Caseload Data 2017, April 14, 2017, https://www.acf.hhs.gov/ofa/programs/tanf/data-reports; and Gerald Falk, "Temporary Assistance for Needy Families (TANF): Size and Characteristics of the Cash Assistance Caseload," Congressional Research Service, January 29, 2016, https://fas.org/sgp/crs/misc/R43187.pdf.

98. Kay E. Brown, "Temporary Assistance for Needy Families: Update on Program Performance," Government Accountability Office, June 5, 2012, 3, http://www.gao.gov/assets/600/591372.pdf.

99. Bryce Covert and Josh Israel, "Mississippi Is Rejecting Nearly All of the Poor People Who Apply for Welfare," Think Progress, April 13, 2017, https://thinkprogress.org/mississippi-reject-welfare-applicants-57701ca3fb13/.

100. See Joe Soss, Richard C. Fording, and Sanford Schram, *Disciplining the Poor: Neoliberal Paternalism and the Persistent Power of Race* (Chicago: University of Chicago Press, 2011), 262–92; and Kathryn J. Edin and H. Luke Shaefer, *$2.00 A Day: Living on Almost Nothing in America* (Boston: Houghton Mifflin Harcourt, 2015), 31–33.

101. Center for Budget and Policy Priorities, "Chart Book: TANF at 20," August 5, 2016, http://www.cbpp.org/sites/default/files/atoms/files/8-22-12tanf_0; see also Peter Germanis, "TANF Is a Massive *Policy* Failure, But Other 'Liberal' Welfare Policies Reduced Poverty: A Response to Scott Winship," August 22, 2016, esp. 8–10, http://mlwiseman.com/wp-content/uploads/2016/05/Winship-Poverty-After-WR.pdf.

102. Patricia Cohen, "A Gaping Hole in the Safety Net," *New York Times*, February 17, 2015.

103. H. Luke Shaefer and Kathryn Edin, "The Rise of Extreme Poverty in the United States," *Pathways* (Summer 2014): 28–32.

104. See Robert Greenstein, "Welfare Reform and the Safety Net," Center on Budget and Policy Priorities," June 6, 2016, https://www.cbpp.org/sites/default/files/atoms/files/6-6-16pov2.pdf; and Monica Potts, "The Social Safety Net Doesn't Exist in America," *The Nation*, October 31, 2016.

105. Institute for Research on Poverty, "TANF Turns 20," *Fast Focus*, March 2017, http://www.irp.wisc.edu/publications/fastfocus/pdfs/FF26-2017.pdf; and Liz Schott, Ladonna Pavetti, and Ife Floyd, "How States Use Federal and State Funds under the TANF Block Grant," Center on Budget and Policy Priorities, October 15, 2015, http://www.cbpp.org/research/family-income-support/how-states-use-federal-and-state-funds-under-the-tanf-block-grant.

106. Center for Budget and Policy Priorities, "Chart Book: TANF at 20."

107. See, e.g., Jane L. Collins and Victoria Mayer, *Both Hands Tied: Welfare Reform and the Race to the Bottom of the Low-Wage Labor Market* (Chicago: University of Chicago Press, 2010); Sandra Morgen, Joan Acker, and Jill Weigt, *Stretched Thin: Poor Families, Welfare Work, and Welfare Reform* (Ithaca, NY: Cornell University Press, 2010); and Laura Lein and Deanna T. Schexnayder, *Life After Welfare Reform and the Persistence of Poverty* (Austin: University of Texas Press, 2007).

108. Committee on Ways and Means, US House of Representatives, *Green Book: Background Material and Data on the Programs within the Jurisdiction of the Committee on Ways and Means*, 2016, ch. 4, "Unemployment Insurance," http://greenbook.waysandmeans.house.gov/2016-green-book/chapter-4-unemployment-insurance.

109. See Lafer, *One Percent Solution*, 75, 122.

110. Rebecca Dixon, "Federal Neglect Leaves State Unemployment Systems in a State of Disrepair," National Employment Law Project, November 2013, http://www.nelp.org/content/uploads/2015/03/NELP-Report-State-of-Disrepair-Federal-Neglect-Unemployment-Systems.pdf.

111. Rachel West, et al., "Where States Are and Where They Should Be on Unemployment Protections," Center for American Progress, July 7, 2016, 7–8, 11–12, tables 1 and 2, https://cdn.americanprogress.org/wp-content/uploads/2016/07/07060320/StateUI-brief.pdf.

112. For proposals intended to alleviate these and other deficiencies, see Claire McKenna, "The Job Ahead: Advancing Opportunity for Unemployed Workers," National Employment Law Project, February 2015, http://www.nelp.org/content/uploads/2015/03/Report-The-Job-Ahead-Advancing-Opportunity-Unemployed-Workers.pdf; and Rachel West et al., "Strengthening Unemployment Protections in America: Modernizing Unemployment Insurance and Establishing a Job Seeker's Allowance," Center for American Progress, June 2016, http://www.nelp.org/content/uploads/Report-Strengthening-Unemployment-Protections-in-America.pdf.

113. West et al., "Where States Are and Where They Should Be," 2; West et al., "Strengthening Unemployment Protections in America," 41–42; and McKenna, "Job Ahead," 10–12.

114. Rebecca Smith, Rich McHugh and Andrew Stettner, "Unemployment Insurance and Voluntary Quits: How States' Policies Affect Today's Families," *Challenge* 46, no. 3 (May–June 2003): 89–107.

115. McKenna, "Job Ahead," 10–12; and Rebecca Smith et al., "Between a Rock and a Hard Place: Confronting the Failure of State Unemployment Insurance Systems to Serve Women and Working Families," National Employment Law Project, July 2003, http://www.nelp.org/content/uploads/2015/03/Between-a-Rock-and-a-Hard-Place-070103.pdf.

116. West et al., "Strengthening Unemployment Protections in America," 37; and Jeffrey B. Wenger, "Divided We Fall: Deserving Workers Slip Through America's Patchwork Unemployment Insurance System," Economic Policy Institute, August 2001, 5–9, http://www.epi.org/publication/briefingpapers_divided/.

117. West et al., "Strengthening Unemployment Protections in America," 55–56.

118. West et al., "Strengthening Unemployment Protections in America," 15–16.

119. Freeman, *America Works*, 15; West et al., "Strengthening Unemployment Protections in America," 55–58; and Julie M. Whittaker and Katelin P. Isaacs, "Unemployment Insurance: Programs and Benefits," Congressional Research Service, October 20, 2016, 5–7, http://greenbook.waysandmeans.house.gov/sites/greenbook.waysandmeans.house.gov/files/RL333 62%20-%20Unemployment%20Insurance%20-%20Programs%20and%20Benefits_0.pdf.

120. Lafer, *One Percent Solution*, 122–25.

121. West et al., "Strengthening Unemployment Protections in America," 39–40; Will Kimball and Rick McHugh, "How Low Can We Go? State Unemployment Insurance Programs Exclude Record Numbers of Jobless Workers," Economic Policy Institute, March 9, 2016, http://www.epi.org/files/2015/how-low-can-we-go-state-unemployment-r3.pdf; and George Wenworth and Claire McKenna, "Ain't No Sunshine: Fewer Than One in Eight Unemployed Workers in Florida Is Receiving Unemployment Insurance," National Employment Law Project, September 21, 2015, http://www.nelp.org/publication/aint-no-sunshine-florida-unemployment-insurance/.

122. West et al., "Strengthening Unemployment Protections in America," 9.

123. US Department of Labor, Wage and Hour Division, *The Fair Labor Standards Act of 1938, as Amended* (revised May 2011), 1, https://www.shrm.org/ResourcesAndTools/tools-and-samples/toolkits/Documents/FairLaborStandAct.pdf.

124. See Bartels, *Unequal Democracy*, 198–228.

125. David Cooper, "Raising the Minimum Wage to $15 by 2024 Would Lift Wages for 41 Million American Workers," Economic Policy Institute, April 2017, 5, figure A, http://www.epi.org/files/pdf/125047.pdf; and Craig K. Elwell, "Inflation and the Real Minimum Wage: A Fact Sheet," Congressional Research Service, January 8, 2014, 2, table 1, https://fas.org/sgp/crs/misc/R42973.pdf.

126. Lafer, *One Percent Solution*, 106–8; Sylvia A. Allegretto and David Cooper, "Twenty-Three Years and Still Waiting for Change: Why It's Time to Give Tipped Workers the Regular Minimum Wage," Economic Policy Institute, July 2014, http://www.epi.org/files/2014/EPI-CWED-BP379.pdf; and US Department of Labor, Wage and Hour Division, "Minimum Wages for Tipped Employees," January 1, 2017, https://www.dol.gov/whd/state/tipped.htm.

127. US Department of Labor, Wage and Hour Division, "Minimum Wage Laws in the States," July 1, 2017, https://www.dol.gov/whd/minwage/america.htm.

128. National Employment Law Project, "City Minimum Wage Laws: Recent Trends and Recent Trends and Economic Evidence," April 2016, http://www.nelp.org/content/uploads/City-Minimum-Wage-Laws-Recent-Trends-Economic-Evidence.pdf.

129. Lafer, *One Percent Solution*, 104–6; and National Employment Law Project, "Fighting Preemption: The Movement for Higher Wages Must Oppose State Efforts to Black Local Minimum Wage Laws," July 2017, http://www.nelp.org/content/uploads/Fighting-Preemption-Local-Minimum-Wage-Laws.pdf.

130. Council of Economic Advisors, "The Economic Case for Raising the Minimum Wage," February 12, 2014, 8, https://www.slideshare.net/whitehouse/the-economic-case-for-raising-the-minimum-wage.

131. Cooper, "Raising the Minimum Wage," 6–7, figure B.

132. Lawrence Mishel, Ross Eisenbrey, and Alyssa Davis, "Top Restaurant Industry CEOs Made 721 Times More than Minimum Wage Workers in 2013," Economic Policy Institute, July 2, 2014, http://www.epi.org/publication/top-restaurant-industry-ceos-721-times-minimum/.

133. John Alpin and Karl Agne, "50 Years After LBJ's War on Poverty: A Study of American Attitudes About Work, Economic Opportunity, and the Social Safety Net," Center for American Progress, January 2014, 28, 30, table 13, https://cdn.americanprogress.org/wp-content/uploads/2014/01/WOP-PollReport2.pdf; National Employment Law Project, "Mini-

mum Wage Basics: Public Opinion on Raising the Minimum Wage," May 2015, http://www. nelp.org/content/uploads/Minimum-Wage-Basics-Polling.pdf; and Drew DeSilver, "5 Facts About the Minimum Wage," Pew Research Center, January 4, 2017, http://www.pewresearch. org/fact-tank/2017/01/04/5-facts-about-the-minimum-wage/.

134. Rick Fantasia and Kim Voss, *Hard Work: Remaking the American Labor Movement* (Berkeley: University of California Press, 2004), 34–77.

135. David Marland, Alex Rowell, and Gordon Laver, "Anti-Democratic Attacks on Unions Hurt Working Americans," Center for American Progress Action Fund, June 22, 2017, https:// cdn.americanprogress.org/content/uploads/sites/2/2017/06/22181720/UnionElection-brief.pdf.

136. Chirag Mehta and Nik Theodore, *Undermining the Right to Organize: Employer Behavior during Union Representation Campaigns* (Chicago: Center for Urban Economic Development, December 2005), http://www.jwj.org/wp-content/uploads/2013/12/UROCUEDcom pressedfullreport.pdf; and Kate Bronfenbrenner, "No Holds Barred: The Intensification of Employer Opposition to Organizing," Economic Policy Institute, May 2009, http://digital commons.ilr.cornell.edu/cgi/viewcontent.cgi?article=1037&context=reports.

137. Bronfenbrenner, "No Holds Barred."

138. John Schmitt and Ben Zipperer, "Dropping the Ax: Illegal Firings during Union Election Campaigns, 1951–2007," Center for Economic and Policy Research, March 2009, 15, http:// cepr.net/documents/publications/unions_2007_01.pdf.

139. See Steven Greenhouse, "Labor Law Is Broken, Economist Says," *New York Times*, October 28, 2010; and Ellen Dannin, "No Rights Without a Remedy: The Long Struggle for Effective National Labor Relations Act Remedies," American Constitution Society for Law and Policy, June 2011, https://www.acslaw.org/sites/default/files/Dannin_No_Rights_With out_Remedy_0.pdf.

140. Lance Compa, *Human Rights and Workers' Rights in the United States* (Washington, DC: AFL-CIO, 2005), https://digitalcommons.ilr.cornell.edu/cgi/viewcontent.cgi?article= 1129&context=laborunions.

141. National Conference of State Legislators, "Right-to-Work Resources," 2017, http:// www.ncsl.org/research/labor-and-employment/right-to-work-laws-and-bills.aspx.

142. Fantasia and Voss, *Hard Work*, 51.

143. Lafer, *One Percent Solution*, 78–99; and Milkman and Luce, "Labor Unions and the Great Recession," 157–58.

144. See Lance Compa, *Unfair Advantage: Workers' Freedom of Association in the United States under International Human Rights Standards* (Ithaca, NY: Cornell University Press, 2004), xix–xx, 29–30, 171–89; and David Madland, "The Future of Worker Voice and Power," Center for American Progress, October 2016, 9, https://cdn.americanprogress.org/wp-content/ uploads/2016/10/06051753/WorkerVoice2.pdf.

145. Jim Grossfeld and John D. Podesta, "A Temporary Fix," *American Prospect*, March 2005, 15–17.

146. Fantasia and Voss, *Hard Work*, 52; and Compa, *Unfair Advantage*, xvii–xix, 31–32, 60.

147. Noam Scheiber, "As Americans Take-Up Populism, Supreme Court Embraces Business," *New York Times*, March 12, 2016, citing Lee Epstein, William M. Landes, and Richard A Posner, "How Business Fares in the Supreme Court," *Minnesota Law Review* 97 (2013): 1431–72; see also Nan Aron and Kyle C. Barry, et al., "The Case Against the Roberts Court," *The Nation* (October 12, 2015), 12–33.

148. See Craig Becker and Judith Scott, "Isolating America's Workers," *The Nation*, October 8, 2012, 27–29; and Aron and Barry, et al., "The Case Against the Roberts Court."

149. Elizabeth Anderson, *Private Government: How Employers Rule Our Lives (and Why We Don't Talk about It)* (Princeton, NJ: Princeton University Press, 2017).

150. Lafer, "Legislative Attack on American Wages," 28–31; and Brady Meixell and Ross Eisenbrey, "An Epidemic of Wage Theft Is Costing Workers Hundreds of Millions of Dollars a Year," Economic Policy Institute, September 11, 2014, http://www.epi.org/files/2014/wage-theft.pdf.

7. THE CULTURAL SYSTEM AND POVERTY

1. Alice O'Connor, *Poverty Knowledge: Social Science, Social Policy, and the Poor in Twentieth-Century U.S. History* (Princeton, NJ: Princeton University Press, 2001).

2. Ann Swidler, "Culture in Action: Symbols and Strategies," *American Sociological Review* 51, no. 2 (April 1986): 273–86.

3. Eduardo Bonilla-Silva, *White Supremacy and Racism in the Post–Civil Rights Era* (Boulder, CO: Lynne Rienner, 2001), 62.

4. Michael I. Norton and Dan Ariely, "Building a Better America—One Wealth Quintile at a Time," *Perspectives on Psychological Science* 6, no. 1 (January 2011): 9–12; Sorapop Kiatpongsan and Michael I. Norton, "How Much (More) Should CEOs Make? A Universal Desire for More Equal Pay," *Perspectives on Psychological Science* 9, no. 6 (November 2014): 587–93; Shai Davidai and Thomas Gilovich, "Building a More Mobile America—One Income Quintile at a Time," *Perspectives on Psychological Science* 10, no. 1 (January 2015): 60–71; and Michael W. Kraus and Jacinth J. X. Tan, "Americans Overestimate Class Mobility," *Journal of Experimental Social Psychology* 58 (May 2015): 101–11.

5. Chrystia Freeland, "The Lottery Mentality," *New York Times*, September 19, 2011, https://www.nytimes.com/roomfordebate/2011/03/21/rising-wealth-inequality-should-we-care/the-lottery-mentality.

6. James R. Kluegel and Eliot R. Smith, *Beliefs about Inequality: Americans' Views of What Is and What Ought to Be* (New York: Aldine De Gruyter, 1986), 44; see also Sandra L. Hanson and John Zogby, "The Polls—Trends: Attitudes About the American Dream," *Public Opinion Quarterly* 74, no. 3 (Fall 2010): 570–84; and Nancy DiTomaso, *The American Non-Dilemma: Racial Inequality Without Racism* (New York: Russell Sage, 2013), 101–36.

7. Richard Wiki, *5 Ways Americans and Europeans Are Different* (Washington, DC: Pew Research Center, April 19, 2016), http://www.pewresearch.org/fact-tank/2016/04/19/5-ways-americans-and-europeans-are-different/.

8. Jim Cullen, *The American Dream: A Short History of an Idea That Shaped a Nation* (New York: Oxford University Press, 2003), 10.

9. Economic Mobility Project, "Findings from a National Survey & Focus Groups on Economic Mobility," March 12, 2009, 21, http://www.pewtrusts.org/~/media/legacy/uploadedfiles/wwwpewtrustsorg/reports/economic_mobility/emp20200920survey20on20economic20mobility20for20print2031209pdf.pdf.

10. Noam Scheiber and Dalia Sussman, "Inequality Troubles Americans Across Party Lines, a Poll Finds," *New York Times*, June 4, 2015; *The New York Times* Poll, December 4–7, 2014, https://assets.documentcloud.org/documents/1377502/poll-finds-a-more-bleak-view-of-american-dream.pdf; and Robert P. Jones, Daniel Cox, Juhem Navarro-Rivera, "Economic Insecurity, Rising Inequality and Doubts About the Future," Public Religion Research Institute, 2014, 14–15, http://www.jewishdatabank.org/Studies/downloadFile.cfm?FileID=3175.

11. Andrew Kohut and Michael Dimock, "Resilient American Values: Optimism in an Era of Growing Inequality and Economic Difficult" (working paper, Council on Foreign Relations, May 2013), 3, https://www.cfr.org/sites/default/files/pdf/2013/03/CFR_WorkingPaper16_Kohut_Dimock.pdf.

12. Jones et al., "Economic Insecurity," 16–17; Pew Research Center, *Most See Inequality Growing, But Partisans Differ over Solutions* (January 23, 2014), 4, http://www.people-press.org/2014/01/23/most-see-inequality-growing-but-partisans-differ-over-solutions/.

13. Jeff Manza and Clem Brooks, "Why Aren't Americans Angrier About Rising Inequality," *Pathways* (Winter 2016): 22–26.

14. Leslie McCall, "Political and Policy Responses to Problems of Inequality and Opportunity: Past, Present, and Future," in *The Dynamics of Opportunity in America: Evidence and Perspectives*, ed. Irwin Kirsch and Henry Braun (New York: Springer, 2016), 415–42; and Leslie McCall, *The Undeserving Rich: American Beliefs about Inequality, Opportunity, and Redistribution* (New York: Cambridge University Press, 2013).

15. Kluegel and Smith, *Beliefs about Inequality*, 37.

16. For an illuminating analysis of the logic of "individualism" and its place in American culture, see Lawrence M. Eppard, "Paved with Good Intentions: Individualism and the Cultural Reproduction of Poverty and Inequality," *Sociation Today* 14, no. 3 (Fall/Winter 2016), http://www.ncsociology.org/sociationtoday/v142/eppard.html.

17. Michael Schudson, "How Culture Works: Perspectives from Media Studies on the Efficacy of Symbols," *Theory and Society* 18, no. 2 (March 1989): 153–80. To explain why some cultural representations are more influential than others, Schudson identifies "five dimensions of cultural power": "retrievability," "rhetorical force," "resonance," "institutional retention," and "resolution." Though I do not use his terminology, my analysis in what follows is a loose application of this framework.

18. Stephen Pimpare, *Ghettos, Tramps, and Welfare Queens: Down and Out on the Silver Screen* (New York: Oxford University Press, 2017), 10, 244, 249, 290–95.

19. Robert C. Bulman, *Hollywood Goes to High School: Cinema, Schools, and American Culture* (New York: Worth, 2005), 43–59; see also Pimpare, *Ghettos, Tramps, and Welfare Queens*, 87–98.

20. Kluegel and Smith, *Beliefs about Inequality*, 247–55.

21. The pioneering work of Joe Feagin set the pattern for subsequent studies; see Joe R. Feagin, *Subordinating the Poor: Welfare and American Beliefs* (Englewood Cliffs, NJ: Prentice-Hall, 1975); and Joe R. Feagin, "Poverty: We Still Believe That God Helps Those Who Help Themselves," *Psychology Today* 6 (1972): 101–10, 129.

22. Besides individualism and structuralism, public opinion research has also found evidence, though less definitive, of other popular theories of poverty, including "fatalism" and "culturalism." See Kevin B. Smith and Lorene H. Stone, "Rags, Riches, and Bootstraps: Beliefs about the Causes of Wealth and Poverty," *Sociological Quarterly* 30, no. 1 (1989): 94–95; Dorota Lepianka, Wim Van Oorschot, and John Belissen, "Popular Explanations of Poverty: A Critical Discussion of Empirical Research," *Journal of Social Policy* 38, no. 3 (July 2009): 421–38; and Matthew O. Hunt and Heather E. Bullock, "Ideologies and Beliefs about Poverty," in *The Oxford Handbook of the Social Science of Poverty*, ed. David Brady and Linda M. Burton (New York: Oxford University Press, 2016), 96–97.

23. Kluegel and Smith, *Beliefs about Inequality*, 100–101; see also Kevin B. Smith, "I Made It Because of Me: Beliefs about the Causes of Wealth and Poverty," *Sociological Spectrum* 5, no. 3 (1985): 255–67.

24. Judith A. Chafel, "Societal Images of Poverty: Child and Adult Beliefs," *Youth and Society* 28, no. 4 (June 1997): 432, 434, 461.

25. Catherine Cozzarelli, Anna V. Wilkinson, and Michael J. Tagler, "Attitudes toward the Poor and Attributions for Poverty," *Journal of Social Issues* 57, no. 2 (Summer 2001): 207–27.

26. Greg M. Shaw and Robert Y. Shapiro, "The Polls-Trends: Poverty and Public Assistance," *Public Opinion Quarterly* 66, no. 1 (Spring 2002): 115–21.

27. Karen Seccombe, Delores James, and Kimberly Battle Walters, "'They Think You Ain't Much of Nothing': The Social Construction of the Welfare Mother," *Journal of Marriage and the Family* 60, no. 4 (November 1998): 849–65; and Liane V. Davis and Jan L. Hagen, "Stereotypes and Stigma: What's Changed for Welfare Mothers," *Affilia* 11, no. 3 (Fall 1996): 319–37.

28. On the variation among individuals in beliefs about the causes of poverty, see Matthew O. Hunt, "The Individual, Society, or Both? A Comparison of Black, Latino, and White Beliefs about the Causes of Poverty," *Social Forces* 75, no. 1 (September 1996): 293–322; Linda Burzotta Nilson, "Reconsidering Ideological Lines: Beliefs about Poverty in America," *Sociological Quarterly* 22 (Autumn 1981): 531–48; and Anup K. Singh, "Attribution Research on Poverty: A Review," *Psychologia* 32 (1989): 143–48.

29. Barrett A. Lee, Sue Hinze Jones, and David W. Lewis, "Public Beliefs about the Causes of Homelessness," *Social Forces* 69, no. 1 (September 1990): 253–65.

30. Martin Gilens, *Why Americans Hate Welfare: Race, Media, and the Politics of Antipoverty Policy* (Chicago: University of Chicago Press, 1999).

31. Catherine Cozzarelli, Michael J. Tagler, and Anna V. Wilkinson, "Do Middle-Class Students Perceive Poor Women and Poor Men Differently?," *Sex Roles* 47, nos. 1–12 (2002): 519–29.

32. Shanto Iyengar, "Framing Responsibility for Political Issues: The Case of Poverty," *Political Behavior* 12, no. 1 (March 1990): 27–28.

33. Martin Gilens, "The American News Media and Public Misperceptions of Race and Poverty," in *Race, Poverty, and Domestic Policy*, ed. C. Michael Henry (New Haven, CT: Yale University Press, 2004), 341–42.

34. Jeffry A. Will, "The Dimensions of Poverty: Public Perceptions of the Deserving Poor," *Social Science Research* 22, no. 3 (September 1993): 312–32.

35. Guy Molyneux, "A Tale of Two Populisms," *American Prospect*, Summer 2017, 35.

36. John B. Judis, *The Populist Explosion: How the Great Recession Transformed American and European Politics* (New York: Columbia Global Reports, 2016), 78–87.

37. Arlie Russell Hochschild, *Strangers in Their Own Land: Anger and Mourning on the American Right* (New York: New Press, 2016), esp. 60–61, 92–94, 135–51; and Theda Skocpol and Vanessa Williamson, *The Tea Party and the Remaking of Republican Conservatism* (New York: Oxford University Press, 2013), esp. 59–77.

38. Pew Research Center, *The Partisan Divide on Political Values Grows Even Wider* (October 5, 2017), 15–16, 49, 51–52, http://assets.pewresearch.org/wp-content/uploads/sites/5/2017/10/05162647/10-05-2017-Political-landscape-release.pdf; and Robert J. Blendon and John M. Benson, "Income Inequality: The Public and the Partisan Divide," *Challenge* 59, no. 1 (2016): 6, table 1.

39. Lee Drutman, "Political Divisions in 2016 and Beyond: Tensions Between and Within the Two Parties," Democracy Fund Voter Study Group, June 2017, 4–8, https://www.voterstudygroup.org/publications/2016-elections/political-divisions-in-2016-and-beyond.

40. Rob Griffin, Ruy Teixera, and John Halpin, "Voter Trends in 2016: A Final Examination," Center for American Progress, November 2017, 6, 18, tables 1 and 7, https://cdn.americanprogress.org/content/uploads/2017/11/02102135/VoterTrends2016-report-update.pdf.

41. See Nelson D. Schwartz, "Mill Town Flipped to Trump, But Jitters Stay Put," *New York Times*, November 25, 2017.

42. See Justin Gest, "The Two Kinds of Trump Voters," *Politico*, February 8, 2017, https://www.politico.com/magazine/story/2017/02/trump-voters-white-working-class-214754; Matthew Yglesias, "The 3 Different Things We Talk About When We Talk About 'Trump Voters'," Vox, December 7, 2016, https://www.vox.com/policy-and-politics/2016/12/7/13854512/who-are-trump-supporters; Shannon Monnat and David L. Brown, "How Despair Helped Drive Trump to Victory," Institute for New Economic Thinking, November 16, 2017, https://www.ineteconomics.org/perspectives/blog/how-despair-helped-drive-trump-victory; Mike Davis, "The Great God Trump and the White Working Class," *Jacobin*, February 7, 2017, https://www.jacobinmag.com/2017/02/the-great-god-trump-and-the-white-working-class/; Keith Orejel, "Why Trump Won Rural America," *Dissent*, October 16, 2017, https://www.dissentmagazine.org/online_articles/rural-vote-trump-economy-manufacturing; and E. J. Dionne Jr., Norman J. Ornstein, and Thomas E. Mann, *One Nation After Trump: A Guide for the Perplexed, the Disillusioned, the Desperate, and the Not-Yet Deported* (New York: St. Martin's Press, 2017), esp. 149–71.

43. See Karen Bernal et al., "Autopsy: The Democratic Party in Crisis," 2017, https://democraticautopsy.org/wp-content/uploads/Autopsy-The-Democratic-Party-In-Crisis.pdf.

44. See, for example, Claudia Strauss, "Not-So-Rugged Individualists: U.S. Americans' Conflicting Ideas about Poverty," in *Work, Welfare, and Politics: Confronting Poverty in the Wake of Welfare Reform*, ed. Frances Fox Piven et al. (Eugene: University of Oregon Press, 2002), 55–69.

45. Lawrence Bobo, "Social Responsibility, Individualism, and Redistributive Policies," *Sociological Forum* 6, no. 1 (March 1991): 71–92.

46. John Halpin and Karl Agne, "50 Years After LBJs War on Poverty: A Study of American Attitudes about Work, Economic Opportunity, and the Social Safety Net," Center for American Progress, January 2014, 28–32, https://www.americanprogress.org/issues/poverty/reports/2014/01/07/81702/50-years-after-lbjs-war-on-poverty/.

47. Kluegel and Smith, *Beliefs about Inequality*, 17, 87–88, 93.

48. Hunt, "The Individual, Society, or Both?," 293–322, 295. In a more recent study of beliefs about black-white inequality, Hunt finds declining support for structural explanations

among both African Americans and Hispanics; see Matthew O. Hunt, "African American, Hispanic, and White Beliefs about Black/White Inequality, 1977–2004," *American Sociological Review* 72, no. 3 (June 2007): 390–415.

49. Lawrence D. Bobo and Ryan A. Smith, "Antipoverty Policy, Affirmative Action, and Racial Attitudes," in *Confronting Poverty: Prescriptions for Change*, ed. Sheldon H. Danziger, Gary D. Sandefur, and Daniel H. Weinberg (New York: Russell Sage and Cambridge, MA: Harvard University Press, 1994), 375.

50. See, for example, Elizabeth L. Beck, Deborah M. Whitley, and James L. Wolk, "Legislators' Perceptions about Poverty: Views from the Georgia General Assembly," *Journal of Sociology and Social Welfare* 26, no. 2 (June 1999): 87–104.

51. Hunt, "The Individual, Society, or Both?," 294–95; see also Hunt and Bullock, "Ideologies and Beliefs about Poverty," 103.

52. Stanley Feldman and John Zaller, "The Political Culture of Ambivalence: Ideological Responses to the Welfare State," *American Journal of Political Science* 36, no. 1 (February 1992): 268–307; and Matthew C. Nisbet, "Communicating about Poverty and Low-Wage Work: A New Agenda," The Mobility Agenda, October 2007, http://www.topospartnership.com/wp-content/uploads/2013/03/USUKPaperFINAL.pdf.

53. Bobo and Smith, "Antipoverty Policy, Affirmative Action, and Racial Attitudes," 372.

54. See McCall, *Undeserving Rich*.

55. Hunt, "The Individual, Society, or Both?," 295; see also Hunt, "African American, Hispanic, and White Beliefs," 394.

56. Tammy Draut, "New Opportunities? Public Opinion on Poverty, Income Inequality, and Public Policy: 1996–2002," Demos, 2002, 6–7, http://www.demos.org/sites/default/files/publications/New_Opportunities.pdf.

57. Eppard, "Paved with Good Intentions," 9–12.

58. Robert V. Robinson and Wendell Bell, "Equality, Success, and Social Justice in England and the United States," *American Sociological Review* 43, no. 2 (April 1978): 125–43.

59. Bobo, "Social Responsibility, Individualism, and Redistributive Policies," 85–88.

60. Christina Fong, "Social Preferences, Self-Interest, and the Demand for Redistribution," *Journal of Public Economics* 82, no. 2 (2001): 225–46.

61. Gilens, "American News Media," 347–49.

62. Robert A. Hackett, "The News Media and Civic Equality: Watch Dogs, Mad Dogs, or Lap Dogs?," in *Democratic Equality: What Went Wrong?*, ed. Edward Broadbent (Toronto: University of Toronto Press, 2001), 197–212; and James Curran, "Rethinking Media and Democracy," in *Mass Media and Society*, 3rd ed., ed. James Curran and Michael Gurevitch (London: Hodder, 2000), 120–54.

63. Earl Wysong, Robert Perrucci, and David Wright, *The New Class Society: Goodbye American Dream?*, 4th ed. (Lanham, MD: Rowman & Littlefield, 2014), 189–215; and John Nichols and Robert W. McChesney, *Dollarocracy: How the Money and Media Election Complex Is Destroying America* (New York: Nation Books, 2013).

64. See James T. Hamilton, *Democracies Detectives: The Economics of Investigative Journalism* (Cambridge: Harvard University Press, 2016); and Bill Moyers, "The Challenge of Journalism Is to Survive in the Pressure Cooker of Plutocracy," Moyers & Company, May 27, 2015, http://billmoyers.com/2015/05/27/bill-moyers-speech-challenge-journalism-survive-plutocracy/.

65. Neil Postman, *Amusing Ourselves to Death: Public Discourse in the Age of Show Business* (New York: Penguin, 1985), 87; see also Thomas E. Patterson, *Informing the News: The Need for Knowledge-Based Journalism* (New York: Vintage, 2013), 20–30.

66. See Jeffrey M. Berry and Sarah Sobieraj, *The Outrage Industry: Political Opinion Media and the New Incivility* (New York: Oxford University Press, 2014).

67. Margaret Sullivan, "Too Little for So Many, Even in *The Times*," *New York Times*, June 2, 2013; Steve Rendell, "A Poverty of Coverage," *Extra!*, September–October 2007, http://fair.org/extra/a-poverty-of-coverage/; Neil deMause and Steve Rendall, "The Poor Will Always Be with Us," *Extra!*, September–October 2007, 9–13, http://fair.org/extra/the-poor-will-always-be-with-us-just-not-on-the-tv-news/; and Heather E. Bullock, Karen Fraser Wyche, and Wendy

R. Williams, "Media Images of the Poor," *Journal of Social Issues* 57, no. 2 (Summer 2001): 232–33.

68. Steven Rendall, Emily Kaufmann, and Sara Qureshi, "Even GOP Attention Can't Make Media Care About Poor," *Extra!*, June 1, 2014, http://fair.org/extra/even-gop-attention-cant-make-media-care-about-poor/.

69. Cited in Dan Froomkin, "It Can't Happen Here: Why Is There So Little Coverage of Americans Who Are Struggling with Poverty," *Nieman Reports* (Winter 2013), 2, http://niemanreports.org/articles/it-cant-happen-here-2/.

70. Cited in Froomkin, "It Can't Happen Here," 1.

71. Andrew R. Cline, "Citizens or Objects: A Case Study in News Coverage of Poverty," *Poverty & Public Policy* 3, no. 4 (2011): 1–8.

72. Miranda Spencer, "'Making the Invisible Visible': Antipoverty Activists Working to Make Their Own Media," *Extra!*, January–February 2003, 21, http://fair.org/extra/quotmaking-the-invisible-visiblequot/.

73. C. Wright Mills, *The Sociological Imagination* (New York: Oxford University Press, 1959), 8–9.

74. See Gregory Mantsios, "Media Magic: Making Class Invisible," in *Race, Class, and Gender in the United States: An Integrated Study*, 5th ed., ed. Paula S. Rothenberg (New York: Worth, 2001), 564–66.

75. Peter Parisi, "A Sort of Compassion: The *Washington Post* Explains the 'Crisis in Urban America,'" *Howard Journal of Communications* 9 (1998), 187.

76. On the concept of "framing," see Robert M. Entman, "Framing: Toward Clarification of a Fractured Paradigm," *Journal of Communication* 43, no. 4 (Autumn 1993): 51–58.

77. Iyengar, "Framing Responsibility," 28–29; see also Carmen L. Manning-Miller, "Media Discourse and the Feminization of Poverty," *Explorations in Ethnic Studies* 17, no. 1 (January 1994): 79–88.

78. Max Rose and Frank R. Baumgartner, "Framing the Poor: Media Coverage and U.S. Poverty Policy, 1960–2008," *Policy Studies Journal* 41, no. 1 (February 2013): 22–53.

79. Parisi, "A Sort of Compassion," 201; see also Nisbet, "Communicating about Poverty," 6–8.

80. Maura Kelly, "Regulating the Reproduction and Mothering of Poor Women: The Controlling Image of the Welfare Mother in Television News Coverage of Welfare Reform," *Journal of Poverty* 14, no. 1 (January-March 2010): 76–96; and Ange-Marie Hancock, *The Politics of Disgust: The Public Identity of the Welfare Queen* (New York: New York University Press, 2004), 65–87.

81. Michael Zweig, *The Working Class Majority: America's Best Kept Secret* (Ithaca, NY: Cornell University Press, 2000), 77–93.

82. Barbara Ehrenreich, "Too Poor to Make the News," *New York Times*, June 14, 2009; and Neil deMause, "The Recession and the 'Deserving Poor': Poverty Finally on the Media Radar—But Only When It Hits the Middle Class," *Extra!*, February 1, 2009, http://fair.org/extra/the-recession-and-the-deserving-poor/.

83. Pimpare cited in deMause, "The Recession and the 'Deserving Poor'."

84. Gilens, *Why Americans Hate Welfare*, 102–32; Gilens, "American News Media," 336–63; Rosalee A. Clawson and Rakuya Trice, "Poverty As We Know It: Media Portrayals of the Poor," *Public Opinion Quarterly* 64, no. 1 (Spring 2000): 53–64; and Bas W. van Doorn, "Pre- and Post-Welfare Reform Media Portrayals of Poverty in the United States: The Continuing Importance of Race and Ethnicity," *Politics & Policy* 43, no. 1 (February 2015): 142–62.

85. Gilens, *Why Americans Hate Welfare*, 121–27; Doorn, "Pre- and Post-Welfare Reform Media Portrayals," 155–56; and Joya Misra, Stephanie Moller, and Marina Karides, "Envisioning Dependency: Changing Media Depictions of Welfare in the 20th Century," *Social Problems* 50, no. 4 (November 2003): 482–504.

86. See Christopher D. DeSante, "Working Twice as Hard to Get Half as Far: Race, Work Ethic, and America's Deserving Poor," *American Journal of Political Science* 57, no. 2 (April 2013): 342–56; and Celeste Watkins-Hayes and Elyse Kovalsky, "The Discourse of Deservingness: Morality and the Dilemmas of Poverty Relief in Debate and Practice," in Brady and Burton, *The Oxford Handbook of the Social Science of Poverty*, 193–220.

87. Sonya Ross and Jennifer Agiesta, "AP Poll: A Slight Majority of Americans Are Now Expressing Negative View of Blacks," *Washington Post*, October 28, 2012, http://www.ign.com/boards/threads/ap-poll-a-slight-majority-of-americans-are-now-expressing-negative-view-of-blacks.452724619/; Tracie McMillan, "Who Do We Think of as Poor?," *New York Times*, July 8, 2017; and Maria Krysan, "Prejudice, Politics, and Public Opinion: Understanding the Sources of Racial Policy Preferences," *Annual Review of Sociology* 26 (2000): 135–68.

88. Charlotte Ryan, *Prime Time Activism: Media Strategies for Grassroots Organizing* (Boston: South End Press, 1991), 189–212; Charlotte Ryan, "Battered in the Media: Mainstream News Coverage of Welfare Reform," *Radical America* 26, no. 1 (January–March 1996): 29–41; and Robert W. McChesney and John Nichols, *People Get Ready: The Fight Against a Jobless Economy and a Citizenless Democracy* (New York: Nation Books, 2016), 139–40; on the "source problem" in the news media, see also Patterson, *Informing the News*, 33–59.

89. Ryan, *Prime Time Activism*, 192–93.

90. Rendall, Kaufmann, and Qureshi, "Even GOP Attention Can't Make Media Care about Poor."

91. Ryan, "Battered in the Media," 34–38, 40; see also Kelly, "Regulating the Reproduction and Mothering of Poor Women," 82–83.

92. Patterson, *Informing the News*, 81–83.

93. Robert M. Entman, "Television, Democratic Theory, and the Visual Construction of Poverty," *Research in Political Sociology* 7 (1995): 149.

94. Michael Schudson, "The Sociology of News Production," *Media, Culture, and Society* 11, no. 3 (July 1989): 278.

95. Nancy Franklin, "Seeing Stars," *New Yorker*, September 26, 2005, 156.

96. For a sustained analysis of how sound bite media work to the advantage of the Right, see Jeffrey Scheuer, *The Sound Bite Society: Television and the American Mind* (New York: Four Walls Eight Windows, 1999).

97. Daniel C. Hallin, "The American News Media: A Critical Theory Perspective," in *Critical Theory and Public Life*, ed. John Forester (Cambridge: MIT Press, 1985), 130.

98. Hallin, "American News Media," 130, 135.

99. For a discussion of media effects, see Herbert J. Gans, *Democracy and the News* (Oxford: Oxford University Press, 2003), 69–89.

100. Leonard Silk and David Vogel, *Ethics and Profits: The Crisis of Confidence in American Business* (New York: Simon and Schuster, 1976), 21–23.

101. Cited in David Vogel, *Fluctuating Fortunes: The Political Power of Business in America* (New York: Basic Books, 1989), 213.

102. Lewis F. Powell, "Attack on American Free Enterprise System," August 23, 1971, http://law2.wlu.edu/deptimages/Powell%20Archives/PowellMemorandumPrinted.pdf. On Powell's memorandum and the onset of the right-wing ideological offensive in the early 1970s, see Jason Stahl, *Right Moves: The Conservative Think Tank in American Political Culture Since 1945* (Chapel Hill: University of North Carolina Press, 2016), 59–64; and Kim Phillips-Fein, *Invisible Hands: The Businessmen's Crusade Against the New Deal* (New York: W. W. Norton, 2009), 156–65.

103. Vogel, *Fluctuating Fortunes*, 145, 194–95, 213–14; and David Brock, *The Republican Noise Machine: Right-Wing Media and How It Corrupts Democracy* (New York: Crown, 2004), 41–42, 45–46.

104. See Richard Meagher, "The 'Vast Right-Wing Conspiracy': Media and Conservative Networks," *New Political Science* 34, no. 4 (January 2012): 469–84.

105. For details on these foundations, their assets, and the role they played in funding the conservative counterrevolution, see John Micklethwait and Adrian Wooldridge, *The Right Nation: Conservative Power in America* (New York: Penguin, 2004), 77–79; and Alice O'Connor, "Financing the Counterrevolution," in *Rightward Bound: Making America Conservative in the 1970s*, ed. Bruce J. Schulman and Julian E. Zelizer (Cambridge, MA: Harvard University Press, 2008), 148–68.

106. See Dan Clawson and Mary Ann Clawson, "Reagan or Business? Foundations of the New Conservatism," in *The Structure of Power in America: The Corporate Elite as a Ruling Class*, ed. Michael Schwartz (New York: Holmes and Meier, 1987), 205–7.

107. For basic information about right-wing think tanks, see Lewis H. Lapham, "Tentacles of Rage: The Republican Propaganda Mills, a Brief History," *Harper's Magazine*, September 2004, 35; and Douglas S. Massey, *Return of the "L" Word: A Liberal Vision for the New Century* (Princeton, NJ: Princeton University Press, 2005), 44–51.

108. Micklethwait and Wooldridge, *Right Nation*, 113.

109. Jennifer Steinhauer and Jonathan Weisman, "In the DeMint Era at Heritage, a Shift from Policy to Politics," *New York Times*, February 24, 2014.

110. Jane Mayer, *Dark Money: The Hidden History of the Billionaires Behind the Rise of the Radical Right* (New York: Anchor Books, 2017), 12.

111. Vogel, *Fluctuating Fortunes*, 214–16.

112. Brock, *Republican Noise Machine*, 74–115.

113. Media Research Center, http://www.mrc.org/about.

114. Stahl, *Right Moves*.

115. Mark Hertsgaard, "How to Fight Fox News and Friends," *The Nation*, March 20, 2017, 15–20, 40; Eric Alterman, *What Liberal Media? The Truth about Bias and the News* (New York: Basic Books, 2003), 28–103.

116. For some data on how the media presence of the Right "overshadows the Left," see Hertsgaard, "How to Fight Fox News and Friends," 17, 20; Jacob S. Hacker and Paul Pierson, *American Amnesia: How the War on Government Led Us to Forget What Made America Prosper* (New York: Simon and Schuster, 2016), 252–53; and Jackie Calmes, "They Don't Give a Damn about Governing: Conservative Media's Influence on the Republican Party," Shorenstein Center on Media, Politics, and Public Policy, July 27, 2015, 18–25, https://shorensteincenter.org/conservative-media-influence-on-republican-party-jackie-calmes/.

117. Cited in Matt Bai, "Notion Building," *New York Times Magazine*, October 12, 2003, 84–85.

118. Lapham, "Tentacles of Rage."

119. Rose and Baumgartner, "Framing the Poor"; Herbert J. Gans, *The War against the Poor: The Underclass and Antipoverty Policy* (New York: Basic Books, 1995); and Michael B. Katz, *The Undeserving Poor: From the War on Poverty to the War on Welfare* (New York: Pantheon, 1989).

120. See Ellen Reese, *Backlash against Welfare Mothers: Past and Present* (Berkeley: University of California Press, 2005), 151–97.

121. Michael Harrington, *The New American Poverty* (New York: Penguin, 1984), 37.

122. Charles Murray, *Losing Ground: American Social Policy, 1950–1980* (New York: Basic Books, 1984), 227–28.

123. Pew Research Center, *Most See Inequality Growing*, 2.

124. Albert O. Hirschman, *The Rhetoric of Reaction: Perversity, Futility, Jeopardy* (Cambridge, MA: Belknap, Harvard University Press, 1991), 11–42. On the centrality of the "perversity thesis" in the welfare reform debate, past and present, see Margaret R. Somers and Fred Block, "From Poverty to Perversity: Ideas, Markets, and Institutions over 200 Years of Welfare Debate," *American Sociological Review* 70, no. 2 (April 2005): 260–87.

125. Sanford D. Schram, *Words of Welfare: The Poverty of Social Science and the Social Science of Poverty* (Minneapolis: University of Minnesota Press, 1995), 101; for a history of the concept of "dependency," see Nancy Fraser and Linda Gordon, "A Genealogy of Dependency: Tracing a Keyword of the U.S. Welfare State," *Signs* 19, no. 2 (Winter 1994): 309–36.

126. Arthur Delaney and Michael McAullif, "Paul Ryan Wants 'Welfare Reform Round 2'," *HuffPost*, March 20, 2012, https://www.huffingtonpost.com/2012/03/20/paul-ryan-welfare-reform_n_1368277.html.

127. See, for example, Sarah Ayres, "The Safety Net Is Good Economic Policy: What Rep. Paul Ryan Gets Wrong about the War on Poverty," March 31, 2014, https://cdn.americanprogress.org/wp-content/uploads/2014/03/RyanBudgetAyresStandard.pdf.

128. David Corn, "Secret Video: Romney Tells Millionaire Donors What He Really Things of Obama Voters," *Mother Jones*, September 17, 2012, http://www.motherjones.com/politics/2012/09/secret-video-romney-private-fundraiser; and Ben Craw and Zack Carter, "Paul Ryan: 60 Percent of Americans Are 'Takers,' Not 'Makers,'" *Huffington Post*, October 5, 2012, https://www.huffingtonpost.com/2012/10/05/paul-ryan-60-percent-of-a_n_1943073.html.

129. Hacker and Pierson, *American Amnesia*, 245–47; Skocpol and Williamson, *Tea Party*, 64–81; Nancy MacLean, *Democracy in Chains: The Deep History of the Radical Right's Stealth Plan for America* (New York: Viking, 2017), esp. 117–19, 211.

130. I am borrowing some wording here from MacLean, *Democracy in Chains*, 1–2.

131. Yascha Mounk, *The Age of Responsibility: Luck, Choice, and the Welfare State* (Cambridge, MA: Harvard University Press, 2017), 4. Much of what I have to say here is indebted to Mounk's engrossing book.

132. Ron Haskins, "The Sequence of Personal Responsibility," Brookings, July 31, 2009, https://www.brookings.edu/articles/the-sequence-of-personal-responsibility/.

133. Mounk, *Age of Responsibility*, 23–26, 29–37, 65, 172–73.

134. Mounk, *Age of Responsibility*, 5, 21–22, 178–79.

135. See O'Connor, *Poverty Knowledge*, 242–83.

136. O'Connor, *Poverty Knowledge*, 15.

137. See David Miller, "Media Power and Class Power: Overplaying Ideology," in *Socialist Register 2002: A World of Contradictions*, ed. Leo Panitch and Colin Leys (London: Merlin Press, 2001), 245–64; and Alfred Stepan and Juan J. Linz, "Comparative Perspectives on Inequality and the Quality of Democracy in the United States," *Perspectives on Politics* 9, no. 4 (December 2011): 841–56, esp. 849–50.

138. Cited in Spencer, "'Making the Invisible Visible,'" 24.

8. THE SOCIAL SYSTEM AND POVERTY

1. Glen C. Loury, "A Dynamic Theory of Racial Income Differences," in *Women, Minorities, and Employment Discrimination*, ed. Phyllis A. Wallace and Annette M. LaMond (Lexington, MA: Lexington Books, 1977), 176.

2. Steven N. Durlauf, "The Memberships Theory of Inequality: Ideas and Implications," in *Elites, Minorities, and Economic Growth*, ed. Elise S. Brezis and Peter Temin (Amsterdam, The Netherlands: Elsevier, 1999), 161–77; and Steven N. Durlauf, "The Memberships Theory of Poverty: The Role of Group Affiliations in Determining Socioeconomic Outcomes," in *Understanding Poverty*, ed. Sheldon H. Danziger and Robert H. Haveman (New York: Russell Sage and Cambridge, MA: Harvard University Press, 2001), 392–416.

3. Durlauf, "Memberships Theory of Poverty," 396.

4. Durlauf, "Memberships Theory of Poverty," 393–94; and Durlauf, "Memberships Theory of Inequality," 162–64.

5. Durlauf, "Memberships Theory of Inequality," 163.

6. See Tommie Shelby, *Dark Ghettos: Injustice, Dissent, and Reform* (Cambridge, MA: Belknap Press, 2016).

7. See Barbara F. Reskin, "The Proximate Causes of Employment Discrimination," *Contemporary Sociology* 29, no. 2 (March 2000): 319–28; and Peggy McIntosh, "White Privilege: Unpacking the Invisible Knapsack," in *Race, Class, and Gender in the United States*, 5th ed., ed. Paula S. Rothenberg (New York: Worth, 2001), 163–68.

8. For one important formulation of this argument, see William A. Darity Jr. et al., "Stratification Economics: A General Theory of Intergroup Inequality," in *The Hidden Rules of Race: Barriers to an Inclusive Economy*, ed. Andrea Flynn et al. (New York: Cambridge University Press, 2017), 35–51.

9. Kim A. Weeden, "Why Do Some Occupations Pay More Than Others? Social Closure and Earnings Inequality in the United States," *American Journal of Sociology* 108, no. 1 (July 2002): 55–101.

10. Charles Tilly, *Durable Inequality* (Berkeley: University of California Press, 1998).

11. Economic Innovation Group, "The 2017 Distressed Community Index," http://eig.org/wp-content/uploads/2017/09/2017-Distressed-Communities-Index.pdf.

12. Eduardo Porter, "Small Cities Are Wilting as Larger Ones Flourish," *New York Times*, October 11, 2017; and Ben Casselman, "Experts Foresee a U.S. Work Force Defined by Ever Widening Divides," *New York Times*, October 25, 2017.

13. Sean F. Reardon, Lindsay Fox, and Joseph Townsend, "Neighborhood Income Composition by Household Race and Income, 1990–2009," *Annals of the American Academy of Political and Social Science* 660 (July 2015): 78–97; Ann Owens, "Inequality in Children's Contexts: Income Segregation of Households With and Without Children," *American Sociological Review* 81, no. 3 (2016): 549–74; George Galster and Patrick Sharkey, "Spatial Foundations of Inequality: A Conceptual Model and Empirical Overview," *Journal of the Social Sciences*, 3, no. 2 (February 2017): 1–33; and Robert D. Putnam, *Our Kids: The American Dream in Crisis* (New York: PublicAffairs, 2015).

14. Douglas S. Massey and Jonathan Tannen, "Segregation, Race, and the Social Worlds of Rich and Poor," in *The Dynamics of Opportunity in America: Evidence and Perspectives*, ed. Irwin Kirsch and Henry Braun (New York: Springer, 2016), 13–33; and John R. Logan, "The Persistence of Segregation in the 21st Century Metropolis," *City & Community* 12, no. 2 (June 2013): 160–68.

15. Paul A. Jargowsky, *Poverty and Place: Ghettos, Barrios, and the American City* (New York: Russell Sage, 1997); and Douglas S. Massey and Nancy A. Denton, *American Apartheid: Segregation and the Making of the Underclass* (Cambridge, MA: Harvard University Press, 1993).

16. Daniel T. Lichter and Kai A. Schafft, "People and Places Left Behind: Rural Poverty in the New Century," in *The Oxford Handbook of the Social Science of Poverty*, ed. David Brady and Linda M. Burton (New York: Oxford University Press, 2016), 317–40; and Linda M. Burton et al., "Poverty," *Pathways: The Poverty and Inequality Report 2017* (Stanford Center on Poverty and Inequality), 9–12, http://inequality.stanford.edu/sites/default/files/Pathways_SOTU_2017_poverty.pdf.

17. Elizabeth Kneebone and Natalie Holmes, "U.S. Concentrated Poverty in the Wake of the Great Recession," Brookings Institution, March 31, 2016, https://www.brookings.edu/research/u-s-concentrated-poverty-in-the-wake-of-the-great-recession/.

18. Durlauf, "Memberships Theory of Inequality," 171.

19. Thomas M. Shapiro, *Toxic Inequality: How America's Wealth Gap Destroys Mobility, Deepens the Racial Divide, and Threatens Our Future* (New York: Basic Books, 2017), 57–58, 68–73.

20. Kneebone and Holmes, "U.S. Concentrated Poverty."

21. Eugenie L. Birch, Harriet B. Newburger, and Susan M. Wachter, Preface to *Neighborhood and Life Chances: How Place Matters in Modern America*, ed. Harriet B. Newburger, Eugenie L. Birch, and Susan M. Wachter (Philadelphia: University of Pennsylvania Press, 2011), xi.

22. Eddie S. Glaude Jr., *Democracy in Black: How Race Still Enslaves the American Soul* (New York: Crown, 2016), 23, 128–29.

23. See Patrick Sharkey, "Neighborhoods, Cities, and Economic Mobility," *Journal of the Social Sciences* 2, no. 2 (May 2016): 159–77; and Raj Chetty et al., "Where Is the Land of Opportunity? The Geography of Intergenerational Mobility in the United States," *Quarterly Journal of Economics* 129, no. 4 (November 2014): 1553–1623.

24. See Steven N. Durlauf, "A Theory of Persistent Income Inequality," *Journal of Economic Growth* 1 (1996): 75–93.

25. My discussion of neighborhood effects draws on several comprehensive overviews of the scholarly research. See Tama Leventhal, Véronique Dupéré, and Elizabeth A. Shuey, "Children in Neighborhoods," in *Handbook of Child Psychology and Developmental Science*, 7th ed., ed. Marc H. Bornstein, Tama Leventhal, and Richard M. Lerner (Hoboken, NJ: Wiley, 2015): 493–533; Mario Luis Small and Katherine Newman, "Urban Poverty after *The Truly Disadvantaged*: The Rediscovery of the Family, the Neighborhood, and Culture," *Annual Review of Sociology* 27 (2001): 23–45; Robert Sampson, Jeffrey D. Morenoff, and Thomas Gannon-Rowley, "Assessing 'Neighborhood Effects': Social Processes and New Directions in Research," *Annual Review of Sociology* 28 (2002): 443–78; Tama Leventhal and Jeanne Brooks-Gunn, "The Neighborhoods They Live In: The Effects of Neighborhood Residence on Child and Adolescent Outcomes," *Psychological Bulletin* 126, no. 2 (2000): 309–37; Anne R. Pebley and Narayan Sastry, "Neighborhoods, Poverty, and Children's Well-Being," in *Social Inequality*, ed. Kathryn M. Neckerman (New York: Russell Sage, 2004), 119–45; and Martha

A. Gephart, "Neighborhoods and Communities as Contexts for Development," in *Neighborhood Poverty*, vol. 1, *Contexts and Consequences for Children*, ed. Jeanne Brooks-Gunn, Greg J. Duncan, and J. Lawrence Aber (New York: Russell Sage, 1997), 1–43.

26. Gephart, "Neighborhoods and Communities," 26–28; Leventhal and Brooks-Gunn, "Neighborhoods They Live In," 315–21.

27. Patrick Sharkey, *Stuck in Place: Urban Neighborhoods and the End of Progress toward Racial Equality* (Chicago: University of Chicago Press, 2013); and Patrick Sharkey and Felix Elwert, "The Legacy of Disadvantage: Multigenerational Neighborhood Effects on Cognitive Ability," *American Journal of Sociology* 116, no.6 (May 2011): 1934–81.

28. For typologies identifying potential causal mechanisms responsible for neighborhood effects, see Sampson, Morenoff, and Gannon-Rowley, "Assessing 'Neighborhood Effects,'" 457–58; Small and Newman, "Urban Poverty," 32–35; Leventhal and Brooks-Gunn, "Neighborhoods They Live In," 322–28; and George C. Galster, "The Mechanism(s) of Neighbourhood Effects: Theory, Evidence, and Policy," in *Neighbourhood Effects Research: New Perspectives*, ed. Maarten van Dam et al. (The Netherlands: Springer, 2012), 23–56.

29. Poor neighborhoods are not all alike of course, and they also vary in quality over time; see Mario Luis Small, *Villa Victoria: The Transformation of Social Capital in a Boston Barrio* (Chicago: University of Chicago Press, 2004); and Mario L. Small, "No Two Ghettos Are Alike," *Chronicle Review* (March 21, 2014): B10–B12.

30. See Pebley and Sastry, "Neighborhoods, Poverty, and Children's Well-Being," 120; Sampson, Morenoff, and Gannon-Rowley, "Assessing 'Neighborhood Effects,'" 458; and Leventhal, Dupéré, and Shuey, "Children in Neighborhoods," 498, 506–8.

31. My terminology here borrows from Leventhal and Brooks-Gunn, "Neighborhoods They Live In," 322.

32. Robin L. Jarrett, "Bringing Families Back In: Neighborhood Effects on Child Development," in *Neighborhood Poverty*, vol. 2, *Policy Implications in Studying Neighborhoods*, ed. Jeanne Brooks-Gunn, Greg J. Duncan, and J. Lawrence Aber (New York: Russell Sage, 1997), 48–64.

33. William Julius Wilson, *The Truly Disadvantaged: The Inner City, the Underclass, and Public Policy* (Chicago: University of Chicago Press, 1987), 39; and William Julius Wilson, *When Work Disappears: The World of the New Urban Poor* (New York: Alfred A. Knopf, 1996), 19, 25–50.

34. Economic Innovation Group, "The 2016 Distressed Communities Index," http://eig.org/wp-content/uploads/2016/02/2016-Distressed-Communities-Index-Report.pdf.

35. For qualitative studies documenting labor market conditions and employment problems in poor communities, see Katherine Newman, *No Shame in My Game: The Working Poor in the Inner City* (New York: Alfred A. Knopf, 1999); and Daniel Dohan, *The Price of Poverty: Money, Work, and Culture in the Mexican American Barrio* (Berkeley: University of California Press, 2003), 37–98.

36. Dohan, *Price of Poverty*, 38.

37. Thomas P. Vartanian, "Adolescent Neighborhood Effects on Labor Market and Economic Outcomes," *Social Service Review* 73, no. 2 (June 1999): 142–67; Manuel Pastor Jr. and Ara Robinson Adams, "Keeping Down with the Joneses: Neighbors, Networks, and Wages," *Review of Regional Studies* 26, no. 2 (1996): 115–45; and Gary P. Green, Leann M. Tigges, and Irene Browne, "Social Resources, Job Search, and Poverty in Atlanta," *Research in Community Sociology* 5 (1995): 161–82.

38. Amy Widestrom, *Displacing Democracy: Economic Segregation in America* (Philadelphia: University of Pennsylvania Press, 2015), 23, 110–13, 140–46; and Matthew Desmond, *Evicted: Poverty and Profit in the American City* (New York: Crown, 2016), 180–82.

39. Small and Newman, "Urban Poverty," 33; and Putnam, *Our Kids*, 213–16.

40. See Robert J. Sampson, Jeffrey D. Morenoff, and Felton Earls, "Beyond Social Capital: Spatial Dynamics of Collective Efficacy for Children," *American Sociological Review* 64, no. 5 (October 1999): 633–60; and Robert J. Sampson, Stephen W. Raudenbush, and Felton Earls, "Neighborhoods and Violent Crime: A Multilevel Study of Collective Efficacy," *Science* 277 (August 15, 1999): 918–24.

41. Putnam, *Our Kids*, 218–21; Leventhal, Dupéré, and Shuey, "Children in Neighborhoods," 498–99, 508–510; and Robert J. Sampson, *Great American City: Chicago and the Enduring Neighborhood Effect* (Chicago: University of Chicago Press, 2012), 152–55, 367–72.

42. Sampson, *Great American City*, 250, 272.

43. Nancy Denton, "Great American Sociology," *City & Community* 12, no. 1 (March 2013): 6.

44. The key early work on social networks is Mark S. Granovetter, *Getting a Job: A Study of Contacts and Careers*, 2nd ed. (Chicago: University of Chicago Press, 1995); for an overview of the literature, see John Field, *Social Capital* (London: Routledge, 2003).

45. On the concept of "institutional agent" in network analysis, see Ricardo D. Stanton-Salazar and Sanford M. Dornbusch, "Social Capital and the Reproduction of Inequality: Information Networks among Mexican-Origin High School Students," *Sociology of Education* 68, no. 2 (April 1995): 116–35.

46. Alejandro Portes, "Social Capital: Its Origins and Applications in Modern Sociology," *Annual Review of Sociology* 24 (1998): 7; and James S. Coleman, "Social Capital in the Creation of Human Capital," *American Journal of Sociology* 94 (Supplement, 1988): S98.

47. Mark S. Granovetter, "A Theoretical Agenda for Economic Sociology," in *The New Economic Sociology: Developments in an Emerging Field*, ed. Mauro F. Guillen et al. (New York: Russell Sage, 2002), 37–38; and Mario Luis Small, *Unanticipated Gains: Origins of Network Inequality in Everyday Life* (Oxford: Oxford University Press, 2009).

48. For a recent overview of the literature, see Sandra Susan Smith, "Job-Finding Among the Poor: Do Social Ties Matter," in Brady and Burton, *The Oxford Handbook of the Social Science of Poverty*, 438–61.

49. On the importance of considering networks as a source of both information *and* influence, see Karen Campbell, Peter V. Marsden, and Jeanne S. Hurlbert, "Social Resources and Socioeconomic Status," *Social Networks* 8 (1986): 97–117.

50. Nan Lin, "Inequality in Social Capital," *Contemporary Sociology* 29, no. 6 (November 2000): 787, 793.

51. Leann M. Tigges, Irene Browne, and Gary P. Green, "Social Isolation of the Urban Poor: Race, Class, and Neighborhood Effects on Social Resources," *Sociological Quarterly* 39, no. 1 (1998): 53–77.

52. On the hard work required of single mothers to maintain reciprocity in their social networks, see Margaret K. Nelson, "Single Mothers and Social Support: The Commitment to, and Retreat from, Reciprocity," *Qualitative Sociology* 23, no. 3 (Fall 2000): 291–317; see also, with reference to the concept of "defensive individualism," Sandra Susan Smith, *Lone Pursuit: Distrust and Individualism among the Black Poor* (New York: Russell Sage, 2007), 22, 97–137.

53. Deborah E. Belle, "The Impact of Poverty on Social Networks and Supports," *Marriage and Family Review* 5, no. 4 (Winter 1982): 91, 94; and Julie E. Miller-Cribbs and Naomi B. Farber, "Kin Networks Among African Americans: Past and Present," *Social Work* 53, no. 1 (January, 2008): 48.

54. Wilson, *Truly Disadvantaged*, 60. For an alternative view, see Melvin L. Oliver, "The Urban Black Community as Network: Toward a Social Network Perspective," *Sociological Quarterly* 29, no. 4 (1988): 623–45.

55. On the social isolation thesis and the disadvantages that accrue to the poor from their lack of contacts with mainstream society, see Massey and Denton, *American Apartheid*, 160–62; Loïc J. D. Wacquant and William Julius Wilson, "The Cost of Racial and Class Exclusion in the Inner City," *Annals of the American Academy of Political and Social Science* 501 (January 1989): 8–25; Tigges, Browne, and Green, "Social Isolation of the Urban Poor," 53–77; and Bruce H. Rankin and James M. Quane, "Neighborhood Poverty and the Social Isolation of Inner-City African American Families," *Social Forces* 79, no. 1 (September 2000): 139–64.

56. William T. Dickens, "Rebuilding Urban Labor Markets: What Community Development Can Accomplish," in *Urban Problems and Community Development*, ed. Ronald F. Ferguson and William T. Dickens (Washington, DC: Brookings Institution Press, 1999), 406–8.

57. Karl Alexander, Doris Entwisle, and Linda Olson, *The Long Shadow: Family Background, Disadvantaged Urban Youth, and the Transition to Adulthood* (New York: Russell Sage, 2014), 161–69; and James R. Elliott, "Social Isolation and Labor Market Insulation: Network and Neighborhood Effects on Less-Educated Urban Workers," *Sociological Quarterly* 40, no. 2 (Winter 1999): 199–216.

58. Deirdre A. Royster, *Race and the Invisible Hand: How White Networks Exclude Black Men from Blue-Collar Jobs* (Berkeley: University of California Press, 2003).

59. Smith, *Lone Pursuit*; Smith, "Job Finding among the Poor," 450–52; and Sandra Susan Smith, "'Don't Put My Name on It': Social Capital Activation and Job-Finding Assistance among the Black Urban Poor," *American Journal of Sociology* 111, no. 1 (July 2005): 1–57.

60. Smith, "'Don't Put My Name on It,'" 27; see also Smith, *Lone Pursuit*, 56–96.

61. Mark S. Granovetter, "The Strength of Weak Ties," *American Journal of Sociology* 78, no. 6 (May 1973): 1360–80; and Mark S. Granovetter, "The Strength of Weak Ties: A Network Theory Revisited," *Sociological Theory* 1 (1983): 201–33.

62. Granovetter, "Network Theory Revisited," 209.

63. Campbell, Marsden, and Hurlbert, "Social Resources and Socioeconomic Status," 98.

64. Granovetter, "Network Theory Revisited," 212–13; Putnam, *Our Kids*, 208–209; but see Smith, "Job-Finding among the Poor," 442–44.

65. Matthew Desmond, "Disposable Ties and the Urban Poor," *American Journal of Sociology* 117, no. 5 (March 2012): 1328–29.

66. Patricia Fernandez Kelly, "Social and Cultural Capital in the Urban Ghetto: Implications for the Economic Sociology of Immigration," in *The Economic Sociology of Immigration: Essays on Networks, Ethnicity, and Entrepreneurship*, ed. Alejandro Portes (New York: Russell Sage, 1995), 220; on the importance of variety in social networks, see also Bonnie Erickson, "Social Networks: The Value of Variety," *Contexts* 2, no. 1 (Winter 2003): 25–31.

67. Campbell, Marsden, and Hurlbert, "Social Resources and Socioeconomic Status," 98–99.

68. Elliott, "Social Isolation and Labor Market Insulation"; Nan Lin, "Social Networks and Status Attainment," *Annual Review of Sociology* 25 (1999): 470–76; and Newman, *No Shame in My Game*, 77–85, 161–74.

69. Pierre Bourdieu, "The Forms of Capital," in *Handbook of Theory and Research for the Sociology of Education*, ed. John G. Richardson (New York: Greenwood Press, 1986), 249.

70. On the relationship between social capital and human capital, see Coleman, "Social Capital in the Creation of Human Capital," S109–S116; Stanton-Salazar and Dornbusch, "Social Capital and the Reproduction of Inequality," 116–35; and Field, *Social Capital*, 45–50.

71. Annette Lareau, *Unequal Childhoods: Class, Race, and Family Life* (Berkeley: University of California Press, 2003).

72. Silvia Domínguez and Celeste Watkins, "Creating Networks for Survival and Mobility: Social Capital among African-American and Latin-American Low-Income Mothers," *Social Problems* 50, no. 1 (February 2003): 111–35.

73. Domínguez and Watkins, "Creating Networks for Survival and Mobility," 125.

74. Julia R. Henly, "Informal Support Networks and the Maintenance of Low-Wage Jobs," in *Laboring Below the Line: The New Ethnography of Poverty, Low-Wage Work, and Survival in the Global Economy*, ed. Frank Munger (New York: Russell Sage, 2002), 179–203.

75. Xavier de Souza Briggs, "Brown Kids in White Suburbs: Housing Mobility and the Many Faces of Social Capital," *Housing Policy Debate* 9, no. 1 (1998): 177–221.

76. Domínguez and Watkins, "Creating Networks for Survival and Mobility," 124, 126–29.

77. Sharon Hicks-Bartlett, "Between a Rock and a Hard Place: The Labyrinth of Working and Parenting in a Poor Community," in *Coping with Poverty: The Social Contexts of Neighborhood, Work, and Family in the African-American Community*, ed. Sheldon H. Danziger and Ann Chih Lin (Ann Arbor: University of Michigan Press, 2000), 27–51.

78. On the "negative" effects of social capital, see Belle, "Impact of Poverty on Social Networks," 91–94; Portes, "Social Capital," 15–18; and Alejandro Portes and Julia Sensenbrenner, "Embeddedness and Immigration: Notes on the Social Determinants of Economic Action," *American Journal of Sociology* 98, no. 6 (May 1993): 1338–44.

79. Portes, "Social Capital," 14.

80. Lewis Coser, *Greedy Institutions: Patterns of Undivided Commitment* (New York: Free Press, 1974), 4, 6.

81. Domínguez and Watkins, "Creating Networks for Survival and Mobility"; Portes and Sensenbrenner, "Embeddedness and Immigration," 1338–40; Belle, "Impact of Poverty on Social Networks," 91–92; and Nelson, "Single Mothers and Social Support," 291–317.

82. Portes and Sensenbrenner, "Embeddedness and Immigration," 1340–44.

83. Newman, *No Shame in My Game*, 92–104.

84. Charles Kadushin, *Understanding Social Networks: Theories, Concepts, and Findings* (Oxford: Oxford University Press, 2012), 168, 172.

85. That gains for some often result in losses for others has led some observers to refer to the "negative," "other," or "dark" side of social resources. See Portes, "Social Capital," 15–16; Field, *Social Capital*, 71–90; and Roger Waldinger, "The 'Other Side' of Embeddedness: A Case-Study of the Interplay of Economy and Ethnicity," *Ethnic and Racial Studies* 18, no. 3 (July 1995): 555–80.

86. Steven N. Durlauf, "Associational Redistribution: A Defense," *Politics & Society* 24, no. 4 (December 1996): 391–410.

9. STRUCTURAL OBSTACLES AND THE PERSISTENCE OF POVERTY (I)

1. C. Wright Mills, *The Sociological Imagination* (Oxford: Oxford University Press, 1959), 8–9.

2. Jessica L. Semega, Kayla R. Fontenot, and Melissa A. Kollar, *Income and Poverty in the United States: 2016*, US Census Bureau, Current Population Reports, P60-259, September 2017, 12–13, table 3, https://www.census.gov/content/dam/Census/library/publications/2017/demo/P60-259.pdf.

3. Paul Jargowsky, "Architecture of Segregation: Civil Unrest, the Concentration of Poverty, and Public Policy," The Century Foundation, August 7, 2015, https://tcf.org/content/report/architecture-of-segregation/.

4. Ta-Nehisi Coates, *We Were Eight Years in Power: An American Tragedy* (New York: One World, 2017), 152.

5. See Ibram X. Kendi, *Stamped from the Beginning: The Definitive History of Racist Ideas in America* (New York: Nation Books, 2016).

6. Melvin L. Oliver and Thomas M. Shapiro, *Black Wealth/White Wealth: A New Perspective on Racial Inequality* (New York: Routledge, 1995), 51.

7. Ira Katznelson, *When Affirmative Action Was White: An Untold History of Racial Inequality in Twentieth-Century America* (New York: W. W. Norton, 2005); and Michael K. Brown et al., *Whitewashing Race: The Myth of a Color-Blind Society* (Berkeley: University of California Press, 2003), 26–33, 76–80.

8. Coates, *We Were Eight Years in Power*, 164–208; Thomas J. Sugrue, *The Origins of the Urban Crisis: Race and Inequality in Postwar Detroit* (Princeton, NJ: Princeton University Press, 1996); and Richard Rothstein, *The Color of Law: A Forgotten History of How Our Government Segregated America* (New York: Liveright, 2017).

9. Lincoln Quillian, "New Approaches to Understanding Racial Prejudice and Discrimination," *Annual Review of Sociology* 32 (2006): 299–328.

10. For a recent analysis, see Andrea Flynn et al., *The Hidden Rules of Race: Barriers to an Inclusive Economy* (New York: Cambridge University Press, 2017).

11. Corrado Giulietti, Mirco Tonin, and Michael Vlassopoulos, "Racial Discrimination in Local Public Services: A Field Experiment in the US," August 2017, forthcoming in the *Journal of the European Economic Association*, https://necpluribusimpar.net/wp-content/uploads/2017/10/Racial-Discrimination-in-Local-Public-Services-A-Field-Experiment-in-the-US.pdf.

12. Marianne Bertrand and Sendhil Mullainathan, "Are Emily and Greg More Employable Than Lakisha and Jamal? A Field Experiment on Labor Market Discrimination," *American Economic Review* 94, no. 4 (September 2004): 991–1013.

13. S. Michael Gaddis, "Discrimination in the Credential Society: An Audit Study of Race and College Selectivity in the Labor Market," *Social Forces* 93, no. 4 (June 2015): 1451–79.

14. For a comprehensive overview of the use of audit studies in testing for employment discrimination, see Devah Pager, "The Use of Field Experiments for Studies of Employment Discrimination: Contributions, Critiques, and Directions for the Future," *Annals of the American Academy of Political and Social Science* 609 (January 2007): 104–33. It is especially noteworthy that audit studies, which measure employer *behavior*, reveal more job discrimination than do survey research studies, which measure employer *attitudes*; see Devah Pager and Lincoln Quillian, "Walking the Talk? What Employers Say versus What They Do," *American Sociological Review* 70, no. 3 (June 2005): 355–80.

15. Devah Pager, Bruce Western, and Bart Bonikowski, "Discrimination in a Low-Wage Labor Market: A Field Experiment," *American Sociological Review* 74, no. 5 (October 2009): 777–99.

16. Devah Pager, "The Mark of a Criminal Record," *American Journal of Sociology* 108, no. 5 (March 2003): 937–75; and Devah Pager, *Marked: Race, Crime and Finding Work in an Era of Mass Incarceration* (Chicago: University of Chicago Press, 2007).

17. Bruce Western, *Punishment and Inequality in America* (New York: Russell Sage, 2006), 85–130.

18. Lincoln Quillian et al., "Meta-Analysis of Field Experiments Shows No Change in Racial Discrimination in Hiring over Time," *Proceedings of the National Academy of Sciences* 114, no. 41 (October 10, 2017): 10870–75.

19. See Valerie Wilson and William M. Rodgers III, "Black-White Wage Gaps Expand with Rising Inequality," Economic Policy Institute, September 19, 2016, http://www.epi.org/files/pdf/101972.pdf; and Kerwin Kofi Charles and Jonathan Guryan, "Prejudice and Wages: An Empirical Assessment of Becker's *The Economics of Discrimination*," *Journal of Political Economy* 116, no. 5 (October 2008): 773–809.

20. William Julius Wilson, *When Work Disappears: The World of the New Urban Poor* (New York: Alfred A. Knopf, 1996), 111–46.

21. Joleen Kirschenman and Kathryn M. Neckerman, "'We'd Love to Hire Them, But . . .': The Meaning of Race for Employers," in *The Urban Underclass*, ed. Christopher Jencks and Paul E. Peterson (Washington, DC: Brookings Institution, 1991), 213.

22. Johanna Shih, "'. . . Yeah, I Could Hire This One, But I Know It's Gonna Be a Problem': How Race, Nativity, and Gender Affect Employers' Perceptions of the Manageability of Job Seekers," *Ethnic and Racial Stu*dies 25, no. 1 (January 2002): 99–119; and Margaret M. Zamudio and Michael I. Lichter, "Bad Attitudes and Good Soldiers: Soft Skills as a Code for Tractability in the Hiring of Immigrant Latina/os Over Native Blacks in the Hotel Industry," *Social Problems* 55, no. 4 (November 2008): 573–589.

23. Philip Moss and Chris Tilly, "'Soft' Skills and Race: An Investigation of Black Men's Employment Problems," *Work and Occupations* 23, no. 3 (August 1996): 260–61.

24. Changhwan Kim and Christopher R. Tamborini, "The Continuing Significance of Race in the Occupational Attainment of Whites and Blacks: A Segmented Labor Market Analysis," *Sociological Inquiry* 76, no. 1 (February 2006): 23–51.

25. Wilson, *When Work Disappears*, 133–34; Kathryn M. Neckerman and Joleen Kirschenman, "Hiring Strategies, Racial Bias, and Inner-City Workers," *Social Problems* 38, no. 4 (November 1991): 437–41.

26. Alex Gold, Edward Rodrigue, and Richard V. Reeves, "Following the Success Sequence: Success Is More Likely If You're White," Brookings, August 6, 2015, https://www.brookings.edu/research/following-the-success-sequence-success-is-more-likely-if-youre-white; Peter Edelman, Harry J. Holzer, and Paul Offner, *Reconnecting Disadvantaged Young Men* (Washington, DC: Urban Institute Press, 2006), 11–36; and Thomas S. Moore, "The Locus of Racial Discrimination in the Labor Market," *American Journal of Sociology* 116, no. 3 (November 2010): 909–42.

27. Vincent J. Roscigno, Lisette M. Garcia, and Donna Bobbitt-Zeher, "Social Closure and Processes of Race/Sex Employment Discrimination," *Annals of the American Academy of Political and Social Science* 609 (January 2007): 28–34; and Vincent J. Roscigno, *The Face of Discrimination: How Race and Gender Impact Work and Home Lives* (Lanham, MD: Rowman & Littlefield, 2007).

28. Donald Tomaskovic-Devey, Melvin Thomas, and Kecia Johnson, "Race and the Accumulation of Human Capital across the Career: A Theoretical Model and Fixed-Effects Application," *American Journal of Sociology* 111, no. 1 (July 2005): 58–89.

29. Thomas M. Shapiro, *Toxic Inequality: How America's Wealth Gap Destroys Mobility, Deepens the Racial Divide, and Threatens Our Future* (New York: Basic Books, 2017), 123–46; and Kerwin Kofi Charles and Erik Hurst, "The Transition to Homeownership and the Black-White Wealth Gap," *Review of Economics and Statistics* 84, no. 2 (May 2002): 281–97.

30. Jeannine Bell, *Hate Thy Neighbor: Move-In Violence and the Persistence of Racial Segregation in American Housing* (New York: New York University Press, 2013); and Roscigno, *Face of Discrimination*, 162–67.

31. William Julius Wilson and Richard P. Taub, *There Goes the Neighborhood: Racial, Ethnic, and Class Tension in Four Chicago Neighborhoods and Their Meaning for America* (New York: Alfred A. Knopf, 2006), 20.

32. Judith N. DeSena, "Local Gatekeeping Practices and Residential Segregation," *Sociological Inquiry* 64, no. 3 (August 1994): 307–21.

33. Richard D. Kahlenberg, "The Walls We Don't Tear Down," *New York Times*, August 6, 2017; and Conor Dougherty, "When Cities Spurn Growth, Equality Suffers," *New York Times*, July 4, 2016.

34. Margery Austin Turner et al., "Housing Discrimination Against Racial and Ethnic Minorities 2012," US Department of Housing and Urban Development, June 2013, xiii, https://www.huduser.gov/portal/Publications/pdf/HUD-514_HDS2012.pdf; and Michael Ewens, Bryan Tomlin, and Liang Choon Wang, "Statistic Discrimination or Prejudice? A Large Sample Field Experiment," *Review of Economics and Statistics* 96, no. 1 (March 2014): 119–134.

35. Margery Austin Turner and Stephen L. Ross, "How Racial Discrimination Affects the Search for Housing," in *The Geography of Opportunity: Race and Housing Choice in Metropolitan America*, ed. Xavier de Souza Briggs (Washington, DC: Brookings Institution, 2005), 81–100; George Galster and Erin Godfrey, "By Words and Deeds: Racial Steering by Real Estate Agents in the U.S. in 2000," *Journal of the American Planning Association* 71, no. 3 (Summer 2005): 251–68; and Shanna L. Smith and Cathy Cloud, "Welcome to the Neighborhood? The Persistence of Discrimination and Segregation," in *The Integration Debate: Competing Futures for American Cities*, ed. Chester Hartman and Gregory D. Squires (New York: Routledge, 2010), 9–21.

36. Margery Austin Turner et al., *Other Things Being Equal: A Paired Testing Study of Mortgage Lending Institutions, Final Report*, US Department of Housing and Urban Development, Office of Fair Housing and Equal Opportunity, April 2002, https://www.urban.org/research/publication/all-other-things-being-equal/view/full_report.

37. Oliver and Shapiro, *Black Wealth/White Wealth*, 136–41; and Michael E. Hodge, Mark C. Dawkins, and Jack H. Reeves, "A Case Study of Mortgage Refinancing Discrimination: African American Intergenerational Wealth," *Sociological Inquiry* 77, no. 1 (February 2007): 23–43.

38. Rachel L. Swarns, "Long Banned, Mortgage Bias Is Back as Issue," *New York Times*, October 31, 2015.

39. William Apgar and Allegra Calder, "The Dual Mortgage Market: The Persistence of Discrimination in Mortgage Lending," in Briggs, *Geography of Opportunity*, 101–23; Richard Williams, Reynold Nesiba, and Eileen Diaz McConnell, "The Changing Face of Inequality in Home Mortgage Lending," *Social Problems* 52, no. 2 (May 2005): 181–208; and Gregory D. Squires and Charis E. Kubrin, *Privileged Places: Race, Residence, and the Structure of Opportunity* (Boulder, CO: Lynne Rienner, 2006), 55–93.

40. Cited in Zoe Greenberg, "Housing Rights Groups Brace for Rollbacks," *New York Times*, January 29, 2017.

41. Squires and Kubrin, *Privileged Places*, 4–17.

42. Thomas Shapiro, *The Hidden Cost of Being African American: How Wealth Perpetuates Inequality* (Oxford: Oxford University Press, 2004), 119–22; and Chenoa Flippen, "Unequal Returns to Housing Investments? A Study of Real Housing Appreciation among Black, White, and Hispanic Households," *Social Forces* 82, no. 4 (June 2004): 1523–51.

43. Jesse Bricker et al., "Changes in U.S. Family Finances From 2013 to 2016: Evidence from the Survey of Consumer Finances," *Federal Reserve Bulletin* 103, no. 3 (September 2017): 13, https://www.federalreserve.gov/publications/files/scf17.pdf; see also Thomas Shapiro, "Wealth," *Pathways: The Poverty and Inequality Report 2017* (Stanford Center on Poverty and Inequality), 36–38, http://inequality.stanford.edu/sites/default/files/Pathways_SOTU_2017_wealth.pdf.

44. Tommie Shelby, *Dark Ghettos: Injustice, Dissent, and Reform* (Cambridge, MA: Belknap, 2016), esp. 19–20.

45. Douglas S. Massey and Jonathan Tannen, "Segregation, Race, and the Social Worlds of Rich and Poor," in *The Dynamics of Opportunity in America: Evidence and Perspectives*, ed. Irwin Kirsch and Henry Braun (New York: Springer, 2016), 13–33; and Sean F. Reardon and Kendra Bischoff, "The Continuing Increase in Income Segregation, 2007–2012," Stanford Center for Education Policy Analysis, March 2016, https://cepa.stanford.edu/sites/default/files/the%20continuing%20increase%20in%20income%20segregation%20march2016.pdf.

46. John R. Logan, "The Persistence of Segregation in the 21st Century Metropolis," *City & Community* 12, no. 2 (June 2013): 160–168.

47. Paul Jargowsky, "Architecture of Segregation"; Elizabeth Kneebone and Natalie Holmes, "U.S. Concentrated Poverty in the Wake of the Great Recession," Brookings Institution, March 31, 2016, https://www.brookings.edu/research/u-s-concentrated-poverty-in-the-wake-of-the-great-recession/.

48. Shelby, *Dark Ghettos*, 278.

49. Maria Krysan, Kyle Crowder, and Michael D. M. Bader, "Pathways to Residential Segregation," in *Choosing Homes, Choosing Schools*, ed. Annette Lareau and Kimberly A. Goyette (New York: Russell Sage, 2014), 27–63; and Camille Zubrinsky Charles, "Can We Live Together? Racial Preferences and Neighborhood Outcomes," in Briggs, *The Geography of Opportunity*, 45–80.

50. On white flight and white avoidance of racially mixed neighborhoods, see Lincoln Quillian, "Why Is Black-White Residential Segregation So Persistent? Evidence on Three Theories from Migration Data," *Social Science Research* 31, no. 2 (June 2002): 197–229; and Maria Krysan, "Whites Who Say They'd Flee: Who Are They, and Why Would They Leave," *Demography* 39, no. 4 (November 2002): 675–96.

51. Bell, *Hate Thy Neighbor*, 53–85; and Sheryll Cashin, *The Failures of Integration: How Race and Class Are Undermining the American Dream* (New York: PublicAffairs, 2004), 17–28.

52. Camille Zubrinsky Charles, "The Dynamics of Residential Segregation," *Annual Review of Sociology* 29 (2003): 191.

53. John Eligon and Robert Gebeloff, "Segregation, the Neighbor That Won't Leave," *New York Times*, August 21, 2016; and David Leonhardt, "Middle-Class Blacks in Poor Neighborhoods," *New York Times*, June 25, 2015.

54. Richard Rothstein, "The Making of Ferguson: Public Policies at the Root of Its Troubles," Economic Policy Institute, October 15, 2014, http://www.epi.org/files/2014/making-of-ferguson-final.pdf.

55. Rothstein, *Color of Law*.

56. Emmanuel Felton, "The Succession Movement in Education," *The Nation*, September 25/October 2, 2017, 13–24; see also Nikole Hannah-Jones, "Dividing Lines," *New York Times Magazine*, September 10, 2017, 40–49, 71–73.

57. Gary Orfield et al., "Brown at 62: School Segregation by Race, Poverty and State," Civil Rights Project, May 16, 2016, 3, https://www.civilrightsproject.ucla.edu/research/k-12-education/integration-and-diversity/brown-at-62-school-segregation-by-race-poverty-and-state; and US Government Accountability Office, "K–2 Education: Better Use of Information Could Help Agencies Identify Disparities and Address Racial Discrimination," April 2016, 6, 10, http://www.gao.gov/assets/680/676745.pdf.

58. Meredith Phillips and Tiffani Chin, "School Inequality: What Do We Know?," in *Social Inequality*, ed. Kathryn M. Neckerman (New York: Russell Sage, 2004), 467–519.

59. Cashin, *Failures of Integration*, 206.

60. George Galster, Ronald Mincy, and Mitch Tobin, "The Disparate Racial Neighborhood Impacts of Metropolitan Economic Restructuring," in *Race, Poverty, and Domestic Policy*, ed. C. Michael Henry (New Haven, CT: Yale University Press, 2004), 188–218.

61. Elizabeth Anderson, *The Imperative of Integration* (Princeton, NJ: Princeton University Press, 2010), 27–28; Laurent Gobillon, Harris Selod, and Yves Zenou, "The Mechanisms of Spatial Mismatch," *Urban Studies* 44, no. 12 (November 2007): 2401–27; and Roberto M. Fernandez and Celina Su, "Space in the Study of Labor Markets," *Annual Review of Sociology* 30 (2004): 545–69.

62. Jomills Henry Braddock II and James M. McPartland, "How Minorities Continue to Be Excluded from Equal Employment Opportunities: Research on Labor Market and Institutional Barriers," *Journal of Social Issues* 43, no. 1 (Spring 1987): 5–39.

63. Anderson, *Imperative of Integration*, 33–34; William Julius Wilson, *The Truly Disadvantaged: The Inner City, the Underclass, and Public Policy* (Chicago: University of Chicago Press, 1987), 60; and Katherine S. Newman, *No Shame in My Game: The Working Poor in the Inner City* (New York: Alfred A. Knopf, 1999), 77–84.

64. Chris Tilly et al., "Space as a Signal: How Employees Perceive Neighborhoods in Four Metropolitan Labor Markets," in *Urban Inequality: Evidence from Four Cities*, ed. Alice O'Connor, Chris Tilly, and Lawrence D. Bobo (New York: Russell Sage, 2001), 304–38.

65. Elijah Anderson, "The Iconic Ghetto," *American Academy of Political and Social Science* 642 (July 2012): 8–24.

66. Shapiro, *Hidden Cost of Being African American*, 119–22; Flippen, "Unequal Returns to Housing Investments?," 523–51.

67. Shapiro, *Hidden Cost of Being African American*, 47–48; Flynn et al., *Hidden Rules of Race*, 15–34.

68. Bricker et al., "Changes in U.S. Family Finances from 2013 to 2016," 13; Shapiro, "Wealth," 36–38.

69. Lawrence Mishel et al., *The State of Working America*, 12th ed. (Ithaca, NY: Cornell University Press, 2012), 68, 385.

70. Shapiro, *Hidden Cost of Being African American*, 36–41; Edward N. Wolff, *A Century of Wealth in America* (Cambridge, MA: Belknap Press of Harvard University, 2017), 529–31; and Lori Latrice Martin, *Black Asset Poverty and the Enduring Racial Divide* (Boulder, CO: First Forum Press, 2013).

71. Anderson, *Imperative of Integration*, 89–111; Douglas S. Massey and Nancy A. Denton, *American Apartheid: Segregation and the Making of the Underclass* (Cambridge, MA: Harvard University Press, 1993), 153–60; and Amy Widestrom, *Displacing Democracy: Economic Segregation in America* (Philadelphia: University of Pennsylvania Press, 2015).

72. Mireya Navarro, "In New York, Having a Job, or 2, Doesn't Mean Having a Home," *New York Times*, September 18, 2013.

73. See Barbara Ehrenreich, *Nickel and Dimed: On (Not) Getting By in America* (New York: Metropolitan Books, 2001), 12, 25–27, 138–41, 170–75, 200–201.

74. Sabrina Tavernise, "A Pipe to the Woods," *New York Times*, September 27, 2016.

75. Kathryn J. Edin and H. Luke Shaefer, *$2.00 A Day: Living on Almost Nothing in America* (Boston: Houghton Mifflin Harcourt, 2015), 72–74.

76. Shaila Dewan, "Evictions Soar in Hot Market; Renters Suffer," *New York Times*, August 29, 2014; see also Matthew Desmond, *Evicted: Poverty and Profit in the American City* (New York: Crown, 2016), 295–99.

77. Meghan Henry et al., "The 2016 Annual Homeless Assessment Report (AHAR) to Congress," US Department of Housing and Urban Development, November 2016, 1, 8–9, https://www.va.gov/homeless/docs/2016-AHAR-Part-1.pdf.

78. Desmond, *Evicted*, 302.

79. Michael E. Stone, "Housing Affordability: One-Third of a Nation Shelter-Poor," in *A Right to Housing: Foundations for a New Social Agenda*, ed. Rachel G. Bratt, Michael E. Stone, and Chester Hartman (Philadelphia: Temple University Press, 2006), 44, 47–57.

80. Andrew Aurand et al., "The Gap: A Shortage of Affordable Homes," National Low Income Housing Coalition, March 2017, 7, http://nlihc.org/sites/default/files/Gap-Report_2017.pdf.

81. Diana Hernández, "Poor Families, Housing, and Health," *Focus* 33, no. 1 (Fall/Winter 2016–2017): 20–21.

82. Desmond, *Evicted*, 300; Rachel G. Bratt, Michael E. Stone, and Chester Hartman, "Why a Right to Housing Is Needed and Makes Sense: Editors' Introduction," in Bratt, Stone, and Hartman, *A Right to Housing*, 1–19.

83. PEW Charitable Trusts, *Household Expenditures and Income* (March 2016, 2–5), http://www.pewtrusts.org/~/media/assets/2016/03/household_expenditures_and_income.pdf.

84. Joint Center for Housing, "The State of the Nation's Housing 2017," Harvard University, 2017, 5, 40, table A-2, http://www.jchs.harvard.edu/sites/jchs.harvard.edu/files/harvard_jchs_state_of_the_nations_housing_2017.pdf.

85. Dionne Searcey, "Home Pricey Home: In a Tepid Market, Builders Cater to the Desires of the Well-Off," *New York Times*, February 25, 2014; and Dionne Searcey, "The Landlord Blues: Homeownership Remains Out of Reach for Many Americans," *New York Times*, June 24, 2015.

86. Joint Center for Housing, "The State of the Nation's Housing 2017," 19, 8; and Richard Fry and Anna Brown, *In a Recovering Market, Homeownership Rates Are Down Sharply for Blacks, Young Adults* (Washington, DC: Pew Research Center, December 15, 2016), http://www.pewsocialtrends.org/2016/12/15/in-a-recovering-market-homeownership-rates-are-down-sharply-for-blacks-young-adults/.

87. Cited in Shaila Dewan, "In Many Cities, Rent Is Rising Out of Reach of Middle Class," *New York Times*, April 15, 2014.

88. Joint Center for Housing, "The State of the Nation's Housing 2017," 31–32; see also Sewin Chan and Gita Khun Jush, "2017 National Rental Housing Landscape: Renting in the Nation's Largest Metros," NYU Furman Center, 2017, http://furmancenter.org/files/NYUFurmanCenter_2017_National_Rental_Housing_Landscape_04OCT2017.pdf.

89. Barry L. Steffen et al., *Worst Case Housing Needs 2015, Report to Congress* (Washington, DC: US Department of Housing and Urban Development, 2015), vii, 1–9, https://www.huduser.gov/portal//Publications/pdf/WorstCaseNeeds_2015.pdf.

90. Andrew Aurand et al., "Out of Reach 2017: The High Cost of Housing," National Low Income Housing Coalition, 2017, 1–7, http://nlihc.org/sites/default/files/oor/OOR_2017.pdf.

91. Desmond, *Evicted*, 4–5, 69, 98, 129, 227, 252, 299, 305–8, 330–31; see also Dewan, "Evictions Soar in Hot Market."

92. Gretchen Purser, "The Circle of Dispossession: Evicting the Urban Poor in Baltimore," *Critical Sociology* 42, no. 3 (2016): 394.

93. Rana Foroohar, *Makers and Takers: The Rise of Finance and the Fall of American Business* (New York: Crown, 2016), 210–36; and Michael Greenberg, "Tenants Under Siege: Inside New York City's Housing Crisis," *New York Review of Books*, August 17, 2017, 75–81.

94. Aurand et al., "Out of Reach 2017," 2, 5.

95. Desmond, *Evicted*, 282–83.

96. Dennis Ventry, cited in James Surowiecki, "The Mortgage Mistake," *New Yorker*, January 12, 2015, 24.

97. Will Fischer and Barbara Sard, "Chart Book: Federal Housing Spending Is Poorly Matched to Need," Center on Budget and Policy Priorities, March 8, 2017, 1–11, https://www.cbpp.org/sites/default/files/atoms/files/12-18-13hous.pdf; see also Matthew Desmond, "How Homeownership Became the Engine of Inequality," *New York Times Magazine*, May 14, 2017, 50; and Shapiro, *Toxic Inequality*, 162–66.

98. On the public housing program in the United States, see Maggie McCarty, "Introduction to Public Housing," Congressional Research Service, January 3, 2014, https://fas.org/sgp/crs/misc/R41654.pdf.

99. Yamiche Alcindor, "Housing Secretary, on a Tour, Says Compassion Is Not About Comfort," *New York Times*, May 4, 2017; and Sarah Lazare, "Trump's Plan to Gut HUD Threatens the Very Survival of America's Poor," Alternet, March 10, 2017, http://www.alternet.org/economy/trumps-plan-gut-hud-threatens-very-survival-working-poor.

100. Peter Marcuse and W. Dennis Keating, "The Permanent Housing Crisis: The Failures of Conservatism and the Limitations of Liberalism," in Bratt, Stone, and Hartman, *A Right to Housing*, 139–62.

101. Valerie E. Lee and David T. Burkam, *Inequality at the Starting Gate: Social Background Differences in Achievement as Children Begin School* (Washington, DC: Economic Policy Institute, 2002); and Timothy M. Smeeding, "Gates, Gaps, and Intergenerational Mobility: The Importance of an Even Start, " in *The Dynamics of Opportunity in America: Evidence and Perspectives*, ed. Irwin Kirsch and Henry Braun (New York: Springer, 2016), 255–295.

102. Gary W. Evans, Jeanne Brooks-Gunn, and Pamela Kato Klebanov, "Stressing Out the Poor: Chronic Physiological Stress and the Income-Achievement Gap," *Pathways* (Winter 2011): 16–21; and Greg J. Duncan and Katherine Magnuson, "The Long Reach of Early Childhood Poverty," *Pathways* (Winter 2011): 22–27.

103. Suzanne Bianchi et al., "Inequality in Parental Investment in Child-Rearing: Expenditures, Time, and Health," in Neckerman, *Social Inequality*, 189–219; Sabino Kornrich and Frank Furstenberg, "Investing in Children: Changes in Parental Spending on Children, 1972–2007," *Demography* 50, no. 1 (February 2013): 1–23; and Bruce Bradbury et al., *Too Many Children Left Behind: The U.S. Achievement Gap in Comparative Perspective* (New York: Russell Sage, 2015), 4–5, 19, 102–5.

104. Smeeding, "Gates, Gaps, and Intergenerational Mobility," 268; and Meredith Phillips, "Parenting, Time Use, and Disparities in Academic Outcomes," in *Whither Opportunity? Rising Inequality, Schools, and Children's Life Chances*, ed. Greg J. Duncan and Richard J. Murname (New York: Russell Sage, 2011), 208–28.

105. Marcia K. Meyers et al., "Inequality in Early Childhood Education and Care: What Do We Know?," in Neckerman, *Social Inequality*, 223–69.

106. Karl Alexander, Doris Entwisle, and Linda Olson, *The Long Shadow: Family Background, Disadvantaged Urban Youth, and the Transition to Adulthood* (New York: Russell Sage, 2014), 1, 49.

107. Bruce Baker et al., "Is School Funding Fair? A National Report Card," 6th ed., Education Law Center, January 2017, http://www.edlawcenter.org/assets/files/pdfs/publications/National_Report_Card_2017.pdf.

108. Executive Office of the President of the United States, Office of Management and Budget, "Major Savings and Reforms Budget of the U.S. Government Fiscal Year 2018," 2017, 17–18, https://www.whitehouse.gov/sites/whitehouse.gov/files/omb/budget/fy2018/msar.pdf; Catherine Brown and Meg Benner, "The Stakes Are Too High to Ignore the Trump-DeVos Agenda," Center for American Progress, September 5, 2017, https://cdn.americanprogress.org/content/uploads/2017/09/01072758/SEAFederalEducation-brief1.pdf; and Diane Ravitch, "When Public Goes Private as Trump Wants: What Happens?," *New York Review of Books*, December 8, 2016, 58–61.

109. Robert D. Putnam, *Our Kids: The American Dream in Crisis* (New York: Simon and Schuster, 2015), 147, 167–68, 174–83; and Catherine Brown, Scott Sargrad, and Meg Benner, "Hidden Money: The Outsized Role of Parent Contributions in School Finance," Center for American Progress, April 8, 2017, https://www.americanprogress.org/issues/education/reports/2017/04/08/428484/hidden-money/.

110. Bradbury et al., *Too Many Children Left Behind*, 110; and Anna K. Chmielewski and Sean F. Reardon, "Education," *Pathways: The Poverty and Inequality Report 2016* (Stanford Center on Poverty and Inequality), 45–50, http://inequality.stanford.edu/sites/default/files/Pathways-SOTU-2016-Education-3.pdf.

111. See Peter Schrag, *Final Test: The Battle for Adequacy in America's Schools* (New York: New Press, 2005), 79.

112. Meredith Phillips and Tiffani Chin, "School Inequality: What Do We Know?," in Neckerman, *Social Inequality*, 510–11; and Cecilia Elena Rouse and Lisa Barrow, "U.S. Elementary and Secondary Schools: Equalizing Opportunity or Replicating the Status Quo?," *The Future of Children* 16, no. 2 (Fall 2006): 116.

113. Gary Orfield et al., "Brown at 62"; US Government Accountability Office, "K–2 Education"; and Gary Orfield, Genevieve Siegel-Hawley, and John Kucsera, "Sorting Out Deepening Confusion on Segregation Trends," Civil Rights Project, March 2014, https://www.

civilrightsproject.ucla.edu/research/k-12-education/integration-and-diversity/sorting-out-deep ening-confusion-on-segregation-trends/Segregation-Trends-Dispute-CRP-Researchers.pdf.

114. Ulrich Boser and Perpetual Baffour, "Isolated and Segregated: A New Look at the Income Divide in Our Nation's Schooling System," Center for American Progress, May 2017, 1, 4, https://cdn.americanprogress.org/content/uploads/2017/05/30124743/SESintegration-report2.pdf.

115. See Putnam, *Our Kids*, 160–73.

116. Sean F. Reardon, "School Segregation and Racial Academic Achievement Gaps," *Journal of the Social Sciences* 2, no. 5 (September 2016): 34–51.

117. The Pell Institute, "Indicators of Higher Education Equity in the United States: 2016 Historical Trend Report," 2016, 18–20, 58–60, http://files.eric.ed.gov/fulltext/ED569199.pdf; and Christopher J. Nelum and Terry W. Hartle, "Where Have All the Low-Income Students Gone?," American Council on Education, December 11, 2015, http://www.acenet.edu/the-presidency/columns-and-features/Pages/Federal-Watch-Where-Have-All-the-Low-Income-Stu dents-Gone.aspx.

118. Gene Nichol, "Educating for Privilege," *Nation*, October 13, 2003, 22.

119. Jeremy Ashkenas, Haeyoun Park, and Adam Pearce, "Affirmative Action Yields Little Progress on Campus for Blacks and Hispanics," *New York Times*, August 25, 2017.

120. Raj Chetty et al., "Minority Report Cards: The Role of Colleges in Intergenerational Mobility," January 2017, 1–2, http://www.equality-of-opportunity.org/assets/documents/coll_mrc_paper.pdf; see also Dimitrios Halikias and Richard V. Reeves, "Ladders, Labs, or Laggards? Which Public Universities Contribute Most," Brookings, July 11, 2017, https://www.brookings.edu/research/ladders-labs-or-laggards-which-public-universities-contribute-most/; and Caroline Hoxby and Christopher Avery, "The Missing 'One-Offs': The Hidden Supply of High-Achieving Low-Income Students," *Brookings Papers on Economic Activity* (Spring 2013): 1–50.

121. Putnam, *Our Kids*, 190; see also Susan Dynarski, "For Poor, Getting to College Is Only Half the Battle," *New York Times*, June 2, 2015.

122. Robert H. Haveman and Timothy M. Smeeding, "The Role of Higher Education in Social Mobility," *The Future of Children* 16, no. 2 (Fall 2006): 126–28; and Daniel Golden, *The Price of Admission: How America's Ruling Class Buys Its Way into Elite Colleges—And Who Gets Left Outside* (New York: Crown, 2006).

123. See Peter Cappelli, *Will College Pay Off? A Guide to the Most Important Financial Decision You'll Ever Make* (New York: PublicAffairs, 2015), 115–44; and Robert Hiltonsmith and Tamara Draut, *The Great Cost Shift Continues: State Higher Education Funding After the Recession* (New York: Demos, 2014), http://www.demos.org/sites/default/files/publications/TheGreatCostShiftBrief2014.pdf.

124. Suzanne Mettler, "College: The Great Unleveler," *New York Times*, March 2, 2014.

125. Chetty et al., "Minority Report Cards," 1–2.

126. The Pell Institute, "Indicators of Higher Education Equity," 41–44.

127. Lawrence E. Gladieux, "Low-Income Students and the Affordability of Higher Education," in *America's Untapped Resource: Low-Income Students in Higher Education*, ed. Richard D. Kahlenberg (New York: Century Foundation Press, 2004), 28–31.

128. Stephanie Saul, "Colleges Chase Out-of-State Students, and Cash," *New York Times*, July 8, 2016; Michelle Goldberg, "The Gentrification of Higher Ed," *The Nation*, June 8, 2015, 22–27; and Jaquette Ozan, Bradley R. Curs, and Julie R. Posselt, "Tuition Rich, Mission Poor: Nonresident Enrollment Growth and the Socioeconomic and Racial Composition of Public Research Universities," *Journal of Higher Education* 87, no. 5 (September/October 2016): 635–673.

129. Cappelli, *Will College Pay Off?*, 128–29; and Stephen Burd, "Undermining Pell: How Colleges Compete for Wealthy Students and Leave the Low-Income Behind," New American Foundation, May 2013, https://static.newamerica.org/attachments/2320-undermining-pell-2/Merit_Aid%20Final.b3b89c275d2249eeb19cb53d3fc049b6.pdf.

130. Donald Heller, cited in Robert Tomsho, "As Tuition Soars, Federal Aid to College Students Falls," *Wall Street Journal*, October 25, 2006.

131. Sean F. Reardon and Erin M. Fahle, "Education," *Pathways: The Poverty and Inequality Report 2017* (Stanford Center on Poverty and Inequality), 20–23, https://inequality.stanford.edu/sites/default/files/Pathways_SOTU_2017_education.pdf.

132. Joseph Berger, "4 Hour Trek across New York for 4 Hours of Work, and $28," *New York Times*, May 6, 2004; David Leonhardt, "Geography Seen as Barrier to Climbing Class Ladder," *New York Times*, July 22, 2013; Katie Rose Quandt, "No One Should Have to Walk 21 Miles to Get to Work," Moyers and Company, February 5, 2015, http://billmoyers.com/2015/02/05/public-transportation/; and Jim Dwyer, "Pushed to Fringes, Needy New Yorkers Face a Long Slog to Work," *New York Times*, November 29, 2017.

133. Mikayla Bouchard, "Transportation Emerges as Key to Escaping Poverty," *New York Times*, May 7, 2015; and Elizabeth Roberto, "Commuting to Opportunity: The Working Poor and Commuting in the United States," Brookings, February 2008, https://www.brookings.edu/wp-content/uploads/2016/06/0314_transportation_puentes.pdf.

134. Charles Craypo and David Cormier, "Job Restructuring as a Determinant of Wage Inequality and Working Poor Households," *Journal of Economic Issues* 34, no. 1 (March 2000): 36.

135. Alan Berube and Steven Raphael, "Access to Cars in New Orleans," Brookings, January 2005, table 3, https://www.researchgate.net/publication/228514891_Access_to_cars_in_New_Orleans.

136. Charles L. Baum, "The Effects of Vehicle Ownership on Employment," *Journal of Urban Economics* 66 (2009): 151–63.

137. Karen Seccombe, Delores James, and Kimberly Battle Walters, "'They Think You Ain't Much of Nothing': The Social Construction of the Welfare Mother," *Journal of Marriage and the Family* 60, no. 4 (November 1998): 858.

138. Robin Pogrebin, "Full Tanks and Empty Wallets Put Squeeze on Working Class," *New York Times*, May 13, 2006.

139. Robert D. Bullard, Introduction to *Highway Robbery: Transportation Racism and New Routes to Equity*, ed. Robert D. Bullard, Glenn S. Johnson, and Angel O. Torres (Cambridge, MA: South End Press, 2004), 3–4.

140. David R. Jones and Nancy Rankin, "Riding Toward Equality: The Fight Against Poverty Includes Busses and Subways," *The Nation*, January 30, 2017, 4; and "Help for Rider Who Can't Afford the Ride," unsigned editorial, *New York Times*, June 6, 2017.

141. Adie Tomer et al., "Missed Opportunity: Transit and Jobs in Metropolitan America," Brookings, May 12, 2011, https://www.brookings.edu/research/missed-opportunity-transit-and-jobs-in-metropolitan-america/.

142. Elizabeth Kneebone and Natalie Holmes, "The Growing Distance Between People and Jobs in Metropolitan America," Brookings, March 2015, https://www.brookings.edu/wp-content/uploads/2016/07/Srvy_JobsProximity.pdf.

143. David C. Phillips, "Do Low-Wage Employers Discriminate Against Applicants with Long Commutes? Evidence from a Correspondence Experiment," August 2015, https://economics.nd.edu/assets/187149/paper_address_experiment_working_paper_8_12_15.pdf.

144. Philip Moss and Chris Tilly, *Stories Employers Tell: Race, Skill, and Hiring in America* (New York: Russell Sage, 2001), 195–96.

145. Mark Garrett and Brian Taylor, "Reconsidering Social Equity in Public Transit," *Berkeley Planning Journal* 13 (1999): 9–10.

146. Harry J. Holzer, Keith R. Ihlanfeldt, and David L. Sjoquist, "Work, Search, and Travel among White and Black Youth," *Journal of Urban Economics* 35, no. 3 (May 1994): 320–45.

147. Brian D. Taylor and Paul M. Ong, "Spatial Mismatch or Automobile Mismatch? An Examination of Race, Residence, and Commuting in U.S. Metropolitan Areas," *Urban Studies* 32, no. 9 (1995): 1453–73.

148. Berger, "4 Hour Trek across New York."

149. Harriet B. Presser, *Working in a 24/7 Economy: Challenges for American Families* (New York: Russell Sage, 2003).

150. On the unique transportation needs of parents, and low-income women in particular, see Evelyn Blumenberg, "En-gendering Effective Planning," *Journal of the American Planning Association* 70, no. 3 (Summer 2004): 269–81; and Evelyn Blumenberg, "Moving Welfare

Participants to Work: Women, Transportation, and Welfare Reform," *Affilia* 15, no. 2 (Summer 2000): 259–76.

151. Cited in Corey M. Abramson, *The End Game: How Inequality Shapes Our Final Years* (Cambridge, MA: Harvard University Press, 2015), 47.

152. Cynthia Needles Fletcher et al., "Small Towns and Welfare Reform," *Poverty Research News* 4, no. 5 (September–October 2000); and April Kaplan, "Transportation and Welfare Reform," *Welfare Information Network: Issue Notes* 1, no. 4 (May 1997): 1.

153. Campbell Robertson, "For Alabama's Poor, the Budget Cuts Trickle Down," *New York Times*, October 10, 2015.

154. Somini Sengupta, "Living on Welfare: A Clock Is Ticking," *New York Times*, April 29, 2001.

155. Erik Eckholm, "In Rural Oregon, These Are the Times That Try Working People's Hopes," *New York Times*, August 20, 2006.

156. Erin Currier et al., *Household Expenditures and Income: Balancing Family Finances in Today's Economy* (Washington, DC: Pew Charitable Trusts, 2016), 8, chart 7, http://www.pewtrusts.org/~/media/assets/2016/03/household_expenditures_and_income.pdf.

157. Kaplan, "Transportation and Welfare Reform"; Rich Stolz, "Race, Poverty, and Transportation," *Poverty and Race* 9, no. 2 (March–April 2000): 1–2, 8–10.

158. Garrett and Taylor, "Reconsidering Social Equity."

159. On the "bus versus rail" battle in Los Angeles, see Eric Mann, "Los Angeles Bus Riders Derail the MTA," in Bullard, Johnson, and Torres, *Highway Robbery*, 33–47.

160. Garrett and Taylor, "Reconsidering Social Equity," 7, 23.

161. Garrett and Taylor, "Reconsidering Social Equity," 23.

10. STRUCTURAL OBSTACLES AND THE PERSISTENCE OF POVERTY (II)

1. Sarah Jane Glynn, "Breadwinning Mothers Are Increasingly the U.S. Norm," Center for American Progress, December 19, 2016, https://www.americanprogress.org/issues/women/reports/2016/12/19/295203/breadwinning-mothers-are-increasingly-the-u-s-norm/.

2. Jessica L. Semega, Kayla R. Fontenot, and Melissa A. Kollar, *Income and Poverty in the United States: 2016*, US Census Bureau, Current Population Reports, P60-259, September 2017, 15, figure 6, https://www.census.gov/content/dam/Census/library/publications/2017/demo/P60-259.pdf.

3. Semega, Fontenot, and Kollar, *Income and Poverty in the United States: 2016*, 41, table A-4; and Ariane Hegewisch and Emma Williams-Baron, "The Gender Wage Gap: 2016: Earnings Differences by Gender, Race, and Ethnicity," Institute for Women's Policy Research, September 2017, 2, https://iwpr.org/wp-content/uploads/2017/09/C459_9.11.17_Gender-Wage-Gap-2016-data-update.pdf.

4. US Bureau of Labor Statistics, *Women in the Labor Force: A Databook*, Report 1065, April 2017, 155, 181–83, tables 20 and 27, https://www.bls.gov/opub/reports/womens-databook/2016/pdf/home.pdf.

5. Semega, Fontenot, and Kollar, *Income and Poverty in the United States: 2016*, 41, table A-4.

6. US Bureau of Labor Statistics, *Women in the Labor Force*, 161–63, table 21; Lonnie Golden, "Still Falling Short on Hours and Pay: Part-Time Work Becoming the New Normal," Economic Policy Institute, December 5, 2016, http://www.epi.org/files/pdf/114028.pdf; and Caroline Fredrickson, *Under the Bus: How Working Women Are Being Run Over* (New York: New Press, 2015), 111–17.

7. Semega, Fontenot, and Kollar, *Income and Poverty in the United States: 2016*, 41, table A-4.

8. Stephen J. Rose and Heidi I. Hartmann, "Still a Man's Labor Market: The Long-Term Earnings Gap," Institute for Women's Policy Research, 2004, https://iwpr.org/wp-content/

uploads/wpallimport/files/iwpr-export/publications/C355.pdf; and Heidi Hartmann, Stephen J. Rose, and Vicky Lovell, "How Much Progress in Closing the Long-Term Earnings Gap?," in *The Declining Significance of Gender?*, ed. Francine D. Blau, Mary C. Brinton, and David B. Grusky (New York: Russell Sage, 2006), 125–55.

9. Elise Gould, Jessica Schieder, and Kathleen Geier, "What Is the Gender Pay Gap and Is It Real?," Economic Policy Institute, October 20, 2016, 7, http://www.epi.org/files/pdf/112962. pdf.

10. Youngjoo Cha, "Overwork and the Persistence of Gender Segregation in Occupations," *Gender & Society* 27, no. 2 (April 2013): 158–84; and Linda Rose Ennis, ed., *Intensive Mothering: The Cultural Contradictions of Modern Motherhood* (Bradford, ON: Demeter Press, 2014).

11. Arlie Hochschild, *The Second Shift* (New York: Avon Books, 1990).

12. Paula England, "Toward Gender Equality: Progress and Bottlenecks," in Blau, Brinton, and Grusky, *Declining Significance of Gender?*, 250–52.

13. David S. Pedulla and Sarah Thébaud, "Can We Finish the Revolution? Gender, Work-Family Ideals, and Institutional Constraints," *American Sociological Review* 80, no. 1 (February 2015): 116–39; and Stephanie Coontz, "Do Millennial Men Want Stay-at-Home Wives?," *New York Times*, April 2, 2017.

14. Martha J. Bailey and Thomas A. DiPrete, "Five Decades of Remarkable but Slowing Change in U.S. Women's Economic and Social Status and Political Participation," *Journal of the Social Sciences* 2, no. 4 (August 2016): 19.

15. Naomi Gerstel, "The Third Shift: Gender and Care Work Outside the Home," *Qualitative Sociology* 23, no. 4 (Winter 2000): 467–83; and Patricia Cohen, "'Care Chasm' Forces Women to Forgo Jobs," *New York Times*, January 25, 2017.

16. Michelle J. Budig, "The Fatherhood Bonus & the Motherhood Penalty: Parenthood and the Gender Gap in Pay," Third Way, September 2, 2014, http://s3.amazonaws.com/content. thirdway.org/publishing/attachments/files/000/000/198/NEXT_-_Fatherhood_Motherhood. pdf?1412698808; and Michelle J. Budig and Melissa J. Hodges, "Differences in Disadvantage: Variations in the Motherhood Penalty across White Women's Earnings Distribution," *American Sociological Review* 75, no. 5 (October 2010): 705–28.

17. Shelley J. Correll, Stephen Benard, and In Paik, "Getting a Job: Is There a Motherhood Penalty?," *American Journal of Sociology* 112, no. 5 (March 2007): 1297–1338.

18. Vincent J. Roscigno, Lisette M. Garcia, and Donna Bobbitt-Zeher, "Social Closure and Processes of Race/Sex Employment Discrimination," *Annals of the American Academy of Political and Social Science* 609 (January 2007): 38.

19. US Bureau of Labor Statistics, "Women in the Labor Force," 61–110, tables 11, 12, and 14.

20. Francine D. Blau and Lawrence M. Kahn, "The Gender Wage Gap: Extent, Trends, and Explanation," *Journal of Economic Literature* 55, no. 3 (September 2017): 789–865, esp. 825–29.

21. Hartmann, Rose, and Lovell, "How Much Progress in Closing the Long-Term Earnings Gap?," 133–39; Asaf Levanon, Paula England, and Paul Allison, "Occupational Feminization and Pay: Assessing Causal Dynamics Using 1950–2000 Census Data," *Social Forces* 88, no. 2 (December 2009): 865–891; and Clair Cain Miller, "Race and Class Define Men Who Take 'Women's Jobs'," *New York Times*, March 10, 2017.

22. Cecilia L. Ridgeway, *Framed by Gender: How Gender Inequality Persists in the Modern World* (Oxford: Oxford University Press, 2011), 56–91; and David Cotter, Joan M. Hermsen, and Reeve Vanneman, "The End of the Gender Revolution? Gender Role Attitudes from 1977 to 2008," *American Journal of Sociology* 117, no. 1 (July 2011): 259–89.

23. Ridgeway, *Framed by Gender*, 92–126

24. Roscigno, Garcia, and Bobbitt-Zeher, "Social Closure," 34–40.

25. Cited in Claire Cain Miller, "Why Women Still Get the Short End of the Dollar," *New York Times*, March 20, 2016.

26. See Donna Bobbitt-Zeher, "Gender Discrimination at Work: Connecting Gender Stereotypes, Institutional Policies, and Gender Composition of Workplace," *Gender & Society* 25, no. 6 (December 2011): 764–86.

27. For a brief summary of studies documenting discrimination against women, including some of those discussed below, see Blau and Kahn, "Gender Wage Gap," 833–35; for a discussion of gender discrimination in the low-wage labor market specifically, see Fredrickson, *Under the Bus*, 43–97.

28. Catherine Saint Louis, "Longtime Nursing Pay Gap Hasn't Budged, Study Says," *New York Times*, March 25, 2015.

29. David Gelles and Rachel Abrams, "Ex-Employees Say Sex Bias Was Common at a Jeweler," *New York Times*, March 1, 2017; and Susan Antilla, "Jeweler's Policies Masked Abuses, Suit Says," *New York Times*, March 7, 2017.

30. US Equal Employment Opportunity Commission, "Checkers Franchise Will Pay $100,000 to Settle EEOC Pay Discrimination Law Suit," Press Release, April 2, 2014, https://www.eeoc.gov/eeoc/newsroom/release/4-2-14.cfm.

31. David Neumark, with Roy J. Bank and Kyle D. Van Nort, "Sex Discrimination in Restaurant Hiring: An Audit Study," *Quarterly Journal of Economics* 111, no. 3 (August 1996): 915–41.

32. Corinne A. Moss-Racusin et al., "Science Faculty's Subtle Gender Biases Favor Male Students," *Proceeding of the National Academy of Sciences* 109, no. 41 (October 9, 2012): 16474–79.

33. Elyse Shaw et al., "Undervalued and Underpaid in America: Women in Low-Wage, Female-Dominated Jobs," Institute for Women's Policy Research, November 17, 2016, https://iwpr.org/wp-content/uploads/wpallimport/files/iwpr-export/publications/D508%20Under valued%20and%20Underpaid.pdf.

34. Laura Lein and Deanna T. Schexnayder, *Live after Welfare: Reform and the Persistence of Poverty* (Austin: University of Texas Press, 2007); Sandra Morgen, Joan Acker, and Jill Weigt, *Stretched Thin: Poor Families, Welfare Work, and Welfare Reform* (Ithaca, NY: Cornell University Press, 2010); and Jane L. Collins and Victoria Mayer, *Both Hands Tied: Welfare Reform and the Race to the Bottom in the Low-Wage Labor Market* (Chicago: University of Chicago Press, 2010).

35. For social policy recommendations to combat gender inequality in the educational system, labor market, and workplace, see Diane Whitmore Schanzenbach and Ryan Nunn, eds., "The 51%: Driving Growth Through Women's Economic Participation," Brookings, The Hamilton Project, October 2017, https://www.brookings.edu/wp-content/uploads/2017/10/es_101917_the51percent_full_book.pdf.

36. US Bureau of Labor Statistics, "Women in the Labor Force," 27, table 5, https://stats.bls.gov/opub/reports/womens-databook/2016/pdf/home.pdf.

37. US Bureau of Labor Statistics, "Families with Own Children: Employment Status of Parents by Age of Youngest Child and Family Type, 2015–2016 Annual Averages," April 20, 2017, https://www.bls.gov/news.release/famee.t04.htm.

38. On the different types of child care arrangements, see Ajay Chaudry, *Putting Children First: How Low-Wage Working Mothers Manage Child Care* (New York: Russell Sage, 2006), 28–84, 224–29; Suzanne W. Helburn and Barbara R. Bergmann, *America's Child Care Problem: The Way Out* (New York: Palgrave, 2002), 87–122; and Brigid Schulte and Alieza Durana, "The New American Care Report," New America, September 2016, 45–47, https://na-production.s3.amazonaws.com/documents/FINAL_Care_Report.pdf.

39. Lynda Laughlin, *Who's Minding the Kids? Child Care Arrangements: Spring 2011*, US Census Bureau, Current Population Reports, P70-135, April 2013, 3–4, table 2, https://www.census.gov/prod/2013pubs/p70-135.pdf.

40. Schulte and Durana, "New American Care Report," 5, 47–52.

41. Helburn and Bergmann, *America's Child Care Problem*, 25–27.

42. Rasheed Malik and Katie Hamm, "Mapping America's Child Care Deserts," Center for American Progress, August 2017, 2, https://cdn.americanprogress.org/content/uploads/2017/08/29111723/Child careDesert-report1.pdf; and Dionne Dobbins et al., "Child Care Deserts: Developing Solutions to Child Care Supply and Demand," Child Care Aware of America, September 2016, http://usa.childcareaware.org/wp-content/uploads/2016/09/Child-Care-Des erts-report-FINAL2.pdf.

43. Leila Schochet and Rasheed Malik, "2 Million Parents Forced to Make Career Sacrifices Due to Problems with Care," Center for American Progress, September 13, 2017, https://www.americanprogress.org/issues/early-childhood/news/2017/09/13/438838/2-million-parents-forced-make-career-sacrifices-due-problems-child-care/.

44. Schulte and Durana, "New American Care Report," 52–57; Helburn and Bergmann, *America's Child Care Problem*, 55–157; and Jane Waldfogel, *What Children Need* (Cambridge, MA: Harvard University Press, 2006), 72–81, 91–106.

45. Elise Gould, Lea J. E. Austin, and Marcy Whitebook, "What Does Good Child Care Reform Look Like?," Economic Policy Institute, March 29, 2017, http://www.epi.org/files/pdf/123954.pdf.

46. Child Care Aware of America, "Parents and the High Cost of Child Care: 2016 Report," 37, http://usa.childcareaware.org/wp-content/uploads/2017/01/CCA_High_Cost_Report_01-17-17_final.pdf.

47. US House of Representatives, Committee on Ways and Means, *2016 Green Book: Background Material and Data on the Programs within the Jurisdiction of the Committee on Ways and Means*, table 9.8, http://greenbook.waysandmeans.house.gov/sites/greenbook.waysandmeans.house.gov/files/Table%209-8.%20Average%20Hourly%20Wages%20for%20Child%20Care%20Workers%20and%20Preschool%20Teacher%2C%20May%202015.pdf; see also Patricia Cohen, "The Wages of Child Care," *New York Times*, July 13, 2016.

48. Sharon Lerner, "The Kid's Aren't Alright," *Nation*, November 12, 2007, 26.

49. Chaudry, *Putting Children First*, 43–46, 70; and Juliet Bromer and Julia R. Henley, "Child Care as Family Support: Caregiving Practices across Child Care Providers," *Children and Youth Services Review* 26 (2004): 941–64.

50. Helburn and Bergmann, *America's Child Care Problem*, 89, 122.

51. For background and information on the CCDBG, see US House of Representatives, Committee on Ways and Means, *2016 Green Book*, ch. 9.

52. Gould, Austin, and Whitebook, "What Does Good Child Care Reform Look Like?," 4; and Stephanie Schmit and Hannah Matthews, "Child Care and Development Block Grant Investment Could Support Bipartisan Reforms, Stop Decline in Children Served," Center for Law and Social Policy, April 2017, http://www.clasp.org/resources-and-publications/publication-1/1.4-Billion-Needed-for-CCDBG-in-2018.pdf.

53. National Women's Law Center, "Child Care for All Families That Need It," February 2017, 2, https://nwlc.org/wp-content/uploads/2017/02/Child-Care-For-All-Families-That-Need-It.pdf.

54. Sabrina Tavernise, "Aid for Child Care Drops When It's Needed Most," *New York Times*, December 14, 2011.

55. Chaudry, *Putting Children First*, 72–76; and Harriet B. Presser, *Working in a 24/7 Economy: Challenges for American Families* (New York: Russell Sage, 2003), 186–88, 191–94.

56. Chaudry, *Putting Children First*, 85–118, 143–45, 154.

57. See Collins and Mayer, *Both Hands Tied*, 83–113; Lein and Schexnayder, *Life After Welfare*, 81–86; Morgen, Acker, and Weigt, *Stretched Thin*, 162–77; and Valerie Polakov, *Who Cares for Our Children: The Child Care Crisis in the Other America* (New York: Teachers College Press, 2007).

58. Presser, *Working in a 24/7 Economy*, 174–213; Lisa Dodson and Wendy Luttrell, "Families Facing Untenable Choice," *Contexts* 10, no. 1 (Winter 2011): 38–42; and Liz Watson, Lauren Frohlich, and Elizabeth Johnston, "Collateral Damage: Scheduling Challenges for Workers in Low-Wage Jobs and Their Consequences," National Women's Law Center, April 2014, https://www.nwlc.org/sites/default/files/pdfs/collateral_damage_scheduling_fact_sheet.pdf.

59. Julie E. Press, "Child Care as Poverty Policy: The Effect of Child Care on Work and Family Poverty," in *Prismatic Metropolis: Inequality in Los Angeles*, ed. Lawrence D. Bobo et al. (New York: Russell Sage, 2000), 341, 373.

60. On how to improve the child-care system, see, for example, Gould, Austin, and Whitebook, "What Does Good Child Care Reform Look Like?"; Katie Hamm and Julie Kashen, "A Blueprint for Child Care Reform: It's Time to Do Better for Children and Families," Center for

American Progress, September 2017, https://cdn.americanprogress.org/content/uploads/2017/09/06134328/Child careReform-report.pdf; and Ms Foundation for Women, "Raising our Nation: Forging a More Robust and Equitable Childcare System in America," 2016, https://philanthropynewyork.org/sites/default/files/resources/Raising-our-Nation.pdf.

61. Joachim O. Hero, Alan M. Zaslavsky, and Robert J. Blendon, "The United States Leads Other Nations in Difference by Income in Perceptions of Health and Health Care," *Health Affairs* 36, no. 6 (June 2017): 1032–40; see also Diane Schanzenbach et al., "Money Lightens the Load," The Hamilton Project, December 2016, 3, figure 2, http://www.hamiltonproject.org/assets/files/money_lightens_the_load_updated.pdf.

62. Rucker C. Johnson, "Health," *Pathways: The Poverty and Inequality Report 2017* (Stanford Center on Poverty and Inequality), 27–31, http://inequality.stanford.edu/sites/default/files/Pathways_SOTU_2017_health.pdf.

63. Cited in Annie Lowrey, "Income Gap, Meet the Longevity Gap," *New York Times*, March 16, 2014.

64. Raj Chetty et al., "The Association Between Income and Life Expectancy in the United States, 2001–2014," *Journal of the American Medical Association* 315, no. 16 (April 26, 2016): 1750–66.

65. Jacob Bor, Gregory H. Cohen, and Sandro Galea, "Population Health in an Era of Rising Income Inequality: USA, 1980–2015," *Lancet* 398, no. 10077 (April 8, 2017): 1475–90.

66. Anne Case and Angus Deaton, "Rising Morbidity and Mortality in Midlife Among White Non-Hispanic Americans in the 21st Century," *Proceedings of the National Academy of Sciences* 112, no. 49 (December 2015): 15078–83; Anne Case and Angus Deaton, "Mortality and Morbidity in the 21st Century," Brookings Papers on Economic Activity, Conference Drafts, May 1, 2017, https://www.brookings.edu/wp-content/uploads/2017/03/casedeaton_sp17_finaldraft.pdf; and Andrew J. Cherlin, "Why Are White Death Rates Rising?," *New York Times*, February 22, 2016.

67. Eric C. Schneider et al., "Mirror, Mirror 2017: International Comparison Reflects Flaws and Opportunities for Better U.S. Health Care," Commonwealth Fund, July 2017, exhibits 1 and 2, appendices 3 and 6, http://www.commonwealthfund.org/~/media/files/publications/fund-report/2017/jul/schneider_mirror_mirror_2017.pdf; and Organisation for Economic Co-operation and Development, *Society at a Glance 2016: OECD Social Indicators*, 8th ed. (Paris: OECD, 2016), 114–15, 123.

68. Nelson D. Schwartz, "Rise of the Red Carpet M.D." *New York Times*, June 4, 2017.

69. Elizabeth Rosenthal, *An American Sickness: How Healthcare Became Big Business and How You Can Take It Back* (New York: Penguin, 2017).

70. Schneider et al., "Mirror, Mirror 2017," appendix 3; and Hero, Zaslavsky, and Blendon, "The United States Leads Other Nations in Difference by Income," 1035.

71. Keenan Dworak-Fisher, Maury Gittleman, and Thomas Moehrle, "Trends in Employment-Based Health Insurance Coverage: Evidence from the National Compensation Survey," *Monthly Labor Review*, Bureau of Labor Statistics, October 2014, tables 1 and 2, https://www.bls.gov/opub/mlr/2014/article/trends-in-employment-based-health-insurance-coverage.htm.

72. Samuel L. Dickman, David U. Himmelstein, and Steffie Woolhandler, "Inequality and the Health-Care System in the USA," *Lancet* 389, no. 10077 (April 8, 2017): 1431–41; and Margot Sanger-Katz, "Medical Debt Often Crushing, Even for Insured," *New York Times*, January 6, 2016.

73. Rabah Kamal and Cynthia Fox, "U.S. Health System is Performing Better, Though Still Lagging Behind Other Countries," Kaiser Family Foundation, May 19, 2017, http://www.healthsystemtracker.org/brief/u-s-health-system-performing-better-though-still-lagging-behind-countries/#item-start.

74. Shefali Luthra, "5 Ways White House Can Use Its Muscle to Undercut Obamacare," *Kaiser Health News*, July 28, 2017, http://khn.org/news/5-ways-white-house-can-use-its-muscle-to-undercut-obamacare/; Dylan Scott, "Trump's Executive Order to Undermine Obamacare, Explained," Vox, October 12, 2017, https://www.vox.com/policy-and-politics/2017/10/12/16458184/trump-obamacare-executive-order-association-health-plans-short-term-insurance; and Robert Pear and Reed Abelson, "President Plots His Own Course on Health Care," *New York Times*, October 13, 2017.

75. Ron Leiber, "Cost of Care for Very Ill Could Rise in Tax Plan," *New York Times*, December 9, 2017; and Charlie Baker et al., "Congress, Please Save CHIP," *New York Times*, December 8, 2017.

76. Helen Epstein, "Enough to Make You Sick?," *New York Times Magazine*, October 12, 2003, 74–81, 98, 102–7; see also, with a focus on how social and environmental factors affect children's health and well-being, Sara Rosenbaum and Robert Blum, "How Healthy Are Our Children?," *The Future of Children* 25, no. 1 (Spring 2015): 11–34.

77. Fred C. Pampel, Patrick M. Krueger, and Justin T. Denney, "Socioeconomic Disparities in Health Behaviors," *Annual Review of Sociology* 36 (2010): 349–70.

78. Zinzi D. Bailey et al., "Structural Racism and Health Inequities in the USA: Evidence and Interventions," *Lancet* 398, no. 10077 (April 8, 2017): 1453–63.

79. Tina Rosenberg, "When Poverty Makes You Sick, A Lawyer Can Be the Cure," *New York Times*, July 17, 2014.

80. Carol Graham, "The Rich Even Have a Better Kind of Stress Than the Poor," Brookings, February 10, 2016, 2, https://www.brookings.edu/research/the-rich-even-have-a-better-kind-of-stress-than-the-poor/; and Carol Graham, *Happiness for All? Unequal Hopes and Lives in Pursuit of the American Dream* (Princeton, NJ: Princeton University Press, 2017), 102–6.

81. S. Leonard Syme and Lisa F. Berkman, "Social Class, Susceptibility, and Sickness," in *The Sociology of Health and Illness: Critical Perspectives*, 7th ed., ed. Peter Conrad (New York: Worth, 2005), 24–30; see also Robert Sapolsky, "Sick of Poverty," *Scientific American* 293 (December 2005): 92–99.

82. Johnson, "Health," 28; Moises Velasquez-Manoff, "Status and Stress," *New York Times*, July 27, 2013; Gary W. Evans, Jeanne Brooks-Gunn, and Pamela Kato Klebanov, "Stressing Out the Poor: Chronic Physiological Stress and the Income-Achievement Gap," *Pathways* (Winter 2011): 16–21; and Greg J. Duncan and Katherine Magnuson, "The Long Reach of Early Childhood Poverty," *Pathways* (Winter 2011): 22–27.

83. Jens Ludwig et al., "Neighborhood Effects on the Long-Term Well-Being of Low-Income Adults," *Science* 337, no. 6101 (September 2012): 1505–10; Janet Currie, "Health and Residential Location," in *Neighborhood and Life Chances: How Place Matters in Modern America*, ed. Harriet B. Newburger, Eugenie L. Birch, and Susan M. Wachter (Philadelphia: University of Pennsylvania Press, 2011), 3–17; and Rucker C. Johnson, "The Place of Race in Health Disparities: How Family Background and Neighborhood Conditions in Childhood Impact Later-Life Health," in Newburger, Birch, and Wachter, *Neighborhood and Life Chances*, 18–36.

84. Alana Rhone et al., *Low-Income and Low-Supermarket-Access Census Tracts, 2010–2015*, US Department of Agriculture, January 2017, https://www.ers.usda.gov/webdocs/publications/82101/eib-165.pdf?v=42752; and Paula Dutko, "Food Deserts Suffer Persistent Socioeconomic Disadvantage," *Choices: The Magazine of Food, Farm, and Resource Issues*, 27, no. 3 (2012), http://ageconsearch.umn.edu/record/138936/files/cmsarticle_252.pdf.

85. Lisa F. Berkman and Thomas Glass, "Social Integration, Social Networks, Social Support, and Health," in *Social Epidemiology*, ed. Lisa Berkman and Ichiro Kawachi (Oxford: Oxford University Press, 2000), 137–73; Ichiro Kawachi and Lisa Berkman, "Social Cohesion, Social Capital, and Health," in Berkman and Kawachi, *Social Epidemiology*, 174–90; and Debra Umberson, Robert Crosnoe, and Corinne Reczek, "Social Relationships and Health Behavior Across the Life Course," *Annual Review of Sociology* 36 (2010): 139–57.

86. John Eligon, "A Question of Environmental Racism in Flint," *New York Times*, January 22, 2016.

87. Ingrid Gould Ellen, Tod Mijanovich, and Keri-Nicole Dillman, "Neighborhood Effects on Health: Exploring the Links and Assessing the Evidence," *Journal of Urban Affairs* 23, nos. 3–4 (2001): 397–98.

88. P. Braverman et al., "Housing and Health," Issue Brief no. 7 (Robert Wood Johnson Foundation, May 2011), http://www.rwjf.org/content/dam/farm/reports/issue_briefs/2011/rwjf70451.

89. Rebekah Levine Coley et al., "Relations Between Housing Characteristics and the Well-Being of Low-Income Children and Adolescents," *Developmental Psychology* 49, no. 9 (September 2013): 1775–89.

90. Matthew Desmond, *Evicted: Poverty and Profit in the American City* (New York: Crown, 2016), 257.

91. Nabihah Magbool, Janet Wiveiros, and Minday Ault, "The Impacts of Affordable Housing on Health: A Research Summary," Center for Housing Policy, April 2015, http://www2.nhc.org/HSGandHealthLitRev_2015_final.pdf.

92. On the relationship between working conditions and health status, see Tores Theorell, "Working Conditions and Health," in Berkman and Kawachi, *Social Epidemiology*, 95–117.

93. Lisa F. Berkman, "The Health Divide," *Contexts* 3, no. 4 (Fall 2004): 41.

94. Rachel Abrams, "Walmart Is Accused of Punishing Workers for Taking Sick Days," *New York Times*, June 2, 2017; and Michael Powell, "For 2 Women in Queens and Many Others, a Sick Day Could Mean They're Fired," *New York Times*, October 23, 2012.

95. Steven Greenhouse, "In Service Sector, No Rest for the Working," *New York Times*, February 22, 2015; Noam Scheiber, "When Shifting Work Schedules Hurt Children's Well-Being," *New York Times*, August 13, 2015; and Leila Morsy and Richard Rothstein, "Parents' Non-Standard Work Schedules Make Adequate Childrearing Difficult," Economic Policy Institute, August 6, 2015, http://www.epi.org/files/pdf/88777.pdf.

96. Yamiche Alcindor, "In Sweltering South, Climate Change Is Workplace Hazard," *New York Times*, August 4, 2017.

97. AFL-CIO, "Death on the Job: The Toll of Neglect," 26th ed., April 2017, 1, https://aflcio.org/sites/default/files/2017-04/2017Death-on-the-Job.pdf; see also Sherry L. Baron et al., "Nonfatal Work-Related Injuries and Illnesses—United States, 2010," Centers for Disease Control and Prevention, *Morbidity and Mortality Weekly Reports*, supp. 62, no. 3 (November 22, 2013): 35–40.

98. AFL-CIO, "Death on the Job," 56; and Barry Meier and Danielle Ivory, "Industry Given a Louder Voice on Job Safety," *New York Times*, June 6, 2017.

99. Michael Marmot, "Harveian Oration: Health in an Unequal World," *Lancet* 368 (December 9–15, 2006): 2082.

100. Semega, Fontenot, and Kollar, *Income and Poverty in the United States: 2016*, 14, figure 5.

101. Liana Fox, *The Supplemental Poverty Measure: 2016*, Current Population Reports P60-261, September 2017, 1, 20, table A-1, https://www.census.gov/content/dam/Census/library/publications/2017/demo/p60-261.pdf.

102. Helen Levy, "Income, Poverty, and Material Hardship Among Older Americans," *Journal of the Social Sciences* 1, no. 1 (2015): 55–77; see also Feeding America, "Senior Hunger Fact Sheet," February 2017, http://www.feedingamerica.org/assets/pdfs/fact-sheets/senior-hunger-fact-sheet.pdf.

103. Joint Center for Housing Studies of Harvard University, *The State of the Nation's Housing 2017* (Cambridge, MA: Joint Center for Housing Studies of Harvard University, 2017), 32, http://www.jchs.harvard.edu/sites/jchs.harvard.edu/files/harvard_jchs_state_of_the_nations_housing_2017.pdf; and Joint Center for Housing Studies of Harvard University, *Projections and Implications for Housing a Growing Population: Older Households 2015–2035* (Cambridge, MA: Joint Center for Housing Studies of Harvard University, 2016), 11, http://www.jchs.harvard.edu/sites/jchs.harvard.edu/files/harvard_jchs_housing_growing_population_2016.pdf.

104. Corey M. Abramson, *The End Game: How Inequality Shapes Our Final Years* (Cambridge, MA: Harvard University Press, 2015), 2.

105. Semega, Fontenot, and Kollar, *Income and Poverty in the United States: 2016*, 51–55, table B-3; see also Wider Opportunities for Women (WOW), "Living Below the Line: Economic Insecurity and Older Americans, No. 3: Race and Ethnicity," http://www.wowonline.org/wp-content/uploads/2015/07/WOW-Living-Below-the-Line-Race-Brief-2015.pdf.

106. Semega, Fontenot, and Kollar, *Income and Poverty in the United States: 2016*, 15, figure 6; and Jason Brown, "Issue Brief Three: The Economic Security of Older Women," The Economic Security of American Households, US Treasury Department, Office of Economic Policy, January 2017, https://www.treasury.gov/resource-center/economic-policy/Documents/The%20Economic%20Security%20of%20American%20Households-The%20Economic%20Security%20of%20Older%20Women.pdf.

107. OECD.Stat, "Pensions at a Glance: Income and Poverty of Older People," Organisation for Economic Co-operation and Development, 2017, http://stats.oecd.org/Index.aspx? DataSetCode=PAG.

108. See Nancy MacLean, *Democracy in Chains: The Deep History of the Radical Right's Stealth Plan for America* (New York: Viking, 2017), 177–82.

109. See The National Academies of Sciences Engineering Medicine, *The Growing Gap in Life Expectancy by Income: Implications for Federal Programs and Policy Responses* (Washington, DC: The National Academy Press, 2015), 3–4; and Sabrina Tavernise, "Life Spans of the Rich Leave the Poor Behind," *New York Times*, February 13, 2016.

110. Rebecca Vallas et al., "The Effect of Rising Inequality on Social Security," Center for American Progress, February 10, 2015, https://cdn.americanprogress.org/wp-content/uploads/ 2015/02/SocialSecurity-brief3.pdf; and Richard Long, "The Real Social Security Crisis Is Income Inequality," Portside, February 25, 2015, https://portside.org/print/2015-02-28/real-social-security-crisis-income-inequality.

111. Jocelyn Fischer and Jeff Hayes, "The Importance of Social Security in the Incomes of Older Americans: Differences in Gender, Age, Race/Ethnicity, and Marital Status," Institute for Women's Policy Research, August 2013, 8–10, figure 4, table 6, https://iwpr.org/wp-content/uploads/wpallimport/files/iwpr-export/publications/D503-ImportanceofSS.pdf.

112. OECD, "2015 Pension Policy Notes: United States," Organisation for Economic Co-operation and Development, 2015, http://www.oecd.org/els/public-pensions/OECD-Pension-Policy-Notes-UnitedStates.pdf.

113. Fischer and Hayes, "Importance of Social Security in the Incomes of Older Americans," 12–14, figure 6.

114. Consumer Financial Protection Bureau, "Snapshot of Older Consumers and Student Loan Debt," January 2017, 3–9, http://files.consumerfinance.gov/f/documents/201701_cfpb_ OA-Student-Loan-Snapshot.pdf.

115. Lori A. Trawinski, "Nightmare on Main Street: Older Americans and the Mortgage Market Crisis," AARP Public Policy Institute, 2012, http://www.aarp.org/content/dam/aarp/ research/public_policy_institute/cons_prot/2012/nightmare-on-main-street-AARP-ppi-cons-prot.pdf; and Elizabeth Olson, "Paying Off the Mortgage Grows Harder for Older Workers," *New York Times*, June 13, 2015.

116. Jessica Silver-Greenberg and Stacy Cowley, "Living on a Borrowed Dime," *New York Times*, October 20, 2017; Andrew L. Yarrow, "A Hidden Time Bomb: Rising Debt among the Elderly," *Tampa Tribune*, December 23, 2014, http://www.tbo.com/list/news-opinion-commentary/a-hidden-time-bomb-rising-debt-among-the-elderly-20141223/; and Amy Traub, "In the Red: Older Americans and Credit Card Debt," AARP Public Policy Institute, 2013), 5, http://www.aarp.org/content/dam/aarp/research/public_policy_institute/security/2013/older-americans-and-credit-card-debt-AARP-ppi-sec.pdf.

117. Keith Miller, David Madland, and Christian E. Weller, "The Reality of the Retirement Crisis," Center for American Progress, January 26, 2015, 2, https://cdn.americanprogress.org/ wp-content/uploads/2015/01/RetirementCrisis1.pdf.

118. Monique Morrissey, "The State of American Retirement: How 401(k)s Have Failed Most American Workers," Economic Policy Institute, March 3, 2016, 12, 16, http://www.epi. org/files/2016/state-of-american-retirement-final.pdf.

119. Miller, Madland, and Weller, "Reality of the Retirement Crisis," 6.

120. For a detailed assessment of this "great transformation" in the retirement system, see Edward N. Wolff, *The Transformation of the American Pension System* (Kalamazoo, MI: W. E. Upjohn Institute for Employment Research, 2011).

121. Nari Rhee and Ilana Boivie, "The Continuing Retirement Savings Crisis," National Institute on Retirement Security, March 2015, 6, figure 3, http://laborcenter.berkeley.edu/pdf/ 2015/RetirementSavingsCrisis.pdf.

122. On the contrast between DB plans and DC plans and the consequences of the ongoing shift from the former to the latter, see Jacob Hacker, "Introduction: The Coming Age of Retirement Insecurity," in *Meeting California's Retirement Security Challenge*, ed. Nari Rhee (Berkeley: UC Berkeley Center for Labor Research and Education, October 2011), 4–20, http:// laborcenter.berkeley.edu/pdf/2011/CAretirement_challenge_1011.pdf.

123. Frank Porcll and Diane Oakley, "The Pension Factor 2012: The Role of Defined Benefit Pensions in Reducing Elderly Economic Hardships," National Institute on Retirement Security, July 2012, 1, http://www.nirsonline.org/storage/nirs/documents/Pension%20Factor%202012/pensionfactor2012_final.pdf.

124. Miller, Madland, and Weller, "Reality of the Retirement Crisis," 13–15; and Alicia H. Munnell, Wenliang Hou, and Anthony Webb, "NRRI Update Shows Half Still Falling Short," Center for Retirement Research at Boston College, December 2014, 3, 5, http://crr.bc.edu/wp-content/uploads/2014/12/IB_14-20-508.pdf.

125. Nari Rhee and Ilana Boivie, "Continuing Retirement Savings Crisis," 1, 20.

126. Drew DeSilver, *More Older Americans Are Working, and Working More, Than They Used To* (Washington, DC: Pew Research Center, 2016), http://www.pewresearch.org/fact-tank/2016/06/20/more-older-americans-are-working-and-working-more-than-they-used-to/; and Paula Span, "The New Old Age," *New York Times*, August 2, 2016.

127. Quoctrung Bui, "As More Older People Look for Work, They Are Put Into 'Old Person Jobs'," *New York Times*, August 18, 2016; and Catherine Rampell, "In Hard Economy for All Ages, Older Isn't Better . . . It's Brutal," *New York Times*, February 13, 2013.

128. Patricia Cohen, "Over 50, Female and Jobless Even as Others Return to Work," *New York Times*, January 2, 2016.

129. Paula Span, "Caregivers Who Are No Spring Chickens," *New York Times*, July 7, 2015.

130. Alexander J. S. Colvin, "The Growing Use of Mandatory Arbitration," Economic Policy Institute, September 27, 2017, http://www.epi.org/files/pdf/135056.pdf; Robert Reich, *Saving Capitalism: For the Many, Not the Few* (New York: Alford A. Knopf, 2015), 54–56; and Jed S. Rakoff, "Why You Won't Get Your Day in Court," *New York Review of Books*, November 24, 2016, 4–6.

131. Brady Meixell and Ross Eisenbrey, "An Epidemic of Wage Theft Is Costing Workers Hundreds of Millions of Dollars a Year," Economic Policy Institute, September 11, 2014, http://www.epi.org/publication/epidemic-wage-theft-costing-workers-hundreds/; and Kim Bobo, *Wage Theft in America: Why Millions of Working Americans Are Not Getting Paid—And What We Can Do About It*, rev. ed. (New York: New Press, 2011).

132. Elizabeth Anderson, *Private Government: How Employers Rule Our Lives (and Why We Don't Talk about It)* (Princeton, NJ: Princeton University Press, 2017); see also Alina Tugend, "Speaking Freely about Politics Can Cost You Your Job," *New York Times*, February 21, 2015.

133. Nicholas Kristof, "Is It a Crime to Be Poor?," *New York Times*, June 12, 2016.

134. Gary Blasi, "How Much Access? How Much Justice?," *Fordham Law Review* 73, no. 3 (December 2004): 879–80.

135. Joseph E. Stiglitz, *The Great Divide: Unequal Societies and What We Can Do About Them* (New York: W. W. Norton, 2015), 155, 170–73.

136. Alan W. Houseman and Linda E. Perle, "Securing Equal Justice for All: A Brief History of Civil Legal Assistance in the United States," Center for Law and Social Policy, December 2013, 7–21, http://www.clasp.org/resources-and-publications/publication-1/Securing-Equal-Justice-for-All-2013-Revision.pdf.

137. On the history of the Legal Services Corporation, see Houseman and Perle, "Securing Equal Justice for All," 21–48; and Michael B. Katz, *The Price of Citizenship: Redefining the American Welfare State* (New York: Metropolitan Books, 2001), 306–14.

138. Katz, *Price of Citizenship*, 308–14; and Alan W. Houseman, "Civil Legal Aid in the United States: An Update for 2015," December 2015; 38–41, https://repository.library.georgetown.edu/bitstream/handle/10822/761858/Houseman_Civil_Legal_Aid_US_2015.pdf?sequence=1&isAllowed=y.

139. Houseman, "Civil Legal Aid in the United States," 43–46.

140. National Center for Access to Justice, "The Justice Index: Measuring Access to Justice," 2016, http://justiceindex.org/; Legal Services Corporation, "Who We Are," http://www.lsc.gov/about-lsc/who-we-are; and Rebecca Buckwalter-Poza, "Making Justice Equal," Center for American Progress, December 8, 2016, 2, https://cdn.americanprogress.org/content/uploads/2016/12/07105805/MakingJusticeEqual-brief.pdf.

141. Alan Houseman, *The Justice Gap: Civil Legal Assistance Today and Tomorrow*, Center for American Progress, June 22, 2011, 3, https://cdn.americanprogress.org/wp-content/uploads/

issues/2011/06/pdf/justice.pdf; John T. Broderick Jr. and Ronald M. George, "A Nation of Do-It-Yourself Lawyers," *New York Times*, January 2, 2010; and Ethan Bronner, "Right to Lawyer Can Be Empty Promise for Poor," *New York Times*, March 16, 2013.

142. Desmond, *Evicted*, 303–5; and Rakoff, "Why You Won't Get Your Day in Court," 4.

143. World Justice Project, "Rule of Law Index 2016," 40–41, 152–53, https://world justiceproject.org/sites/default/files/documents/RoLI_Final-Digital_0.pdf.

144. Earl Johnson Jr., "Lifting the 'American Exceptionalism' Curtain: Options and Lessons from Abroad," *Hastings Law Review* 67 (2016): 1225–32.

145. Earl Johnson Jr., "Equal Access to Justice: Comparing Access to Justice in the United States and Other Industrial Democracies," *Fordham International Law Journal* 24 (2001): 98.

146. Office of Management and Budget, "Major Savings and Reforms, Budget of the U.S. Government, Fiscal Year 2018," 98, https://www.whitehouse.gov/sites/whitehouse.gov/files/omb/budget/fy2018/msar.pdf; and Tom McCarthy and Molly Redden, "Legal Services in Unprecedented Danger under Trump's Budget Proposal," *The Guardian*, March 16, 2017, https://www.theguardian.com/us-news/2017/mar/16/legal-aid-services-cut-trump-budget-proposal.

147. Dorothy Samuels, "Trump Targets the Legal Services Corporation," *The American Prospect*, April 11, 2017, http://prospect.org/article/trump-targets-legal-services-corporation.

148. US Department of Justice, Civil Rights Division, "Investigation of the Ferguson Police Department," March 4, 2015, https://www.justice.gov/sites/default/files/opa/press-releases/attachments/2015/03/04/ferguson_police_department_report.pdf; and US Department of Justice, Civil Rights Division, "Investigation of the Baltimore City Police Department," August 10, 2016, https://www.justice.gov/opa/file/883366/download. On Ferguson and Baltimore, and the killings of Michael Brown and Freddie Gray, see also Keeanga-Yamahtta Taylor, *From #BlackLivesMatter to Black Liberation* (Chicago: Haymarket, 2016), 75–80, 153–68.

149. On class and race disparities in the criminal justice system, see Michelle Alexander, *The New Jim Crow: Mass Incarceration in the Age of Colorblindness* (New York: New Press, 2012); and Mark Peffley and Jon Hurwitz, *Justice in America: The Separate Realities of Blacks and Whites* (Cambridge, MA: Cambridge University Press, 2010).

150. Samuel R. Gross, Maurice Possley, and Klara Stephens, "Race and Wrongful Convictions in the United States," National Registry of Exonerations, March 7, 2017, https://www.law.umich.edu/special/exoneration/Documents/Race_and_Wrongful_Convictions.pdf; and Niraj Chokshi, "Race Bias Is Found in Wrongful Convictions," *New York Times*, March 8, 2017.

151. Alexander, *New Jim Crow*, 84–86; John F. Pfaff, *Locked In: The True Causes of Mass Incarceration and How to Achieve Real Reform* (New York: Basic Books, 2017), 136–38; and Sara Mayeux, "Gideon v. Wainwright in the Age of a Public Defense Crisis," Talk Poverty, May 9, 2016, https://talkpoverty.org/2016/05/09/gideon-wainwright-age-public-defense-crisis/.

152. Adam Liptak, "County Says It's Too Poor to Defend the Poor," *New York Times*, April 15, 2003; and Jacob Carpenter, "Wisconsin Pays Nation's Lowest Rate to Defend Poor: Lawyers Say It's Time for a Raise," Portside, May 24, 2017, http://portside.org/2017-05-24/wisconsin-pays-nations-lowest-rate-defend-poor-lawyers-say-its-time-raise.

153. Buckwalter-Poza, "Making Justice Equal," 3, 5–6; Timothy Williams, "In South Carolina, No Money and No Lawyer Often Means Jail Time for Minor Crimes," *New York Times*, October 13, 2017; Erik Eckholm, "Citing Workload, Public Lawyers Reject New Cases," *New York Times*, November 9, 2008; and Monica Davey, "Budget Woes Hit Defense Lawyers for the Indigent," *New York Times*, September 10, 2010.

154. Erik Eckholm, "Court Costs Put Extra Burden on Poor, Nonwhite and Young," *New York Times*, September 1, 2016; and John Pfaff, "A Mockery of Justice for the Poor," *New York Times*, April 30, 2016.

155. Richard Faussey, "Suit Describes 'Waiting List' for Legal Aid in New Orleans," *New York Times*, January 16, 2016; and Derwyn Bunton, "No Lawyers to Spare for Poor in New Orleans," *New York Times*, February 19, 2016.

156. Bryce Covert, "The Injustice of Cash Bail," *The Nation*, November 6, 2017, 12–17; and Peter Edelman, *Not a Crime to Be Poor: The Criminalization of Poverty in America* (New York: New Press, 2017).

157. Alexander, *New Jim Crow*, 40–48; Elizabeth Hinton, *From the War on Poverty to the War on Crime: The Making of Mass Incarceration in America* (Cambridge, MA: Harvard University Press, 2016).

158. Danielle Kaeble and Lauren Glaze, *Correctional Populations in the United States, 2015* (US Department of Justice, Office of Justice Programs, Bureau of Justice Statistics, December 2016), 2, https://www.bjs.gov/content/pub/pdf/cpus15.pdf; and Devah Pager, *Marked: Race, Crime, and Finding Work in an Era of Mass Incarceration* (Chicago: University of Chicago Press, 2007), 11–15.

159. Kaeble and Glaze, *Correctional Populations in the United States, 2015*; The Sentencing Project, "Trends in U.S. Corrections," 2016, http://sentencingproject.org/wp-content/uploads/2016/01/Trends-in-US-Corrections.pdf.

160. The Sentencing Project, "Trends in U.S. Corrections," 4.

161. The Sentencing Project, "Trends in U.S. Corrections," 3; and E. Ann Carson and Elizabeth Anderson, *Prisoners in 2015* (US Department of Justice, Office of Justice Programs, Bureau of Justice Statistics, December 2016), 3, https://www.bjs.gov/content/pub/pdf/p15.pdf.

162. Jonathan Rothwell, "Drug Offenders in American Prisons: The Critical Distinction Between Stock and Flow," Brookings, November 25, 2015, https://www.brookings.edu/blog/social-mobility-memos/2015/11/25/drug-offenders-in-american-prisons-the-critical-distinction-between-stock-and-flow/.

163. Alexander, *New Jim Crow*, 59–139; and Michael Tonry, *Punishing Race: A Continuing American Dilemma* (Oxford: Oxford University Press, 2011), 3–76.

164. Pfaff, *Locked In*, especially chapter 5; and Alexander, *New Jim Crow*, 84–86.

165. Jeffrey Reiman and Paul Leighton, *The Rich Get Richer and the Poor Get Prison: Ideology, Class, and Criminal Justice*, 10th ed. (Boston: Pearson, 2013).

166. David K. Shipler, *The Working Poor: Invisible in America* (New York: Alfred A. Knopf, 2004), 252.

167. Richard V. Reeves, Edward Rodrigue and Elizabeth Kneebone, "Five Evils: Multidimensional Poverty and Race in America," Brookings Institution, April 2016, https://www.brookings.edu/wp-content/uploads/2016/06/ReevesKneeboneRodrigue_Multidimensional Poverty_FullPaper.pdf; and Paul A. Jargowsky, "The Architecture of Segregation: Civil Unrest, the Concentration of Poverty, and Public Policy," The Century Foundation, August 9, 2015, https://s3-us-west-2.amazonaws.com/production.tcf.org/app/uploads/2015/08/07182514/Jargowsky_ArchitectureofSegregation-11.pdf.

168. Board of Governors of the Federal Reserve System, *Report on the Economic Well-Being of U.S. Households in 2016* (May 2017), 25–29, https://www.federalreserve.gov/publications/files/2016-report-economic-well-being-us-households-201705.pdf; and Jonathan Morduch and Rachel Schneider, *The Financial Diaries: How American Families Cope in a World of Uncertainty* (Princeton, NJ: Princeton University Press, 2017), esp. 65–84.

169. Jacob S. Hacker, *The Great Risk Shift* (New York: Oxford University Press, 2006); and Rachel E. Dwyer and Lora A. Phillips Lassus, "The Great Risk Shift and Precarity in the U.S. Housing Market," *The Annals of the American Academy of Political and Social Science* 660, no. 1 (July 2015): 199–216.

11. CONCLUSION

1. Steven Lukes, "Power," *Contexts* 6, no. 3 (Summer 2007): 59.

2. C. Wright Mills, *The Power Elite* (New York: Oxford University Press, 1956), 4.

3. On poverty as a "problem of power," see also Michael B. Katz, *The Undeserving Poor: America's Enduring Confrontation with Poverty*, 2nd ed. (Oxford: Oxford University Press, 2013), 273–77.

4. Economic Policy Institute, "A Real Agenda for Working People," December 7, 2016, http://www.epi.org/files/2017/real-workers-agenda.pdf; Melissa Boteach, Rebecca Vallas, and Eliza Schultz, "A Progressive Agenda to Cut Poverty and Expand Opportunity," June 2016, https://cdn.americanprogress.org/wp-content/uploads/2016/06/03081022/RoadmapOpportunity

-report.pdf; and Carmel Martin, Andy Green, and Brendan Duke, "Raising Wages and Rebuilding Wealth," Center for American Progress, September 2016, https://cdn.americanprogress.org/wp-content/uploads/2016/09/06131608/RaisingWagesRebuildingWealth.pdf.

5. See, for example, David Rolf, *The Fight for $15: The Right Wage for a Working America* (New York: New Press, 2016), 234–58; E. J. Dionne Jr., Norman J. Ornstein, and Thomas E. Mann, *One Nation After Trump: A Guide for the Perplexed, the Disillusioned, the Desperate, and the Not-Yet Deported* (New York: St. Martin's Press, 2017), 175–201; Thomas M. Shapiro, *Toxic Inequality: How America's Wealth Gap Destroys Mobility, Deepens the Racial Divide & Threatens Our Future* (New York: Basic Books, 2017), 181–218; and Lane Kenworthy, *Social Democratic America* (Oxford: Oxford University Press, 2014).

6. Michelle Jackson, "Don't Let 'Conversation One' Squeeze Out 'Conversation Two'," *Pathways* (Spring 2017): 33–36, http://inequality.stanford.edu/sites/default/files/Pathways_Spring2017_Conversation-Two.pdf.

7. See Kenworthy, *Social Democratic America*, 141–42.

8. See Robert W. McChesney and John Nichols, *People Get Ready: The Fight Against a Jobless Economy and a Citizenless Democracy* (New York: Nation Books, 2016), 245–76.

9. Joe Soss, "The Poverty Fight," *Contexts* 11, no. 2 (Spring 2011): 84.

10. Frances Fox Piven, *Challenging Authority: How Ordinary People Change America* (Lanham, MD: Rowman & Littlefield, 2006), 20–21; Frances Fox Piven, "The Prospects for Resistance," *The Nation*, February 6/13, 2017, 13–15; and Frances Fox Piven and Lorraine C. Minnite, "Poor People's Politics," in *The Oxford Handbook of the Social Science of Poverty*, ed. David Brady and Linda M. Burton (New York: Oxford University Press, 2016), 751–73; see also Aldon Morris and Dan Clawson, "Lessons of the Civil Rights Movement for Building a Worker Rights Movement," *Working USA* 8, no. 6 (December 2005): 681–704.

11. Earl Wysong, Robert Perrucci, and David Wright, *The New Class Society: Goodbye American Dream?*, 4th ed. (Lanham, MD: Rowman & Littlefield, 2014), 126–27, 270–71, 290–91.

12. Democratic Socialists of America, http://www.dsausa.org/.

13. Family Values @ Work, http://familyvaluesatwork.org/; Forward Together, http://forwardtogether.org/; and iMomsRising, https://www.momsrising.org/.

14. Center for Community Change, https://www.communitychange.org/.

15. Immigrant Solidarity Network, http://www.immigrantsolidarity.org/.

16. Environmental Justice Resource Center, http://sustainable.org/creating-community/justice-a-equity/574-environmental-justice-resource-center-ejrc.

17. See Black Lives Matter, http://blacklivesmatter.com/; and The Movement for Black Lives, https://policy.m4bl.org/. On the killings of Trayvon Martin and Michael Brown, and for an indispensable study of the historical and political setting of Black Lives Matter, see Keeanga-Yamahtta Taylor, *From #BlackLivesMatter to Black Liberation* (Chicago: Haymarket, 2016).

18. On the labor movement, see Jane F. McAlevey, *No Shortcut: Organizing for Power in the New Gilded Age* (New York: Oxford University Press, 2016); Rick Fantasia and Kim Voss, *Hard Work: Remaking the American Labor Movement* (Berkeley: University of California Press, 2004); and Dan Clawson, *The Next Upsurge: Labor and the New Social Movements* (Ithaca, NY: Cornell University Press, 2003).

19. For a survey of new forms of activism and "emerging institutions" within the labor movement, see Richard B. Freeman, "What Can Labor Organizations Do for U.S. Workers When Unions Can't Do What Unions Used to Do?," in *What Works for Workers: Public Policies and Innovative Strategies for Low-Wage Workers*, ed. Stephanie Luce et al. (New York: Russell Sage, 2014), 50–78.

20. United Workers Congress, "The Rise of Worker Centers and the Fight for a Fair Economy," April 2014, 4, http://www.unitedworkerscongress.org/uploads/2/4/6/6/24662736/__uwc_rise_of_worker_centers-_sm.pdf; see also Janice Fine, *Worker Centers: Organizing Communities at the Edge of the Dream* (Ithaca, NY: Cornell University Press, 2006).

21. See Freeman, "What Can Labor Organizations Do," 63–66; and Steven Greenhouse, "In Florida Tomato Fields, a Penny Buys Progress," *New York Times*, April 25, 2014.

22. Spencer Woodman, "ROC vs the NRA" *The Nation*, May 31, 2010, 21–24; and Laura Flanders, "Serving Up Justice: The Movement for Restaurant Workers' Rights Heats Up," *The Nation*, September 2/9, 2013. For information about ROC, see http://rocunited.org.

23. Cited in Noam Scheiber, "Fight for $15 Shifts Focus," *New York Times*, November 30, 2016. Fight for $15, http://fightfor15.org/?; affiliate organization, Raise the Minimum Wage, http://raisetheminimumwage.com/. See also Rolf, *The Fight for $15*; and Irene Tung, Yannet Lathrop, and Paul Sonn, "The Growing Movement for $15," National Employment Law Project, November 2015, http://www.nelp.org/content/uploads/Growing-Movement-for-15-Dollars.pdf.

24. Cited in Steven Greenhouse, "A Broader Strategy on Wages," *New York Times*, March 31, 2015.

25. On "new unionism" or "social movement unionism," see Fantasia and Voss, *Hard Work*, 120–59.

26. Vanessa Tait, *Poor Workers' Unions: Rebuilding Labor from Below* (Cambridge, MA: South End Press, 2005), 5.

27. On the contribution of Jobs With Justice to this effort, see Steve Early and Larry Cohen, "Jobs With Justice: Mobilizing Labor-Community Coalitions," *WorkingUSA*, November–December 1997, 49–57. For information on Jobs With Justice, see http://www.jwj.org.

28. On the concept of "fusion," see Clawson, *Next Upsurge*, 13–14, 194–99.

29. Martin Luther King Jr., *Where Do We Go from Here: Chaos or Community?* (New York: Harper & Row, 1967), 166.

Selected Bibliography

Abel, Jaison R., Richard Deitz, and Yaqin Su. "Are Recent College Graduates Finding Good Jobs?" *Current Issues in Economics and Finance* 20, no. 1 (2014): 1–8.

Abramson, Corey M. *The End Game: How Inequality Shapes Our Final Years.* Cambridge, MA: Harvard University Press, 2015.

Acemoglu, Daron, David Autor, David Dorn, Gordon H. Hansen, and Brendan Price. "Import Competition and the Great US Employment Sag of the 2000s." *Journal of Labor Economics* 34, no. 1, pt. 2 (2015): S141–S198.

Alesina, Alberto, and Edward L. Glaeser. *Fighting Poverty in the U.S. and Europe: A World of Difference.* New York: Oxford University Press, 2004.

Alexander, Karl, Doris Entwisle, and Linda Olson. *The Long Shadow: Family Background, Disadvantaged Urban Youth, and the Transition to Adulthood.* New York: Russell Sage, 2014.

Alexander, Michelle. *The New Jim Crow: Mass Incarceration in the Age of Colorblindness.* New York: New Press, 2012.

Alterman, Eric. *What Liberal Media? The Truth about Bias and the News.* New York: Basic Books, 2003.

Alverado, Facundo, Anthony B. Atkinson, Thomas Piketty, and Emmanuel Saez. "The Top 1 Percent in International and Historical Perspective." *Journal of Economic Perspectives* 27, no. 3 (Summer 2013): 3–20.

Amy, Douglas J. *Behind the Ballot Box: A Citizen's Guide to Voting Systems.* Westport, CT: Praeger, 2000.

———. *Real Choices/New Voices: How Proportional Representation Elections Could Revitalize American Democracy.* 2nd ed. New York: Columbia University Press, 2002.

Anderson, Carol. *White Rage: The Unspoken Truth of Our Racial Divide.* New York: Bloomsbury, 2016.

Anderson, Elijah. *Code of the Street: Decency, Violence, and the Moral Life of the Inner City.* New York: W. W. Norton, 1999.

———. "The Iconic Ghetto." *The American Academy of Political and Social Science* 642 (July 2012): 8–24.

Anderson, Elizabeth. *The Imperative of Integration.* Princeton, NJ: Princeton University Press, 2010.

———. *Private Government: How Employers Rule Our Lives (and Why We Don't Talk About It).* Princeton, NJ: Princeton University Press, 2017.

Atkinson, Anthony B. *Inequality: What Can Be Done?* Cambridge, MA: Harvard University Press, 2015.

Autor, David H., David Dorn, and Gordon H. Hansen. "The China Shock: Local Labor Market Effect of Import Competition in the United States." *American Economic Review* 103, no. 6 (October 2013): 2121–68.

Bailey, Martha J., and Thomas A. DiPrete. "Five Decades of Remarkable but Slowing Change in U.S. Women's Economic and Social Status and Political Participation." *Journal of the Social Sciences* 2, no. 4 (August 2016): 1–32.

Bailey, Zinzi D., et al. "Structural Racism and Health Inequities in the USA: Evidence and Interventions." *Lancet* 398, no. 10077 (April 8, 2017): 1453–63.

Bane, Mary Jo, and Lawrence M. Mead, eds. *Lifting Up the Poor: A Dialogue on Religion, Poverty, and Welfare Reform*. Washington, DC: Brookings Institution Press, 2003.

Banfield, Edward C. *The Unheavenly City Revisited*. Boston: Little, Brown, 1974.

Bartels, Larry M. *Unequal Democracy: The Political Economy of the New Gilded Age*. 2nd ed. New York: Russell Sage Foundation; Princeton, NJ: Princeton University Press, 2016.

Beaudry, Paul, David A. Green, and Benjamin M. Sand. "The Great Reversal in the Demand for Skill and Cognitive Tasks." *Journal of Labor Economics* 34, no. 1, pt. 2 (January 2016): S199–S247.

Bell, Jeannine. *Hate Thy Neighbor: Move-In Violence and the Persistence of Racial Segregation in American Housing*. New York: New York University Press, 2013.

Berkman, Lisa F. "The Health Divide." *Contexts* 3, no. 4 (Fall 2004): 38–43.

Bernhardt, Annette, Martina Morris, Mark S. Handcock, and Marc A. Scott. *Divergent Paths: Economic Mobility in the New American Labor Market*. New York: Russell Sage, 2001.

Berry, Jeffrey M. *The New Liberalism: The Rising Power of Citizen Groups*. Washington, DC: Brookings Institution Press, 1999.

Berry, Jeffrey M., and Sarah Sobieraj. *The Outrage Industry: Political Opinion and the New Incivility*. New York: Oxford University Press, 2014.

Blau, Francine D., and Lawrence M. Kahn. "The Gender Wage Gap: Extent, Trends, and Explanation." *Journal of Economic Literature* 55, no. 3 (September 2017): 789–865.

Blinder, Alan. "Offshoring: The Next Industrial Revolution?" *Foreign Affairs* 85, no. 2 (March–April 2006): 113–28.

Bluestone, Barry, and Bennett Harrison. *The Deindustrialization of America: Plant Closings, Community Abandonment, and the Dismantling of Basic Industry*. New York: Basic Books, 1982.

Bobbott-Zeher, Donna. "Gender Discrimination at Work: Connecting Gender Stereotypes, Institutional Policies, and Gender Composition of the Workplace." *Gender & Society* 25, no. 6 (December 2011): 764–86.

Bobo, Kim. *Wage Theft in America: Why Millions of Working Americans Are Not Getting Paid—And What We Can Do About It*. New York: New Press, 2011.

Bobo, Lawrence D. "Social Responsibility, Individualism, and Redistributive Policies." *Sociological Forum* 6, no. 1 (March 1991): 71–92.

Bobo, Lawrence D., and Ryan A. Smith. "Antipoverty Policy, Affirmative Action, and Racial Attitudes." In *Confronting Poverty: Prescriptions for Change*, edited by Sheldon H. Danziger, Gary D. Sandefur, and Daniel H. Weinberg, 365–95. New York: Russell Sage and Cambridge, MA: Harvard University Press, 1994.

Bonilla-Silva, Eduardo. *Racism Without Racists: Color-Blind Racism and the Persistence of Racial Inequality in the United States*. 4th ed. Lanham, MD: Rowman & Littlefield, 2014.

———. *White Supremacy and Racism in the Post–Civil Rights Era*. Boulder, CO: Lynne Rienner, 2001.

Bourdieu, Pierre. "The Forms of Capital." In *Handbook of Theory and Research for the Sociology of Education*, edited by John G. Richardson, 241–58. New York: Greenwood Press, 1986.

Bradbury, Bruce, Miles Corak, Jane Waldfogel, and Elizabeth Washbrook. *Too Many Children Left Behind: The U.S. Achievement Gap in Comparative Perspective*. New York: Russell Sage, 2015.

Bradley, David, Evelyne Huber, Stephanie Moller, François Nielsen, and John D. Stephens. "Distribution and Redistribution in Postindustrial Democracies." *World Politics* 55, no. 2 (January 2003): 193–228.

Brady, David. "The Politics of Poverty: Left Political Institutions, the Welfare State, and Poverty." *Social Forces* 82, no. 2 (December 2003): 557–82.

———. *Rich Democracies, Poor People: How Politics Explains Poverty*. New York: Oxford University Press, 2009.

Brady, David, Regina S. Baker, and Ryan Finnigan. "When Unionization Disappears: State-Level Unionization and Working Poverty in the United States." *American Sociological Review* 78, no. 5 (October 2013): 872–96.

Brady, David, Agnes Blome, and Hanna Kleider. "How Politics and Institutions Shape Poverty and Inequality." In *The Oxford Handbook of the Social Science of Poverty*, edited by David Brady and Linda M. Burton, 117–40. New York: Oxford University Press, 2016.

Brady, David, and Lane M. Destro. "Poverty." In *The Oxford Handbook of U.S. Social Policy*, edited by Daniel Béland, Kimberly J. Morgan, and Christopher Howard, 585–602. New York: Oxford University Press, 2014.

Brady, David, Andrew S. Fullerton, and Jennifer Moren Cross. "More Than Just Nickels and Dimes: A Cross-National Analysis of Working Poverty in Affluent Democracies." *Social Problems* 57, no. 4 (November 2010): 559–85.

Bratt, Rachel G., Michael E. Stone, and Chester Hartman, eds. *A Right to Housing: Foundations for a New Social Agenda*. Philadelphia: Temple University Press, 2006.

Briggs, Xavier de Souza. "Brown Kids in White Suburbs: Housing Mobility and the Many Faces of Social Capital." *Housing Policy Debate* 9, no. 1 (1998): 177–221.

———, ed. *The Geography of Opportunity: Race and Housing Choice in Metropolitan America*. Washington, DC: Brookings Institution, 2005.

———. "Moving Up Versus Moving Out: Neighborhood Effects in Housing Mobility Studies." *Housing Policy Debate* 8, no. 1 (1997): 195–234.

Brock, David. *The Republican Noise Machine: Right-Wing Media and How It Corrupts Democracy*. New York: Crown, 2004.

Budig, Michelle J., and Melissa J. Hodges. "Differences in Disadvantage: Variations in the Motherhood Penalty across White Women's Earnings Distribution." *American Sociological Review* 75, no. 5 (October 2010): 705–28.

Bullock, Heather E., Karen Fraser Wyche, and Wendy R. Williams. "Media Images of the Poor." *Journal of Social Issues* 57, no. 2 (Summer 2001): 229–46.

Bulman, Robert C. *Hollywood Goes to High School: Cinema, Schools, and American Culture*. New York: Worth, 2005.

Burtless, Gary, and Christopher Jencks. "American Inequality and Its Consequences." In *Agenda for the Nation*, edited by Henry J. Aaron, James M. Lindsay, and Pietro S. Nivola, 61–108. Washington, DC: Brookings Institution Press, 2003.

Cappelli, Peter. "Skill Gaps, Skill Shortages, and Skill Mismatches: Evidence and Arguments for the United States." *ILR Review* 68, no. 2 (March 2015): 251–90.

———. *Will College Pay Off? A Guide to the Most Important Financial Decision You'll Ever Make*. New York: PublicAffairs, 2015.

Carnes, Nicholas. *White-Collar Government: The Hidden Role of Class in Economic Policy Making*. Chicago: University of Chicago Press, 2013.

Case, Anne, and Angus Deaton. "Rising Morbidity and Mortality in Midlife Among White Non-Hispanic Americans in the 21st Century." *Proceedings of the National Academy of Sciences* 112, no. 49 (December 2015): 15078–83.

Cashin, Sheryll. *The Failures of Integration: How Race and Class Are Undermining the American Dream*. New York: PublicAffairs, 2004.

Cha, Youngjoo. "Overwork and the Persistence of Gender Segregation in Occupations." *Gender & Society* 27, no. 2 (April 2013): 158–84.

Chafel, Judith A. "Societal Images of Poverty: Child and Adult Beliefs." *Youth and Society* 28, no. 4 (June 1997): 432–63.

Charles, Camille Zubrinsky. "The Dynamics of Racial Residential Segregation." *Annual Review of Sociology* 29 (2003): 167–207.

Charles, Kerwin Kofi, and Jonathan Guryan. "Prejudice and Wages: An Empirical Assessment of Becker's *The Economics of Discrimination*." *Journal of Political Economy* 116, no. 5 (October 2008): 773–809.

Chaudry, Ajay. *Putting Children First: How Low-Wage Working Mothers Manage Child Care*. New York: Russell Sage, 2006.

Chernomas, Robert, and Ian Hudson. *Economics in the Twenty-First Century: A Critical Perspective*. Toronto: University of Toronto Press, 2016.

Chetty, Raj, Nathaniel Hendren, Patrick Kline, and Emmanuel Saez. "Where Is the Land of Opportunity? The Geography of Intergenerational Mobility in the United States." *Quarterly Journal of Economics* 129, no. 4 (November 2014): 1553–1623.

Chetty, Raj, et al. "The Association Between Income and Life Expectancy in the United States, 2001–2014." *Journal of the American Medical Association* 315, no. 16 (April 26, 2016): 1750–66.

Clawson, Dan. *The Next Upsurge: Labor and the New Social Movements*. Ithaca, NY: Cornell University Press, 2003.

Clawson, Dan, and Mary Ann Clawson. "Reagan or Business? Foundations of the New Conservatism." In *The Structure of Power in America: The Corporate Elite as a Ruling Class*, edited by Michael Schwartz, 201–17. New York: Holmes and Meier, 1987.

Clawson, Dan, Alan Neustadtl, and Denise Scott. *Money Talks: Corporate PACs and Political Influence*. New York: Basic Books, 1992.

Clawson, Dan, Alan Neustadtl, and Mark Weller. *Dollars and Votes: How Business Campaign Contributions Subvert Democracy*. Philadelphia: Temple University Press, 1998.

Clawson, Rosalee A., and Rakuya Trice. "Poverty as We Know It: Media Portrayals of the Poor." *Public Opinion Quarterly* 64, no. 1 (Spring 2000): 53–64.

Coates, Ta-Nehisi. *We Were Eight Years in Power: An American Tragedy*. New York: One World, 2017.

Coleman, James S. "Social Capital in the Creation of Human Capital." *American Journal of Sociology* 94 (supp. 1988): S95–S120.

Collins, Jane L., and Victoria Mayer. *Both Hands Tied: Welfare Reform and the Race to the Bottom in the Low-Wage Labor Market*. Chicago: University of Chicago Press, 2010.

Corak, Miles. "Do Poor Children Become Poor Adults? Lessons from a Cross-Country Comparison of Generational Earnings Mobility." *Research on Economic Inequality* 13, no. 1 (2006): 143–88.

———. "Income Inequality, Equality of Opportunity, and Intergenerational Mobility." *Journal of Economic Perspectives* 27, no. 3 (Summer 2013): 79–102.

Corcoran, Mary, Greg J. Duncan, Gerald Gurin, and Patricia Gurin. "Myth and Reality: The Causes and Persistence of Poverty." *Journal of Policy Analysis and Management* 4, no. 4 (Summer 1985): 516–36.

Corcoran, Mary, and Jordan Matsudaira. "Is It Getting Harder to Get Ahead? Economic Attainment for Two Cohorts." In *On the Frontier of Adulthood: Theory, Research, and Public Policy*, edited by Richard A. Settersten Jr., Frank F. Furstenberg Jr., and Ruben C. Rumbaut, 356–95. Chicago: University of Chicago Press, 2005.

Correll, Shelley J., Stephen Benard, and In Paik. "Getting a Job: Is There a Motherhood Penalty?" *American Journal of Sociology* 112, no. 5 (March 2007): 1297–1338.

Cowie, Jefferson, and Joseph Heathcott, eds. *Beyond the Ruins: The Meanings of Deindustrialization*. Ithaca, NY: Cornell University Press, 2003.

Cozzarelli, Catherine, Michael J. Tagler, and Anna V. Wilkinson. "Do Middle-Class Students Perceive Poor Women and Poor Men Differently?" *Sex Roles* 47, nos. 11–12 (2002): 519–29.

Cozzarelli, Catherine, Anna V. Wilkinson, and Michael J. Tagler. "Attitudes toward the Poor and Attributions for Poverty." *Journal of Social Issues* 57, no. 2 (Summer 2001): 207–27.

Craypo, Charles, and David Cormier. "Job Restructuring as a Determinant of Wage Inequality and Working-Poor Households." *Journal of Economic Issues* 34, no. 1 (March 2000): 21–42.

Cullen, Jim. *The American Dream: A Short History of an Idea That Shaped a Nation*. New York: Oxford University Press, 2003.

Currie, Janet, and Duncan Thomas. "The Intergenerational Transmission of 'Intelligence': Down the Slippery Slope of *The Bell Curve*." *Industrial Relations* 38, no. 3 (July 1999): 297–330.

Dahl, Robert. *On Political Equality*. New Haven, CT: Yale University Press, 2006.

Daley, David. *Ratf**cked: The True Story Behind the Secret Plan to Steal America's Democracy*. New York: Liveright, 2016.

Darity, William, Jr. "What's Left of the Economic Theory of Discrimination?" In *The Question of Discrimination: Racial Inequality in the U.S. Labor Market*, edited by Steven Shulman and William Darity Jr., 335–74. Middletown, CT: Wesleyan University Press, 1989.

Darity, William A., Jr., et al. "Stratification Economics: A General Theory of Intergroup Inequality." In *The Hidden Rules of Race: Barriers to an Inclusive Economy*, edited by Andrea Flynn, Susan R. Holmberg, Dorian T. Warren, and Felicia J. Wong, 35–51. New York: Cambridge University Press, 2017.

Davis, Gerald F. "After the Corporation." *Politics & Society* 41, no. 2 (2013): 288–89.

———. *Managed by the Market: How Finance Reshaped America*. New York: Oxford University Press, 2009.

Davis, Liane V., and Jan L. Hagen. "Stereotypes and Stigma: What's Changed for Welfare Mothers." *Affilia* 11, no. 3 (Fall 1996): 319–37.

Dean, Adam. "Power Over Profits: The Political Economy of Workers and Wages." *Politics & Society* 43, no. 3 (2015): 333–60.

Desmond, Matthew. "Disposable Ties and the Urban Poor." *American Journal of Sociology* 117, no. 5 (March 2012): 1295–335.

———. *Evicted: Poverty and Profit in the American City*. New York: Crown, 2016.

———. "Severe Deprivation in America: An Introduction." *Journal of the Social Sciences* 1, no. 1 (2015): 1–11.

Devlin, Bernie, Stephen E. Fienberg, Daniel P. Resnick, and Kathryn Roeder, eds. *Intelligence, Genes, and Success: Scientists Respond to "The Bell Curve."* New York: Copernicus, Springer-Verlag, 1997.

Dickman, Samuel L., David U. Himmelstein, and Steffie Woolhandler. "Inequality and the Health-Care System in the USA." *Lancet* 389, no. 10077 (April 8, 2017): 1431–41.

Dionne, E. J., Jr., Norman J. Ornstein, and Thomas E. Mann. *One Nation After Trump: A Guide for the Perplexed, the Disillusioned, the Desperate, and the Not-Yet Deported*. New York: St. Martin's Press, 2017.

DiTomaso, Nancy. *The American Non-Dilemma: Racial Inequality Without Racism*. New York: Russell Sage, 2013.

Dohan, Daniel. *The Price of Poverty: Money, Work, and Culture in the Mexican American Barrio*. Berkeley: University of California Press, 2003.

Domínguez, Silvia, and Celeste Watkins. "Creating Networks for Survival and Mobility: Social Capital among African-American and Latin-American Low-Income Mothers." *Social Problems* 50, no. 1 (February 2003): 111–35.

Drutman, Lee. *The Business of America Is Lobbying: How Corporations Became Politicized and Politics Became More Corporate*. New York: Oxford, 2015.

D'Souza, Dinesh. *The End of Racism: Principles for a Multiracial Society*. New York: Free Press, 1995.

Duneier, Mitchell. *Ghetto: The Invention of a Place, the History of an Idea*. New York: Farrar, Straus and Giroux, 2016.

Durlauf, Steven N. "The Memberships Theory of Inequality: Ideas and Implications." In *Elites, Minorities, and Economic Growth*, edited by Elise S. Brezis and Peter Temin, 161–77. Amsterdam, Netherlands: Elsevier, 1999.

———. "The Memberships Theory of Poverty: The Role of Group Affiliations in Determining Socioeconomic Outcomes." In *Understanding Poverty*, edited by Sheldon H. Danziger and Robert H. Haveman, 392–416. New York: Russell Sage; Cambridge, MA: Harvard University Press, 2001.

———. "A Theory of Persistent Income Inequality." *Journal of Economic Growth* 1 (1996): 75–93.

Dwyer, Rachel E., and Lora A. Phillips Lassus. "The Great Risk Shift and Precarity in the U.S. Housing Market." *Annals of the American Academy of Political and Social Science* 660, no. 1 (July 2015): 199–216.

Edelman, Peter. *Not a Crime to Be Poor: The Criminalization of Poverty in America*. New York: New Press, 2017.

Edin, Kathryn, and Maria Kefalas. *Promises I Can Keep: Why Poor Women Put Motherhood Before Marriage*. Berkeley: University of California Press, 2005.

Edin, Kathryn, and H. Luke Shaefer. *$2.00 a Day: Living on Almost Nothing in America*. Boston: Houghton Mifflin Harcourt, 2015.

Edin, Kathryn, and Timothy J. Nelson. *Doing the Best I Can: Fatherhood in the Inner City*. Berkeley: University of California Press, 2013.

Edsall, Thomas Byrne. *The New Politics of Inequality*. New York: W. W. Norton, 1984.

Edwards, Richard C. "Individual Traits and Organizational Incentives: What Makes a 'Good' Worker?" *Journal of Human Resources* 11, no. 1 (Winter 1976): 51–68.

Ehrenreich, Barbara. *Nickel and Dimed: On (Not) Getting By in America*. New York: Henry Holt, Metropolitan, 2001.

England, Paula. "The Gender Revolution: Uneven and Stalled." *Gender & Society* 24, no. 2 (April 2010): 149–66.

Entman, Robert M. "Television, Democratic Theory, and the Visual Construction of Poverty." *Research in Political Sociology* 7 (1995): 139–59.

Eppard, Lawrence M. "Paved with Good Intentions: Individualism and the Cultural Reproduction of Poverty and Inequality." *Sociation Today* 14, no. 3 (Fall/Winter 2016).

Erickson, Bonnie. "Social Networks: The Value of Variety." *Contexts* 2, no. 1 (Winter 2003): 25–31.

Fantasia, Rick, and Kim Voss. *Hard Work: Remaking the American Labor Movement*. Berkeley: University of California Press, 2004.

Farber, Naomi. "The Significance of Aspirations among Unmarried Adolescent Mothers." *Social Service Review* 63, no. 4 (December 1989): 518–32.

———. "The Significance of Race and Class in Marital Decisions among Unmarried Adolescent Mothers." *Social Problems* 37, no. 1 (February 1990): 51–63.

Feagin, Joe R. "America's Welfare Stereotypes." *Social Science Quarterly* 52, no. 4 (March 1972): 921–33.

———. "Poverty: We Still Believe That God Helps Those Who Help Themselves." *Psychology Today* 6 (1972): 101–10, 129.

———. *Subordinating the Poor: Welfare and American Beliefs*. Englewood Cliffs, NJ: Prentice-Hall, 1975.

Fields, Karen E., and Barbara J. Fields. *Racecraft: The Soul of Inequality in American Life*. London: Verso, 2012.

Fischer, Claude S., Michael Hout, Martin Sanchez Jankowski, Samuel R. Lucas, Ann Swidler, and Kim Voss. *Inequality by Design: Cracking the Bell Curve Myth*. Princeton, NJ: Princeton University Press, 1996.

Flavin, Patrick. "Income Inequality and Policy Representation in the American States." *American Politics Research* 40, no. 1 (January 2012): 29–59.

Flynn, Andrea, Susan R. Holmberg, Dorian T. Warren, and Felicia J. Wong, *The Hidden Rules of Race: Barriers to an Inclusive Economy*. New York: Cambridge University Press, 2017.

Foroohar, Rana. *The Rise of Finance and the Fall of American Business*. New York: Crown, 2016.

Ford, Martin. *Rise of the Robots. Technology and the Threat of a Jobless Future*. New York: Basic Books, 2015.

Frank, Thomas. *Listen, Liberal: Or Whatever Happened to the Party of the People?* New York: Picador, 2017.

Fraser, Steve. *The Age of Acquiescence: The Life and Death of American Resistance to Organized Wealth and Power*. New York: Little, Brown, 2015.

Fraser, Steven, ed. *The Bell Curve Wars: Race, Intelligence, and the Future of America*. New York: Basic Books, 1995.

Fredrickson, Caroline. *Under the Bus: How Working Women Are Being Run Over*. New York: New Press, 2015.

Freeman, Richard B. *America Works: The Exceptional U.S. Labor Market*. New York: Russell Sage, 2007.

————. "Globalization and Inequality." In *The Oxford Handbook of Economic Inequality*, edited by Wiemer Salverda, Brian Nolan, and Timothy M. Smeeding, 575–99. New York: Oxford University Press, 2009.

Fukuyama, Francis. *Political Order and Political Decay: From the Industrial Revolution to the Globalization of Democracy*. New York: Farrar, Straus and Giroux, 2014.

Galbraith, James K. *The End of Normal: The Great Crisis and the Future of Growth*. New York: Simon & Schuster, 2014.

————. *Inequality: What Everyone Needs to Know*. New York: Oxford University Press, 2016.

Galster, George, and Patrick Sharkey. "Spatial Foundations of Inequality: A Conceptual Model and Empirical Overview." *Journal of the Social Sciences*, 3, no. 2 (February 2017): 1–33.

Galston, William A., and Elaine C. Kamarck. "Against Short-Termism." *Democracy: A Journal of Ideas* 38 (Fall 2015): 10–24.

Gans, Herbert J. *Democracy and the News*. New York: Oxford University Press, 2003.

————. *The War against the Poor: The Underclass and Antipoverty Policy*. New York: Basic Books, 1995.

Gerstel, Naomi. "The Third Shift: Gender and Care Work Outside the Home." *Qualitative Sociology* 23, no. 4 (Winter 2000): 467–83.

Gilder, George. *Wealth and Poverty*. New York: Basic Books, 1981.

Gilens, Martin. *Affluence and Influence: Economic Inequality and Political Power in America*. New York: Russell Sage; Princeton, NJ; Princeton University Press, 2012.

————. "The American News Media and Public Misperceptions of Race and Poverty." In *Race, Poverty, and Domestic Policy*, edited by C. Michael Henry, 336–63. New Haven, CT: Yale University Press, 2004.

————. "Inequality and Democratic Responsiveness." *Public Opinion Quarterly* 69, no. 5 (2005): 778–96.

————. "Preference Gaps and Inequality in Representation." *PS: Political Science and Politics* 42, no. 2 (April 2009): 335–41.

————. *Why Americans Hate Welfare*. Chicago: University of Chicago Press, 1999.

Glaude, Eddie S., Jr. *Democracy in Black: How Race Still Enslaves the American Soul*. New York: Crown, 2016.

Gordon, David M. *Fat and Mean: The Corporate Squeeze of Working Americans and the Myth of Managerial "Downsizing"*. New York: Free Press, 1996.

Gordon, Robert J. *The Rise and Fall of American Growth: The U.S. Standard of Living Since the Civil War*. Princeton, NJ: Princeton University Press, 2016.

Gornick, Janet C., and Marcia K. Meyers. *Families That Work: Policies for Reconciling Parenthood and Employment*. New York: Russell Sage, 2005.

Gornick, Janet C., and Markus Jäntti. "Child Poverty in Cross-National Perspective: Lessons from the Luxembourg Income Study." *Children and Youth Services Review* 34 (2012): 558–68.

Graham, Carol. *Happiness for All? Unequal Hopes and Lives in Pursuit of the American Dream*. Princeton, NJ: Princeton University Press, 2017.

Granovetter, Mark S. *Getting a Job: A Study of Contacts and Careers*. 2nd ed. Chicago: University of Chicago Press, 1995.

————. "The Strength of Weak Ties." *American Journal of Sociology* 78, no. 6 (May 1973): 1360–80.

————. "The Strength of Weak Ties: A Network Theory Revisited." *Sociological Theory* 1 (1983): 201–33.

Green, Gary P., Leann M. Tigges, and Irene Browne. "Social Resources, Job Search, and Poverty in Atlanta." *Research in Community Sociology* 5 (1995): 161–82.

Hacker, Jacob C. *The Great Risk Shift: The Assault on American Jobs, Families, Health Care, and Retirement—And How You Can Fight Back*. New York: Oxford University Press, 2006.

Hacker, Jacob C., and Paul Peirson. *American Amnesia: How the War on Government Led Us to Forget What Made America Prosper*. New York: Simon & Schuster, 2016.

————. *Winner-Take-All Politics: How Washington Made the Rich Richer—And Turned Its Back on the Middle Class*. New York: Simon & Schuster, 2010.

Hallin, Daniel C. "The American News Media: A Critical Theory Perspective." In *Critical Theory and Public Life*, edited by John Forester, 121–46. Cambridge, MA: MIT Press, 1985.

Halpern-Meekin, Sarah, Kathryn Edin, Laura Tach, and Jennifer Sykes. *It's Not Like I'm Poor: How Working Families Make Ends Meet in a Post-Welfare World.* Oakland: University of California Press, 2015.

Hancock, Ange-Marie. *The Politics of Disgust: The Public Identity of the Welfare Queen.* New York: New York University Press, 2004.

Hanson, Sandra L., and John Zogby. "The Polls—Trends: Attitudes About the American Dream." *Public Opinion Quarterly* 74, no. 3 (Fall 2010): 570–84.

Harrington, Michael. *The New American Poverty*. New York: Penguin, 1984.

———. *The Other America: Poverty in the United States*. New York: Macmillan, 1993 [1962].

Harrison, Lawrence E. *Who Prospers? How Cultural Values Shape Economic and Political Success*. New York: Basic Books, 1992.

Hart, Betty, and Todd R. Risley. *Meaningful Differences in the Everyday Experience of Young American Children*. Baltimore, MD: Paul H. Brookes Publishing, 1995.

Hays, Sharon. *Flat Broke with Children: Women in the Age of Welfare Reform*. New York: Oxford University Press, 2003.

Helburn, Suzanne W., and Barbara R. Bergmann. *America's Child Care Problem: The Way Out*. New York: Palgrave, 2002.

Hero, Joachim O., Alan M. Zaslavsky, and Robert J. Blendon. "The United States Leads Other Nations in Difference by Income in Perceptions of Health and Health Care." *Health Affairs* 36, no. 6 (June 2017): 1032–40.

Herrnstein, Richard J., and Charles Murray. *The Bell Curve: Intelligence and Class Structure in American Life*. New York: Free Press, 1994.

Hicks-Bartlett, Sharon. "Between a Rock and a Hard Place: The Labyrinth of Working and Parenting in a Poor Community." In *Coping with Poverty: The Social Contexts of Neighborhood, Work, and Family in the African-American Community*, edited by Sheldon H. Danziger and Ann Chih Lin, 27–51. Ann Arbor: University of Michigan Press, 2000.

Hill, Steven. *Fixing Elections: The Failure of America's Winner Take All Politics*. New York: Routledge, 2002.

———. *Raw Deal: How the "Uber Economy" and Runaway Capitalism Are Screwing American Workers*. New York: St. Martin's Press, 2015.

Hinton, Elizabeth. *From the War on Poverty to the War on Crime: The Making of Mass Incarceration in America*. Cambridge, MA: Harvard University Press, 2016.

Hochschild, Arlie Russell. *Strangers in Their Own Land: Anger and Mourning on the American Right*. New York: New Press, 2016.

Hochschild, Jennifer L. *Facing Up to the American Dream: Race, Class, and the Soul of the Nation*. Princeton, NJ: Princeton University Press, 1995.

Hunt, Matthew O. "African American, Hispanic, and White Beliefs about Black/White Inequality, 1977–2004." *American Sociological Review* 72, no. 3 (June 2007): 390–415.

———. "The Individual, Society, or Both? A Comparison of Black, Latino, and White Beliefs about the Causes of Poverty." *Social Forces* 75, no. 1 (September 1996): 293–322.

Hunt, Matthew O., and Heather E. Bullock. "Ideologies and Beliefs About Poverty." In *The Oxford Handbook of the Social Science of Poverty*, edited by David Brady and Linda M. Burton, 93–116. New York: Oxford University Press, 2016.

Iversen, Roberta Rehner, and Annie Laurie Armstrong. *Jobs Aren't Enough: Toward a New Economic Mobility for Low-Income Families*. Philadelphia: Temple University Press, 2006.

Iversen, Roberta Rehner, and Naomi Farber. "Transmission of Family Values, Work, and Welfare among Poor Urban Black Women." *Work and Occupations* 23, no. 4 (November 1996): 437–60.

Iyengar, Shanto. "Framing Responsibility for Political Issues: The Case of Poverty." *Political Behavior* 12, no. 1 (March 1990): 19–40.

Jacoby, Russell, and Naomi Glauberman, eds. *The Bell Curve Debate: History, Documents, Opinions*. New York: Times Books, 1995.

Jargowsky, Paul A. *Poverty and Place: Ghettos, Barrios, and the American City*. New York: Russell Sage, 1997.

Jarrett, Robin L. "Living Poor: Family Life among Single Parent, African American Women." *Social Problems* 41, no. 1 (February 1994): 30–49.

Jencks, Christopher, and Meredith Phillips, eds. *The Black-White Test Score Gap*. Washington, DC: Brookings Institution Press, 1998.

Jones, Rachel K., and Ye Luo. "The Culture of Poverty and African-American Culture: An Empirical Assessment." *Sociological Perspectives* 42, no. 3 (1999): 439–58.

Judis, John B. *The Populist Explosion: How the Great Recession Transformed American and European Politics*. New York: Columbia Global Reports, 2016.

Jung, Jiwook. "Shareholder Value and Workforce Downsizing." *Social Forces* 93, no. 4 (June 2015): 1335–68.

Kalleberg, Arne L. *The Mismatched Worker*. New York: W. W. Norton, 2007.

———. *Good Jobs, Bad Jobs: The Rise of Polarized and Precarious Employment Systems in the United States, 1970s to 2000s*. New York: Russell Sage, 2011.

Kamerman, Sheila B. "Europe Advanced While the United States Lagged." In *Unfinished Work: Building Equality and Democracy in an Era of Working Families*, edited by Jody Heymann and Christopher Beem, 309–347. New York: New Press, 2005.

Kantor, Harvey, and Robert Lowe. "Educationalizing the Welfare State and Privatizing Education: The Evolution of Social Policy Since the New Deal." In *Closing the Opportunity Gap*, edited by Prudence L. Carter and Kevin G. Welner, 25–39. New York: Oxford University Press, 2013.

Katz, Michael B. *The Undeserving Poor: America's Enduring Confrontation with Poverty*. 2nd ed. New York: Oxford University Press, 2013.

———. *The Undeserving Poor: From the War on Poverty to the War on Welfare*. New York: Pantheon, 1989.

Katznelson, Ira. *When Affirmative Action Was White: An Untold History of Racial Inequality in Twentieth-Century America*. New York: W. W. Norton, 2005.

Kelly, Maura. "Regulating the Reproduction and Mothering of Poor Women: The Controlling Image of the Welfare Mother in Television News Coverage of Welfare Reform." *Journal of Poverty* 14, no. 1 (January–March 2010): 76–96.

Kelly, Patricia Fernandez. "Social and Cultural Capital in the Urban Ghetto: Implications for the Economic Sociology of Immigration." In *The Economic Sociology of Immigration: Essays on Networks, Ethnicity, and Entrepreneurship*, edited by Alejandro Portes, 213–47. New York: Russell Sage, 1995.

Kelso, William A. *Poverty and the Underclass: Changing Perceptions of the Poor in America*. New York: New York University Press, 1994.

Kendall, Diana. *Framing Class: Media Representations of Wealth and Poverty in America*. Lanham, MD: Rowman & Littlefield, 2005.

Kendi, Ibram X. *Stamped from the Beginning: The Definitive History of Racist Ideas in America*. New York: Nation Books, 2016.

Kenworthy, Lane. *Progress for the Poor*. New York: Oxford University Press, 2011.

———. *Social Democratic America*. New York: Oxford University Press, 2014.

Kincheloe, Joe L., Shirley R. Steinberg, and Aaron D. Gresson III, eds. *Measured Lies: The Bell Curve Examined*. New York: St. Martin's Press, 1996.

King, Martin Luther Jr. *Where Do We Go from Here: Chaos or Community?* New York: Harper & Row, 1967.

Kluegel, James R., and Eliot R. Smith. *Beliefs about Inequality: Americans' Views of What Is and What Ought to Be*. New York: Aldine De Gruyter, 1986.

Knapp, Peter, Jane C. Kronick, R. William Marks, and Miriam G. Vosburgh. *The Assault on Equality*. Westport, CT: Praeger, 1996.

Kohn, Melvin L. "Two Visions of the Relationship between Individual and Society: The Bell Curve versus Social Structure and Personality." In *A Nation Divided: Diversity, Inequality, and Community in American Society*, edited by Phyllis Moen, Donna Dempster-McClain, and Henry A. Walker, 34–51. Ithaca, NY: Cornell University Press, 1999.

Kollmeyer, Christopher. "Market Forces and Workers' Power Resources: A Sociological Account of Real Wage Growth in Advanced Capitalism." *International Journal of Comparative Sociology* 58, no. 2 (2017): 99–119.

Kotz, David M. *The Rise and Fall of Neoliberal Capitalism*. Cambridge, MA: Harvard University Press, 2015.

Krysan, Maria, Kyle Crowder, and Michael D. M. Bader. "Pathways to Residential Segregation." In *Choosing Homes, Choosing Schools*, edited by Annette Lareau and Kimberly A. Goyette, 27–63. New York: Russell Sage, 2014.

Krysan, Maria, Reynolds Farley, Mick P. Couper, and Tyrone A. Forman. "Does Race Matter in Neighborhood Preferences? Results from a Video Experiment." *American Journal of Sociology* 115, no. 2 (September 2009): 527–59.

Lafer, Gordon. *The Job Training Charade*. Ithaca, NY: Cornell University Press, 2002.

———. *The One Percent Solution: How Corporations Are Remaking America One State at a Time*. New York: ILR Press, 2017.

Lamont, Michèle, and Annette Lareau. "Cultural Capital: Allusions, Gaps and Glissandos in Recent Theoretical Developments." *Sociological Theory* 6 (Fall 1988): 153–68.

Lapham, Lewis H. "Tentacles of Rage: The Republican Propaganda Mills, a Brief History." *Harper's Magazine*, September 2004, 31–41.

Lee, Cheol-Sung. "Labor Unions and Good Governance: A Cross-National Comparative Analysis." *American Sociological Review* 72, no. 4 (August 2007): 585–609.

Lee, Valerie E., and David T. Burkam. *Inequality at the Starting Gate: Social Background Differences in Achievement as Children Begin School*. Washington, DC: Economic Policy Institute, 2002.

Lein, Laura, Sandra K. Danziger, H. Luke Shaefer, and Amanda Tillotson. "Social Policy, Transfers, Programs, and Assistance." In *The Oxford Handbook of the Social Science of Poverty*, edited by David Brady and Linda M. Burton, 733–50. New York: Oxford University Press, 2016.

Lein, Laura, and Deanna T. Schexnayder. *Life After Welfare: Reform and the Persistence of Poverty*. Austin: University of Texas Press, 2007.

Leventhal, Tama, and Jeanne Brooks-Gunn. "The Neighborhoods They Live In: The Effects of Neighborhood Residence on Child and Adolescent Outcomes." *Psychological Bulletin* 126, no. 2 (2000): 309–37.

Leventhal, Tama, Véronique Dupéré, and Elizabeth A. Shuey. "Children in Neighborhoods." In *Handbook of Child Psychology and Developmental Science*, 7th ed., edited by Marc H. Bornstein, Tama Leventhal, and Richard M. Lerner, 493–533. Hoboken, NJ: Wiley, 2015.

Levy, Helen. "Income, Poverty, and Material Hardship Among Older Americans." *Journal of the Social Sciences* 1, no. 1 (2015): 55–77.

Lewis, Oscar. "The Culture of Poverty." In *Explosive Forces in Latin America*, edited by John J. TePaske and Sydney Nettleton Fisher, 149–73. Columbus: Ohio State University Press, 1964.

———. "The Culture of Poverty." In *On Understanding Poverty: Perspectives from the Social Sciences*, edited by Daniel P. Moynihan, 187–200. New York: Basic Books, 1968.

———. "The Culture of Poverty." *Scientific American*, October 1966, 19–25.

Lichter, Daniel T., Christie D. Batson, and J. Brian Brown. "Welfare Reform and Marriage Promotion: The Marital Expectations and Desires of Single and Cohabiting Mothers." *Social Service Review* 78, no. 1 (March 2004): 2–25.

Lin, Ken-Hou, and Donald Tomaskovic-Devey. "Financialization and U.S. Income Inequality, 1970–2008," *American Journal of Sociology* 118, no. 5 (March 2013): 1291–94.

Lin, Nan. "Inequality in Social Capital." *Contemporary Sociology* 29, no. 6 (November 2000): 785–95.

———. "Social Networks and Status Attainment." *Annual Review of Sociology* 25 (1999): 467–87.

Livingstone, D. W. *The Education-Jobs Gap: Underemployment or Economic Democracy*. Boulder, CO: Westview Press, 1998.

Logan, John R. "The Persistence of Segregation in the 21st Century Metropolis." *City & Community* 12, no. 2 (June 2013): 160–68.

Luce, Stephanie, Jennifer Luff, Joseph A. McCartin, and Ruth Milkman, eds. *What Works for Workers: Public Policies and Innovative Strategies for Low-Wage Workers*. New York: Russell Sage, 2014.

Ludwig, Jens, and Susan Mayer. "'Culture' and the Intergenerational Transmission of Poverty: The Prevention Paradox." *Future of Children* 16, no. 2 (Fall 2006): 175–96.

Lukes, Steven. "Power." *Contexts* 6, no. 3 (Summer 2007): 59–61.

MacLean, Nancy. *Democracy in Chains: The Deep History of the Radical Right's Stealth Plan for America*. New York: Viking, 2017.

Magnet, Myron. *The Dream and the Nightmare: The Sixties' Legacy to the Underclass*. New York: William Morrow, 1993.

Mandle, Jay. *Democracy, America, and the Age of Globalization*. New York: Cambridge University Press, 2008.

———. "The Politics of Democracy." *Challenge* 47, no. 1 (January–February 2004): 53–63.

Mann, Thomas E., and Norman J. Ornstein. *It's Even Worse Than It Looks: How the American Constitutional System Collided with the New Politics of Extremism*. New York: Basic Books, 2016.

Manning-Miller, Carmen L. "Media Discourse and the Feminization of Poverty." *Explorations in Ethnic Studies* 17, no. 1 (January 1994): 79–88.

Manza, Jeff. "Unequal Democracy in America: The Long View." In *The New Gilded Age: The Critical Inequality Debates of Our Time*, edited by David B. Grusky and Tamar Kricheli-Katz, 131–58. Stanford, CA: Stanford University Press, 2012.

Marchevsky, Alejandra, and Jeanne Theoharis. *Not Working: Latina Immigrants, Low Wage Jobs, and the Failure of Welfare Reform*. New York: New York University Press, 2006.

Martin, Lori Latrice. *Black Asset Poverty and the Enduring Racial Divide*. Boulder, CO: First Forum Press, 2013.

Massey, Douglas S. *Return of the "L" Word: A Liberal Vision for the New Century*. Princeton, NJ: Princeton University Press, 2005.

Massey, Douglas S., and Nancy A. Denton. *American Apartheid: Segregation and the Making of the Underclass*. Cambridge, MA: Harvard University Press, 1993.

Massey, Douglas S., and Jonathan Tannen. "Segregation, Race, and the Social Worlds of Rich and Poor." In *The Dynamics of Opportunity in America: Evidence and Perspectives*, edited by Irwin Kirsch and Henry Braun, 13–33. New York: Springer, 2016.

Mayer, Jane. *Dark Money: The Hidden History of the Billionaires Behind the Rise of the Radical Right*. New York: Anchor Books, 2017.

McAlevey, Jane F. *No Shortcuts: Organizing for Power in the New Gilded Age*. New York: Oxford University Press, 2016.

McCall, Leslie. "Political and Policy Responses to Problems of Inequality and Opportunity: Past, Present, and Future." In *The Dynamics of Opportunity in America: Evidence and Perspectives*, edited by Irwin Kirsch and Henry Braun, 415–442. New York: Springer, 2016.

———. *The Undeserving Rich: American Beliefs about Inequality, Opportunity, and Redistribution*. New York: Cambridge University Press, 2013.

McChesney, Robert W. and John Nichols. *People Get Ready: The Fight Against a Jobless Economy and a Citizenless Democracy*. New York: Nation Books, 2016.

McNamee, Stephen J., and Robert K. Miller Jr. *The Meritocracy Myth*. 3rd ed. Lanham, MD: Rowman & Littlefield, 2014.

Mead, Lawrence M. *The New Paternalism: Supervisory Approaches to Poverty*. Washington, DC: Brookings Institution Press, 1997.

———, ed. *The New Politics of Poverty: The Nonworking Poor in America*. New York: Basic Books, 1992.

Meagher, Richard. "The Vast Right-Wing Conspiracy: Media and Conservative Networks." *New Political Science* 34, no. 4 (January 2012): 469–84.

Micklethwait, John, and Adrian Wooldridge. *The Right Nation: Conservative Power in America*. New York: Penguin, 2004.

Milkman, Ruth, and Stephanie Luce. "Labor Unions and the Great Recession." *Journal of the Social Sciences* 3, no. 3 (April 2017): 145–65.

Mills, C. Wright. *The Sociological Imagination*. New York: Oxford University Press, 1959.

Mishel, Lawrence, Josh Bivens, Elise Gould, and Heidi Shierholz. *The State of Working America*. 12th ed. Ithaca, NY: Cornell University Press, 2012.

Misra, Joy, Stephanie Moller, and Marina Karides. "Envisioning Dependency: Changing Media Depictions of Welfare in the 20th Century." *Social Problems* 50, no. 4 (November 2003): 482–504.

Moore, Thomas S. "The Locus of Racial Discrimination in the Labor Market." *American Journal of Sociology* 116, no. 3 (November 2010): 909–42.

Morduch, Jonathan, and Rachel Schneider. *The Financial Diaries: How American Families Cope in a World of Uncertainty.* Princeton, NJ: Princeton University Press, 2017.

Morgen, Sandra, Joan Acker, and Jill Weight. *Stretched Thin: Poor Families, Welfare Work, and Welfare Reform.* Ithaca, NY: Cornell University Press, 2010.

Mounk, Yascha. *The Age of Responsibility: Luck, Choice, and the Welfare State.* Cambridge, MA: Harvard University Press, 2017.

Murray, Charles. *Losing Ground: American Social Policy, 1950–1980.* New York: Basic Books, 1984.

Newman, Katherine S. *No Shame in My Game: The Working Poor in the Inner City.* New York: Alfred A. Knopf, 1999.

Nichols, John, and Robert W. McChesney. *Dollarocracy: How the Money and Media Election Complex Is Destroying America.* New York: Nation Books, 2013.

Nilson, Linda Burzotta. "Reconsidering Ideological Lines: Beliefs about Poverty in America." *Sociological Quarterly* 22 (Autumn 1981): 531–48.

Nisbet, Richard E. *Intelligence and How to Get It: Why Schools and Culture Matter.* New York: W. W. Norton, 2009.

Noble, Charles. *The Collapse of Liberalism: Why America Needs a New Left.* Lanham, MD: Rowman & Littlefield, 2004.

———. *Welfare as We Knew It: A Political History of the American Welfare State.* New York: Oxford University Press, 1997.

Nolan, Brian, and Ive Marx. "Economic Inequality, Poverty, and Social Exclusion." In *The Oxford Handbook of Economic Inequality,* edited by Wiemer Salverda, Brian Nolan, and Timothy M. Smeeding, 315–41. New York: Oxford University Press, 2009.

O'Connor, Alice. "Financing the Counterrevolution." *In Rightward Bound: Making America Conservative in the 1970s,* edited by Bruce J. Schulman and Julian E. Zelizer, 148–68. Cambridge: Harvard University Press, 2008.

———. *Poverty Knowledge: Social Science, Social Policy, and the Poor in Twentieth-Century U.S. History.* Princeton, NJ: Princeton University Press, 2001.

———. "Poverty Knowledge and the History of Poverty Research." In *The Oxford Handbook of the Social Science of Poverty,* edited by David Brady and Linda M. Burton, 21–46. New York: Oxford University Press, 2016.

———. "Poverty Research and Policy for the Post-Welfare Era." *Annual Review of Sociology* 26 (2000): 547–62.

Oliver, Melvin L., and Thomas M. Shapiro. *Black Wealth/White Wealth: A New Perspective on Racial Inequality.* New York: Routledge, 1995.

Owens, Ann. "Inequality in Children's Contexts: Income Segregation of Households With and Without Children." *American Sociological Review* 81, no. 3 (2016): 549–574.

Page, Benjamin I., Larry M. Bartels, and Jason Seawright. "Democracy and the Policy Preferences of Wealthy Americans." *Perspectives on Politics* 11, no. 1 (March 2013): 51–73.

Pager, Devah. "The Mark of a Criminal Record." *American Journal of Sociology* 108, no. 5 (March 2003): 937–75.

———. *Marked: Race, Crime, and Finding Work in an Era of Mass Incarceration.* Chicago: University of Chicago Press, 2007.

Pager, Devah, Bruce Western, and Bart Bonikowski. "Discrimination in a Low-wage Labor Market: A Field Experiment." *American Sociological Review* 74, no. 5 (October 2009: 777–99.

Pampel, Fred C., Patrick M. Krueger, and Justin T. Denney. "Socioeconomic Disparities in Health Behaviors." *Annual Review of Sociology* 36 (2010): 349–70.

Parisi, Peter. "A Sort of Compassion: The *Washington Post* Explains the 'Crisis in Urban America.'" *Howard Journal of Communications* 9 (1998): 187–203.

Patterson, Orlando, with Ethan Fosse, eds. *The Cultural Matrix: Understanding Black Youth.* Cambridge, MA: Harvard University Press, 2015.

Patterson, Thomas E. *Informing the News: The Need for Knowledge-Based Journalism.* New York: Vintage Books, 2013.

———. *The Vanishing Voter: Public Involvement in an Age of Uncertainty.* New York: Vintage, 2003.

Pebley, Anne R., and Narayan Sastry. "Neighborhoods, Poverty, and Children's Well-Being." In *Social Inequality*, edited by Kathryn M. Neckerman, 833–847. New York: Russell Sage, 2004.

Pedulla, David S., and Sarah Thébaud. "Can We Finish the Revolution? Gender, Work-Family Ideals, and Institutional Constraints." *American Sociological Review* 80, no. 1 (February 2015): 116–39.

Petterson, Stephen M. "Are Young Black Men Really Less Willing to Work?" *American Sociological Review* 62, no. 4 (August 1997): 605–13.

Pfaff, John F. *Locked In: The True Causes of Mass Incarceration and How to Achieve Real Reform.* New York: Basic Books, 2017.

Phillips, Meredith, and Tiffani Chin. "School Inequality: What Do We Know?" In *Social Inequality*, edited by Kathryn M. Neckerman, 467–519. New York: Russell Sage, 2004.

Phillips-Fein, Kim. *Invisible Hands: The Businessmen's Crusade Against the New Deal.* New York: W. W. Norton, 2009.

Picketty, Thomas. *Capital in the Twenty-First Century.* Translated by Arthur Goldhammer. Cambridge, MA: Belknap Press of Harvard University Press, 2014.

Pimpare, Stephen. *Ghettos, Tramps, and Welfare Queens: Down and Out on the Silver Screen.* New York: Oxford University Press, 2017.

———. *A People's History of Poverty in America.* New York: New Press, 2008.

Piven, Frances Fox. *Challenging Authority: How Ordinary People Change America.* Lanham, MD: Rowman & Littlefield, 2006.

Piven, Frances Fox, and Lorraine C. Minnite. "Poor People's Politics." In *The Oxford Handbook of the Social Science of Poverty*, edited by David Brady and Linda M. Burton 751–73. New York: Oxford University Press, 2016.

Polakov, Valerie. *Who Cares for Our Children: The Child Care Crisis in the Other America.* New York: Teachers College Press, 2007.

Portes, Alejandro. "Social Capital: Its Origins and Applications in Modern Sociology." *Annual Review of Sociology* 24 (1998): 1–24.

Press, Julie E. "Child Care as Poverty Policy: The Effect of Child Care on Work and Family Poverty." In *Prismatic Metropolis: Inequality in Los Angeles*, edited by Lawrence D. Bobo, Melvin L. Oliver, James H. Johnson Jr., and Abel Valenzuela Jr., 338–82. New York: Russell Sage, 2000.

Presser, Harriet B. *Working in a 24/7 Economy: Challenges for American Families.* New York: Russell Sage, 2003.

Pryor, Frederic L., and David L. Schaffer. *Who's Not Working and Why: Employment, Cognitive Skills, Wages, and the Changing U.S. Labor Market.* New York: Cambridge University Press, 1999.

Purser, Gretchen. "The Circle of Dispossession: Evicting the Urban Poor in Baltimore." *Critical Sociology* 42, no. 3 (2016): 393–415.

———. "'Still Doin' Time': Clamoring for Work in the Day Labor Industry." *Journal of Labor and Society* 15, no. 3 (September 2012): 397–415.

Putnam, Robert D. *Bowling Alone: The Collapse and Revival of American Community.* New York: Simon and Schuster, 2000.

———. *Our Kids: The American Dream in Crisis.* New York: PublicAffairs, 2015.

Quillian, Lincoln. "New Approaches to Understanding Racial Prejudice and Discrimination." *Annual Review of Sociology* 32 (2006): 299–328.

Quillian, Lincoln, Devah Pager, Ole Hexel, and Arnfinn H. Midtbøen. "Meta-Analysis of Field Experiments Shows No Change in Racial Discrimination in Hiring over Time." *Proceedings of the National Academy of Sciences* 114, no. 41 (October 10, 2017): 10870–75.

Radcliff, Benjamin, and Patricia Davis. "Labor Organizations and Electoral Participation in Industrial Democracies." *American Journal of Political Science* 44, no. 1 (January 2000): 132–41.

Rainwater, Lee, and William L. Yancey, eds. *The Moynihan Report and the Politics of Controversy.* Cambridge, MA: MIT Press, 1967.

Rank, Mark Robert. "As American as Apple Pie: Poverty and Welfare." *Contexts* 2, no. 3 (Summer 2003): 41–49.

———. *Living on the Edge: The Realities of Welfare in America.* New York: Columbia University Press, 1994.

———. *One Nation, Underprivileged: Why American Poverty Affects Us All.* New York: Oxford University Press, 2004.

———. "Toward a New Paradigm for Understanding Poverty." In *The Oxford Handbook of the Social Science of Poverty,* edited by David Brady and Linda M. Burton, 866–83. New York: Oxford University Press, 2016.

Rank, Mark Robert, and Thomas A. Hirschl. "Rags or Riches? Estimating the Probabilities of Poverty and Affluence across the Adult American Life Span." *Social Science Quarterly* 82, no. 4 (December 2001): 651–69.

Rank, Mark Robert, Thomas A. Hirschl, and Kirk A. Foster. *Chasing the American Dream: Understanding What Shapes Our Fortunes.* Oxford: Oxford University Press, 2014.

Rankin, Bruce H., and James M. Quane. "Neighborhood Poverty and the Social Isolation of Inner-City African American Families." *Social Forces* 79, no. 1 (September 2000): 139–64.

Reardon, Sean F., and Kendra Bischoff. "Income Inequality and Income Segregation." *American Journal of Sociology* 116, no. 4 (January 2011): 1092–153.

Reardon, Sean F., Lindsay Fox, and Joseph Townsend. "Neighborhood Income Composition by Household Race and Income, 1990–2009." *Annals of the American Academy of Political and Social Science* 660 (July 2015): 78–97.

Reese, Ellen. *Backlash against Welfare Mothers: Past and Present.* Berkeley: University of California Press, 2005.

———. *They Say Cut Back, We Say Fight Back! Welfare Activism in an Era of Retrenchment.* New York: Russell Sage, 2011.

Reich, Robert B. *Saving Capitalism: For the Many, Not the Few.* New York: Alfred A. Knopf, 2015.

Reskin, Barbara F. "The Proximate Causes of Employment Discrimination." *Contemporary Sociology* 29, no. 2 (March 2000): 319–28.

Ridgeway, Cecilia L. *Framed by Gender: How Gender Inequality Persists in the Modern World.* Oxford: Oxford University Press, 2011.

Rigby, Elizabeth, and Gerald C. Wright. "Political Parties and Representation of the Poor in the American States." *American Journal of Political Science* 57, no. 3 (July 2013): 552–65.

Rivera, Lauren A. *Pedigree: How Elite Students Get Elite Jobs.* Princeton, NJ: Princeton University Press, 2015.

Robert, Stephanie A. "Socioeconomic Position and Health: The Independent Contribution of Community Socioeconomic Context." *Annual Review of Sociology* 25 (1999): 489–516.

Rodríguez-Muñiz, Michael. "Intellectual Inheritances: Cultural Diagnostics and State of Poverty Knowledge." *American Journal of Cultural Sociology* 3, no. 1 (2015): 89–122.

Rodrik, Dani. *The Globalization Paradox: Democracy and the Future of the World Economy.* New York: W. W. Norton, 2011.

———. *Has Globalization Gone Too Far?* Washington, DC: Institute for International Economics, 1997.

Rolf, David. *The Fight for $15: The Right Wage for a Working America.* New York: New Press, 2016.

Roscigno, Vincent J. *The Face of Discrimination: How Race and Gender Impact Work and Home Lives.* Lanham, MD: Rowman & Littlefield, 2007.

Roscigno, Vincent J., Lisette M. Garcia, and Donna Bobbitt-Zeher. "Social Closure and Processes of Race/Sex Employment Discrimination." *Annals of the American Academy of Political and Social Science* 609 (January 2007): 17–48.

Rose, Max, and Frank R. Baumgartner. "Framing the Poor: Media Coverage and U.S. Poverty Policy, 1960–2008." *Policy Studies Journal* 41, no. 1 (February 2013): 22–53.

Rosenfeld, Jake. *What Unions No Longer Do.* Cambridge, MA: Harvard University Press, 2014.

Rosenfeld, Jake, and Jennifer Laird. "Unions and Poverty." In *The Oxford Handbook of the Social Science of Poverty*, edited by David Brady and Linda M. Burton, 800–19. New York: Oxford University Press, 2016.

Rosenthal, Howard. "Politics, Public Policy, and Inequality: A Look Back at the Twentieth Century." In *Social Inequality*, edited by Kathryn M. Neckerman, 861–92. New York: Russell Sage, 2004.

Roth, Zachary. *The Great Suppression: Voting Rights, Corporate Cash, and the Conservative Assault on Democracy.* New York: Crown, 2016.

Rothstein, Jesse. "The Great Recession and Its Aftermath: What Role for Structural Changes." *Journal of the Social Sciences* 3, no. 3 (April 2017): 22–49.

Rothstein, Richard. *The Color of Law: A Forgotten History of How Our Government Segregated America.* New York: Liveright, 2017.

Royster, Deirdre A. *Race and the Invisible Hand: How White Networks Exclude Black Men from Blue-Collar Jobs.* Berkeley: University of California Press, 2003.

Russo, John, and Sherry Lee Linkon. "The Social Costs of Deindustrialization." In *Manufacturing a Better Future for America*, edited by Richard McCormack, 183–215. New York: Alliance for American Manufacturing, 2009.

Ryan, Charlotte. "Battered in the Media: Mainstream News Coverage of Welfare Reform." *Radical America* 26, no. 1 (January–March 1996): 29–41.

———. *Prime Time Activism: Media Strategies for Grassroots Organizing.* Boston: South End Press, 1991.

Ryan, William. *Blaming the Victim.* Rev., upd. ed. New York: Vintage, 1976.

Sampson, Robert J. *Great American City: Chicago and the Enduring Neighborhood Effect.* Chicago: University of Chicago Press, 2012.

Sampson, Robert J., Jeffrey D. Morenoff, and Thomas Gannon-Rowley. "Assessing 'Neighborhood Effects': Social Processes and New Directions in Research." *Annual Review of Sociology* 28 (2002): 443–78.

Scarbrough, Jacquelin W. "Welfare Mothers' Reflections on Personal Responsibility." *Journal of Social Issues* 57, no. 2 (Summer 2001): 261–76.

Scheuer, Jeffrey. *The Sound Bite Society: Television and the American Mind.* New York: Four Walls Eight Windows, 1999.

Schiller, Bradley R. *The Economics of Poverty and Discrimination.* 9th ed. Upper Saddle River, NJ: Pearson Prentice Hall, 2004.

Schlozman, Kay Lehman, Sidney Verba, and Henry E. Brady. *The Unheavenly Chorus: Unequal Political Voice and the Broken Promise of American Democracy.* Princeton, NJ: Princeton University Press, 2012.

Schram, Sanford D. *Words of Welfare: The Poverty of Social Science and the Social Science of Poverty.* Minneapolis: University of Minnesota Press, 1995.

Schudson, Michael. "How Culture Works: Perspectives from Media Studies on the Efficacy of Symbols." *Theory and Society* 18, no. 2 (March 1989): 153–80.

Schutz, Eric A. *Inequality and Power: The Economics of Class.* New York: Routledge, 2011.

Schwartz, Joel. *Fighting Poverty with Virtue: Moral Reform and America's Urban Poor, 1825–2000.* Bloomington: Indiana University Press, 2000.

Scruggs, Lyle, and James P. Allan. "The Material Consequences of Welfare States: Benefit Generosity and Absolute Poverty in 16 OECD Countries." *Comparative Political Studies* 39, no. 7 (September 2006): 880–904.

Seccombe, Karen, Delores James, and Kimberly Battle Walters. "'They Think You Ain't Much of Nothing': The Social Construction of the Welfare Mother." *Journal of Marriage and the Family* 60, no. 4 (November 1998): 849–65.

Shah, Anuj K., Sendhil Mullainathan, and Eldar Shafir. "Some Consequences of Having Too Little." *Science* 338 (November 2012): 682–85.

Shapiro, Thomas M. *The Hidden Cost of Being African American: How Wealth Perpetuates Inequality*. Oxford: Oxford University Press, 2004.

———. *Toxic Inequality: How America's Wealth Gap Destroys Mobility, Deepens the Racial Divide & Threatens Our Future*. New York: Basic Books, 2017.

Sharkey, Patrick. "Neighborhoods, Cities, and Economic Mobility." *Journal of the Social Sciences* 2, no. 2 (May 2016): 159–77.

———. *Stuck in Place: Urban Neighborhoods and the End of Progress toward Racial Equality*. Chicago: University of Chicago Press, 2013.

Sharkey, Patrick, and Felix Elwert. "The Legacy of Disadvantage: Multigenerational Neighborhood Effects on Cognitive Ability." *American Journal of Sociology* 116, no.6 (May 2011): 1934–81.

Sheak, Bob, and Melissa Morris. "The Limits of the Job Supply in U.S. Capitalism." *Critical Sociology* 28, no. 3 (2002): 389–415.

Shelby, Tommie. *Dark Ghettos: Injustice, Dissent, and Reform*. Cambridge, MA: Belknap Press of Harvard University Press, 2016.

———. "Liberalism, Self-Respect, and Troubling Cultural Patterns in Ghettos." In *The Cultural Matrix: Understanding Black Youth*, edited by Orlando Patterson, with Ethan Fosse, 498–532. Cambridge, MA: Harvard University Press, 2015.

Shipler, David K. *The Working Poor: Invisible in America*. New York: Alfred A. Knopf, 2004.

Skocpol, Theda. "Civic Transformation and Inequality in the Contemporary United States." In *Social Inequality*, edited by Kathryn M. Neckerman, 729–67. New York: Russell Sage, 2004.

———. "Voice and Inequality: The Transformation of American Civic Democracy." *Perspectives on Politics* 2, no. 1 (March 2004): 3–20.

Skocpol, Theda, and Morris P. Fiorina, eds. *Civic Engagement in American Democracy*. Washington, DC: Brookings Institution, 1999.

Skocpol, Theda, and Vanessa Williamson. *The Tea Party and the Remaking of Republican Conservativism*. Oxford: Oxford University Press, 2013.

Small, Mario Luis. "No Two Ghettos Are Alike." *Chronicle Review* (March 21, 2014): B10–B12.

———. *Villa Victoria: The Transformation of Social Capital in a Boston Barrio*. Chicago: University of Chicago Press, 2004.

Small, Mario Luis, David J. Harding, and Michèle Lamont. "Reconsidering Culture and Poverty." *American Academy of Political and Social Science* 629 (May 2010): 6–27.

Small, Mario Luis, and Katherine Newman. "Urban Poverty after *The Truly Disadvantaged*: The Rediscovery of the Family, the Neighborhood, and Culture." *Annual Review of Sociology* 27 (2001): 23–45.

Smeeding, Timothy M. "Gates, Gaps, and Intergenerational Mobility: The Importance of an Even Start." In *The Dynamics of Opportunity in America: Evidence and Perspectives*, edited by Irwin Kirsch and Henry Braun, 255–95. New York: Springer, 2016.

———. "Poor People in Rich Nations: The United States in Comparative Perspective." *Journal of Economic Perspectives* 20, no. 1 (Winter 2006): 69–90.

———. "Poverty Measurement." In *The Oxford Handbook of the Social Science of Poverty*, edited by David Brady and Linda M. Burton, 21–46. New York: Oxford University Press, 2016.

Smith, Kevin B., and Lorene H. Stone. "Rags, Riches, and Bootstraps: Beliefs about the Causes of Wealth and Poverty." *Sociological Quarterly* 30, no. 1 (1989): 93–107.

Smith, Mark A. *The Right Talk: How Conservatives Transformed the Great Society into the Economic Society*. Princeton, NJ: Princeton University Press, 2007.

Smith, Sandra Susan. "'Don't Put My Name on It': Social Capital Activation and Job-Finding Assistance among the Black Urban Poor." *American Journal of Sociology* 111, no. 1 (July 2005): 1–57.

———. "Job-Finding Among the Poor: Do Social Ties Matter?" In *The Oxford Handbook of the Social Science of Poverty*, edited by David Brady and Linda M. Burton, 438–61. New York: Oxford University Press, 2016.

————. *Lone Pursuit: Distrust and Defensive Individualism Among the Black Poor*. New York: Russell Sage, 2007.

Somers, Margaret R., and Fred Block. "From Poverty to Perversity: Ideas, Markets, and Institutions over 200 Years of Welfare Debate." *American Sociological Review* 70, no. 2 (April 2005): 260–87.

Soss, Joe, Richard C. Fording, and Sanford Schram. *Disciplining the Poor: Neoliberal Paternalism and the Persistent Power of Race*. Chicago: University of Chicago Press, 2011.

Soss, Joe, and Lawrence R. Jacobs. "The Place of Inequality: Non-Participation in the American Polity." *Political Science Quarterly* 124, no. 1 (Spring 2009): 95–125.

Squires, Gregory D., and Charis E. Kubrin. *Privileged Places: Race, Residence, and the Structure of Opportunity*. Boulder, CO: Lynne Rienner, 2006.

Stahl, Jason. *Right Moves: The Conservative Think Tank in American Culture Since 1945*. Chapel Hill: University of North Carolina Press, 2016.

Stanton-Salazar, Ricardo D., and Sanford M. Dornbusch. "Social Capital and the Reproduction of Inequality: Information Networks among Mexican-Origin High School Students." *Sociology of Education* 68, no. 2 (April 1995): 116–35.

Steinberg, Stephen. *The Ethnic Myth: Race, Ethnicity, and Class in America*. Upd. and exp. ed. Boston: Beacon Press, 1989.

Stepan, Alfred, and Juan J. Linz. "Comparative Perspectives on Inequality and the Quality of Democracy in the United States." *Perspectives on Politics* 9, no. 4 (December 2011): 841–56.

Stier, Haya, and Marta Tienda. *The Color of Opportunity: Pathways to Family, Welfare, and Work*. Chicago: University of Chicago Press, 2001.

Stiglitz, Joseph E. *The Great Divide: Unequal Societies and What We Can Do About Them*. New York: W. W. Norton, 2015.

————. *The Price of Inequality: How Today's Divided Society Endangers Our Future*. New York: W. W. Norton, 2012.

Strauss, Claudia. *Making Sense of Public Opinion: American Discourses About Immigration and Social Programs*. New York: Cambridge University Press, 2012.

————. "Not-So-Rugged Individualists: U.S. Americans' Conflicting Ideas about Poverty." In *Work, Welfare, and Politics: Confronting Poverty in the Wake of Welfare Reform*, edited by Frances Fox Piven, Joan Acker, Margaret Hallock, and Sandra Morgen, 55–69. Eugene: University of Oregon Press, 2002.

Streib, Jessi, Juhi Verma, Whitney E. Welsh, and Linda M. Burton. "Life, Death, and Resurrections: The Culture of Poverty Perspective." In *The Oxford Handbook of the Social Science of Poverty*, edited by David Brady and Linda M. Burton, 247–69. New York: Oxford University Press, 2016.

Stricker, Frank. *Why America Lost the War on Poverty—And How to Win It*. Chapel Hill: University of North Carolina Press, 2007.

Sugrue, Thomas J. *The Origins of the Urban Crisis: Race and Inequality in Postwar Detroit*. Princeton, NJ: Princeton University Press, 1996.

Tait, Vanessa. *Poor Workers' Unions: Rebuilding Labor from Below*. Cambridge, MA: South End Press, 2005.

Taylor, Keeanga-Yamahtta. *From #BlackLivesMatter to Black Liberation*. Chicago: Haymarket Books, 2016.

Teixeira, Ruy A., and Lawrence Mishel. "Whose Skills Shortage—Workers or Management?" *Issues in Science and Technology* 9, no. 4 (Summer 1993): 69–74.

Tigges, Leann M., Irene Browne, and Gary P. Green. "Social Isolation of the Urban Poor: Race, Class, and Neighborhood Effects on Social Resources." *Sociological Quarterly* 39, no. 1 (1998): 53–77.

Tilly, Charles. *Durable Inequality*. Berkeley: University of California Press, 1998.

Tomaskovic-Devey, Donald, Ken-Hou Lin, and Nathan Meyers. "Did Financialization Reduce Economic Growth?" *Socio-Economic Review* (May 2015):1–24.

Tomaskovic-Devey, Donald, Melvin Thomas, and Kecia Johnson. "Race and the Accumulation of Human Capital across the Career: A Theoretical Model and Fixed-Effects Application." *American Journal of Sociology* 111, no. 1 (July 2005): 58–89.

Tonry, Michael. *Punishing Race: A Continuing American Dilemma.* New York: Oxford University Press, 2011.

Vaisey, Stephen. "Education and Its Discontents: Overqualification in America, 1972–2002." *Social Forces* 85, no. 2 (December 2006): 835–64.

Valenzuela Jr., Abel. "Day Labor Work." *Annual Review of Sociology* 29 (2003): 307–33.

Van Doorn, Bas W. "Pre- and Post-Welfare Reform Media Portrayals of Poverty in the United States: The Continuing Importance of Race and Ethnicity." *Politics & Policy* 43, no. 1 (February 2015): 142–62.

Vance, J. D. *Hillbilly Elegy: A Memoir of a Family and Culture in Crisis.* New York: Harper, 2016.

Vogel, David. *Fluctuating Fortunes: The Political Power of Business in America.* New York: Basic Books, 1989.

Waldinger, Roger, and Michael I. Lichter. *How the Other Half Works: Immigration and the Social Organization of Labor.* Berkeley: University of California Press, 2003.

Watkins-Hayes, Celeste, and Elyse Kovalsky. "The Discourse of Deservingness: Morality and Dilemmas of Poverty Relief in Debate and Practice." In *The Oxford Handbook of the Social Science of Poverty*, edited by David Brady and Linda M. Burton, 193–220. New York: Oxford University Press, 2016.

Weeden, Kim A. "Why Do Some Occupations Pay More than Others? Social Closure and Earnings Inequality in the United States." *American Journal of Sociology* 108, no. 1 (July 2002): 55–101.

Weil, David. *The Fissured Workplace: Why Work Became So Bad for So Many and What Can Be Done to Improve It.* Cambridge, MA: Harvard University Press, 2014.

———. "Income Inequality, Wage Determination, and the Fissured Workplace." In *After Piketty: The Agenda for Economics and Inequality*, edited by Heather Boushey, J. Bradford DeLong, and Marshall Steinbaum, 209–31. Cambridge, MA: Harvard University Press, 2017.

Western, Bruce. *Punishment and Inequality in America.* New York: Russell Sage, 2006.

Western, Bruce, and Jake Rosenfeld. "Unions, Norms, and the Rise in U.S. Wage Inequality." *American Sociological Review* 76, no. 4 (August 2011): 513–37.

Widestrom, Amy. *Displacing Democracy: Economic Segregation in America.* Philadelphia: University of Pennsylvania Press, 2015.

Williams, Joan C. *White Working Class: Overcoming Cluelessness in America.* Boston: Harvard Business Review Press, 2017.

Wilson, William Julius. *The Truly Disadvantaged: The Inner City, the Underclass, and Public Policy.* Chicago: University of Chicago Press, 1987.

———. *When Work Disappears: The World of the New Urban Poor.* New York: Alfred A. Knopf, 1996.

Wilson, William Julius, and Richard P. Taub. *There Goes the Neighborhood: Racial, Ethnic, and Class Tension in Four Chicago Neighborhoods and Their Meaning for America.* New York: Alfred A. Knopf, 2006.

Winters, Jeffrey A., and Benjamin I. Page. "Oligarchy in the United States." *Perspectives on Politics* 7, no. 4 (December 2009): 731–51.

Wise, Tim. *Under the Affluence: Shaming the Poor, Praising the Rich and Sacrificing the Future of America.* San Francisco, CA: City Lights Books, 2015.

Wolff, Edward N. *A Century of Wealth in America.* Cambridge, MA: Belknap Press of Harvard University, 2017.

———. *Does Education Really Help? Skill, Work, and Inequality.* Oxford: Oxford University Press, 2006.

———. "Household Wealth Trends in the United States, 1962 to 2013: What Happened Over the Great Recession?" *Journal of the Social Sciences* 2, no. 6 (October 2016): 24–43.

Wood, Adrian. "How Trade Hurts Unskilled Workers." *Journal of Economic Perspectives* 9, no. 3 (Summer 1995): 57–80.

Wysong, Earl, Robert Perrucci, and David Wright. *The New Class Society: Goodbye American Dream?* 4th ed. Lanham, MD: Rowman & Littlefield, 2014.

Young, Alford A., Jr. *The Minds of Marginalized Black Men: Making Sense of Mobility, Opportunity, and Future Life Chances*. Princeton, NJ: Princeton University Press, 2004.

Young, Kevin, and Michael Schwartz. "Healthy, Wealthy, and Wise: How Corporate Power Shaped the Affordable Care Act." *New Labor Forum* 23, no. 2 (May 2014): 30–40.

Zamudio, Margaret M., and Michael I. Lichter. "Bad Attitudes and Good Soldiers: Soft Skills as a Code for Tractability in the Hiring of Immigrant Latina/os Over Native Blacks in the Hotel Industry." *Social Problems* 55, no. 4 (November 2008): 573–589.

Zuberi, Dan. *Differences That Matter: Social Policy and the Working Poor in the United States and Canada*. Ithaca, NY: Cornell University Press, 2006.

Zweig, Michael. *The Working Class Majority: America's Best Kept Secret*. Ithaca, NY: Cornell University Press, 2000.

Index

globalization and, 92, 121; policy recommendations on, 250; power shift and, 123–124

Lafer, Gordon, 74–75, 120, 137, 139

Lapham, Lewis, 166

Latinos. *See* Hispanic Americans

Lazonick, William, 73, 100–101

left-wing populism, 150

legal deprivation, 20, 237–241

Legal Services Corporation (LSC), 10, 238–239

Lerner, Sharon, 225

Levin, Mark, 166

Levy, Helen, 232

Lewis, Oscar, 40

liberalism: changes in, 124–125; poverty and, 45

Lichter, Michael, 68

Limbaugh, Rush, 166

Livingstone, D. W., 75

lobbyists, 118, 120, 128, 129–130, 138

local government, 136–137, 138

Loury, Glen, 172

Lowe, Robert, 77

Low Income Home Energy Assistance Program, 10

low-wage jobs, 113; experiences with, 81; health and, 231; personal traits and, 69; poverty trap and, 8; transportation and, 215, 217; unions and, 253; women and, 221

LSC. *See* Legal Services Corporation

Ludwig, Jens, 48

Lukes, Steven, 245–246

Luo, Ye, 52

Magnet, Myron, 42, 45, 50–51

Maguire, Terry, 170

makers and takers, 144, 168

Malkin, Michelle, 166

managerialism, 99

Mandle, Jay, 129

Manjoo, Farhad, 97

manufacturing sector, 86, 87, 88, 106

Manyika, James, 96

Manza, Jeff, 146

marriage, 55–56

Martin, Trayvon, 252, 323n17

matriarchal family structure, of African Americans, 44

Mayer, Susan, 48

McChesney, Robert, 97, 123

Mead, Lawrence, 41–42, 44

media, 156; cultural system and, 147, 155–164; daily news issues with, 161–162; FAIR study of, 156–157, 161; framing poverty in news stories, 158; political disengagement and, 123; poverty and welfare racialization, 160–161; poverty coverage lacking in, 1, 155, 156–157, 162; purpose of, 155–156; recommendations for, 249, 250; right wing and, 164, 165–166; sound bite bias, 162; sources used by, 161; storylines and, 157, 159, 160; storytelling and, 158–159; technical focus of, 163; victim-blaming and, 163–164

Media Research Center, 165

Medicaid, 9–10, 140

membership organizations, 125

memberships theory, 174

men: earnings mobility of, 8; higher wages of, 67

meritocracy, 33–34, 35, 61, 65, 172

Mettler, Suzanne, 213

Meyerson, Harold, 83

middle class: education and, 64, 76; liberalism and, 124–125; political system and, 128, 137; status of, 14, 56; transportation and, 218

Milkman, Ruth, 88

minimum wage, 10, 136–138, 197, 248

Mishel, Lawrence, 75

mobility optimism, 146

Molyneux, Guy, 149–150

MomsRising, 252

Mounk, Yascha, 169

moral reform, 46, 47, 58–59, 269n26

Morduch, Jonathan, 11

Morris, Melissa, 109

Morrow, Lance, 107

motherhood penalty, 221

mothers: household responsibilities of, 220–221; pay gap and, 220. *See also* single mothers

The Movement for Black Lives, 253

About the Author

Edward Royce is professor emeritus of sociology at Rollins College, where he was a recipient of the Cornell Distinguished Faculty Award. In addition to *Poverty and Power*, he is also the author of *The Origins of Southern Sharecropping* (1993) and *Classical Social Theory and Modern Society: Marx, Durkheim, Weber* (2015). He currently lives in Northampton, Massachusetts.